D1559701

New Directions in Philosophy and Cognitive Science

Series Editors: **John Protevi**, Louisiana State University and **Michael Wheeler**, University of Stirling

This series brings together work that takes cognitive science in new directions. Hitherto, philosophical reflection on cognitive science – or perhaps better, philosophical contribution to the interdisciplinary field that is cognitive science – has for the most part come from philosophers with a commitment to a representationalist model of the mind.

However, as cognitive science continues to make advances, especially in its neuroscience and robotics aspects, there is growing discontent with the representationalism of traditional philosophical interpretations of cognition. Cognitive scientists and philosophers have turned to a variety of sources – phenomenology and dynamic systems theory foremost among them to date – to rethink cognition as the direction of the action of an embodied and affectively attuned organism embedded in its social world, a stance that sees representation as only one tool of cognition, and a derived one at that.

To foster this growing interest in rethinking traditional philosophical notions of cognition – using phenomenology, dynamic systems theory, and perhaps other approaches yet to be identified – we dedicate this series to "New Directions in Philosophy and Cognitive Science."

Titles include:

Robyn Bluhm, Anne Jaap Jacobson and Heidi Lene Maibom
NEUROFEMINISM
Issues at the Intersection of Feminist Theory and Cognitive Science

Michelle Maiese
EMBODIMENT, EMOTION, AND COGNITION

Richard Menary
COGNITIVE INTEGRATION
Mind and Cognition Unbounded

Zdravko Radman
KNOWING WITHOUT THINKING
Mind, Action, Cognition and the Phenomenon of the Background

Matthew Ratcliffe
RETHINKING COMMONSENSE PSYCHOLOGY
A Critique of Folk Psychology, Theory of Mind and Stimulation

Jay Schulkin
ACTION, PERCEPTION AND THE BRAIN

Forthcoming titles:

Anne Jaap Jacobson
KEEPING THE WORLD IN MIND
Biologically Embodied Representations and the New Sciences of the Mind

Hanne De Jaegher
PARTICIPATION SENSE-MAKING
An Enactive Approach to Intersubjectivity

Robert Welshon
NIETZSCHE, PSYCHOLOGY, AND COGNITIVE SCIENCE

New Directions in Philosophy and Cognitive Science
Series Standing Order ISBN 978–0–230–54935–7 Hardback
                    978–0–230–54936–4 Paperback
(*outside North America only*)

You can receive future titles in this series as they are published by placing a standing order. Please contact your bookseller or, in case of difficulty, write to us at the address below with your name and address, the title of the series and one of the ISBNs quoted above.

Customer Services Department, Macmillan Distribution Ltd, Houndmills, Basingstoke, Hampshire RG21 6XS, England

Also by Anne Jaap Jacobson

FEMINIST INTERPRETATIONS OF DAVID HUME

Neurofeminism

Issues at the Intersection of Feminist Theory and Cognitive Science

Edited by

Robyn Bluhm
Assistant Professor of Philosophy, Old Dominion University, USA

Anne Jaap Jacobson
Professor of Philosophy and Electrical and Computer Engineering, University of Houston, USA

and

Heidi Lene Maibom
Associate Professor of Philosophy, Carleton University, Canada

First published 2012 by
PALGRAVE MACMILLAN

Palgrave Macmillan in the UK is an imprint of Macmillan Publishers Limited,
registered in England, company number 785998, of Houndmills, Basingstoke,
Hampshire RG21 6XS.

Palgrave Macmillan in the US is a division of St Martin's Press LLC,
175 Fifth Avenue, New York, NY 10010.

Palgrave Macmillan is the global academic imprint of the above companies
and has companies and representatives throughout the world.

Palgrave® and Macmillan® are registered trademarks in the United States,
the United Kingdom, Europe and other countries.

ISBN: 978–0–230–29673–2

This book is printed on paper suitable for recycling and made from fully
managed and sustained forest sources. Logging, pulping and manufacturing
processes are expected to conform to the environmental regulations of the
country of origin.

A catalogue record for this book is available from the British Library.

A catalog record for this book is available from the Library of Congress.

10 9 8 7 6 5 4 3 2 1
21 20 19 18 17 16 15 14 13 12

Transferred to Digital Printing in 2013

Contents

List of Illustrations   vii

Acknowledgments   ix

List of Contributors   x

Introduction   1
Robyn Bluhm, Anne Jaap Jacobson, and Heidi Lene Maibom

1   The Politics of Pictured Reality: Locating the Object
    from Nowhere in fMRI   11
    Letitia Meynell

2   What, If Anything, Can Neuroscience Tell Us About
    Gender Differences?   30
    Ginger Hoffman

3   In a Different Voice?   56
    Heidi Lene Maibom

4   The Role of Fetal Testosterone in the Development of the
    "Essential Difference" Between the Sexes:
    Some Essential Issues   73
    Giordana Grossi and Cordelia Fine

5   Hardwired for Sexism? Approaches to Sex/Gender
    in Neuroscience   105
    Rebecca M. Jordan-Young and Raffaella I. Rumiati

6   Re-Queering the Brain   121
    Isabelle Dussauge and Anelis Kaiser

7   Situated Neuroscience: Exploring Biologies of Diversity   145
    Gillian Einstein

8   Cosmopolitics and the Brain: The Co-Becoming of
    Practices in Feminism and Neuroscience   175
    Deboleena Roy

9   Linking Neuroscience, Medicine, Gender and Society
    through Controversy and Conflict Analysis: A "Dissensus
    Framework" for Feminist/Queer Brain Science Studies   193
    Cynthia Kraus

10   Seeing as a Social Phenomenon: Feminist Theory and
     the Cognitive Sciences   216
     Anne Jaap Jacobson

11   Beyond Neurosexism: Is It Possible to Defend
     the Female Brain?   230
     Robyn Bluhm

Bibliography   246

Name Index   281

Subject Index   282

Illustrations

Figures

1.1   A 2-D fetal ultrasound image, printed with permission
from 3D Miracles – 3D Ultrasound, Halifax, Nova Scotia   15

1.2   A 3-D fetal ultrasound image, printed with permission
from 3D Miracles – 3D Ultrasound, Halifax, Nova Scotia   15

1.3   A figure comparing fMR images from 16 men and
16 women purporting to show "ample differences in
brain activation patterns underlying anticipation of
different reward types between men and women" from
Spreckelmeyer et al. (2009: 164), by permission of
Oxford University Press   23

2.1   Image from Price and Friston (2002), showing differential
brain activation during a semantic task, by permission
from Elsevier Press   41

2.2   Image from Keller and Menon (2009), showing areas
where brain activation was significantly greater in
male subjects than female subjects during performance
of an arithmetic task, by permission from Elsevier Press   44

5.1   Associations predicted by brain-organization theory.
Reprinted by permission of the publisher from
Brain Storm: The Flaws in the Science of Sex Differences
by Rebecca M. Jordan-Young (p. 177, Cambridge, MA:
Harvard University Press), Copyright © 2010 by the
President and Fellows of Harvard College   112

5.2   Associations observed among (genetic) females.
Reprinted and adapted by permission of the publisher
from *Brain Storm: The Flaws in the Science of Sex Differences*
by Rebecca M. Jordan-Young (p. 190, Cambridge, MA:
Harvard University Press), Copyright © 2010 by the
President and Fellows of Harvard College   114

5.3   Associations observed among (genetic) males.
Reprinted and adapted by permission of the publisher from
Brain Storm: The Flaws in the Science of Sex Differences by Rebecca
M. Jordan-Young (p. 191, Cambridge, MA: Harvard University

Press), Copyright © 2010 by the President and
Fellows of Harvard College   116

Table

4.1   Summary of studies investigating aT/ mT and E/S ability   92

Acknowledgments

The editors would like to thank Sharon Crasnow for organizing a panel on Neuroscience and Feminism for the Society of Analytical Feminism at the APA, at which we first discussed the possibility of this volume, and John Protevi for encouraging us to submit the book proposal to Palgrave Macmillan's "New Directions in Philosophy and Cognitive Science" series. We would also like to thank Lynn Randolph for permission to use her painting *Immeasurable Results* on the cover of this volume.

Contributors

Robyn Bluhm – Assistant Professor of Philosophy and Co-Director of the Institute for Ethics and Public Affairs, Old Dominion University.

Isabelle Dussauge – Assistant Professor, Department of Thematic Studies – Technology and Social Change, Linköping University.

Gillian Einstein – Associate Professor, Department of Psychology and the Dalla Lana School of Public Health, University of Toronto.

Cordelia Fine – Associate Professor, Melbourne Business School, University of Melbourne.

Giordana Grossi – Associate Professor of Psychology, SUNY New Paltz.

Ginger Hoffman – Assistant Professor of Philosophy, Loyola University New Orleans.

Anne Jaap Jacobson – Professor of Philosophy and Electrical and Computer Engineering, University of Houston and Engineering and Director of the UH Center for Neuro-Engineering and Cognitive Science.

Rebecca M. Jordan-Young – Assistant Professor of Women's, Gender & Sexuality Studies, Barnard College.

Anelis Kaiser – Visiting Professor, Psychology, Science, and Gender, Institute of Pedagogical Psychology/Centre for Interdisciplinary Women's and Gender Studies Technical University Berlin, Germany.

Cynthia Kraus – Tenured Senior Lecturer and Researcher, Institute of Social Sciences, University of Lausanne, Switzerland.

Heidi Lene Maibom – Associate Professor, Department of Philosophy, Carleton University.

Letitia Meynell – Associate Professor, Department of Philosophy, cross-appointed with the Gender and Women's Studies Program, Dalhousie University.

Deboleena Roy – Associate Professor of Women's Studies and Neuroscience and Behavioral Biology, Emory University.

Raffaella I. Rumiati – Associate Professor, SISSA Cognitive Neuroscience Sector, Trieste, Italy.

Introduction

Robyn Bluhm, Anne Jaap Jacobson, and Heidi Lene Maibom

Neurofeminism is the first collection of essays to bring a critical feminist perspective to the recent brain sciences. The authors come from several different academic disciplines, and the essays often include insights and material from more than one area of study. The work can be seen as addressing issues in four large areas within neurofeminism: sex and gender differences, ethics, philosophy of science, and embodiment. Many of the essays address topics from two or even three of these areas. Accordingly, the editors have decided not to divide this book into sections; rather, this introduction will delineate themes from each of the areas as they appear in the chapters.

1 Sex and gender

1.1 Terminological questions

Most people who are familiar with feminist scholarship recognize a distinction between sex and gender. This distinction can be traced back to the works of two psychologists, John Money (Money 1955) and Robert Stoller (Stoller 1968) (see Fausto-Sterling 2000a; Mikkola 2008). Stoller was interested in the question of gender identity, and separated sex and gender so as to be able to discuss the experiences of individuals whose biological appearance (sex) was at odds with their experiences of being female or male (gender). Money, being a sexologist, focused on the development of gender identity in individuals born with ambiguous genitalia and raised as either female or male. From these two bodies of work arose the use of 'sex' as referring to biological characteristics, particularly those that are relevant to reproduction, whereas 'gender' came to refer to psychological or behavioral characteristics. Gender identity was thought to be the result of socialization as female or as male.

1

Second-wave feminists began using the distinction in the late 1960s and early 1970s to emphasize that psychological and behavioral characteristics associated with masculinity and femininity were the products of differences in socialization and experiences. These are *gender* characteristics, unlike the physical characteristics associated with being male or female. This emphasis on socialization was meant to combat earlier notions of biological determinism, which argued that stereotypical male and female characteristics were as much the results of biology as physical differences. By attributing gender differences to culture or environment, feminists wanted to emphasize that "it was social institutions, themselves designed to perpetuate gender inequality, that produced most of the differences between women and women" (Fausto-Sterling 2000a: 638). Moreover, they argued that changes designed to eliminate gender inequality in these social institutions would also eliminate gender differences. If that were true, the social origin of most differences between men and women would be well established.

Despite the clarity of this argument and the rationale for distinguishing between gender and sex, the *use* of the terms has not been consistent. In addition to the usage described above, the terms have been used in at least two other ways.[1] First, they are often used interchangeably, as synonyms. Although Money has been credited with being the first to use the term 'gender' outside of its linguistic context, the use of 'gender' as a synonym for 'sex' has a long history. David Haig (2004) notes that the *Oxford English Dictionary* contains examples of this usage from as long ago as the fifteenth century. He also notes that, in the early 1970s, feminist works sometimes used the terms synonymously (e.g. Holter 1970) or even reversed the association, so that 'gender' was used to refer to innate characteristics, while sex roles were learned (Chafetz 1974; discussed in Haig 2004: 93). Biologists still talk of sex differences or gender differences without meaning to imply anything about the cause of these differences. As a result, Haig points out, papers examining differences in animals sometimes refer to gender differences.

Second, 'gender' is sometimes used as an alternative for 'women.' In an influential discussion the use of gender in historical analysis, Joan W. Scott notes that "[i]n its simplest usage, 'gender' is a synonym for 'women.' Any number of books and articles whose subject is women's history have, in the past few years, substituted 'gender' for 'women' in their titles" (1986: 1056). Scott notes that this practice achieves at least two ends. One is to underscore the distinction between sex and gender described above. The other is to indicate "the scholarly seriousness of a work, for 'gender' has a more neutral and objective sound than does 'women'" (1986: 1056). The use of the term 'gender,' Scott suggests, avoids the political connotations of 'women's history,' which was seen as being associated with "the (supposedly strident) politics of feminism" (1986: 1056). Similarly, Haig suggests that contemporary authors may use 'gender' as a euphemism for 'sex,' either to avoid the connotation of copulation or simply to use a more academic-sounding term.

In summary, even if sexologists and feminist writers consider the distinction between sex and gender to be clear, the actual use of the terms varies enough to obscure the distinction. It is particularly important in interdisciplinary work to take note of this variability, since the conventions of one discipline may not be those of another. There is yet another important problem with the use of the terms 'sex' and 'gender': the distinction itself is open to question, particularly in the case of biological, including neuroscientific, research.

2   Sex and gender, biology, and brains

The distinction between sex and gender, as noted above, was intended to be part of an argument against the idea that physical or behavioral differences between men and women are biologically determined, and therefore 'natural' and unchangeable. Certainly some differences, such as physical differences associated with reproduction, do not seem to be amenable to change. Differences in social roles and intellectual achievements, however, were held to be the result of differences in the socialization of girls and boys. The sex/gender distinction thus became associated with the distinctions between biology and culture, or between nature and nurture.

However, associating biology with sex differences is problematic. Biological characteristics are thought to be innate and unchangeable. If this is true, then biological differences between men and women must also be innate and immutable. So if behavioral differences can be associated with biological differences, they, too, become natural and immutable. Ruth Doell and Helen Longino (1988) characterize this type of reasoning as rooted in the "linear model" of development. Genetic differences in the XX versus XY chromosomal makeup lead to gonadal differences in a developing fetus. Gonadal differences determine the production of different levels of sex hormones, which affect the development of the brain. This is ultimately the source of the easily observable differences in the behaviors of girls and boys and the women and men they become. More recently, Rebecca Jordan-Young (2010) has shown that the linear model, which she calls "brain organization theory," still dominates much of developmental neurobiology. Given the influence of this line of explanation and the equation of sex differences with biological differences, it is clear why people are tempted to conclude that the kinds of psychological and behavioral differences claimed by feminists to be gender differences, and thus due to social factors, are actually sex differences, and the result of the unfolding of inevitable biological processes.

Yet a number of feminist scientists have argued that because the body, and especially the brain, is changed by experiences, 'biological' should not be taken to mean 'natural,' or 'innate,' or the product of sex rather than gender (e.g. Bleier 1984; Fausto-Sterling 1992, 2000a; Hubbard 1992). It is impossible, they argue, to disentangle the effects of sex from those of gender on differences in the brain. Thus, the very utility of the distinction between sex and gender has been called into question.[2]

Because of the difficulty of distinguishing between sex and gender in discussions of the brain (see below), we have not enforced a consistent use of the terms in this volume. Instead, the authors should make clear any potentially confusing or contradictory uses in their contributions.

3   Ethics

Sex and gender differences are also relevant in feminist approaches to ethics. Unwittingly perhaps, traditional ethics embodies a man's perspective on what morality is about (power relations, negotiation, etc.), what its central concepts are (harms, rights, and justice), its structure (rules and regulations), the nature of moral agency (rational reflection), and so on (Jaggar 1983). Men's moral experience traditionally takes place in a society in which they dominate public life and where women are largely subjugated to them. The prototypical picture of the moral sphere is of a public forum where men negotiate a reasonable coexistence among themselves as independent and more-or-less equal agents. Social contract theory is a case in point (Hobbes, Locke, Rousseau). Kant's moral realm of rational agents respecting each other *qua* purely rational agents is, perhaps, a rather extreme version of such a vision. Evolutionary accounts of human social organization and morality insist that humans are naturally egalitarian, without considering that more than half of the human population has historically enjoyed little, or no, equality (e.g. Boehm 1993; Wilson 2002).

Game theoretic models of human cooperation and altruism likewise present a typical male perspective. This is particularly clear in the prisoner's dilemma, which is often used to model human cooperation and altruism (Axelrod 1984; Frank 1988). In the classic formulation, two suspects have been arrested by the police, who have insufficient evidence to convict either of them for the crime in question. Apart from cooperating in their criminal activities, the subjects are relatively independent; they have no familial, friendship, or emotional ties to one another (which would complicate matters). To encourage a confession, the police offer each of them, separately, the following deal. If one testifies against the other and the other remains silent, that prisoner goes free and the silent one gets 10 years. If both refuse to testify, they get only 6 months in jail each (for another, minor, charge). If both agree to testify, they get 5 years each. They must decide in ignorance of the other's decision. The rational course of action for either agent is to defect, i.e. to agree to testify against the other. If this dilemma is used as a model of human cooperation, an apparently unsolvable problem arises about how human cooperation came about. Only iterated forms of the dilemma allow a rational solution in terms of cooperation, but this presupposes that people interact with largely the same individuals (cf. Trivers 1971). Whether such conditions can be assumed to have held back in the Pleistocene is unclear. There are also issues concerning migration between groups, which makes it hard to avoid infiltration of cooperative individuals by non-cooperative ones, unsettling the delicate balance required for cooperation and altruism (Sterelny 2003; Richerson and Boyd 2005).[3]

Recently people have begun to question whether game theoretic models are evolutionarily realistic. Thinking of cooperating individuals as having no affective ties may simplify matters from an abstract, scientific point of view, but may seriously misrepresent the state of human relations in the period we are interested in modeling. Consider first of all that our *raison d'être* is to produce viable offspring. With young that require as many as 18 years of parental care, humans find themselves with a challenge not faced by most other animals. A mother cannot reasonably hope to raise an infant on her own, for instance. Consequently, the model of the origin of human cooperation and altruism where the independent and unattached individual pairs off against the other is not very useful (Hrdy 2009). Furthermore, parental nurturance is found in our closest ancestors, indicating that something other than rational self-interest was available for evolution to work with. Charles Darwin, himself, suggested that parental nurturance might be the root of many of our moral characteristics (Darwin 1871). It is not hard to see that if we start with parental nurturance – which likely involves altruistic motivation (Sober and Wilson 1998) – current game theoretical models are a poor fit. Perhaps they can account for the rise of large-scale societies out of small-scale ones, but they do not provide good models for the origin of human cooperation or altruism. One suspects that this ignoring of the relevance of the parental connection to the field of ethics – be it evolutionary ethics, moral theory, or meta-ethics – is the fruit of a culture that historically has dominated and undervalued women and their work. Women have been delegated the work of the household and childrearing which, in their turn, have been regarded as being of little relevance to public life or serious intellectual occupations, like philosophy.

By contrast to the male perspective outlined above, many feminists have argued that morality extends into the personal sphere traditionally understood to be that of the female. Furthermore, they argue, this sphere may be more basic and constitute a better model for societal morality than the traditional male-dominated one (Gilligan 1982; Noddings 1984; Robinson 1999). For instance, Carol Gilligan's (1982) care ethics was originally a response to Lawrence Kohlberg's moral stage theory which, being deeply inspired by Kantian moral thinking, is plausibly construed as a predominantly male-oriented approach to morality (Kohlberg 1976). It is interesting to note that the care approach has close affinities with Buddhist ethics, which is one of the oldest in the world, but has not been much considered in Western ethical thought until relatively recently.

4   Philosophy of science

Feminist neuroscientists were among the first to critique androcentric theories and assumptions in their disciplines, making neuroscience an important site for what Harding (1986) called "spontaneous feminist empiricism." Since that time, feminist epistemology and philosophy of science has become an established area of research, and has provided a theoretical basis for these criticisms. Elizabeth Anderson (2011) suggests that the central concept of feminist epistemology and philosophy of science is that knowers are situated (and, therefore, so is their knowledge). What can be known by an individual or a group depends on a number of factors relevant to the knower's situation, including aspects of their social location, their background beliefs and world views, their values and interests, and their relationships to other inquirers and areas of inquiry. These factors are, of course, not independent of each other.

Gender is a particular type of social situation that can have important effects on the type of scientific theories that are developed. Working out the effects of gender on neuroscience research was an important part of the early feminist critiques mentioned above. A number of authors pointed out ways in which gender stereotypes and gender roles influenced the development of evolutionary theory and the emerging field of sociobiology. For example, Longino and Doell (1983) examined the biases resulting from evolutionary theories that were based on the idea of "man the hunter" but largely ignored women's potential roles in shaping human evolution. Birke (1986) showed the influence of gender roles, as understood in the mid-twentieth century, on sociobiological theories, as well as how sociobiologists reinforced those theories.

Other feminists highlighted problems with sex difference research. Anne Fausto-Sterling (1992) reviewed the sizable body of work that attempted to show sex differences in the size or shape of the corpus callosum, the fibrous structure connecting the two hemispheres of the brain. She pointed out that despite the failure to find consistent differences across studies, researchers continue to develop new methods of measurement and to look at different parts of the structure in order to find a difference that they were certain *must* exist.

Philosophers of science attempted to gain a better understanding of the way that social values and background assumptions influenced science, and also to develop a cure for cases in which their effects were pernicious. Although a review of the details of these theories is beyond the scope of this introduction (see Anderson 2011 for an analysis), a key insight is that the development of theories that are more empirically adequate depends on the social structure of science. Specifically, diverse perspectives are necessary in order to overcome the biases associated with particular positions (e.g. Longino 1992; Harding 2004). In the case of neuroscience research, which is complex and multidisciplinary, and which aims to link biology with psychology and behavior, these aspects of feminist philosophy of science are particularly useful and important.

5 Embodiment

Feminist approaches to neuroscience also have important implications for questions about embodied cognition. The idea that cognition is embodied is gaining popularity in mainstream Anglophone philosophy (Noë 2004, 2009; Hutto 2007; Menary 2010; Rowlands 2010; Shapiro 2011), yet it remains hotly debated (Block 2005; Prinz 2006; Adams and Aizawa 2008; Rupert 2009). In such philosophy, embodied cognition is contrasted with cognition that is wholly within the brain. If cognition is housed in our skulls, it may have causes beyond the brain, but they are not really part of it. They do not form constitutive parts of cognition. Theories of embodied cognition, then, are foes of reductionism as it is traditionally understood.

Anglophone philosophy has a cultural context in which the idea that the mind is all in the head has gained a hold on theorists. This is partly due to the impact Turing and the digital computer have had on philosophy of mind. From Turing we get a model of what wholly physical thinking might be; namely, symbolic computations. At the same time, we all know that computers are largely unmoving, lifeless objects. We need, then, to add into our understanding of the culture the fact that philosophers found it easy to think of minds in such objects. Though a lack of ease with the body has ancient roots, the usual suspect for European philosophy's conviction that the mind is independent of bodily action today is Descartes. According to him, we can easily conceive of the mind without the body. Indeed, he thought the highest forms of thinking did not involve the body at all. Centuries of subsequent worries about the relationship between minds and bodies, including others' bodies and supposed minds, have had their impact.

Feminist thought on embodiment is far ahead of mainstream philosophy, as Meynell's fine introduction to *Embodiment and Cognition* makes clear (Campbell, Meynell et al. 2009). For feminists, both the individual body and one's society, often interacting, are potent factors in shaping cognition. The external factors may be merely causal, but they can also be constitutive, as when one's identity incorporates factors beyond one's brain or one counts as possessing information that goes beyond what could be held in any one head. For some feminists the rules and norms important to cognition cannot be the invention of individuals acting on their own (Baier 1997).

There is a particularly interesting difference between embodiment in mainstream philosophy and that in feminist thought. Mainstream thought's forays into embodiment are often relatively asocial. Few feminists have found plausible the idea that the body can be seen as a somehow purely natural product, fundamentally unaltered by the distinguishing characteristics of the society in which it is placed (Bordo 1993; Young 2005). The social nature of the embodied mind starts early and perhaps even precedes birth. For many philosophers, then, the self remains very like the scholar alone in a study. On the other hand, feminists have often taken social interactions to provide parts or aspects of cognition that are very important factors to be considered in theories of cognition. These effects of society on cognition may be mediated by mild or by fairly strong actions affecting the body.

6 The chapters

As previously noted, many of the essays in this volume address more than one of the above themes. Letitia Meynell draws on work in aesthetics to analyze the production of images in neuroimaging research on sex/gender differences. Ginger Hoffman also addresses work on sex/gender differences, using discussions of multiple realizability in philosophy and in biology to argue that finding a physical difference between the brains of women and men may not be evidence for behavioral differences. Her analysis also raises problems for the traditional view that cognition is "all in the head." Heidi Lene Maibom assesses claims that women are more empathetic than men and considers the effects that recent research on empathy and sympathy have had on an ethics of care approach. Giordana Grossi and Cordelia Fine are also concerned with debunking the feminizing of empathy, in their case in the shape of Baron-Cohen's extreme male brain hypothesis of autism. Baron-Cohen (2003) posits an essential difference between males and females centered on the two constructs of systematizing and empathizing. However, the evidence for this theory, as Grossi and Fine show, is distinctly lacking.

Following this trend towards similarity rather than difference, Rebecca Jordan-Young and Raffaella Rumiati argue that, since the evidence of male/female differences is highly problematic, and there are many more similarities than differences in any case, it is morally questionable for researchers to continue to focus their research on differences (see also Jordan-Young 2010). The chapter by Isabelle Dussauge and Anelis Kaiser also moves beyond consideration of sex/gender differences in the brain, but shows how this distinction has shaped research on sexuality and sexual orientation, arguing that queer theory provides valuable resources to allow researchers to move beyond this simplistic framework.

Several other essays in this volume address the question of appropriate frameworks and methods for neuroscience research. Einstein uses both her methods and work in feminist philosophy of science to offer some suggestions for the development of a feminist neuroscience, highlighting the ethical implications of background assumptions about the nature of the nervous system and of research methods. Deboleena Roy and Cynthia Kraus also address questions about methodology and interdisciplinarity. Kraus argues against the current focus on consensus across disciplines and promotes the idea of a "dissensus framework," while Roy draws on work by Isabelle Stengers to develop an ecology of practices that is rooted in both feminism and neuroscience.

Problems with the traditional sex/gender binary also show the necessity of finding better ways to understand the relationship between the mind, the body, and the environment (including the social environment). As such, they relate to questions about the nature of embodiment and cognition. Anne Jacobson undertakes an analytic exploration of a view that disrupts our understanding of the social nature of cognitive competence and she argues against it in the case of vision. Questions about embodiment are also central in Gillian Einstein's chapter, which describes her research on the physiological effects of female genital circumcision.

The final paper, by Robyn Bluhm, looks at the way that scientific studies of sex/gender differences are used in self-help books that purport to be based on neuroscience. She shows that the oversimplified (and often even erroneous) picture presented in these books greatly influences the popular understanding of the brain and (gendered) behavior, and underscores the need for the kind of critical, feminist, nuanced approaches to neuroscience that the essays in this volume present.

Notes

1. We will ignore here the use of the terms in linguistics, focusing only on their use to describe characteristics of human beings.
2. This criticism echoes arguments by feminist theorists (e.g. Spelman 1988; Butler 1990, 1993; Gatens 1995) who argue that the distinction between sex and gender is problematic; however, a detailed discussion of these issues is beyond the scope of this introduction. Mikkola (2008) provides a good overview of these criticisms.
3. Part of the problem here is that evolutionary altruism is defined as behavior that reduces the fitness of the individual. As such, no behavior aimed at increasing the fitness of offspring, siblings, etc. counts as altruistic. The trouble starts when this sense of altruism is not clearly distinguished from that of psychological altruism. Psychological altruism is the idea that organisms are sometimes motivated to do something for another for their sake, without this motivation being based on another, more ultimate egoistic motivation (Sober and Wilson 1998). The prisoner's dilemma might be a good model for the problem of evolutionary altruism, but not for that of psychological altruism.

1
The Politics of Pictured Reality: Locating the Object from Nowhere in fMRI

Letitia Meynell

1 Introduction

In *Sexing the Body*, Anne Fausto-Sterling recounts the late twentieth-century taming of the corpus callosum in the name of sexing the brain. This three-dimensional bridge, which transfers signals between lobes of the living brain, was domesticated to make it scientifically tractable: dead, preserved brains were physically sectioned, then conceptually divided into five parts and studiously measured. As she explains, "One is left to assign meaning to an abstraction, and the space opened up for mischief becomes enormous" (2000b: 130).

In a similar vein, here I explore the 'space for mischief' that opens up in applications of current neuroimaging technologies that continue the tradition of sexing the brain. The particular way that pictures are constructed with fMR imaging technologies combine with the implicit rhetoric of science and mechanical objectivity to present constructed abstractions as if they were concrete particulars. These neuroscientific 'objects from nowhere' present images of *the* female brain and *the* male brain that essentialize *the* feminine mind and *the* masculine mind. Concerns about essentialist tendencies in neuroimaging are familiar to feminists (Schinzel 2006a, 2006b; Kaiser et al. 2007), but what has been lacking to date is a generic account of the pictorial function of scientific, machine-made images as a crucial component in understanding the persuasive power of fMRI studies of gender difference. While perhaps the scientists who use these devices have a more nuanced understanding of the content and epistemic status of these images, it is in the popular media and lay understanding where I think the space for mischief is particularly troubling. It is, after all, in these contexts that public opinion is made and gender is enacted.

In what follows, I characterize a conceptual landscape for understanding machine-made images in which I locate the object from nowhere. Though my account shares much with Adina Roskies' (2008) explanation of the ways in which the actual inferential gap between the brain and brain image in fMRI is much larger than the apparent inferential gap, it does, I hope, offer itself more naturally to generalization to other machine-made images. Drawing on Kendall Walton's work (1990, 2008) I develop a general account of this hidden epistemic difference in distance. I then show how it facilitates the presentation of constructed abstractions as concrete particulars. I argue that the persuasive power of these objects from nowhere derives from their *apparent* transparency. The mistaken belief that fMR images are transparent rests on their depictive character and the fact that they are machine made. Once we understand the persuasive power of the object from nowhere we can see how it exerts itself in gender construction.

2   Representation, depiction and transparency

In order to develop a general account we need to have a clear analysis of how pictures and especially machine-made pictures present their content.[1] In this section I give a brief overview of Walton's theory of representation and explain depiction, a type of pictorial representation, as a degreed notion, employing the example of fetal ultrasound. I then consider the distinct epistemic character of machine-produced images (like ultrasound and fMRI) addressing their apparent transparency as windows on to real objects and past states of affairs. Following Walton, I show how depictiveness and transparency are fundamentally different in character and conceptually distinct, despite often being correlated. This lays the conceptual groundwork for the explication of the object from nowhere in the following section and offers a more detailed and more general analysis than is suggested by Roskies.

2.1   Representation and depiction

Although primarily designed for aesthetics, Walton's theory of representation can be usefully extended to non-artistic images (see Meynell 2008a, 2008b). For Walton, 'representation' is a functional term identifying objects that act as props for the imagination. So, for instance, while one could use the *Mona Lisa* or a copy of *Daniel Deronda* as doorstops, qua representations, they have the function of prompting their viewers/readers to imagine that they are looking at a woman with an enigmatic smile and to imagine a young English gentleman discovering his Jewish identity, respectively. One might suppose that one is free to imagine whatever one likes when viewing these works and, of course, in a certain sense this is trivially true. However, just as it is a kind of mis-use of the *Mona Lisa* to use it as a doorstop, it is also a misuse to imagine in viewing it that one is looking at a pizza or a hippopotamus (Walton 1990: 60; Meynell 2008b). Authorized imaginings are constrained by principles of generation that determine what the viewer/reader is meant to imagine in the act of viewing (or reading) the representation. These principles range from stipulated conventions and tacit rules to psycho-logical capacities and cognitive constraints; they determine the content of the world of the representation. Principles of generation are what the viewer/reader brings to the representation that enable her to com-prehend its content. If a viewer/reader cannot understand or misun-derstands a representation – attributing to it content that it does not possess – this is probably because she lacks the appropriate principles of generation. Many of these principles are tacitly learned through repeated application, which becomes increasingly nuanced with prac-tice. Learning to see the content of a representation of a certain type helps us to properly glean the content of similar representations in the future (Walton 1990: 40–41).

Now, there are many obvious ways in which authorized *Mona Lisa* imaginings are different in character from those that happen on read-ing *Daniel Deronda*. The difference is not *simply* that one is visual art while the other is narrative as the distinction remains if we compare the *Mona Lisa* with, say, some of Mark Rothko's later works.[2] As a piece of figurative art, the *Mona Lisa* depicts things as they might be perceived in the world; there are recognizable objects in specific spatial relations. Rothko's later works, no matter how magnificent or evocative, are not intended to represent things as they might be directly *visually* experi-enced in life.[3] In Walton's terms, what makes the *Mona Lisa* different is that it is a depiction. In depictions the peculiarly visual character of the image is wound up in its viewing, prompting the viewer to imagine that she is seeing the scene or object that is represented. In the very act of viewing the *Mona Lisa* we *make-believe* that we are viewing a woman; she appears relaxed, her hair is parted in the middle, her plump hands are crossed. "The seeing and the imagining are inseparably bound together, integrated into a single complex phenomenological whole'" (Walton 1990: 295). The works that Rothko painted for the Four Seasons restaurant in New York may have been intended to "'ruin the appetite of every son of a bitch who ever eats in that room'" (Banville 2006), but not by prompting diners to imagine a specific object or scene in the act of viewing the paintings.

Despite its ties to visual experience, depiction does not rest on similarity or visual similarity and thus does not reduce to a two-place resemblance relation between the object represented and the representation. Because Walton is interested in the representation of non-existent objects and states of affairs (e.g. Zeus, unicorns, the Loch Ness monster eating acorns) he needs an account of both representation and depiction where the ontological status of what is represented is irrelevant to its status as a representation. So, rather than resting depictiveness on the similarity between image and object,[4] he bases it on the similarity of the way the viewer would visually inspect the object or state of affairs if it existed in reality to decipher what is true with how the viewer visually inspects the representation to decipher its content. Walton explains, "I do not mean to compare the visual sensations or phenomenological experiences which viewers and observers of things enjoy…The analogies I am interested in hold…between visual investigations of picture worlds and visual investigations of the real world" (Walton 1990: 304). So, for instance, if I want to know if a person in my vicinity is yawning or has a nose piercing I look at her face. Similarly, if I have the same questions about Leonardo's subject I look at her depicted face. My perceptual and cognitive systems make use of light and shadow to determine three-dimensional shape and, analogously, they make use of pale and dark paint to decipher three-dimensional shape information from a two-dimensional surface.[5]

When we have no experience of visually investigating a depicted object (whether it exists or not), we draw on principles of generation from similar objects and representations of those objects to generate our imaginings. The ease of doing this depends on our familiarity with the type of object and the degree of conformity between the principles of generation that we bring to the image and the principles of generation that are required to glean the content. The analogies between viewing the object itself and the depiction may be many or few and these analogies can be more or less crucial to gleaning the content, so depictiveness comes in degrees.

Usefully, we can see that the recent move from 2-D to 3-D ultrasound is an advance in degree of depictiveness and some of the ways in which depictiveness increases in this case are instructive for understanding depictiveness generally. Comparing the 2-D image in Figure 1.1 with the 3-D image in Figure 1.2, we can see that Figure 1.1 has the appearance of an X-ray image or perhaps a poor print from an old or poorly

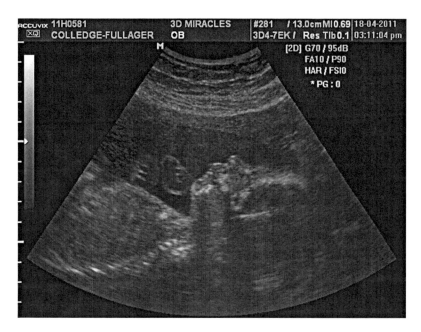

Figure 1.1 A 2-D fetal ultrasound image, printed with permission from 3D Miracles – 3D Ultrasound, Halifax, Nova Scotia

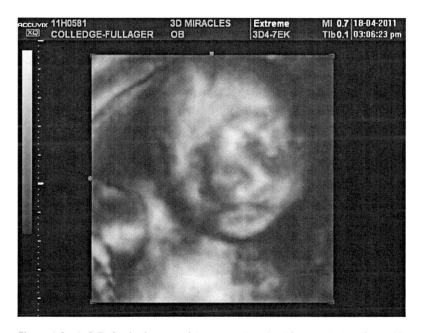

Figure 1.2 A 3-D fetal ultrasound image, printed with permission from 3D Miracles – 3D Ultrasound, Halifax, Nova Scotia

made press. The projection system employed is orthogonal, presenting a cross-section of the fetal body. The line style works with the projection system to represent the shape of the body as an outline. Because most lay viewers are relatively unfamiliar with orthogonal projection, cross-sections of fetuses, fetal environments, and seeing outlines through the line style employed, specialized interpretation – in Walton's terms, principles of generation unfamiliar to the typical lay viewer – is often required to glean the content of images of this type. Currently, the general public in the global North are somewhat familiar with the basic appearance of late-term fetuses, trained by multiple popular culture and popular science sources (Petchesky 1987). So, because in Figure 1.1 the cross-section looks like a profile and noise and confusing elements are minimal, even non-expert viewers can, without assistance, decipher the content and imagine in their viewing of the image that they are viewing a fetus. Of course, the pregnant woman whose insides are being imaged by the ultrasound typically has an expert viewer (the technician) to assist her in generating the right imaginings, telling her what part of the image should be understood as what part of the fetal body (Mitchell and Georges 1997: 376). Interestingly, prospective parents may even interact with the image rather than the fetus itself, housed inside the pregnant woman's body (Mitchell and Georges 1997: 378). This imaginative interaction with the image is itself suggestive of its depictiveness.

However, the 3-D ultrasound is considerably more depictive; the contrast with Figure 1.2 is striking. The initial impression is of a slightly tinted, somewhat blurry black and white photograph. This is facilitated through the use of perspective projection and the presentation of shape information in this system through shadows and hotspots. The hotspot on the brow of the fetus suggests a light source coming from the viewer, as if from the flash on a camera. Even the relatively untrained eye can easily decipher a human head with facial features against a background. No expert intervention is required to help us to imagine seeing a fetus here. Although Figure 1.1 is a depiction, it is less depictive than Figure 1.2.

It is worth remembering that depictiveness does not reduce to a two-place resemblance relationship between the image and the object or the appearance of the object. Arguably, the 3-D ultrasound image prompts one to imagine a baby, not a fetus (though this depends on the principles of generation brought to the image). It is pretty obvious that the pregnancy, which is constitutive of the fetus being a fetus, is not visible. Rather than being in the total darkness of the gravid body, 3-D ultrasound images show an individual in an open space with a light shining on it. The individual does not appear to be attached to another human body as there is no human body depicted, just a shadowy background that one must make some effort to remember is a woman.[6]

2.2 Transparency and machine-made images

If depictiveness is about the way that viewers understand the content of images, transparency addresses the way that viewers assess the veridicality[7] of images. It is widely recognized that machine-produced images and those directly rendered by humans are epistemically different and that the difference concerns the production and causal history of the images themselves. The epistemic status conferred on the image – whether we take it to reveal some fact(s) of the matter – depends in large part on the method of its construction. In science, machine-made depictions might be thought of as visual prosthetics, extending our perceptual capacities and allowing us to see what would otherwise be unobservable (Haraway 1991). Walton explicates the epistemic character of photographs in a way that both naturally extends to machine made, scientific images and offers a method for analyzing the extent to which machine-construction can appropriately be taken to confer this epistemic success. Thus, although his account of transparency is in a sense absolute, with production by machine being a necessary, though not sufficient, condition, it also admits of degrees with some machine-made images being more or less transparent.

"Photographs," Walton writes, "are transparent. We see the world through them" (2008: 86). In contrast, when looking at a human-rendered picture we see what the artist believed she saw. Walton offers the example of an explorer who emerges from the jungle with a set of dinosaur pictures and he challenges us to compare what our epistemic assessment of the pictures would be if they were photographs versus if they were sketches. The question is not which we would find most convincing, but the evidential path upon which our judgments would rest: "in the case of the sketches we rely on the picture maker's belief that there is a dinosaur in a way in which we don't in the case of the photographs" (2008: 99). The sketches show that the explorer believed there was a dinosaur, whereas "if the photographs *do* convince us that he believed in the dinosaur, they do so because they convince us that there was a dinosaur, not the other way around" (2008: 98).

One useful way of characterizing transparent images is through the language of counterfactual dependence. Suppose that the explorer had been hallucinating the dinosaur when making the picture. In the case of the sketch the hallucinations determine the content of the image, whereas in the case of the photograph they would make no difference at all. "[P]hotographs... have 'natural' counterfactual dependence on the photographed scenes, whereas handmade paintings possess only 'intentional' counterfactual dependence on what they portray" (following Walton 2008: 127). The camera captures the scene and thus the photograph's content does not depend on and will not counterfactually vary on the basis of the explorer's beliefs about the scene. Of course, this is something of an oversimplification. Beliefs do have *some* role to play in determining the content of a photograph as they inform the design of the camera, the exposure of the film, the choice of the subject, and so forth. But with these provisos, the content of photographs depends significantly on the contingent facts about the photographed scenes. The important question to our epistemic assessment is the ways in which the content of a machine-made image counterfactually rests on these beliefs rather than the features of the imaged object.

The implicit acceptance that machine-made images have counterfactual independence from the machine operator's beliefs seems to ground what Lorraine Daston and Peter Galison (2007) call "mechanical objectivity." As they explain, mechanization itself has been thought to ensure objectivity through instantiating a "set of procedures that... as it were, move nature to the page through a strict protocol, if not automatically" (2007: 121). The machine, "free from the will" is seen as free from distorting subjectivity, making it a more reliable communicator and granting it epistemic authority denied to human drawing. Through this lens, machine-made images appear to be ideal scientific tools. The epistemic authority granted to science is enhanced through mechanical objectivity and thus machine-made scientific images become exemplars for conveying "the facts," free from bias.

This approach to machine-made pictorial content is by no means inevitable. While mechanical objectivity reached its zenith during the Victorian era, the ever-increasing power and complexity of imaging technology, led to "a strategy that explicitly acknowledged the need to employ *trained judgment* in making and using images" (Daston and Galison 2007: 311) in the early twentieth century. Daston and Galison suggest that these two regulative ideals – mechanical objectivity and trained judgment – have come to shape the way that scientists understand their own image-making activities, with different scientists taking one attitude or the other towards their work (2007: 318–321).

Whichever ideal characterizes a given scientist's approach, the scientific image retains epistemic authority. The machine captures a part or aspect of the world. In one case it is obvious for all to see and in the other case expert skill is required in both an image's capture and its interpretation. Put in this way, we can see that mechanical objectivity, where the machine operates free from any subjective influence, takes machine-made images to be more transparent than trained judgment, where the image is understood to be, at least in part, counterfactually dependent on the actions of the scientist. Moreover, through the lens of trained judgment, the image is only fully transparent to the scientist; only she can properly interpret what the image says about the world.

While Daston and Galison nicely elucidate the ways in which new technologies complicate the epistemic authority of scientific images, Walton provides a method of analysis that can be applied in the assessment of the epistemic status of machine-made images. We can investigate an image and the mechanism that made it and identify whether (or to what extent) a given aspect of the content of the image depends on human choices made in the construction of the machine or on the object itself. Moreover, we can articulate the principles of generation required to understand the content of a particular image and so decide whether trained judgment is properly required to understand it.

2.3   Transparency vs. depictiveness

It should now be clear that transparency is quite distinct from depictiveness (Walton 2008: 113–114). Transparency is a feature only of machine-made images that addresses the causal path between the object of knowledge and the knower. The method of construction is irrelevant to depictiveness, which addresses the degree to which the way the viewer organizes her imagining of seeing the depicted object matches the way that the same viewer *would* organize her perception of the object itself. Whereas an object must exist for a representation to be transparent, a depiction need not be of an existent object (consider depictions of Zeus).

Now, it happens to be the case that the vast majority of photographs presented for viewing (especially before the advent of digital photography and Photoshop (see Walton's discussion 2008: 114–116)) combine transparency with depictiveness and are considered to be epistemically useful because they do so. Witness the fact that photographs are favored in journalism and criminal trials, not just for their transparency but also for their depictiveness; together they make photographs epistemologically powerful. After all, a fuzzy snapshot of Piccadilly Circus is transparent but fails to be ideally depictive and thus fails to be particularly epistemically useful; I cannot use it to gain much knowledge about

Piccadilly Circus. I can only visually inspect it to get to know some of the basic architectural features of the intersection, rather than inspect it as I might visually inspect Piccadilly Circus itself in order to get to know things about it.

Because many of the principles of generation that we apply to representations have been tacitly gleaned from past practices of viewing representations, it seems plausible to suppose that a familiarity with photography's transparency, depictiveness, and epistemic power leads us to view other machine-made depictions in a similar light. This tendency will only be reinforced in light of common transparent machine-made depictions, like X-rays. When we can make out the content of a machine-made depiction – in other words, when, as lay viewers, we can apply principles of generation so as to make a depiction meaningful – and when this content coheres with (or at least does not contradict) what we already believe of the depicted object, it is natural to suppose that we are transparently seeing the object through the image. This process will be self-reinforcing and may become habitual and tacit. In such cases, trained judgment *appears* not to be needed by virtue of the fact that we can decipher the image at all. In this way there may be a tendency to assume that machine-made depictiveness implies transparency. In scientific contexts, this assumption combines with mechanical objectivity and scientific authority and orients the viewer to treat machine-made depictions, like fMR images, as powerful epistemic devices that present us directly with states of affairs, without bias or subjective influence.

That a correlation between degree of depictiveness and degree of transparency, even if common, is far from necessary is clearly illustrated in the comparison between 2-D and 3-D fetal ultrasound. As I have argued above, 3-D ultrasound is more depictive than 2-D ultrasound, and depictiveness in machine-made images is often a sign of transparency, thus we might tacitly assume that 3-D ultrasound is more transparent than 2-D ultrasound. However, while 3-D ultrasound has greater *apparent* transparency, it is in fact less transparent. This is because there are more components between object and image and, if not a greater number of human minds, then certainly more theory, more programming and a greater number of representational choices. 3-D ultrasound images are constructed from several 2-D images, adding a layer of data processing on top of what is already required to produce the 2-D ultrasound image.

The language of counterfactual dependence provides a method for analyzing degrees of transparency. It allows us to specify which aspects of an image have "natural counterfactual dependence" on the represented state of affairs in contrast to those that have counterfactual dependence on human beliefs or assumptions. The machines that mediate signal and visual output are themselves designed by human agents and as they become increasingly complex, the human judgments – informed by background knowledge, conceptual schemas, judgments of saliency, and conventions – become increasingly relevant for determining their transparency and thus the appropriate epistemic attitude toward the content of the image. Thus, even when trained judgment is not needed to glean the content of an image, it may be required to assess the relation between its content and the method of production, upon which judgments of epistemic status should rest. The problem is that machine-made depictions implicitly suggest transparency, even when they are not in fact correlated. When this judgment of transparency is added to the epistemic authority of science the space opens up for mischief.

3   The object from nowhere located and the mischief that it makes

Adina Roskies has identified something akin to this gap between actual and apparent transparency in fMRI, characterizing it through the language of inferential distance. In the terms outlined above, inferential distance widens as engineers' and software designers' beliefs become salient in the construction of an image, such that an aspect of the depicted content is counterfactually dependent on those beliefs and decisions, rather than directly on the imaged object itself (Roskies 2008: 22). Roughly, as with fetal ultrasound, *apparent* inferential proximity of fMR images to the imaged brain rests on the degree of depictiveness, the *actual* inferential distance depends on transparency[8] and the validity of the assumptions made about the brain in order to render the images informative. Roskies illustrates the power of this analysis by taking her readers step by step through the multiple assumptions that form the *actual* inferential distance.

She begins by noting that fMRI, as a tool of cognitive neuroscience, is designed to "map functional components of mind to neural structures," achieving this through revealing "the neural activity underlying cognitive and/or behavioral tasks" (2008: 23). So, what the images depict is neural activity, which in turn is correlated with mental activity (an assumption that is already vague and fraught with difficulties). The gaps that particularly concern us occur in what Roskies calls the causal stream that relates the actual neural activity to the visual display of data on a screen.[9] The design of the machine and data analysis are premised on a set of correlations: neural activity (excitatory or inhibitory) is correlated with increased blood flow; blood flow is correlated with an increased level of oxygenated blood; an increase in oxygenated blood is associated with an increase in the BOLD signal (the signal that fMRI detects); and a decrease in oxygenated blood is associated with a decrease in the BOLD signal.

While these correlations are well confirmed, they are far from endowing the visually constructed data derived from them with transparency. There are certain types of differences in the neural state that would not register a change in the brain image. First, many neural states give rise to the same signal; the same net magnetic susceptibility changes can result from different combinations of changes in blood flow, volume, and oxygen extraction and, indeed, the same signal might appear with either inhibitory or excitatory synaptic activity. Secondly, it is not clear that fMRI machines can distinguish large changes in the firing of a few neurons from small changes in the firing of many neurons from changes in neuronal synchrony. Third, the spatial and temporal resolution of fMRI is orders of magnitude coarser than neural firings and fourth, signal to noise ratios are quite low (Roskies 2008: 25). The question is whether there are good reasons to think that these differences between the brain state and its fMR representation are salient; a question that has no straightforward, theory independent answer.

Now, it is important to note that the above assumptions are peculiar to fMRI and they rest on top of a whole other range of assumptions and data manipulations embedded in MRI technology. Britta Schinzel usefully brings the perspective of a computer scientist to the analysis. She writes:

> between these data collected on the wall, interpreted as grey or colour level pixels, and the final images a lot of computational steps and algorithms have to be performed, many of which are already interpreting steps [i.e. steps that require theoretical commitments and thus depend on the designers' beliefs]. These include corrections of the inhomogeneous strength of the magnetic field, corrections of different kinds of noise, stemming from the apparatus as well as from the patient's tissue, up to the selection and preparation of parameters according to which varied images can be produced from the data set of one and the same person. Tissue noise on the molecular level is ruled out using physiological models, won by empirical experience. As the molecular tissue properties are varying not only according to the kind of tissue (organ differences, normal or pathological tissue), but also individually, it is not sure that the uniform modelling is adequate in every individual case. (2006b: 192)

For fMRI data the signal to noise ratio is low enough that the experiment must be set up so that data exposure is repeated a number of times (Schinzel 2006b: 193) and often images are averaged across multiple individuals.

Each of these steps in the causal stream marks a point where we might reasonably raise a question about whether an aspect of the image is dependent on a human decision behind the machine's design or is dependent on the brains being imaged. In Roskies' terms, each step marks an inferential move where the beliefs of the scientist/engineer/programmer have a role in determining what information is retained from one component of the system to the next. In this light, we can see that these images are not very transparent. They are, however, depictive. It is easy to see the brain in the image and just as it is natural to point out and name parts of the fetal body in an ultrasound image; it is natural to point to parts of the brain in the fMR image in much the same spirit.

While there are many different ways of creating depictions from raw fMRI data, the most familiar to the lay public are the black and white cross-sections with lit up patches of color indicating neural activity (see Figure 1.3 for a black and white version). Although these images are data maps of the BOLD signal, it is tempting to collapse the inferential distance and read the bright colors as pictures of neural functioning. Unlike some of the colorful 3-D fMR images, this mode of presentation looks serious and scientific. The 2-D sections are tantalizingly reminiscent of X-rays or even 2-D ultrasound and it is natural to bring principles of generation practiced on these more familiar medical imaging

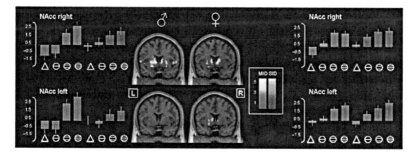

Figure 1.3   A figure comparing fMR images from 16 men and 16 women purporting to show "ample differences in brain activation patterns underlying anticipation of different reward types between men and women" from Spreckelmeyer et al. (2009: 164), by permission of Oxford University Press

technologies to bear on fMR images, particularly if one has little else to go on.[10] As an X-ray or ultrasound image reveals the structure of a real object and states of affairs actually occurring at a particular place and time, it is natural to read fMR images this way also.

However, unlike X-rays and ultrasounds, fMR images from cognitive studies of sex differences do not depict an extant object at a particular time; fMR images must be averaged across multiple instances or individuals in order to get reliable data out of the noise. As Roskies notes, "although what results from this averaging procedure is a brain image, it is not an image of a brain" (2008: 26). Moreover, it is not only the lit up areas marking the BOLD response that are averaged; because human brains come in a variety of different shapes, structures and structure to function relationships, when images are averaged the data from each brain image must be warped to fit it into a common space (Roskies 2008: 26). So, both the black and white image of the brain and the representation of activity in the brain, though appearing to be a transparent picture of an actual brain are representations of a fiction. The brain image is a constructed abstraction in the same way that the average Canadian household, with its 1.5 children, or the splenium of the corpus callosum is. But it is more than this; it is an object from nowhere.

That the average Canadian family *is* an abstraction and does not actually *exist* is obvious through its method of presentation. Real families may have vague boundaries but their members can only be counted in whole numbers, actual families do not admit part members (unless we are speaking metaphorically). With an fMR image, the mode of presentation – depictive and machine made – obscures its real nature, presenting it as if it were a transparent representation of a real object. In this sense fMR images present 'an object' 'from nowhere.' While clearly the object from nowhere is misleading – it presents a fictional abstraction as if it were a real object – it is not until it is put to the service of sexing the brain that its mischievous nature becomes clear. While fMRI studies of sex differences are presented in such a way as to suggest that they are *discovering* sex differences, visually they display and methodologically they presuppose a kind of absolute sex dimorphism and thus implicitly support sex essentialism.

Anelis Kaiser and colleagues show how fMRI has been used to investigate differences between the neurological function behind men and women's language processing, olfactory processing, facial perception, emotional sensation, and even satiety reaction to chocolate (Kaiser et al. 2007, 2009; Kaiser 2010: 198). While Kaiser et al. consider a variety of ways in which many of these fMRI studies of sex differences are problematic (Kaiser et al. 2009), my focus rests on the visual construction of sex dimorphism. First, the neuroimages used in these studies are often objects from nowhere. Although they look like transparent images of actual male and female brains, they are statistical maps displayed in a fictional generic space. A second issue arises in light of the inherently mathematical nature, and in particular the statistical status, of fMR images. Many of these studies have small numbers of participants – sometimes as few as ten men and ten women (Kaiser et al. 2007: 193). Supposing that the general population varies in the neuro-correlates of the studied task, then no matter how one divides the 20 individuals, one is likely to get two quite different brain images. Given what we know about development and neuroplasticity, there is good reason to think there will almost always be variation within the population for anything having to do with the brain. Thus, whenever scientists compare two fMR images produced from two small groups of men and women, they may well find two distinct images, even if there is no average difference between men and women in the population at large. If there is variability in the population, one requires much higher numbers of participants for the random variation to wash out.[11] Arguably, the only way you could justify using such small numbers statistically, is if you are already committed to a strong sex dimorphism and you are confident of capturing male and female natures in your study.

Third, despite the empirical importance of variation to the study of sex differences, the mode of presentation totally elides variation. Even if there are average group differences between the brains of women and men, the methods of data presentation obscure variance in the data and the amount of overlap between groups. Thus visually the question is begged against current feminist theorizing that emphasizes the contingency and complexity of sex/gender expression and argues for either multiple sex/genders or that sex/gender should be understood as a spectrum or even a set of relatively independent spectra (along which specific traits of particular organisms can be found) (Fausto-Sterling 2000b). It might be objected that because the signal to noise ratio is low it is not clear that it would be possible to separate variation in neural processing from noise. However, if this is the case, all the more reason to visually highlight the margins of error in the data and clearly represent the uncertainty that both noise and variation bring to the image What is required is a pictorial equivalent of error bars, not a visual presentation that obscures and implicitly denies both error and variation.

Of course, if what you are really looking to characterize is male and female essences, then variation *is* noise. Indeed, the very design of the research – the use of fMRI to find differences between men and women for a variety of different cognitive states – assumes and reifies the idea that there are essential cognitive differences between the sexes/genders. (After all, experiments might be designed to make many sexes/genders visible in the brain (Kaiser 2010: 208) or might be designed to corre-late gendered behavior with brain states regardless of the sex of sub-jects who embody them.) It appears that this research program seeks to uncover mysterious sex differences deep in the functioning brain. In short, when fMRI is applied to sexing the brain it tends to create two objects from nowhere – the male brain and the female brain – where the constructed lack of continuity between the two suggests an absolute sex dimorphism – two objects that are two distinct forms of brain, two fundamentally different kinds of people – despite the fact that typically the raw data do not.

As with the studies of the corpus callosum that Fausto-Sterling cri-tiques (2000b), the institutional context for fMRI studies of sex differ-ence is not neutral. fMRI studies that reveal sex differences are favored because science journals favor publishing positive results and a finding of no difference between sexes is taken to be the null hypothesis (Schinzel 2006a: 23; Kaiser et al. 2007: 197–198). Furthermore, the current studies are legitimized by being consistent, both in their background assump-tions and their results, with a long history of scientific studies on the essential differences between males and females (Schiebinger 1989; Fausto-Sterling 2000b). So, the very studies of the corpus callosum that Fausto-Sterling suggests are scientifically suspect effectively legitimize the current fMRI studies on sex differences. Thus the feminist voices that criticize the background assumptions and experimental methods of these studies are relegated to the ideological fringe, simply by virtue of the inherent conservatism of science. Ironically, this marginalization robs the science itself of one of its most powerful tools in the search for valid results – control for sexist bias (Biology and Gender Study Group 1988).

4   The object from nowhere and gendered reality outside the lab

It is natural for the non-expert to read fMR images as showing absolute differences between 'men's brain' and 'women's brain' (especially given conflation of neuronal differences to evolved differences that can be found in the presentation of this science in the popular media (e.g., Marsa 2007)). However, there is an ambiguity about how this should be understood. Is it a factual claim about all women and all men or is it in some sense normative? The factual claim that brains differ in some absolute sense on the basis of sex is clearly false. But the normative claim is at best morally and politically suspect, at least from a feminist perspective. Though there are many different ways of reading images of the dimorphic human brain normatively, all are troubling. Is the picture of the normative woman's brain that of *real* women, *properly functioning* women, *healthy* women, *normal* women, or *average* women? Feminists will, of course, reject this construction of women as singular in kind and be skeptical of the normative version of the claim suspecting many of the normative terms as covers for heterosexism, classism, racism, agism, and ablism. Since the late 1980s feminists have generally accepted that sex essentialism is factually mistaken, exclusionary, and damaging and where there is actual diversity among women it is not only false but morally wrong to claim that there isn't (Alcoff 1988; Spelman 1988). The rhetorical function of fMR images in the service of sexing the brain is thus antithetical to feminist values.

Moreover, sex-gender essentialism, especially related to cognitive and affective functioning, is predictably used to explain the under-representation and differential success of women in various desirable and powerful positions. The studies of sex differences thereby support 'common knowledge' that our society is just and egalitarian, but women and men are simply inherently and irremediably different, which is why sex differences in wealth, power, and status persist. We no longer only have the scientists' word to go on as this common knowledge is presented with the apparent transparency and mechanical objectivity of fMR images for everyone to see. The implicit message is that anyone, including the layperson, can look at two images of man's brain and woman's brain performing the same function and see that they display different neural activity. Indeed, 'common sense' suggests that to deny as much against clear fMRI evidence displays an absurd ideological prejudice.

The above analysis shows how neuroimaging technologies can be complicit in the construction of our social imaginary in ways that reinforce a belief in gender essentialism. Crucially, it is the particular character of these images – machine made, depictive, averaged abstractions – that makes them capable of producing objects from nowhere. Certainly, fMRI has legitimate and important clinical (and perhaps even non-clinical) applications and it would be ludicrous to advocate scrapping this technology. However, we need to be far more attentive to the motivations and institutional structures behind its various applications because they may both reflect and reinforce regressive social attitudes. Moreover, we must be attuned to the ways in which their depictive character and apparent transparency influences their uptake and proliferation in the popular media and among the general public.

Thinking more broadly, we need conceptual tools to analyze the content and epistemic adequacy of images in general. While currently, lay viewers and scientists are all too often impressed by mechanical objectivity and scientific authority to question scientific images, especially when as depictions they "wear their content on their sleeves" (Roskies 2008: 21), a cynical rejection of all scientific images as constructed is equally problematic. Instead, we need the awareness that depictiveness is conceptually entirely distinct from transparency and an analytic strategy that investigates the distinct assumptions, idealizations, and abstractions that constitute the inferential distance and the degree of transparency actually enjoyed by a given technology. Importantly, this cannot be a totally decontextualized epistemological project. Rather, we need the conceptual and analytic tools to grapple with what, borrowing from Marilyn Frye, we might think of as the politics of pictured reality.

Notes

1. The following explication of Walton's account of depiction and representation follows accounts that I have given elsewhere, see Meynell (2008a, 2008b).
2. I refer here to the works that are most associated with Rothko – the enormous canvases with horizontal blocks of color.
3. I must emphasize that this is not intended as a criticism, but as a claim about artistic style.
4. Nelson Goodman argues persuasively that resemblance cannot be the criterion for representation as there is no one way that any given object is or appears (1968: 6–15; see Meynell forthcoming: section 3c for a more detailed discussion).
5. For an in-depth account of how marks on a surface construct three-dimensional shape information see Willats (1997) and Meynell's brief introduction to Willats' system (forthcoming).
6. This is an ongoing theme in feminist discussions of ultrasound (see, for instance, Petchesky 1987; Mitchell and Georges 1997; Birke 1999).
7. 'Veridicality' is meant as a provisional epistemic success term for images, akin to the role of truth as an epistemic success term for propositions. What exactly the appropriate epistemic success term is for images is an issue that lies beyond the scope of this chapter.
8. Roskies follows Cohen and Meskin's (2004) account of the epistemic status of photographs, which is grounded on a rejection of literal transparency that Walton defends.

9. Roskies also discusses the functional stream, where a number of problematic assumptions about the functional organization of the brain, the nature of cognitive tasks, and mental content are discussed. Roskies identifies the gaps in the functional stream as more problematic as she believes the problems in the causal stream may ultimately be remedied, whereas those in the functional stream cannot (2008: 29).

10. Kelly Joyce explains that MR images resemble X-rays as a matter of historical accident. As MRI entered clinical practice it became the domain of radiologists whose training in X-ray image interpretation predisposed them to prefer neuroimages that resembled X-rays (2008: 38–41).

11. Suggestively, Kaiser and colleagues report that while sex differences for language processing have been found in a number of studies, some of the largest studies and at least one meta-analysis of studies have found no differences (2007: 192–194). I recommend Kaiser and colleagues' review article for a more sophisticated analysis of statistical and data analysis problems than can be found in some of these studies (2009). Thirion and colleagues (2007) have found that although small numbers of subjects may be standard in fMRI studies, there are reasons to doubt the reliability of their results.

2

What, If Anything, Can Neuroscience Tell Us About Gender Differences?

Ginger Hoffman

1 Introduction

There exists a widespread belief that men and women are very, very different – even to the point of being like different species, or like inhabitants of different planets.[1] This idea is ubiquitous: it can be found in scientific journal articles, newspapers, movies, TV shows, songs, stand-up comedy, self-help literature, and our everyday remarks and behaviors. To get a flavor of the intensity and character that this idea can acquire, consider this quotation from *Why Men Don't Listen and Women Can't Read Maps*, a popular book authored by Barbara and Allan Pease:

> Men and women are different…They live in different worlds, with different values and according to quite different sets of rules. Everyone knows this, but very few people, particularly men, are willing to admit it…Men dominate TV remote controls and flick through the channels; women don't mind watching the commercials. Under pressure, men drink alcohol and invade other countries; women eat chocolate and go shopping. Women criticize men for being insensitive, uncaring, not listening, not being warm and compassionate, not talking, not giving enough love, not being committed to relationships, wanting to have sex rather than make love, and leaving the toilet seat up. Men criticize women about their driving, for not being able to read street directories, for turning maps upside down, for their lack of a sense of direction, for talking too much without getting to the point, for not initiating sex often enough, and for leaving the toilet seat down. (Pease and Pease 2001: 3)

Many of the familiar gender stereotypes are invoked here: women are more sensitive, are better listeners, and have no sense of direction, and men are aggressive, uncaring, and more interested in sex. There is clearly a lot to vehemently challenge here, even if one believes that there are, indeed, some average mental and behavioral differences between women and men. However, although it is extremely tempting to do so, I will not challenge the content of this claim directly. Instead, I will challenge it indirectly by tackling one of its most widely used evidence bases: neuroscientific evidence of gendered brain differences. Especially in the last fifteen or so years, neuroscience has been increasingly used to support the claim that there are fundamental mental and behavioral differences between women and men.[2] Consider this promise by the Peases: "In this book, you will see how science confirms that men and woman [*sic*] are profoundly different both physically and mentally. They are *not* the same" (Pease and Pease 2001: 6–7). The idea has generally been that, if there are indeed differences in the brains of men and women, then the mental and behavioral differences between them are more "substantiated," more "real," or more "fundamental." Thus, neuroscientific data have been taken to greatly substantiate and strengthen claims of fundamental gender differences. My task in this chapter is to examine whether it actually succeeds in this goal. I will argue that it does not, at least, not without relying on the truth of certain assumptions which are highly questionable. Thus, my task is to challenge the following claim:

NEUROSCIENCE BOLSTERS: Neuroscientific data ('neuro-data,' for short)[3] provide *special* or *additional*[4] evidence for fundamental mental and behavioral differences between genders.

In other words, my main thesis is that NEUROSCIENCE BOLSTERS is true much less often than we think.[5]

It is not difficult to see how claims of fundamental gender differences (and, consequently, the strength and legitimacy of the evidence that supports them, including the veracity of NEUROSCIENCE BOLSTERS) have serious ramifications for how we relate to and understand those around us: our spouses, partners, friends, parents, children, co-workers, and various strangers we encounter. Nor is it difficult to see how these claims can have serious ramifications for gender equity. Although 'fundamentally different' does not strictly imply 'having a different worth' or 'having different rights,' this is often forgotten in everyday practice. Take just one of many examples: if women are seen as 'fundamentally' less capable in math and science (see, for example, the Larry Summers hullabaloo (Dillon and Rimer 2005)), then this will presumably make it harder for women to be able to pursue careers in these areas, even if it is their passion. Their self-image could suffer, as could their concrete possibilities for success and fair compensation, etc. Thus I take it as a starting point that various claims of differences between genders have been, are, and likely will be used in ways that aid the oppression of women (and men, albeit in different ways).

I will argue my thesis in roughly two steps. First, I hone in on the idea that neuro-data provide 'special' evidence for fundamental gender differences. I look at a number of possibilities for what sort of special evidence neuro-data have been presumed to provide (evidence of permanence, evidence of innateness, etc.) and contest each one. Much of this first half of the chapter is a review and reinterpretation of points made elsewhere (for example, see Eliot 2009), points that are nevertheless extremely helpful to recap here. In the second part of the chapter, I go a step further and question whether neuro-data provide *any* evidence of fundamental gender differences. Here, I appeal to basic distinctions in the philosophy of mind to argue that a difference in brain activity or structure may not necessarily imply a difference in mental activity or behavior. To my knowledge, this argument has *not* been made elsewhere.

2 Part I: Neuro-data fail to provide *special* evidence of fundamental gender differences

2.1 What sort of special evidence might neuro-data provide?

In order to assess whether neuro-data succeed in bolstering claims of gender difference, it is necessary to try to understand what type of 'bolstering' they are purportedly providing. Here, I examine the idea that neuro-data provide *special* evidence of fundamental gender differences. What might this mean? I will consider a few possibilities in turn. They are:

1. Neuro-data bolster claims of fundamental mental and behavioral differences between genders by providing evidence that those differences are physical.
2. Neuro-data bolster claims of fundamental mental and behavioral differences between genders by providing evidence that those differences are permanent.

3. Neuro-data bolster claims of fundamental mental and behavioral differences between genders by providing evidence that those differences are innate.
4. Neuro-data bolster claims of fundamental mental and behavioral differences between genders by providing evidence that those differences are 'hard-wired.'

2.1.1 Option 1: neuro-data provide evidence of physical differences

First, one might think that neuro-data bolster the idea that women and men are fundamentally different by showing that the mental and behavioral differences between them are also *physical* ones. That is, one might think that purported differences between the sexes (e.g. take your favorite stereotypes: women are better at communicating, men are better at analytical problem-solving, etc.) are more *real* if they can be shown to exist in the body or brain – in physical entities such as neurons, ions, levels of deoxyhemoglobin, and the like. But I reject this contention. Once (and if) we acknowledge a mental or behavioral difference between the genders, claims of a physical difference are unsurprising.

How are they unsurprising? They are unsurprising if we believe that mental states are identical to physical states. That is, if we are physicalists,[6] once (and if) we accept that there are mental differences between genders, then it is absolutely unsurprising that there would be physical (brain) differences too: mental differences just *are* physical differences![7] That is, assuming we have evidence for a mental difference, neuro-data do not give us any 'special' or 'extra' evidence for the 'realness' of this difference by providing us with physical evidence – we had that evidence from the start! If we are dualists, then the presence of brain differences might be a *little* more surprising (it doesn't *automatically* follow from the fact that there are mental differences), but not much. Most dualists (known as dualist_interactionists) assume a fairly tight causal relationship between the brain and the mind, so if women's and men's mental processes differed, it would make sense that these differences were caused by differences in the brain, and/or were themselves causing brain differences. In the remainder of the chapter, for simplicity, I tend to assume a physicalist stance, but also often spell out options for the dualist_interactionist.

2.1.2 Option 2: neuro-data provide evidence of permanent differences

Another way in which neuro-data may bolster evidence of fundamental mental and behavioral gender differences may be by showing those differences to be *permanent* or *enduring*. That is, it may seem that seeing a

difference between genders 'in the brain' would mean that that difference is unchangeable. The term 'hard-wired' is used again and again in
these (and other) discussions, and if one takes it literally, one may indeed
think that everything in the brain is 'wired together' in an utterly permanent way (I will say more about the notion of 'hard-wiring' below).

But this assumption has very little backing. To see why, it is helpful to
consider both structural and functional categories of neuro-data. First,
consider functional data. Does this type of data provide evidence of
permanent gender differences? It seems very clear that it does not. Brain
activity changes from second to second (more precisely, millisecond
(or less) to millisecond (or less)), which is to be expected if one thinks
that brain activity is either identical to, or intimately causally linked to,
mental activity. According to physicalists (and usually dualist$_{interaction-}$
$_{ists}$), when someone moves from calm to complete surprise, the activity
of her brain changes. When someone sees a roller coaster, and then
looks over to a Ferris wheel, the activity of her brain changes. (In fact,
the pattern of activity in the visual cortex corresponds topographically
to the image one perceives (see Kandel, Schwartz, and Jessell 1991: 426).
So, when one is looking at a Ferris wheel, there will be, roughly, a Ferris
wheel-shaped pattern of activity in the visual cortex. For this pattern
of brain activity to change, all one needs to do is shift one's gaze to a
differently shaped object.) Clearly, assessing brain activity at any given
point in time in no way implies that that activity will be there forever,
or even for a long time.

Now, one might object that these are not the sorts of functional
brain changes one sees when one looks at functional studies of gender
differences in the brain. In these studies, brain activity is compared
between women and men when they are performing a certain task.
Thus, here, the sort of brain activity measured presumably corresponds
to a *skill* or *ability* instead of some occurrent experience like seeing a
roller coaster. Still, there is no reason to think that this type of brain
activity is immune to change. People gain and refine skills all the time.
There is nothing about the brain, *per se*, that indicates that its activity is
unchangeable (for example, see Pascual-Leone et al. 2005).

Even in the case of *structural* differences in the brain, change is very
possible. The brain is *plastic*, which means that it is malleable: it can
change and respond to environmental influences throughout its lifetime
(Kandel, Schwartz, and Jessell 1991; Pascual-Leone et al. 2005). Indeed,
there is an abundance of empirical evidence showing that the environment can have profound effects on brain structure. The environment

has been shown to alter the following: the overall weight and size of the brain, neurogenesis (the 'birth' of new neurons), gliogenesis (the 'birth' of new glial cells), dendritic branching (the number of branches one part of a neuron has – thus, the shape of a neuron), and synaptogenesis (the formation of new synapses (or "connections between neurons")) (Mora, Segovia, and del Arco 2007: 80–81; see also Jacobs, van Praag, and Gage 2000; Ming and Song 2005; Pascual-Leone et al. 2005). For example, environmental 'enrichment' has been shown to increase all of the above properties in rats (Mora, Segovia, and del Arco 2007: 80–81). Specifically, rats who are reared in cages that have more space, ramps, platforms, wheels for exercise, and toys have increased neurogenesis in certain regions of their brains, as well as increased branching of pre-existing neurons and other structural changes. Inversely, certain types of environmental stress have been shown to *inhibit* neurogenesis (Jacobs, van Praag, and Gage 2000).

Now, I grant that the structure of the brain is almost certainly not infinitely malleable. And, it might be that some structural differences observed across sexes may tend to remain fixed. But this is a claim that requires further investigation. Barring such investigation, simply seeing a difference in the brain speaks no more to its permanence than does seeing a mental difference.

2.1.3 *Option 3: neuro-data provide evidence of innate differences*

Even if neuro-data do not necessarily provide special evidence of gender differences by demonstrating the *permanence* of those differences, one might think that they provide a different sense of 'special' evidence – evidence of the *innateness* of those differences. In other words, one may think that they provide evidence that gender differences have been 'genetically programmed' or 'genetically determined' in individuals since before birth, and that such differences are therefore inevitable (and even, some may go on to claim, therefore 'natural' or 'good').

But neuro-data also fail to necessarily provide this sort of special evidence – special evidence of innateness. As we saw in the section above, neither the structure nor the function of the brain is a product of genes alone. On the contrary, the environment can have a profound impact on both brain structure and function (for example, as mentioned, an 'enriched' environment can cause changes in neurogenesis and neuronal morphology). Recall that the brain is made of cells, which are made of proteins (among other things). One's DNA provides (according to the ubiquitous metaphor) the 'blueprint' for how proteins are made, but these proteins, at every point in their manufacturing process and beyond, are continually altered, modified, or destroyed by a variety of factors, many of them caused by environmental 'inputs' to the cell. For example, increased levels of corticosterone, 'the stress hormone,' can result in myriad changes in protein form, abundance, and other properties (Yan et al. 1999; Prager and Johnson 2009). In other words, the genes ('blueprints') themselves provide a *starting point* for determining how the end product looks, but a lot can and does happen between what is on the blueprint and what the end product looks and acts like (changes can even be made that directly contradict the instructions on the blueprint (Smith and Sowden 1996)). So the brain is a complex product of both genes *and* the environment. Therefore, brain differences between genders likely reflect both genetic *and* environmental/experiential differences. Lise Eliot puts it this way:

> I want to point out one particularly insidious way in which neuroscience has been misused; this is the idea that the brain's sex differences – most of which have been demonstrated in adults only – are necessarily innate. Ignoring the fundamental plasticity by which the brain learns anything, several popular authors confuse *brain* with *nature*, promoting the view that differences between the sexes are fixed, hard-wired, and predetermined biological facts. (Eliot 2009: 8–9)

2.1.4   Option 4: neuro-data provide evidence of 'hard-wired' differences

Finally, one might think that neuro-data are able to provide special evidence of gender differences by showing these differences to be 'hard-wired.' In order to judge whether this is right, it is first necessary to understand what is meant by 'hard-wired.' This is not easy. I think that, in some contexts, 'hard-wired' is meant to signify 'permanent.' Presumably this is what the 'hard' in 'hard-wired' stands for. At other times, I believe it is meant to signify 'genetically determined' or 'innate' (the idea, I think, being that one's genes caused the brain to be 'wired' a certain way from the start). And yet other times, I think it is meant to signify both of these things. But, as discussed above, neuro-data do not necessarily provide any evidence of the permanence of a difference. Nor do they necessarily provide any evidence of the innateness of a difference. So, if these translations of 'hard-wired' are accurate, neuro-data do not necessarily provide any evidence that gender differences are hard-wired.[8]

3   Part II: neuro-data often fail to provide *any* evidence of fundamental gender differences

3.1   What sort of additional evidence might neuro-data provide?

Thus far, I have explored and rejected some senses in which neuro-data might be thought to provide *special* evidence of fundamental gender differences, such as evidence of their permanence or innateness. But even if neuro-data can't provide *special* evidence of gender differences, it might be thought that they can nevertheless provide *additional* evidence of them. How? Assuming physicalism, *prima facie*, we would think that, since brain states and mental states are identical, a gender difference seen between brain states would indicate a gender difference between mental states.[9] If this is true, then experiments that reveal a brain difference between genders would ostensibly reveal a mental difference as well. Assuming this is right, NEUROSCIENCE BOLSTERS would be true because neuro-data would provide an *additional* method for exposing mental differences between genders. And this is important: since any given methodology for gathering data almost certainly has some limitations or flaws, the more methods (or 'routes') one can use to arrive at the same result, the better evidence one has for that result.

I do believe that this is a good example of the usefulness of neuro-data for illuminating gender differences, but – and this is a big but – *only if* we grant that a difference in brain state implies a difference in mental state. And I am not convinced that we can always grant this, *even* if we insist that brain states are identical to mental states. This is because of the possibility of what philosophers of mind call '*multiple realization*.'[10] I will explain this concept in the following section, but the take-home message is this: mental states may be identical to brain states, but may, say, be identical to one *type* of brain state in women, and to a different *type* of brain state in men.[11] Below, I will explain how, if multiple realization (hereafter 'MR') is true for the particular gender differences in which we are interested, neuro-data may fail to provide *any* evidence of these differences (much less evidence of their permanence or innateness). This is very significant. If true, it means that the neuroscientific studies designed to detect such differences are giving *no information at all* about whether men and women are mentally different. This is very far indeed from the popular perception that seeing a difference in the brain 'cements' or bolsters the idea of fundamental gender differences.

3.2   Multiple realization: a background

What is MR? MR is, roughly, the idea that "it is possible for minds to be built in various distinct ways" (Shapiro 2004: 1).[12] In other words, mental states can be constituted by or constructed from different types of brain states. Often the best way to understand MR is to consider examples of other, non-mental, things that are multiply realized. Mousetraps, for example, are multiply realized. A mousetrap can be made of wood, cheese, and a metal spring and clamp configured in the right way (to yield what many think of as a 'traditional' mouse-trap), or it can be made from plastic, a dab of peanut butter, batteries, and something that generates an electric shock, also configured in the right way (an 'electronic' mousetrap). In fact, as long as something successfully lures and traps live mice, it counts as a mousetrap, no matter what it's made of or how it's configured.[13] A corkscrew is also multiply realized. There are, for example, 'waiter's corkscrews' (like the kind one might find on a Swiss army knife) and 'winged corkscrews' (which have two levers that one is meant to pull down simultaneously) (Shapiro 2004: 2). Obviously, there are scores of other things that are multiply realized.

Transitioning from mousetraps and corkscrews to mental states like pain and hunger, let's examine what exactly it means for a mental state to be multiply realized. Take the mental state of a particular breed of jealousy. This jealousy could be identical to (i.e. 'realized by') activity in brain area P in one individual, and identical to (i.e. 'realized by') activity in brain area Q in another. Here, if we were to investigate what was happening in both the brains and the minds of these individuals, we would see a brain difference but no mental difference. That is, we would see activity in brain area P in person 1, and activity in brain area Q in person 2, but both people would be experiencing the *same type* of jealousy. Note that MR is perfectly compatible with physicalism. The mental state of jealousy in both individuals is identical to a brain state – it's just that it happens to be identical to different *types* of brain states in each of the different individuals (just like a mousetrap is identical to a certain configuration of wood, metal, and cheese in one instance, and identical to a certain configuration of plastic, batteries, and peanut butter in another). In other words, we might say that this mental state is 'realized' differently in different people, or that it is 'multiply realized.'

Another common way to understand MR is to appeal to the idea that our brains are like computers: we can envision our brains as the hardware and our minds as the software.[14] Here, it is not difficult to see how the same software can be 'realized' differently on different machines (Photoshop, for example, has both Macintosh and PC versions – as do most pieces of software).[15]

3.3   Multiple realization across genders

The above example of jealousy is what we would call a case of MR 'across individuals.' There can, ostensibly, also be MR within a given individual across times (the same type of mental state is realized differently in the same individual at different times), across species (the same type of mental state is realized differently in different species), or even across different life forms (the same type of mental state is realized differently in different life forms, e.g. humans and aliens). In this chapter, I wish to suggest that the very same type of mental state may be realized differentially across different *genders*. For example, a particular type of pain in women may be identical to activity in brain area C, whereas this type of pain in men may be identical to activity in brain area D. I call this 'multiple realization across genders' (MR_{gender}):

> MR_{gender} **for mental state X:** Mental state X is realized differently in men and women.

The significance of MR_{gender} for NEUROSCIENCE BOLSTERS is immense: if MR_{gender} is true in any particular instance, then we have an excellent reason to doubt NEUROSCIENCE BOLSTERS in that instance. That is, if a certain mental state is MR_{gender}, then finding a corresponding gender difference in brain activity or structure will *not* indicate that there is a gender difference in this mental state. This is because, if the mental state is MR_{gender}, then it has different realizations (or 'incarnations') in different genders, and we would *expect* to see a brain difference when one and the same type of mental state is occurring. In the example above, if we want to know whether a group of men and women are experiencing the same type of pain, we would actually look for a *difference* in their patterns of brain activity – activation in brain area C in women, and in brain area D in men. This is because the mental state in question will simply have different realizations (or 'incarnations') in different genders, just as mousetraps can have different realizations or incarnations in houses that use traditional mousetraps and in houses that use electronic mousetraps. In this analogy, if we wanted to know if two houses were both set up to trap live mice, we would look for a configuration of wood, metal springs, and cheese in one house, and plastic, batteries, and peanut butter in the other.

3.4   Why think that there is MR across genders?

I believe that simply introducing the *possibility* of MR$_{gender}$, as I have just done above, is enough to give us at least some reason to hesitate before embracing NEUROSCIENCE BOLSTERS. As I explained, neuro-scientific evidence of a brain difference between genders might not give us *any* evidence of a mental (what I have assumed to be a 'funda-mental') difference between genders, depending on whether MR$_{gender}$ is true. But the undermining of NEUROSCIENCE BOLSTERS can be that much more effective if there is reason to think that MR$_{gender}$ is not just a remote possibility, but is, instead, quite likely. Thus, in this section I will offer three main considerations in favor of the idea that MR$_{gender}$ is, indeed, likely.

3.4.1   *Consideration 1: MR is widespread in biological systems*

One reason to think MR$_{gender}$ is likely is that MR in general is pervasive throughout biology. In recent years, the likelihood of actual MR has been attacked by a number of philosophers of science; most agree that MR is *possible* in theory, but several question whether there are actually any legitimate examples of it in real life (Bechtel and Mundale 1999; Shapiro 2004; Polger 2009). In response to this worry, Carrie Figdor defends the 'empirical viability' of MR by appealing to work in biology and cognitive neuroscience (Figdor 2010: 420). Figdor points out that (1) throughout biology at all levels (molecular, cellular, at the level of the whole organism), there are examples of more than one structure sub-serving the exact same function (for example, there are multiple codons for each amino acid, there are multiple antibodies for every antigen, etc.), and (2) many of these examples likely count as MR. Biologists even have their own technical term for this phenomenon: 'degeneracy.'[16]

Because degeneracy is widespread throughout biology, it would be strange to think that somehow brain states and mental states were the exception. In fact, Figdor mentions a few putative instances of degen-eracy (and hence MR) in brain and mental states, one of which draws from the work of Cathy Price and Karl Friston (Price and Friston 2002). In this example, individual subjects display activation in different brain areas when they are completing the *same* task (a semantic task of match-ing words to pictures) (see Figure 2.1). According to Price and Friston, this type of inter-subject variation in fMRI studies is not uncommon, although it is rarely reported. Price and Friston remark:

> functional imaging studies normally discard these 'idiosyncratic' activations and treat them as random error. Nevertheless, we cannot

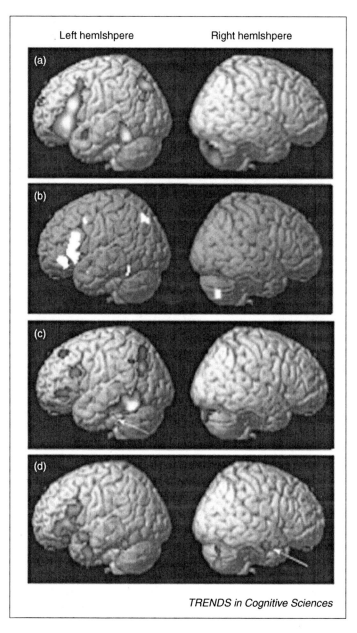

Left hemlshpere   Right hemlshpere

(a)

(b)

(c)

(d)

TRENDS in Cognitive Sciences

Figure 2.1 Image from Price and Friston (2002), showing differential brain activation during a semantic task, by permission from Elsevier Press. (a) shows activity averaged across 12 subjects. (b) shows (in white) only those areas that were activated in *all* subjects. (c) shows activation in Subject #1, and (d) shows activation in Subject #2. Focusing on (c) and (d), we can see a putative instance of the mental state needed for the semantic task being differentially realized in different individuals.

exclude the possibility that they are not random but reflect degener-
ate mechanisms for performing the same function. (Price and Friston
2002: 418)

Although this happens to be an example of evidence for MR across *individuals*, and not across *genders*, there is plenty of evidence specifically
for the latter, which I present below.

3.4.2   Consideration 2: men's and women's brains develop differently

There is another reason to think it is likely that certain mental states
are multiply realized across genders: brain development tends to happen very differently in female and male members of the same species.
Because of this, there might be different structures within female and
male brains that end up getting 'recruited' to subserve the same type of
mental state. For example: *in utero*, male and female brains are exposed
to different levels of estrogen and testosterone, and estrogen and testosterone differentially affect neurogenesis and cell death (Simerly 2002).
Differential neurogenesis and cell death, in turn, can lead to the development of different structures (or, if we prefer, different 'circuitry'), and
different structures may indeed end up serving as different realizations
of the same mental state. Throughout the neuroscientific literature,
there are indeed several structural differences reported between male
and female brains (overall brain volume, percentage of gray matter to
white matter, size of the corpus callosum, etc.).[17]

3.4.3   Consideration 3: there is empirical evidence of MR across genders

We have just reviewed two reasons to think that MR_{gender} is more than a
remote possibility: (1) MR *in general* is widespread throughout biological
systems, and (2) men's and women's brains have different developmental histories and thus some structural differences, and these differences
may converge to subserve the same mental state. Now, I introduce a
third reason, one which I believe is especially compelling: there is
actual empirical evidence for MR_{gender}. More specifically, there are actual
studies which likely show a brain difference, but no mental difference,
between women and men. Although there may be some limitations to
these studies, and they therefore don't yet constitute irrefutable *proof*
of MR_{gender}, I think that they nevertheless provide very good evidence
for it.

First, I will describe one of these studies in some detail. Next, I will discuss, also in detail, some possible objections to the idea that this study
(and others like it) are real-life examples of MR_{gender}. I will dismiss some

of these objections, but recognize that others are not fully addressed at this time. Finally, as another, independent response to these objections, I will present some separate evidence in favor of counting this study as an actual real-life example of MR_{gender}.

Before I launch into a synopsis of one of these studies, it is important to note that it is not the only study which purports to show gendered brain differences in the absence of a mental difference. Studies have also claimed to show such results in the context of working memory (Bell et al. 2006), motor control of finger movements (Bell et al. 2006), visual guidance of reaching (Gorbet and Sergio 2007), and the influence of emotion on working memory (Koch et al. 2007), to name a few.

3.5 A case study: mathematical skills

In 2009, Katherine Keller and Vinod Menon, using fMRI, measured brain activity in male and female human subjects engaged in a specific type of mathematical reasoning (looking at equations like $8 + 3 - 4 = 5$ and deciding whether they were correct or incorrect) (Keller and Menon 2009). Thus, in this study, the 'mental state' being measured was a particular type of arithmetical reasoning or cognition, and it was measured by looking at performance on the arithmetic task: specifically, how accurately the subjects performed, and how quickly. In this study, female and male subjects, on average, completed the task with the same degree of accuracy, and with equal rapidity. In other words, no difference was found between the mental states of females and males. However, there *were* statistically significant brain differences between males and females. Males showed greater activation than females in the right hemisphere of the intra-parietal sulcus, angular gyrus, parahippocampal gyrus, and lingual gyrus. In contrast, females did not show greater activation than males in any brain regions (Figure 2.2).

3.6 Interpretation of Keller and Menon

This study, combined with the others like it referenced above (e.g. Bell et al. 2006; Gorbet and Sergio 2007; Koch et al. 2007), provide examples of reported brain differences between men and women without mental differences. Therefore, they seem to serve as *actual examples* of mental states being multiply realized across genders. But it is important to point out that this conclusion may be a little too hasty; there may be alternate interpretations of these studies that do not invoke MR. It is these objections that I will explore now.

In the philosophy of science literature, there are two especially prominent strands of objection to the idea that MR is demonstrated

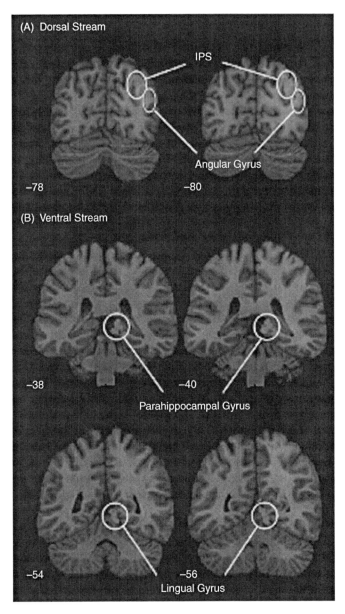

(A) Dorsal Stream

IPS

Angular Gyrus

−78   −80

(B) Ventral Stream

−38   −40

Parahippocampal Gyrus

−54   −56
Lingual Gyrus

Figure 2.2 Image from Keller and Menon (2009), showing areas where brain activation was significantly greater in male subjects than female subjects during performance of an arithmetic task, by permission from Elsevier Press. The areas are marked in red and circled and labeled. Note that there were no observed mental differences between females and males during performance of this task. Thus activity in the denoted areas *may* represent a realization of arithmetic cognition that occurs in one gender only.

empirically (Bechtel and Mundale 1999; Shapiro 2004). Recall, in order for something to count as actual MR, there must be (1) an actual multiplicity of realizations (i.e. an actual difference in brain states), and (2) an actual sameness or identity of types of mental states (because MR is a phenomenon where *one* type of mental state is multiply realized). The two strands of objection correspond to each of these requirements; the first strand is that (1) is not met: in other words, that there is actually *not* a brain difference between genders. The second strand is that (2) is not met: in other words, that there actually *is* a difference in mental states. I will now consider how these possible strands of objection might apply to MR_{gender} and the Keller and Menon study.

3.6.1 *Objection 1: there is actually not a brain difference between women and men*

One way to challenge the conclusion that the Keller and Menon study provides a real-life example of MR_{gender} is to question whether the brain differences reported therein were actually 'legitimate' ones. Why might an objector think that these brain differences fail to count as 'legitimate'? First, it may be that the reported differences themselves were over-exaggerated or fictitious; the studies might have erroneously detected a difference when there was none. In other words, the parameters used to process and present the final fMRI data may have ended up producing 'false positives.'

Second (and this point has been made by Shapiro (2004) and Polger (2009) in the context of other studies), even though these studies reported what may have been a true difference in brain *location* across genders, it could have been that the exact same type of brain *structure* (the same neuronal connections, the same cytoarchitecture, the same types of neurotransmitters) was active at each location. And, according to some (Shapiro 2004; Polger 2009), this sort of difference – a difference in location alone – does not count as a legitimate difference. Instead – according to this objection – what's necessary for a legitimate difference is something like a different material (thinking back to the mousetrap, wood as opposed to metal) or a different arrangement of components (as is seen in the two types of corkscrews). In the brain, a difference in material would presumably be something like a difference in cell types, or a difference in the neurotransmitters used for communication. And a different arrangement of components would presumably be a different configuration of synaptic connections.

I have two related responses to the above concerns that the observed brain differences are not legitimate. First, whether or not these reported differences are indeed 'legitimate' according to the criteria set forth by Shapiro and other objectors, they are indeed the very types of differences that are ubiquitously *counted* as such by other parties. These very types of difference – e.g. activation in one brain region versus another – are just the type that neuroscientists declare as legitimate in fMRI studies. They are also the type that become cited and celebrated in self-help books and other sources of popular media as 'real' or 'legitimate' differences, and that become paraded as evidence of fundamental differences between men and women.

Second, even if we grant that these differences are *not* legitimate, we can still leverage a very different type of response to our objector. This response is as follows. First, we must concede that these studies actually do *not* succeed in demonstrating actual examples of MR_{gender}. So we must agree with our objector on this count, and we cannot, in this case, argue against NEUROSCIENCE BOLSTERS using the possibility of MR. But we *can* argue against NEUROSCIENCE BOLSTERS in a different way. Recall that NEUROSCEINCE BOLSTERS says that neuro-data provide special or additional evidence for fundamental differences across genders. But here, if neuro-data are not showing any legitimate differences across genders, then it is hard to see how they could be providing evidence for fundamental differences across genders: because, in a sense, they are not showing a difference at all (at least, not a *legitimate* one).

Here is another way to put this. Note that there are two options here: the differences found in the Keller and Menon study, and those like it, either do or do not count as legitimate differences. If they *do* count as legitimate differences, then this is consistent with the possibility of one mental state being MR across genders. And we can thus use MR_{gender} to undercut the truth of NEUROSCIENCE BOLSTERS. Second, if the supposed brain differences *do not* count as legitimate differences, in this case the neuro-data *also* add nothing to the claim of a fundamental difference, since they show what counts as a *similarity* (and not a difference). Either way, neuroscience is failing to furnish evidence of what we have deemed to be 'fundamental' gender differences.

3.6.2   *Objection 2: there are actually mental differences between women and men*

A second way an objector could challenge the contention that the Keller and Menon study (and the others like it) supplies an actual example of MR_{gender} would be to contest the supposed mental similarity between genders. Again, in order for something to count as a case of MR, there must be: (1) *different* types of brain states, and (2) the *same* type of mental state. And it is possible that, in the studies mentioned above, (2) was not fulfilled. That is, it is possible that there actually *were* mental differences between genders, but that they went undetected. If this were the case, then the brain differences reported could have corresponded to these undetected mental differences, instead of serving as different realizations of one and the same type of mental state.

The main candidate for an undetected mental difference is a difference in arithmetic *strategy*. That is, it may have been that women and men performed equally accurately and equally quickly on the arithmetic task, but that they used completely different mental *strategies* to achieve this performance. This objection, however, seems rather shaky in the case of the arithmetic task. This is because, in this particular study, there is no *prima facie* reason to think that women and men employed different strategies to assess the correctness of equations like $8 + 1 - 7 = 2$, at least according to Keller and Menon. Keller and Menon remark: "given that our study contains well-educated participants, from a relatively gender-equal society … it is unlikely that males and females applied different strategies to solve the fairly simply MA [mental arithmetic] tasks that we used here" (Keller and Menon 2009: 351). Note that subjects were recruited from the "Stanford University community," so this claim of being "well-educated" is not unreasonable. And Keller and Menon added that, to their knowledge, no other study has reported a gender difference in strategy on these types of mathematical problems, at least for adults.

Still, there might be ways for an objector to get around this response. First, just because no study has reported a gender difference in arithmetic strategy doesn't mean there isn't one. And Keller and Menon simply could have been wrong in their presumption that women and men employed similar strategies. Additionally, it could be that there was a mental difference aside from a difference in strategy. For example, women and men could have had, on average, different types of subjective experiences, like different emotions or moods during the task.

I believe these are all caveats to be taken seriously, and that, because of them, we should not over-zealously declare to have definitively found a real-life example of MR_{gender} (or, real-life examples, if we consider the other studies). Still, these caveats are not necessarily insurmountable; further investigation can help assess whether or not they actually pose a threat. For example, subjects can be tested on whether they actually are employing different strategies, or experiencing different emotions. And, depending on the results of such further investigations, it could well be that we have an actual bona fide case of MR_{gender} on our hands.

At the very least, then, these studies are a large step to demonstrating not just the likelihood, but the actuality, of MR$_{gender}$ (at least for some mental states).

3.6.3   Evidence in favor of the idea that MR$_{gender}$ is actual

I have just presented two possible objections to the idea that the Keller and Menon study reveals a real-life example of MR$_{gender}$. I believe that we can sidestep the first (that there were no brain differences), but the other (that there might have been undetected mental differences) may present a legitimate problem for us. Further investigation is needed to assess its threat. On a more positive note, I want to turn to some evidence *in support of* the idea that the Keller and Menon study provides a real-life example of MR$_{gender}$. Keller and Menon themselves believe that the reason there is a brain difference without a mental difference is that women's and men's brains have a different *structure*. This echoes what I briefly mentioned above as one reason to believe that MR$_{gender}$ may be likely (at least, for some mental states): women's and men's brains develop differently, and thus it may be the case that different structures get recruited to subserve the same function. Keller and Menon tested whether there were, in fact, average structural differences between men's and women's brains. They found such differences, including many in those specific areas where they had found a difference in brain activity between men and women. They explain:

> A more likely reason [than a difference in strategy] for the observed gender differences in functional [brain] responses[18] is that there are significant structural differences between male and female brains in these regions. Our VBM [voxel based morphometry] analysis provides strong evidence that this may indeed be the case. We found that females had greater gray matter density in both dorsal and ventral stream regions where...task-related gender differences were observed [in the brain]. Specifically, within the dorsal stream, females showed greater gray matter density in and around the right IPS and angular gyrus regions where males showed greater functional [brain] responses. Within the ventral stream, a similar pattern was observed, with females showing significantly greater gray matter density in and around the right parahippocampal cortex regions where males showed greater functional [brain] activation. In addition, females showed greater gray matter volume in dorsal stream regions where males showed greater functional [brain] responses. (Keller and Menon 2009: 351)

So this evidence is consistent with the idea that different structures could have developed in men and women to subserve the same mental function, and thus supports the thesis of MR_{gender}.

In this last section, I have examined whether we are licensed to conclude that the Keller and Menon study, and those like it, provide real-life examples of MR across genders. First, I explored two general ways in which the Keller and Menon study could have *failed* to furnish an actual example of MR_{gender}: it could have failed to demonstrate a brain difference, and/or it could have failed to demonstrate a mental similarity. I argued that the former possibility was not a threat. I then assessed the latter possibility, and concluded that it *may* present a threat – that, even though it *appeared* that mental states were the same across genders, they might not have been. Therefore, I believe this possible objection deserves further investigation. Nevertheless, I believe this study, and the several others like it, are, at the very least, a very promising step to demonstrating real-life MR_{gender}. Additionally, before discussing the Keller and Menon study, I mentioned other positive evidence for MR_{gender} as well. Not only is MR fairly ubiquitous in biological systems, as Figdor points out, but there is also reason to think that women's and men's brains develop differently, and so it is not difficult to see how structural differences might 'converge' to realize the same mental state. In fact, Keller and Menon found structural differences (in, for example, the percentage of gray matter) in the brains of women and men, and they found them in the particular brain areas that showed differential activation during the same performance level of the arithmetic task. So there are certainly good reasons to think that MR_{gender} is much more than just a conceptual possibility. And thus there are good reasons to think that MR_{gender} can pose a serious threat to NEUROSCIENCE BOLSTERS.

3.7   A last objection

At this point, I want to address a final, broader, objection to my claims thus far. My main task in this chapter has been to challenge the truth of NEUROSCIENCE BOLSTERS. In doing this, however, one may think I've gone too far. That is, one may think that there are clearly at least *some* cases where neuroscientific data can provide additional evidence of fundamental differences between genders. My quick response to this objection is one of agreement. My goal here is not to claim that NEUROSCIENCE BOLSTERS can *never* be true. I am claiming, instead, that, in order for it to be true in any given case, we must *first* rule out the possibility of MR_{gender} in that particular case.

Consider the following example. Say we have a multitude of evidence (and we do) that the hippocampus is related to (either identical to (if physicalism is true) or intimately causally linked to (if dualism$_{interactionism}$ is true)) certain types of spatial memory in humans. Let's imagine (here is where I am dramatically departing from reality) that *all* women tested thus far have been found to have extremely poor spatial memory, almost to the point of lacking it altogether. Let's also imagine that all of these women have also been found to have tiny hippocampi. And let us suppose that all men tested thus far, on the other hand, do have spatial memory, and do possess good-sized hippocampi. Here, then, it seems that this would be a clear example of neuroscientific data being able to provide additional evidence of a fundamental difference between genders: here, the size of hippocampi would provide additional evidence for the degree of spatial memory, and thus for differences in spatial memory between men and women. As such, this seems to be one example of NEUROSCIENCE BOLSTERS being true.

I think that this may be correct, but that its correctness relies upon the assumption that spatial memory is *not* realized by a *different* brain area in women than it is in men. For example, assume that spatial memory is realized by the hippocampus in men. But in women, in contrast, imagine that spatial memory is realized by brain area S. That is, it could be that, in all of the women who were tested who lack spatial memory, not only do they have minuscule hippocampi, but they *also* happen to have minuscule brain area S's. In this case, then, it would be the smallness of brain area S, and *not* the smallness of the hippocampus, that would explain the mental difference in spatial memory between men and women. Thus, if this were the case, and spatial memory was, indeed, MR$_{gender}$, then the neuro-data concerning the hippocampus alone would *not* be providing additional evidence of a mental difference between genders. Because in this case, the fact that these women have tiny hippocampi would be (I am assuming) completely independent of the fact that they have tiny brain area S's.[19]

However, in this example, the neuro-data showing the largeness of *hippocampi* in men and the smallness of *brain area S* in women *would* provide additional evidence of a spatial memory difference between genders. Thus, in this case, once we addressed the possibility of MR$_{gender}$, and gathered the evidence necessary to determine that brain area S was, indeed, responsible for spatial memory in women, we could presumably use neuro-data to 'bolster' claims of a gender difference in spatial memory.

Or consider a different case. Let's say the size of brain area X has an extremely tight correlation with the mental feature of IQ, so that every cubic mm of area X is correlated with one IQ point. If we have found that this correlation held in every individual tested, in an enormous number of individuals, in both men and women, then this would seem to count as a solid case of NEUROSCIENCE BOLSTERS. For example, Man 1 has an IQ of 100 and a volume of brain area X of 15 cubic mm; Man 2 has an IQ of 110 and a volume of 25 cubic mm; Woman 1 has an IQ of 100 and a volume of 15 cubic mm; Woman 2 has an IQ of 99 and a volume of 14 cubic mm, etc. And let's say that men have, on average, a 2 point lower IQ than do women, and that the volume of brain area X, is, on average, 2 cubic mm smaller than the volume of brain area X in women. This, then, would presumably be an excellent example of NEUROSCIENCE BOLSTERS.

I agree that this would be a case in which NEUROSCIENCE BOLSTERS was almost certainly true. But cases like this seem rare indeed. And one (among many) reasons for this rarity could be that mental states are multiply realized (either across genders, or across individuals, or both). For example, the brain may simply be configured differently in different genders (and in different individuals) such that slightly different brain areas contribute to the same mental function in slightly different ways. For example, imagine that IQ was MR_{gender}, such that, in women, IQ was realized by brain area X alone, whereas in men, it was realized by both brain area X and brain area Q. That is, in men, brain area X would be principally responsible for IQ, but brain area Q would be able to provide 'backup' if brain area X faltered. Women, in contrast, have no 'backup' region. So, if *this* were the case, reduced size of brain area X of men wouldn't necessarily correlate with a lower IQ, because brain area Q could be compensating.[20] Thus in this case, we wouldn't have that incredibly tight correlation to begin with. But if we did, in fact, have that tight correlation, it seems that we would have a case where NEUROSCIENCE BOLSTERS was true.

4   Conclusions

In this paper, I have offered serious reasons to doubt the ability of neuroscience to offer extra or special evidence of fundamental differences between genders. I did so as follows:

(1) First, I acknowledged that neuro-data indeed provide evidence of a *physical* difference between genders, but that this is unsurprising

if we have already accepted that there are mental differences, *and* have adopted a physicalist stance within the philosophy of mind. (It is also unsurprising if we have adopted a dualist$_{interactionist}$ stance).

(2) Next, I offered reasons to doubt that neuro-data provide any evidence of a *permanent* gender difference. Just because we see a difference in the brain doesn't mean that it is unchangeable. In fact, the brain itself is highly plastic (malleable).

(3) Similarly, neuro-data do not necessarily provide evidence of *innate* gender differences. Just because we see a difference in the brain doesn't mean that that difference is genetically determined. It could have been just as easily been 'determined' by the environment (in all likelihood, it has both genetic and environmental factors in its causal history).

(4) Also, neuro-data fail to necessarily provide evidence of 'hard-wiring' of gender differences. 'Hard-wiring' seems to simply mean 'permanent' and/or 'innate,' and I challenged these types of evidence in previous sections.

(5) Finally, in many situations, it may not even be the case that neuroscience provides *any* evidence for mental differences between women and men. This is because the mental states of interest may be *multiply realized* across genders. That is, the very same mental state could be instantiated by one brain area in women and by a different brain area in men. If this is the case, neuro-data showing a brain difference would give no evidence of a mental difference whatsoever.

(6) Multiple realization across genders is not unlikely. There are many examples of multiple realization throughout biology, and we have additional reason to think that there may be MR across genders, since men and women exhibit various structural differences in brain development.

(7) More striking, there are several examples in the neuroscientific literature of what may actually be MR across genders. That is, there are several studies reporting a brain difference between genders with no mental difference. I discussed one such study – that of Keller and Menon – in some detail. Although there are certainly reasons to be cautious about hastily concluding that this proves MR across genders (and I discussed the most worrisome of these reasons), it is at least a very promising step in this direction.

(8) Finally, I noted that NEUROSCIENCE BOLSTERS may be true in some cases, and laid out a few such hypothetical cases. The key to these cases is that MR$_{gender}$ (of the relevant brain regions) does *not*

obtain. In other words, MR_{gender} must be ruled out from the outset in order to uphold NEUROSCIENCE BOLSTERS.

All in all, there are several reasons to question the ability of neuroscience to provide special or additional evidence of fundamental differences between genders. Seeing a 'brain difference' between sexes, I maintain, *may* do little or nothing to support the idea that genders are essentially or importantly different from one another.[21,22]

Notes

1. cf. John Gray's mega-bestseller *Men are from Mars, Women are from Venus* (Gray 1992).
2. In what follows, I will often use the shorthands 'fundamental differences' or 'fundamental gender differences' instead of 'fundamental mental and behavioral differences' to signify those putative fundamental differences between genders that are specifically mental (psychological), and/or behavioral (for example: women are more empathic, men are more competitive, etc.). That is, I am not talking about *anatomical* gender differences (e.g. women have bigger breasts; men have testicles). I take it that 'fundamental' signifies something of social, moral, and political importance for gender equity. Although a case could be made that certain anatomical differences are fundamental in this sense, it is, I believe, much more obvious to think of mental and behavioral differences as fundamental in this sense. Additionally, I will often use 'mental' to signify both mental and behavioral states (e.g. internal mental states like desires, beliefs, emotions, sensations, moods, rational and cognitive activities, *and* states that are more external, like behaviors or personality traits).
3. What sort of neuro-data am I talking about here? Generally, neuro-data fall into one of two broad categories. First, there are structural data, which include techniques like structural MRI and post-mortem brain examination, and yield information about the morphology of the brain. They include things like the size and shape of the brain and its various regions, the cellular makeup of the brain (e.g. the percentage of gray and white matter), the shapes of the neurons and the numbers of connections they have with one another, the number of neurons in different brain regions, etc. Second, there are functional data, which include functional MRI (fMRI), PET, EEG recordings, and the like. These techniques provide information about the *activity* of the brain – which brain regions are active, the extent to which they are active, etc. For example, fMRI is a technique that measures the relative activity of different areas of the brain by looking at the magnetic signal produced by the amount of deoxygenated hemoglobin in those areas. It is assumed that higher levels of deoxygenated hemoglobin indicate greater blood flow to the region of interest, and thus more activity in that region.
4. 'Special evidence' refers to evidence of various *properties* of gender differences (e.g. their innateness, their permanence, etc.). In contrast, 'additional evidence' refers to evidence for the *existence* of those differences.

5. Thus, officially, in this chapter I am not contesting the claim that men and women are mentally different. I am contesting the idea that neuroscience can substantiate or add anything to it; at least, as often as we think it does. Although there are certainly arguments one can make against the broader claim that men and women are mentally different (for example, some of the reported psychological differences may be over-exaggerated, or false due to biased data collection), and that other authors have, indeed, made, such arguments are outside the scope of this chapter.

6. To review some elementary concepts in philosophy of mind, *physicalism* is one of the two main answers to the question 'How is the mind related to the body?' (a terminological note: sometimes 'mental states' are substituted for 'the mind' and 'brain states' for 'the body'). Physicalism says that the mind (or, mental states) and the body (or, brain states) are *identical*: a mental state like hunger just *is* a certain brain state. They are one and the same. *Dualism*, the other main answer, says that the mind and body are separate metaphysical entities. One example of this would be if the mind were part of a spirit or soul, different from the physical matter that makes up the brain. Note that (most) dualists allow that these two entities (mind and brain) can causally interact with one another. This brand of dualism is called 'interactionism' or 'dualism$_{interactionism}$.'

7. Lise Eliot makes a similar point. She says: "Yes, men and women are different. Yes, their brains are different. (They pretty much have to be, if you take the modern scientific view that the brain is responsible for all thoughts and feelings.)" (Eliot 2009: 9). Note that her "modern scientific view" is consistent with both physicalism and dualism$_{interactionism}$.

8. For the record, because of this ambiguity, I think the term 'hard-wired' is horribly confusing, and perhaps, because of this, should no longer continue to be used. I think its usage very often reflects a conflation of 'permanent,' 'innate,' and 'seen in the brain.' This conflation is in error. As I've partially reviewed, all of these things are separable (one example: something can be seen in the brain without being innate, or permanent).

9. Note: for those already familiar with the distinction within philosophy of mind, this would be assuming a specific type of physicalism, called 'type–type physicalism.' This is the type of physicalism most people assume when they first think of physicalism.

10. Putnam is usually considered to be the first to have explored and labeled this idea (Putnam 1967).

11. This corresponds to a different type of physicalism than that mentioned above; this corresponds to 'token–token physicalism.'

12. Most authors accept a distinction between 'multiple realization' and 'multiple realizability.' The former refers to the actual state of affairs of being multiply realized, and the latter refers to a capability or possibility for something to be multiply realized. In this chapter, I will use the abbreviation 'MR' to signify either one, and will trust the context will make it clear which use is intended.

13. Note: some would disagree here, and insist that not just 'any old' configuration will count. They adopt stricter standards for what counts as MR, and require that two putative realizations, in order to count as distinct, have substantially different configurations or designs. Thus, for them, a difference

in material alone is not sufficient for MR; there must also be a difference in design (see Shapiro 2004 and Polger 2009).

14. This idea is very often associated or equated with the doctrine of functionalism in philosophy of mind. Functionalism defines mental states as functional states, in much the same way that a software program is a functional state (the program Microsoft Word is a function of accepting input in the form of letters, numbers, and certain commands, and producing output in the form of organized text documents).

15. Here, we assume that Photoshop (or whatever software we are considering) is exactly 'the same' on different computers. However, what criteria make software count as 'the same' is open to debate; we might think that they would have to perform the exact same functions, at the exact same speed, and perhaps would have to have the exact same appearance. Indeed, if we adopt a very stringent set of criteria for 'sameness,' then we might not count Photoshop on a Mac as 'the same' as Photoshop on a PC (indeed, we may not count Photoshop on my Mac as the same as Photoshop on your Mac if they run at different speeds). In response, however, it is not impossible to think that sameness of software would be less stringent – that it would only concern the constellation of functions performed and not the speed or appearance of their performance.

16. Although the definition of 'degeneracy' is slightly different from MR, the two are very close to one another, and I will assume they are one and the same for the purposes of this chapter.

17. Although it is important to note that many of these are highly contested and even purportedly disproven, some of them are presumably reliable (see Eliot 2009).

18. 'Functional' here refers to the function of the brain, *not* mental function. This is a standard usage for neuroscientists.

19. Of course, it would be a fairly remarkable coincidence that women who had smaller areas of 'their own' for spatial memory (brain area S) *just so happened* to, independently, also have smaller 'men's areas' for spatial memory (hippocampi). And one may well think that we could harness the unlikeliness of this scenario to claim that the smallness of hippocampi in women could, after all, provide *some* evidence of a mental difference between genders (assuming we knew nothing about brain area S, or the possibility of MR_{gender} for spatial memory). I am comfortable with this suggestion. I simply wish to claim that, *until* we have ruled out MR_{gender}, this evidence is on shakier ground and that, *if* MR_{gender} is true, it will no longer count as evidence.

20. This is assuming, of course, that a *smaller* area indicates *lower* function in the first place. This assumption does not always hold.

21. Note: many of the above arguments need not be restricted to the idea of differences across *genders*. Using neuroscience to substantiate differences between, say, depressed and non-depressed individuals, or individuals with particular personality traits, etc., falls prey to many (but not all) of the worries I have articulated above.

22. Many thanks to Robyn Bluhm, Lauren Ashwell, Jon Altschul, Bhob Rainey, and several anonymous reviewers for their helpful suggestions on earlier versions of this chapter. This material is partially based upon work supported by the National Science Foundation under Grant No. 0135559.

3
In a Different Voice?

Heidi Lene Maibom

Are women more caring than men, as the ethics of care tradition suggests? Do they think more, feel more, and do more for, others than men? Most people seem to think so, be they researchers or lay people, men or women. However, the evidence from psychology and neuroscience does not support this conclusion. Matching the cognitive and emotional traits most obviously related to caring, we find few, if any, differences between male and female capacities and propensities. In addition, this chapter throws doubt on some of the characterizations of care in the ethics of care tradition. For instance, greater emotional enmeshing with the other does not seem to lead to more prosocial or altruistic behavior.

1 An ethics of care

The best-known feminist ethics is, perhaps, the ethics of care. In her landmark work, Carol Gilligan argues that women and men have different moral outlooks and that traditional ethics have tended to sideline and devalue the feminine perspective. Where traditional male ethics focuses on justice, rights, and principles, women think more in terms of care, relationships, and responsibilities (Gilligan 1982). Gilligan attempts to tell a story about women's development – including their moral development – that departs from the typical Freudian story, where the formation of the superego is tied to castration anxiety. As women are anatomically unequipped to experience such anxiety, the resultant female superego is not "so inexorable, so impersonal, so independent of its emotional origins as we require it to be in men" Freud writes (quoted in Gilligan 1982: 7). Consequently, women have a deficient sense of justice, and their moral outlook is under the constant sway of their emotions.

Where Freud sees deficiency, Gilligan sees difference. The female moral outlook that Freud identified in such scathing terms embodies different, but equally morally important, concerns to that of the traditional justice, rights, and principles perspective. And instead organizing moral development around the penis, Gilligan, following Nancy Chodorow (1974), has it revolve around the child's experience of intimate relationships. Where the male child is encouraged to separate from the mother early and to develop autonomously, the female child is kept enmeshed in close emotional bonds to her mother. This difference in socialization and attachment to the mother leads to the emergence of "two perspectives on morality": one typically male, the other typically female (Gilligan and Wiggins 1987: 704). The latter perspective is characterized by a concern about *caring* for intimate others (Gilligan 1982; Noddings 1989). It is, therefore, tempting to think of an ethics of care as an ethics of the household. And, indeed, many of the criticisms leveled against this tradition focus exactly on this seeming narrowness of the approach (Koehn 1998). The focus here, however, is on whether care is well understood as characterizing a *female* moral orientation toward others.

Gilligan does not mean to suggest that men do not, at times, adopt an ethics of care perspective or that women deploy 'traditional' ethics. Nevertheless, the examples – which are mainly of women – and the terminology – listening to *women's* voices and taking the *feminine* perspective on morality – indicate that Gilligan and feminists like Noddings and Meyers regard care as particularly characteristic of the female perspective (Gilligan 1982; Noddings 1989; Meyers 1994). The story from Chodorow focuses on the environmental factors of child development, suggesting that that the ethics of care concerns gender more than sex. Most studies on differences in cognition and emotion between men and women divide the subjects according to biological sex alone. Since those are the studies that I will use, it might seem that this chapter can only talk to sex differences, where Gilligan and others are concerned with gender. Although issues concerning sex and gender are vexed (see introduction), I don't think they create serious problems for my argument. Assuming that biological females, by and large, are subjected to the environmental factors that Chodorow suggests they are, they should be more likely to adopt an ethics of care perspective than what I have called a traditional perspective. Consequently, these studies are useful when evaluating the suggestions arising from the ethics of care tradition.

My focus in this chapter is on the psychological underpinnings of care primarily. However, it is worth noting that the evidence does not support the idea that care considerations are more characteristic of women's moral reasons and justifications than of men's. Whereas some studies, using the so-called Ethics of Care Interview (ECI, Skoe and Diessner 1994) have shown women superior at things like role-taking, most studies have found no significant differences between the sexes in moral orientation. In Sara Jaffee and Janet Shibley Hyde's (2000) meta-study of 113 studies, 72–73 percent found no difference in care and justice reasoning. Those that found differences favoring women had very modest effect sizes accounting for between 0.9–2.4 percent of the variance (Jaffee and Hyde 2000; Walker 2006). In short, there is little empirical support for a substantial difference between the sexes in moral orientation or thinking.

It is conceivable that part of the problem finding support for Gilligan's hypothesis is the difficulty translating the care approach into an empirically testable hypothesis. Perhaps this has been done badly; perhaps 'care' is not a well-defined construct. Ultimately, I argue that 'care' covers an array of attitudes, motivations, and feelings that, although they have, individually, their counterpart in human psychology, do not combine in the way that much of the care literature proposes. Furthermore, they do not show the sex dimorphism that the care tradition suggests that they should. This raises questions about the validity and usefulness of the care approach. But first, we need to consider what care is, exactly, and how it maps on to known psychological traits.

2   Care, empathy, and sympathy

For Gilligan and Noddings, care is something like an affectively infused attention to others' welfare combined with a motivation to promote such welfare. It is profoundly interpersonal in that the agent becomes enmeshed – cognitively and affectively – with the other person:

> For the care ethicist, true caring – or at least caring in the highest and most interesting sense – is an affective stance in which both the care-giver and the cared-for put themselves at risk as part of a process of committing to the forging of a shared self. This is the kind of care one sees in intimate caring relations. (Koehn 1998: 25)

Bringing the individuality of the person into moral reflection is of paramount importance. By contrast to the masculine justice approach, which stresses the acting in accordance with moral principles, care ethicists point out that the focus on principles and rules risks sidelining the concerns and thoughts of the people who are affected by the moral choices. Principles subsume everyone equally, as if each person were interchangeable. They largely ignore the individuality of persons. As such, traditional rule-based ethics shows disrespect for the individual by its one-fits-all approach to morality. By contrast, care ethics stresses listening to the other and receiving her in her otherness (Noddings 1984: 30–35). In that way, we can administer to the other person's actual needs and desires, not merely to those that we, or a defunct patriarchy, project onto them.

Care ethicists – or certainly a number of them – stress that caring for others does not involve pure self-sacrifice. The caring person must speak for herself, find her own voice, and "care with autonomy" (Blum et al. 1979: 191; see also Gilligan 1982: 67–68). Some even claim that there a fundamental reciprocity to caring (Koehn 1998: 24). While caring is a fundamentally other-oriented approach where, as Noddings puts it, the other comes to "fill the firmament" (1984: 114), an *ethics* of care recommends balancing caring for the other and being cared for by the other in return. It also involves some self-care, although this can hardly be construed as reciprocity. The elimination of one of the forms of caring violates the basic principles of this form of ethics. Care, then, would be understood as the activity of caring, while an ethics of care balances care for the other, care for the self, and care reciprocation. Our question concerns care; does caring characterize women more than men? To answer this question, some translation is required. The psychological literature is replete with discussion of the more caring, prosocial, and altruistic emotions and attitudes of people, but the term 'care' is rarely used, and certainly does not play the role here that it does in the ethics of care literature. We should therefore look for the traits that psychologists most often connect with activities that are characteristic of caring.

Prominent researchers on empathy and mothering have argued that empathy and/or sympathy evolved out of the capacity for parental care. For instance, Daniel Batson argues that:

> [G]eneralized parental nurturance now seems the most likely evolutionary basis of empathic concern – even for strangers. Human parental nurturance is far more flexible and future-oriented than the parental instincts found in most – perhaps all – other mammalian species. It is need-oriented, emotion-based, and goal-directed. And it can be generalized well beyond our own children – in the case of pets, even to members of other species. (Batson 2009)

Elliott Sober and David Sloan Wilson (1998) also argue that empathy has evolved from parental care. Sarah Hrdy, who is famous for her anthropological work on mothers and mothering, agrees that human altruism and empathy has its roots in parental care and nurturance. Being one of a small number of species that engage in cooperative breeding, humans combine altruistic caring with the capacity to think of others in terms of their inner mental states, thereby creating the particular empathetic relating to others that is so characteristic of the human species (Hrdy 2009). There is therefore prodigious support by experts in the fields concerned with speculations about our evolved capacities that empathy and/or sympathy have their roots in parental caring. We might therefore look to empathy or sympathy as the emotions that underlie care.

Although there is some disagreement of nomenclature in the literature, it is safe to say that sympathy is an emotion, which is concerned with the wellbeing of others. Thus:

> *A* sympathizes with *B* if *A* believes something bad has happened to *B* or *B* is in a bad situation, and this makes *A* feels bad for *B*.

Empathy, on the other hand, is sometimes understood to be the ability to understand what others think or feel or to take up their perspective – often known as cognitive empathy – and sometimes as a way of feeling for others – called affective empathy (Davis 1983; Mehrabian 1997; Sober and Wilson 1998). By contrast to cognitive empathy, which is not assumed to involve an affective component, affective empathy is the experiencing of an emotion *for* another *because* that other person is feeling it. The emotion experienced for the other must involve some sort of consonance with that experienced by the other to count as empathy.[1] We can express this idea so:

> Person *A* empathizes with person *B* if *A* feels emotion E_1 for *B* because *A* perceives, believes, or imagines that *B* feels E_2, where E_1 and E_2 are consonant, but not necessarily identical, emotions.

Consonant emotions have the same emotional tone (positive/negative) and are close in intentional content. For instance, apprehensiveness and fear are consonant emotions, whereas jealousy and surprise are not.

This philosophical distinction between sympathy and empathy has found empirical support. The experience of pain and disgust for others has been found to activate many of the same brain areas that are activated when the subject feels pain or disgust, and people tend to report experiencing these emotions (Wicker et al. 2003; Keysers et al. 2004; Singer et al. 2004; Jackson, Meltzoff, and Decety 2005). By contrast, when people sympathize, they report feeling warmhearted or soft-hearted even as the subject of their sympathy is experiencing distress, fear, and so on. A sympathetic or compassionate orientation toward others is also – more or less consistently – associated with lowered heart rate, whereas the distressed reaction to others in distress has been linked with increased heart rate (Eisenberg et al. 1988).

Although the literature on morally relevant emotions tends to focus on empathy and sympathy, witnessing or imagining others' plight also causes emotional contagion and/or so-called personal distress. In emotional contagion, a person feels an emotion as a result of some-body else feeling an emotion of the same general type. For instance, by being around a very anxious co-worker, one might come to feel anxious oneself. Put this way, emotional contagion looks a lot like empa-thy. In contradistinction to empathy, however, the emotion here is not experienced *for* the other person. It is felt as if for the self. When my co-worker makes me anxious by being anxious, *I'm* anxious; I'm not anxious *for* her. Defined this way, emotional contagion of distress is indistinguishable from so-called personal distress. Personal distress is distress at another's distress that is self-oriented. It is usually con-trasted with empathic distress, which is theorized to be other-directed. Personal distress is an emotion we shall return to later. It is generally taken to be an egocentric emotion with little, or no, moral relevance. Emotional contagion, by contrast, is often thought to precede, or to be a precursor to, empathy. The capacity for emotional contagion, many think, is a sign of our profoundly social natures (Hatfield, Cacioppo, and Rapson 1994).

3   Mapping care

The four most prominent features of care appear to be: (1) concern with the other's welfare, (2) motivation to act so as to improve, or at least not impoverish, someone's welfare, (3) a relatively profound understanding of the other's thoughts, feelings, desires, and needs, characterized by a sharing of perspective, and (4) a deep emotional involvement with the other person in which one feels *with* the other. Does any known cog-nitive or emotional capacity, or set of capacities, fit all these features? I shall argue that there is no good fit between (1)–(4) in any of the cognitive-emotional capacities most associated with altruism, helping, and nurturing.

Sympathy, as I have described it, is the best candidate for (1) and (2). Sympathy is an affectively infused concern for the other's welfare with relatively well-documented behavioral effects. The nomenclature here is likely to give rise to some confusion, so let me point out that much of the evidence of the prosocial or altruistic effects of sympathy comes from Batson's work on what he calls empathic concern. Batson's empathic concern refers to a warmhearted, soft, tender, or compassionate feeling toward others, *not* to an emotion that is consonant with the emotion of the person for whom one feels empathic concern. That person is likely to be distressed, and empathizing with her would involve some form of empathic distress. It would be an unpleasant, more acute emotion, not a warm, soft one. Batson's empathic concern is directed at the others' welfare, not how they feel, just like sympathy. It is this emotion, specifically, that has been shown to give rise to helping behavior (Batson 1991).

One problem with thinking of sympathy as being one of the emotions involved in care is that it appears to involve a type of distance from the suffering other that many writers in the care tradition strenuously object to. For instance, Daryl Koehn (1998) argues that care cannot be too distanced emotionally from the object of care, and thus rejects sympathy as a candidate for care:

> Sympathy could be defined as the acknowledgement by the sympathizer of someone else's presumed unwelcome feelings (e.g. gut-wrenching grief at the loss of a loved one), coupled with the sympathizer's simultaneous awareness that these feelings are the other person's and not necessarily the sympathizer's own. My sympathy will be uncaring if I project what I think my friend ought to be feeling without bothering to converse with her and to enter imaginatively into her situation as she describes it.... Moreover, sympathy always introduces a distance between the sympathizer and the object of her sympathy. This distance from the other's presumed plight can easily slip into condescension. The pitying self may fail to create a shared self in which the parties are mutually vulnerable to each other....
>
> For these reasons, the female ethicist insists that, while sympathy may be a spectator sport, ethical caring never is. We must "feel" with the other. There must be an affective component to our caring for another, a feeling of engagement arising in part because the caregiver knows the stakes are high. Our very selves are at stake when we care because we are working at creating a shared self, invented as we proceed. (Koehn 1998: 26)

The stress on *listening* to the other (Gilligan 1982), becoming "engrossed" in the other (Noddings 1984), or feeling *with* the other person (Blum as quoted in Koehn 1998: 26) stands in some tension with the more distanced approach that is implicated in deep consideration for others' welfare (Darwall 1998). Whereas I think it is uncharitable to construe sympathy as a 'spectator sport,' it is certainly true that there is a clear differentiation between the self and the other in sympathy. Sympathy is experienced *for* another, and is usually qualitatively distinct from what the other is likely to feel. By comparison to other emotions routinely experienced under the same, or similar, circumstances, i.e. empathetic distress and personal distress, sympathy appears to be the one involving most distance from what the other person is experiencing. Nonetheless, sympathy's pro-social effects are well documented (Batson 1991).

If care must satisfy the demand for emotion matching, then affective empathy is a better match than sympathy. When we empathize with someone who is sad, say, we are sad *for* them. In that sense, we are directly involved or implicated in their sadness. Affective empathy involves sensitivity to how the other person *feels* and motivation to alleviate unpleasant emotions. Consequently, to the extent that empathy motivates actions that improve others' wellbeing, it is by means of improving their affective state. Researchers tend to agree that the focus on others' wellbeing is a development from empathy toward something like sympathy (Darwall 1998; Hoffman 2000). So while fitting (4), affective empathy is not a great match for (1) or (2), and does not directly implicate (3). Cognitive empathy, or perspective taking, matches (3), but not (1), (2), or (4).[2] However, the perspective one takes on a person who is in need or distress helps induce either sympathy (thus leading to (1) and (2)) or personal distress. Batson and colleagues (1997) found that when instructed to think about how someone would think or feel in their situation people tend to experience a preponderance of sympathy (what he calls 'empathic concern'). By contrast, subjects instructed to imagine how they, themselves, would feel were they in the other person's situation experience a mix of sympathy and personal distress.

Personal distress is distress experienced at someone else's distress or distressing situation and is directed at the self, i.e. is experienced as ordinary distress even if it is recognized that the cause of the distress is the fact that the other person is distressed or is in a distressing situation. It motivates helping behavior just like sympathy does. However, if escape from the situation in which one is exposed to the others' distress is relatively easy, personal distress increases the likelihood that one will do so rather than help the person in need. As such, personal distress is usually conceptualized as leading to egoistic motivation to escape distress by contrast to sympathy, which appears to lead to altruistic motivation to help the one in need (Batson 1991; Eisenberg 2000; Hoffman 2000). Personal distress, however, is perhaps the closest one can imagine coming to an emotion springing from the joint self that some care ethicists want us to create. Here we literally feel each other's distress as if it were our own. Unfortunately, personal distress is not as useful as a more distanced approach to the other when it comes to motivation to help, and the motivation appears to be egoistic to the extent that one is motivated to alleviate the other's distress only to the extent that it alleviates one's own.

It seems that imagining being in the other's situation, even *being* the other, leads to the experience of greater distress, and increases the risk that the subject will attempt to escape the situation rather than help the other. Here again, the closeness and intimacy of the attitude to the other appears to interfere with, rather than aid, a moral orientation toward others. It increases the focus on oneself as the subject of distress and reduces helping relative to a more distanced approach that focuses on the feelings of the other *as* the other. It seems that the more one attempts to mesh oneself with the other, the more this triggers emotional self-involvement, personal distress, and willingness to escape the distressing situation. It would therefore be odd indeed if the care ethics tradition were to prefer personal distress to sympathy as a candidate for care.

Before concluding that the notion of care does not show a good fit with any of the psychological categories most closely associated with caring for others, a couple of caveats are in order. First, I have talked as if people experience either empathy or sympathy or personal distress at any one time. In effect, people often feel a mix of sympathy and personal distress when presented with a person in need. The same is true of many other emotions. For instance, subjects commonly report feeling *both* guilt and shame (Tangney and Dearing 2002). Nevertheless, it seems that the emotion that is felt predominantly is a good predictor of subsequent motivation, even if it is not the only one felt. Experiencing a preponderance of sympathetic feelings toward another disposes a person to help. By contrast, once someone experiences as much distress as sympathy, they become disposed to escape the situation, one way or another (Batson, Early, and Salvarini 1997). Thus, even if several emotions are felt at the same time, it still seems that there are problems with care mapping on to real-life emotions. A second important point concerns the distress at the others' distress or needful situation. In Batson's et al. (1997) experiment, all subjects reported experiencing distress, both for themselves and the other, when presented with the person in need, with most distress being felt *for* the other. However, subjects in the imagine-self scenario experienced more distress for themselves than people in the other two conditions did, but just as much, possibly even more,[3] distress for the subject. So, it may be that it is not the experience of distress *per se* – be it for the other or personal distress – that is the problem. It is how much such distress one experiences, particularly self-oriented distress.

If care is characterized by (1) concern with the other's welfare, (2) motivation to act so as to improve, or at least not impoverish, someone's welfare, (3) a relatively profound understanding of the other's thoughts, feelings, desires, and needs, characterized by a sharing of perspective, and (4) a deep emotional involvement with the other person in which one feels *with* the other, it does not fit the traditional nurturing/helping emotions of psychological theory particularly well. While sympathy incorporates care for another's welfare with attendant motivation, it need not involve much of an understanding of the other's thoughts, feelings, etc. Further, one who sympathizes feels *for*, not necessarily *with*, the other. There is no commonly forged self in evidence in sympathy. Sympathy, then, satisfies (1) and (2) only. The more intimate connection with the other can be found in empathetic distress or personal distress, but the latter, at least, is associated with a tendency to avoid being exposed to the other if it is easy to do so, and does not seem to address (1), (2), or (3). Cognitive empathy is a better candidate for psychological understanding of the other, but perspective taking is independent from concern with someone's welfare and emotional involvement with them. Certain types of perspective taking do seem to induce sympathy and, thereby, altruistic motivation, but others are more likely to induce personal distress. So whereas cognitive empathy addresses (3), it is only loosely associated with (1), (2), and (4). It may seem, then, that the best candidate is empathy or empathic distress. Empathy clearly satisfies (4). Its fit with (1)–(3) is questionable, however. In empathetic distress, the person is concerned with the fact that the other person is distressed and is motivated to alleviate that distress. Concern with welfare is the specific domain of sympathy, where empathy focuses on the other's emotions. Of course, being concerned with someone's distress may mean being concerned with their welfare, and helping to alleviate that distress often increases their welfare. However, a narrow focus on making people feel better might ultimately lead to actions that do *not* further their welfare. Affective empathy also does not guarantee any deep understanding of the other. In conclusion, the notion of care shows an uneasy fit with psychological structures known to underlie emotional consonance, emotions of nurturance, and so on. This raises questions about the notion of care as it tends to be used in the ethics of care tradition. Nevertheless, even if the fit is imperfect, we may still ask whether any of the candidate traits for underlying care are experienced more by women than by men.

4   Sex differences in empathy, sympathy, and perspective taking

The question of whether there are sex differences in empathy, sympathy, or perspective taking is vexed. Some studies show significant differences (e.g. Eisenberg et al. 1987; Baron-Cohen and Wheelwright 2004), and quite a few show no differences at all (Eisenberg-Berg and Lennon 1980; Graham and Ickes 1997; Ickes, Gesn, and Graham 2000). Measures of empathy vary across different studies, and this is thought to be the cause of some of the discrepancy (Carlo 2006; Eisenberg, Spinrad, and Sadovsky 2006). Indeed, Nancy Eisenberg and Randy Lennon argue that:

> In general, sex differences in empathy were a function of the methods used to assess empathy. There were large sex differences favoring women when the measure of empathy was self-report scales; moderate differences (favoring females) were found for reflexive crying and self-report measures in laboratory situations; and no sex differences were evident when the measure of empathy was either physiological or unobtrusive observations of nonverbal reactions to another's emotional state. (1983: 100)

Since females outperform males primarily on tests where it is clear that empathy/sympathy is being tested and there often is no difference in less obtrusive tests, it seems that females are primed to *appear* more caring and empathetic than men without necessarily being so. The evidence, however, is mixed.

Starting with sex differences in cognitive empathy, understood as mental state attribution, there are some areas in which females appear to be superior. Judith Hall (1978) found that women outperform men at identifying emotion using nonverbal cues. Sex, however, only explained 4 percent of the variance, making this difference decidedly small. Evin McClure (2000) found significant sex differences in discrimination of facial expressions favoring females in infants, children, and adolescents. By contrast, Roland Erwin et al. (1992) found that men were superior to women in discriminating facial expressions of happiness and sadness, apparently due to women being worse than men at discriminating sadness in women's faces, but not men's. Similarly, Naomi and George Rotter (1988) found that men were better than women at identifying anger in faces, although women performed better on the individuation of other facially expressed emotions.[4] Other studies have found no difference in ability (Schulte-Rüther et al. 2008). For instance, Sherman Lee and colleagues found no effect of gender on the ability to ascribe mental states on the basis of the expression in someone's eyes (Lee et al. 2010). Jonathan Silas and colleagues (2010) report significant sex differences in the activation of what is assumed to be the human mirror neuron system when subjects perform and observe movement, with women showing increased activation by comparison to men, but those differences were not reflected in people's self-reports. Men reported making as many, and as diverse, psychological ascriptions as women did. Therefore, these differences in brain activation may not reflect differences in ability to ascribe psychological properties to others.

When it comes to accuracy in ascribing mental states, researchers have found relatively few differences, and those that were found were attributable to women attempting to conform to the gender or sex ideal of being understanding, empathetic, etc. (Graham and Ickes 1997; Ickes, Gesn, and Graham 2000). Kristi Klein and Sara Hodges (2001) showed that when provided with monetary rewards, men perform as well as women. This suggests that when there are differences in accuracy between males and females, that difference is due more to differences in motivation than difference in ability. Summing up, there is some evidence of slight female superiority in ascribing mental states based on nonverbal evidence, but no consistent differences (other than slight differences in motivation) are observed in other areas of mental state ascription.

Perspective taking is central to the question of empathy and care. The designer of the Ethics of Care Interview (ECI) Eva Skoe argues that perspective taking uniquely predicts care-based moral levels. People who take others' perspective more often show a greater care orientation. But Skoe (2010) discovered *no* gender differences on perspective taking.[5] Birgit Derntl and colleagues (2010) also found no difference in perspective taking between males and females, although they found differences in the brain areas that were activated (see below).

Moving on to evidence of differences in empathic responding between men and women, we face the problem that most of the tests that psychologists use to gage levels of empathy do not differentiate between affective empathy and sympathy and, as Batson (1991) points out, offer no reliable way of separating these attitudes from compassion or pity. Females *report* experiencing more affective empathy than men (Mestre et al. 2009; Skoe 2010) and girls facially express more empathy/sympathy than boys (Eisenberg, Spinrad, and Sadovsky 2006) though the difference apparently is not large. Erno Hermans and colleagues (2009) have found that women who score low on autistic traits exhibit the most facial mimicry of the emotions of others. There two difficulties with interpreting the data as supporting increased affective empathy in females as things stand. First, it is unclear that what is measured is empathy rather than sympathy, personal distress, or emotional contagion. There is, for instance, good evidence that women experience more personal distress than men in response to others in need, as I will discuss below. Second, although women sometimes report experiencing more empathy, such self-reports do not align with other correlates of empathy. Physiological correlates of the empathy/sympathy/personal distress reaction – e.g. heart rate – do not indicate that women experience more empathy than men (Eisenberg, Spinrad, and Sadovsky 2006) and studies that show increased female empathic distress show no increased female helping behavior compared to men. This is curious since empathic distress is supposed to be correlated with increased helping (Greeno and Maccoby 1986). Lack of extra helping in women despite higher empathy ratings was also reported by Michael Morgan and colleagues in a study on helping the homeless (1997) and by Patricia Oswald (2000) in an empathy-helping study. All we can conclude for now, therefore, is that women *claim* to be more empathetic than men do, but there is little evidence suggesting that they actually are.

With the advent of more sophisticated brain scanning devices, it is now possible to individuate more specific brain areas involved in the processing of certain information. Here some sex differences have shown up. Singer et al. (2006) found that women have the same neural empathic response to fair and unfair players in pain in a sequential prisoner's dilemma game. By contrast, men experience no empathy for unfair players in pain; in fact, they have increased activity in their reward centers. It is hard to draw any sweeping conclusions from a study of such a specific empathy difference, particularly given the small sample size (16 men vs. 16 women).

In a study by Martin Schulte-Rüther (2008) and colleagues, women reported experiencing stronger affect than men in response to angry or fearful faces. There were no sex differences in accuracy of identification or in latency of recognition. Differences were noticed in the brain activation pattern, where women showed stronger activation of the right inferior frontal gyrus and right superior temporal sulcus of the mirror neuron system (particularly the inferior frontal gyrus), and men more activation in the temporo-parietal junction (TPJ) (Schulte-Rüther et al. 2008). The mirror neuron system is thought to be involved in action identification, contagion, and empathy. The TPJ is implicated in theory of mind tasks generally, particularly belief ascription, and self-other differentiation. Schulte-Rüther et al. interpret this result to signify that men use more cognitive resources to identify their own emotional responses to others, in particular, *and* that they exhibit more distancing from the emotions of others. By contrast, women are strongly emotionally engaged by others and are more absorbed by their experiences in a less self–other differentiated way. The authors conclude that this suggests that their study supports the idea that women are more empathetic than men. However, their design makes it impossible to distinguish between empathy, emotional contagion, and personal distress. And whereas the evidence that women experience more empathy than men is weak, there is consistent evidence that women experience more personal distress than men. This study could support that idea further.

In line with the above studies, Birgit Derntl and colleagues (2010) found no behavioral differences between men and women on tasks testing emotion recognition, perspective taking, and affective responsiveness (empathy, sympathy, or personal distress), but significant differences in brain activation. Females showed more activation than men of emotion-related areas, including the amygdala, across all empathy measures. Although it is tempting to conclude that this provides evidence that women are more empathetic in the sense of being more emotionally responsive to others, we do not know enough about how to interpret the brain data yet. The fact that women and men report the same levels of emotion recognition, perspective taking, and affective responsiveness should make us hesitant to draw such a conclusion.

This leaves us with evidence for sex differences in personal distress. And here the situation seems less equivocal overall. Eisenberg et al. (1988) found that girls experienced more personal distress than boys, but not more empathy. Skoe's (2010) study shows more personal distress in females than males. Of special interest to the care ethics tradition here is the fact that personal distress is uniquely *negatively* correlated with ECI scores. In other words, the tendency to experience more personal distress in response to others' difficult situation or negative emotionality is associated with less of an ethics of care orientation. Again, in a study of people's neurological responses to seeing people in pain, Chia Yen-Yang and colleagues (2009) discovered increased mu rhythm suppression – which is used "as a reliable indicator of the sensorimotor cortical resonance of empathy for pain" (2009: 177) – in females compared to males. In this study, mu suppression was correlated with the personal distress subscale of IRI in women, but not in men although other research supports the idea that mu suppression is a marker of personal distress. Women, therefore, appear to be more emotionally reactive to the distress of others than men. By contrast to empathy and sympathy, experiencing personal distress makes the person focus on herself and, therefore, on doing something about her own distress. As Batson has shown, escaping the distressing situation, if such escape is easy, is one favored way of relieving personal distress (Batson 1991). Where I tend to think personal distress is overly maligned in the literature, it clearly bears a much more complex relationship to maintaining and furthering personal relationships than empathy does. And though some ethics of care proponents are enthusiastic about breaking down the boundary between the self and the other, particularly in emotional matters, personal distress is not well related to pro-social behavior.

To conclude, there is little evidence of female superiority in the broad area of empathic relating to others. The evidence shows that both men and women *think* that women are more sympathetic, empathetic, and experience more emotional contagion, than men. But even here, the differences are typically not large. Once studies deploy measures that either do not rely on self-reports or do not obviously tap into empathy/ sympathy, the difference between men and women generally disappears. Women may be superior to men in ascribing mental states based on purely facial information and they may experience more emotional contagion or personal distress than men, but on the majority of empathy and sympathy measures, no consistent significant differences have been found. In conclusion, there is little support for the cultural stereotype of female empathic superiority. Furthermore, care does not correlate so well with facial expression recognition or emotional contagion to justify calling a care orientation a typically female ethical orientation.

I have said that there are no male/female differences in broad empathetic responding, but it should be noted that there *is* a difference in self-conception. It appears, however, to be a self-conception that has curiously little effect on *actual* empathic responding. This could be an artifact of the experimental structure. It would be interesting to explore further the power of self-conception to affect cognitive-emotional responding to others. For the moment, however, we have no evidence that it makes a difference.

5 Conclusion

Determining what psychological structures care is supposed to reflect presents with substantial difficulties. Those that have attempted to test the hypothesis that an ethics of care reflects a female orientation toward ethics have failed to find support for the idea. Male and female reasoning deploy care considerations equally. Unsurprisingly, when moral dilemmas concern personal relationships, both men and women use care constructs to reason about them. By contrast, when they concern conflicts with strangers, institutions, etc., both men and women tend to reason more in terms of rights and justice (Jaffee and Hyde 2000; Walker 2006). If we try to analyze the suggestion of care ethicists in terms of the types of cognitive and emotional reactions and attitudes to the feelings and wellbeing of others that are typically associated with care and nurturance, the situation is not much improved. Although both sexes agree that women are more empathetic than men, actual differences are hard to find. Further, some of the differences that we do find may not be particularly hospitable to an ethics of care position. The way that care is described vacillates between a sympathetic – i.e. welfare oriented – approach to others, and an almost emotional unification with them. The psychological literature suggests that getting so emotionally enmeshed with the other that the boundaries between self and other begin to break down is *not* useful. It leads to increased personal distress, which is associated with egoistic motivation to relieve that distress, e.g. removing oneself from the person in need. In addition to the empirical difficulties with the idea that an ethics of care approach is more typical of women than men, there are difficulties mapping this structure on to the emotions and attitudes associated with nurturance and caring. This raises questions about the notion of care. We may want to reconsider the validity and usefulness of this particular ethical construct.

Notes

1. Some require type-identity (Sober and Wilson 1998) or isomorphism (Singer and Lamm 2009), but this seems too demanding. On the other hand, the more permissive understanding of empathy promoted by Martin Hoffman

(2000) may be *too* broad. For instance, I may happen to feel very upset for no apparent reason while my friend, who has just been fired from his job, feels just fine. This does not empathy make.

2. Note, though, that the perspective taking that care theorists have in mind is often a great deal more onerous than that explored by social psychologists, as it does not simply involve trying to take up the perspective of another; it involves taking in the other in their alterity and feeling what they are feeling.

3. In the study at hand, the difference was not statistically significant.

4. Incidentally, one of the emotions that women were better than men at identifying in this study was sadness, contrasting with the findings of Erwin et al. (1992). This encapsulates the difficulty of the sex and gender difference research generally. The findings often fail to give a consistent picture of sex or gender differences.

5. On the perspective taking subscale of IRI (Interpersonal Reactivity Index) see Davis (1983).

4

The Role of Fetal Testosterone in the Development of the "Essential Difference" Between the Sexes: Some Essential Issues

Giordana Grossi and Cordelia Fine

1 Introduction

The Empathizing/Systemizing (E/S) hypothesis developed by Baron-Cohen and colleagues has two main goals: first, to explain the presence of brain, cognitive, and behavioral differences between the sexes; and second, to explain the pattern of symptoms associated with autistic syndromes. These two goals are connected, since Baron-Cohen argues that autism is the expression of an "extreme male brain" (e.g. Baron-Cohen 2002). Briefly, the E/S hypothesis proposes that levels of fetal testosterone (fT) influence brain development in such a way that lower levels of fT (more common in females) result in a 'female brain' that is "predominantly hard-wired for empathy" (Baron-Cohen 2003: 1). Empathizing is defined as "the drive to identify another's mental states and to respond to these with an appropriate emotion, in order to predict and to respond to the behavior of another person" (Baron-Cohen, Knickmeyer, and Belmonte 2005: 820). By contrast, higher levels of fT (more common in males) result in a 'male brain' that is "predominantly hard-wired for understanding and building systems" (Baron-Cohen 2003: 1). Systemizing is defined as "the drive to analyze a system in terms of the rules that govern the system, in order to predict the behavior of the system" (Baron-Cohen, Knickmeyer, and Belmonte 2005: 820). The "extreme male brain" of autism thus manifests as poor empathizing abilities twinned with superior systemizing abilities.

The social and political implications of the E/S hypothesis are readily apparent. While Baron-Cohen (e.g. Baron-Cohen 2003) is clear that a person of one sex may have the brain of the other (thus a woman may have a 'male' brain, and vice versa), on average the sexes will differ in their hardwired cognitive predispositions. This implies that gender inequalities are not due solely to gender discrimination or socialization, but at least partially to an "essential difference" (Baron-Cohen 2003), on average, between the sexes. (For an explicit argument of this kind with respect to sex ratios in math and physics, see Baron-Cohen 2007: 169.) Indeed, Baron-Cohen (2003: 185) argues that individuals with a 'female brain' are biologically predisposed toward occupations that, currently at least, are performed mostly by women, and thus "make the most wonderful counsellors, primary-school teachers, nurses, carers, therapists, social workers, mediators, group facilitators or personnel staff." By contrast, those with a 'male brain' supposedly enjoy a hardwired facility for traditionally male occupations, for example in science, engineering, business, law, and plumbing, all of which, it is argued, involve constructing and analyzing systems. The real-world implications of acceptance of the E/S hypothesis make it especially important that its assumptions, claims, and data are examined with care. In this chapter we focus on data and arguments regarding the relationship between fT, brain, and behavioral differences between the sexes. In the first section we evaluate the evidence for sex differences in Empathizing and Systemizing (herein E and S) abilities. In the second section we assess the arguments that fT organizes brain 'type.' We focus especially on the evidence presented by Baron-Cohen and colleagues in *Science* (Baron-Cohen, Knickmeyer, and Belmonte 2005), which we note is a prestigious journal with a wide circulation. In both sections we highlight numerous empirical, methodological, and conceptual inadequacies.

2   Sex differences in systemizing and empathizing

The E/S hypothesis asserts sex differences in E and S abilities. By way of support for this position, Baron-Cohen et al. (2005: 819) argue that:

> Although males and females do not differ in general intelligence, specific cognitive tasks reveal sex differences. Differences favoring males are seen on the mental rotation test (Shepard and Metzler 1971),[1] spatial navigation including map reading (Kimura 1999), targeting (Watson and Kimura 1991), and the embedded figures test (Witkin et al. 1962),[2] although there are conflicting studies regarding

the latter (Hyde, Geiringer, and Yen 1975). Males are also more likely to play with mechanical toys as children (Hines, Allen, and Gorski 1992),[3] and as adults, they score higher on engineering and physics problems (Lawson, Baron-Cohen, and Wheelwright 2004). In contrast, females score higher on tests of emotion recognition (McClure 2000), social sensitivity (Baron-Cohen et al. 1999), and verbal fluency (Hyde and Linn 1988). They start to talk earlier than boys do (Fenson et al. 1994) and are more likely to play with dolls as children (Hines, Allen, and Gorski 1992). [For ease of reference, numbered citations in original have been replaced with author/date citations.]

Difficulties with these assertions fall into three types. First, in some cases it is contentious whether the tasks in which sex differences are observed fall under the purview of S or E ability. Second, the asserted sex difference may be under dispute, or contingent on social-contextual factors. Third, the potential role of experiential factors in the sex difference may be under-acknowledged.

2.1 Is it actually systemizing or empathizing?

We consider first the supposed greater male interest and skill in domains requiring systemizing. As noted earlier, systemizing is defined as the drive to analyze the rules that govern a system, with a view to predicting its behavior. This 'drive' is assumed to be content-free, that is, it applies to a variety of domains of systems, including technical, natural, abstract, social, organizable, and motoric systems (see Baron-Cohen 2002: 248). Systemizing interests would thus include grammar, physics, architecture, sociology, quilting, hair-dressing, and knitting; for some of which, we note, there is no evidence of greater male skill or interest.

Notwithstanding the imprecision of the definition, it is not immediately obvious to us that superior performance on mental rotation, spatial navigation, targeting, or embedded figures tasks constitutes convincing evidence of superiority in understanding and predicting systems. In fact, Baron-Cohen et al. (2005: 820) note that "it is unclear if the [embedded figures test] is really a test of systemizing or simply a test of good attention to detail". Unfortunately, this lack of clarity with regards to the specific cognitive operations involved in the cited tasks, or systemizing itself, creates rather too much leeway when it comes to empirical tests of the E/S hypothesis. For instance, Baron-Cohen has argued that the mental rotation test "involves systemizing because it is necessary to treat each feature in a display as a variable that can be transformed (e.g., rotated) and then predict the output, or how it will appear after transformation" (Baron-Cohen 2007: 167, reference removed). Yet he and colleagues later questioned the validity of mental rotation as a systemizing measure, on the grounds that mental rotation ability does not correlate with proxies of fT exposure, stating that "mental rotation is not an ideal task for testing the elevated foetal testosterone (fT) hypothesis of [autism spectrum conditions]" (Knickmeyer et al. 2008: 995). Clearly, this is not a scientifically acceptable approach. If the hypothesis is that higher levels of fT create a more strongly systemizing brain, then cognitive tests should be defined *a priori* as systemizing or not. If a cognitive test that has been defined as systemizing fails to show an association with fT, then this constitutes lack of empirical support for the hypothesis.

Similar, although fewer, issues arise with regards to whether some of the skills cited by Baron-Cohen et al. (2005) as being superior in females actually constitute evidence of superiority in empathizing. Verbal fluency, for example – the ability to list as many words as possible from a particular category (like 'animals' or 'words beginning with the letter *p*') in a given period of time – bears no obvious link to empathizing ability. In addition, while it's certainly plausible that an ability to understand a caregiver's thoughts and intentions will facilitate language development, this doesn't imply that a relative delay in language development necessarily has poorer empathizing ability as its cause.[4] It is also not clear whether the superior performance of girls on the 'social sensitivity' task (Baron-Cohen et al. 1999, as cited in Baron-Cohen et al. 2005) is best explained in terms of superior female empathizing. This study found that while boys and girls aged seven, nine, and eleven years old were generally able to understand the erroneous mental states that led to faux pas, girls were more likely to identify when someone had said something she or he shouldn't have said. It's unclear, however, whether this difference arose because boys were less sensitive to the story characters' feelings, or whether they were simply more forgiving of the accidental and non-malicious hurting of others' feelings.

Exacerbating the imprecision of Baron-Cohen's approach in defining systemizing and empathizing is his use of self-report questionnaires – the Empathy Quotient (EQ, Baron-Cohen and Wheelwright 2004) and Systemizing Quotient (SQ, Baron-Cohen et al. 2003) – to measure E and S tendencies, or brain 'type.' This approach is problematic for two reasons. First, as Levy (2004: 322) has noted, the statements in the EQ and SQ are "often testing for the gender of the subject, by asking whether the subject is interested in activities which tend to be disproportionately associated with males or with females (cars, electrical wiring, computers and other machines, sports and stock markets, on the one hand, and friendships and relationships, on the other)." The questionnaires are thus likely to make gender salient. Importantly, social psychological work has shown that priming gender increases self-stereotyping (e.g. Hogg and Turner 1987; James 1993; Steele and Ambady 2006; Chatard, Guimond, and Selimbegovic 2007). Indeed, even noting one's sex at the beginning of a questionnaire, as the EQ and SQ both require participants to do, can increase self-stereotyping (Sinclair, Hardin, and Lowery 2006). A serious concern, then, is that the responses on these self-report tests are significantly biased by gender-primed self-stereotyping.

Furthermore, self-report questionnaires do not measure actual behavior and often fail to predict behavior. For example, a now substantial literature shows that self-report measures of social sensitivity bear little relation to actual empathic accuracy. A review by Davis and Kraus (1997: 162) found that self-ratings of social sensitivity, empathy, femininity, and thoughtfulness had "minimal value" in the identification of good and poor social judges. More recent studies have also found only weak or non-significant correlations between self-estimates of ability and actual performance (Realo et al. 2003; Ames and Kammrath 2004; Voracek and Dressler 2006).

2.2 Is the sex difference real and reliable?

Two further issues arising from the evidence of sex differences cited by Baron-Cohen and colleagues are: first, some of these behavioral differences are under dispute; second, their existence is surprisingly sensitive to social-contextual factors. With regards to the first point, while there is support for a male advantage in mental rotation (e.g. Voyer, Voyer, and Bryden 1995), recent meta-analyzes have cast doubts on sex differences in spatial navigation and the embedded figure test (for a discussion of such literature, see Newcombe 2010). Similarly, the female advantages in verbal fluency and proficiency are not just of dubious relevance to the E/S hypothesis, but have also been questioned; differences may exist in children, but they tend to disappear with age (see Wallentin 2009). Female superiority in the cognitive component of empathizing (that is, inferring the thoughts and feelings of others) is also under question. Meta-analyzes have found superior decoding of nonverbal expressions of emotion in girls and women (Hall 1984; McClure 2000). However, research using the empathic accuracy test – a more realistic test of mindreading that assesses ability to infer a partner's thoughts and feelings in a genuine, unscripted social interaction – calls into question the assumption that females have an advantage in real-world mindreading

(Graham and Ickes 1997; Ickes 2003). Extensive use of this test has reliably found equivalent performance in the sexes (except in conditions to be discussed shortly; Ickes, Gesn, and Graham 2000).

With regards to the second issue, a growing body of social psychological research has demonstrated that sex differences can be significantly influenced by the social context in which the task is presented (for summary see Fine 2010a). Specifically, sex differences in performance are decreased or even eliminated when either the 'gendered' nature of the task, or the gender of the participant, is made less salient. Thus, sex differences in the performance of mental rotation tasks – the largest cognitive sex difference – have been significantly reduced and even eliminated altogether by simple changes such as presenting the task as associated with skill on 'feminine' compared with 'masculine' tasks (Sharps, Price, and Williams 1994), asking people to rotate stick figures rather than shapes (Alexander and Evardone 2008), or informing participants that women show superior performance (Moè 2009). A large literature on 'stereotype threat' (Steele 1997) has similarly shown significant effects of the social context on sex differences in math performance (for meta-analysis, see Nguyen and Ryan 2008). Briefly, stereotype threat refers to the detrimental effect on performance of a social context that highlights a relevant negative stereotype about one's social group (e.g. the stereotype that women are bad at math, during a math test). A recent meta-analysis of stereotype threat studies found that females, matched with males on real-world academic tests like the SAT, performed worse in math under stereotype threat (Walton and Spencer 2009). Moreover, the meta-analysis indicated that when stereotype threat was removed – generally by making gender seem less relevant to the task at hand – women actually outperformed their male peers who, from real-world tests, purportedly had the same mathematical ability.

Similar effects of task 'degendering' have been observed for both cognitive and affective components of empathizing. As noted earlier, research with the empathic accuracy test has reliably failed to find sex differences, regardless of whether the interacting dyads are strangers, friends, or romantic partners. However, when the test form was changed slightly to ask participants to rate the accuracy of their empathic judgments, female performance was enhanced (Ickes et al. 2000; Ickes 2003). Ickes (2003) suggested that this small change reminds women of the social expectation that women should be empathic. Similarly, Koenig and Eagly (2005) successfully closed the gender gap on a social sensitivity task by presenting it as a test of complex information processing.

Providing extra motivation to men to do well on empathizing tasks by offering social or financial incentives has also been successful in increasing male performance (Thomas and Maio 2008) and equalizing male/female performance (Klein and Hodges 2001), respectively. With regards to the affective component of empathizing (that is, experiencing an appropriate emotional response to another's mental state), Eisenberg and Lennon (1983) concluded from a meta-analysis that the female empathic advantage becomes vanishingly small as it becomes less and less obvious to the participant that something to do with empathy is being assessed. Thus, sex differences were greatest on self-report tests, smaller differences were seen when the purpose of the testing was less obvious, and few consistent differences were found for studies using unobtrusive physiological or facial/gestural measures as an index of empathy (although it should be noted that it's not clear how well such measures actually index affective empathy). Likewise, while Fabes and Eisenberg (1998) concluded that overall there is evidence of greater affective empathy in girls than boys, as with adults, this difference was smaller when based on observations rather than self-report or report by another (such as a parent).

The salience of participants' gender-identity also influences performance on gender-typed tasks. Thus females' mental rotation (McGlone and Aronson 2006) and math performance (Rydell, McConnell, and Beilock 2009) is improved, or becomes similar to that of males (Hausmann et al. 2009) when participants are primed to think of themselves in terms of a math-positive and/or non-gendered identity. Ryan, David, and Reynolds (2004) found that making a student- rather than gender-identity salient eliminated sex differences in care-based versus justice-based moral reasoning, and females asked to take the first-person perspective of a male character performed as poorly as males on emotion-knowledge tasks (Marx and Stapel 2006).

It is, we would suggest, problematic to attribute to differences between the 'female brain' and the 'male brain' sex differences in E and S that can be so readily reduced and even eliminated by simple social manipulations that diminish the salience of stereotypical expectations.

2.3 The purported 'innateness' of sex differences

Finally, sex differences in empathizing and systemizing abilities and interests, when present, might stem from experiential factors. While Baron-Cohen acknowledges that culture plays a "major role," he regards gender socialization factors as "amplifying...partly innate differences" (Baron-Cohen 2007: 169). Baron-Cohen et al. (2005: 819–820) cite three lines of research as evidence that there is a "biological foundation" to purported sex differences:

> Male rats perform significantly better than females do on the radial arm and Morris water maze (Roof et al. 1993). This sex difference is eliminated by castrating males or by treating females with testosterone neonatally (De Vries and Simerly 2002). Human males also commit fewer errors and require less time to complete a 'virtual' maze (Moffat, Hampson, and Lee 1998). Young male vervet monkeys prefer to play with toy trucks, whereas young female vervets prefer dolls (Alexander and Hines 2002). This finding suggests that sex differences in toy preferences in children result, in part, from innate biological differences. Biological contributions to social interest are suggested by studies of human infants. When one-day-old babies are presented with either a live face or a mechanical mobile, girls spend more time looking at the face, whereas boys prefer the mechanical object (Connellan et al. 2001).[5] [For ease of reference, numbered citations in original have been replaced with author/date citations.]

Examination of these three lines of evidence – from maze performance in rats and humans, toy preferences in monkeys, and newborn preferences for mechanical versus social stimuli – in each case yields conceptual and empirical difficulties, which we discuss in turn.

2.3.1   *Maze performance in rats and humans*

First, Baron-Cohen et al. cite data from non-human animals – rats – as evidence that similar sex differences in spatial navigation in humans are biologically inherent. We begin by noting that the study cited as evidence of superior male rat performance on the radial arm and Morris water maze task (Roof et al. 1993) was a lesion study that found no sex differences in neurologically intact animals.[6] Moreover, DeVries and Simerly (2002) do not mention studies of spatial skills in the rat. Moffat et al. (1998) was an MRI investigation of planum temporale and corpus callosum morphology in left handers, and did not involve a virtual maze task. Baron-Cohen et al. may instead be referring to Moffat, Hampson, and Hatzipentalis (1998), who found sex differences in a task requiring participants to navigate a virtual maze. However, we note that participants were asked to fill out a demographic questionnaire before performing the behavioral test. It is therefore plausible that behavior was influenced by stereotype threat.

Moreover, no justification is provided for selecting rats as an appropriate comparison with humans. Humans are cognitively and neurologically dissimilar to rats in potentially important ways (see Hines 2004: 215), and it is not known whether the same mechanisms are involved in spatial navigation in the two species. Underlining the need for caution in extrapolating from rats from humans is research showing that it is impossible to generalize even within the same species. For example, in a meta-analysis of spatial behavior in rodents, Jonasson (2005) found a sex difference favoring male rats in two different types of mazes (water and radial arm), but the difference varied depending on the strain of rats. Importantly, the difference disappeared, or was reversed, in mice.

2.3.2 Toy preferences in monkeys

Baron-Cohen et al. (2005: 820) next cite an observational study of vervet monkeys' toy play behavior (Alexander and Hines 2002) as evidence that human sex differences in children's play behavior is due in part to "innate biological differences." This study compared contact time with 'masculine' toys (a ball and a police car), 'feminine' toys (a toy pan and a doll), and 'neutral' toys (a picture book and a stuffed dog), presented serially in the vervet enclosure. Between-sex contrasts showed greater male interest in the 'masculine' toys, and greater female interest in the 'feminine' toys. The sexes showed equal interest in the 'neutral' toys. Within-sex contrasts found only that females had greater percentage contact with 'feminine' toys than with 'masculine' toys. More recently, Hassett et al. (2008) ran a similar study with male and female rhesus monkeys, in which they compared interaction (using two dependent variables, total frequency and total duration of contact) with 'masculine' wheeled toys versus 'feminine' stuffed toys. Between-sex contrasts found that males and females were equally interested in the wheeled toys. Males and females also spent a similar duration of time with the stuffed toys, but females had a greater total frequency of interaction with these toys. Within-sex contrasts revealed that males preferred wheeled toys over stuffed toys, while females showed no preference.

There are two important points to be made about these findings (see Fine 2010a and for a further critique of the earlier study, see also Jordan-Young 2010). First, there are issues regarding the choice of 'feminine' toys. Although in human culture cooking utensils are associated with females due to their role in domestic caretaking, it is entirely unclear why a female predisposition toward a toy pan should be anticipated in monkey populations, which do not enjoy the art of heated cuisine. The pan was, however, the most popular toy for female vervets, and

Alexander and Hines (2002) suggested that this may have been due to the appeal of its red color. This raises the possibility that other sex differences in toy preferences may have been due to confounding factors. It is also worth noting that a stuffed animal (a dog) was used as a 'neutral' stimulus by Alexander and Hines (and was in fact the most popular toy with male vervets), yet stuffed animals were used as 'feminine' stimuli by Hassett et al. even though, as Hines and Alexander (2008) point out, boys and girls like stuffed animals equally.

Second, the results from the two studies are somewhat contradictory with each other. Alexander and Hines (2002) found greater male than female interest in 'masculine' toys, while Hassett et al. (2008) found that males and females were equally interested in 'masculine' toys. Moreover, while Hassett et al. found that rhesus males spent significantly more time with 'masculine' toys than with 'feminine' ones, Alexander and Hines found no such preference in vervets. Likewise, Hassett et al.'s observation of greater female than male interest in stuffed animals (significant for only one dependent measure) was not observed by Alexander and Hines. In other words, the studies together leave some uncertainty regarding the reliability of both between- and within-sex differences in gendered toy preferences.

2.3.3   *Newborn preferences for mechanical versus social stimuli*

As a final line of evidence for the 'innateness' of sex differences in empathizing/systemizing tendencies, Baron-Cohen et al. (2005) refer to a study of newborn looking preferences which compared neonates' looking time at a live face versus a mobile (Connellan et al. 2000). Male and female babies spent equal amounts of time looking at the face (that of the first author): both sexes, on average, spent just under half the total presentation time (approximately a minute) looking at Connellan's face.[7] However, males looked longer at the mobile than did females (51.9 percent of presentation time versus 40.6 percent for females) and females looked longer at the face than the mobile (49.4 percent versus 40.6 percent of presentation time). A detailed critique of the methodological flaws of this study has been provided by Nash and Grossi (2007). These flaws range from the many differences between the stimuli (each of which could have been responsible for the observed differences), to experimenter expectancy effects (the first author was herself the live face, and controlled the movement of the mobile), to the authors' non-standard procedure for measuring looking time preference (serial presentation rather than the simultaneous presentation methodology that is standard in infant visual preference research). These serious methodological issues render questionable the study's contribution to the scientific literature; notably, the findings have not been replicated. Moreover, no attempt is made by the authors to justify the assumption that newborn looking preferences anticipate future propensity for complex, culture-dependent skills such as physics or empathizing (Levy 2004; Nash and Grossi 2007).

2.4 Summary of evidence for sex differences in E and S

The claim for the existence of strong and reliable sex differences in E and S is not supported by the extant evidence. The imprecision in defining E and S (as 'drives,' not as sets of specific cognitive abilities) has made it difficult to find cognitive tasks that convincingly capture these constructs; furthermore, when sex differences are present they are not reliable and can be explained by other mechanisms. The strongest evidence for sex differences in E and S comes from self-report questionnaires which are, as discussed, fraught with methodological problems. The argument that some of these differences have a biological foundation because they are observed in other animals and in newborns is also not convincing. The choice of the species used to support data on humans is generally not properly justified. Moreover, data from monkey and newborn studies are ambiguous or have not been replicated. By contrast, the role of gender socialization processes in gendered preferences is well documented (e.g. Bussey and Bandura 1999; Martin and Ruble 2004; Miller, Trautner, and Ruble 2006; Leaper and Friedman 2007).

3   Fetal testosterone organizes functional brain 'type'

The E/S hypothesis predicts that differences in fT levels are associated with differences in specific brain structures that are, in turn, associated with differences in cognitive style or behavior. Our discussion of this body of evidence falls into three parts. We begin by discussing the conceptual roots of this aspect of the E/S hypothesis and the assumptions about the nature of the developmental process implicit in such an account. Next, we evaluate the strength of empirical support for the prediction that fT levels correlate with later E and S abilities. Third, we discuss the evidence regarding sex differences in the brain in relation to the prediction that fT influences brain structure in ways that have functional implications for E and S ability.

3.1   The conceptual roots of the E/S hypothesis

The conceptual roots of the E/S hypothesis lie in what has been termed the "orthodox view of brain sexual differentiation" (Breedlove, Cooke, and Jordan 1999). Briefly, this view holds that the gene-directed development of testes in the male fetus results in high levels of gonadal fT that direct the development of male genitalia, and 'organize' a male brain that produces male behavior (in some cases after these brain structures are 'activated' by circulating sex hormones in pubescence and adulthood). The organizational-activational hypothesis, first proposed by Phoenix et al. (1959), seeks to account for sexually dimorphic behavior – in particular, behavior tied to reproduction (for example, frequency of mounting and lordosis) – and empirical tests of the hypothesis are usually conducted with non-primate mammals. The hormonal environment is manipulated during the critical period that masculinization of the external genitalia takes place, and the effects on brain organization and/or sexually dimorphic behavior are observed (for a brief summary, see Breedlove et al. 1999). (The timing of the critical period varies across species; for example, in rats the critical period for sexual differentiation includes the early postnatal period. Thus for simplicity, we sometimes use the term 'early' to encompass both prenatal and neonatal testosterone levels.)

In a highly influential proposal, Geschwind and colleagues extrapolated such accounts of brain sexual differentiation in animals to humans. Research by Diamond and colleagues showed that high levels of neonatal testosterone in male rats were associated with a relatively thicker right hemisphere cortex: in castrated male rats, the normal right-thicker-than-left cortical asymmetry was reversed (see Diamond 1991). Partly on the basis of such findings in rats, Geschwind and Behan (1982) proposed that similarly in humans the higher levels of fT in males stimulates growth of the right hemisphere while inhibiting growth of the left. Further, Geschwind and Galaburda (1987) proposed cognitive sequelae to these differences in brain development, suggesting that these structural differences enable greater male facility for visuospatial and mathematical processing, but delay language development, compared with females.

Baron-Cohen and colleagues cite Geschwind's work as supportive of a role for fT in sexual differentiation of the brain (e.g. Lutchmaya, Baron-Cohen, and Raggatt 2002a; Chapman et al. 2006). However, numerous differences in the way that early hormones affect rodents and humans have led to the conclusion that the "dominant rat and mouse models of sexual differentiation seem unlikely to apply to human sexual differentiation" (Wallen 2005: 8). Hines (2004), moreover, has noted that rat brains differ to human brains in important ways, with proportionally more area devoted to sensory functions and fewer association areas devoted to more complex, higher-order cognition. Thus, it cannot be assumed that the brain changes wrought by early testosterone in rats would be preserved in humans. In line with these concerns, fT does not appear to have the same effect on right hemisphere growth in humans as it does in rats. Neither a large post-mortem study of fetal brains (Chi, Dooling, and Gilles 1977; see discussion in Bleier 1986) nor a structural neuroimaging study of 74 newborns found evidence for a relatively larger right hemisphere in human males (Gilmore et al. 2007). Moreover, as Nash and Grossi (2007) note, post-mortem and neuroimaging studies of adult brains have also failed to demonstrate a relatively larger right hemisphere in males, either overall, or specifically in the parts of the brain thought to be involved in spatial processing.

Beyond the difficulty of extrapolating from non-primate mammals, it's also unclear whether the orthodox view provides an adequate account of brain sexual differentiation even in these animals. It has been noted that establishing a simple causal pathway from early T to structural brain differences to behavioral differences in mammals has so far proved impossible at a higher level than the brainstem (see, for example, brief discussions in Breedlove et al. 1999; De Vries 2004). This failure may be explained by research showing that the effects of early testosterone on brain and behavior may be indirect. For instance, Moore et al. (1992) have shown that the higher level of neonatal testosterone in male rat pups produces odor cues (in the pup urine) that elicit differential treatment from the mother (greater anogenital licking), and that this maternal behavior contributes to brain and behavioral differences between the sexes. In other words, early T may affect brain and behavior indirectly, via social environmental effects.

As Moore (2002) points out, the orthodox view of brain sexual differentiation is premised on a 'development to' perspective, according to which the environment merely influences the individual's progress 'to' a genetically encoded phenotype, via gene-directed effects on hormones and, thus, the brain. Such a perspective is implicit in Baron-Cohen's writing, in which he refers to socialization factors influencing (for example, "amplifying"; Baron-Cohen 2007: 169) what is innately or biologically specified (see Levy 2004: 323). The 'development to' perspective is predominant in psychological science (although see, for example, Karmiloff-Smith 2007, and Westermann et al. 2007, for overviews of cognitive neurodevelopmental approaches that explicitly reject a 'development to' perspective). However, as Lickliter and Honeycutt (2003: 819) have noted, in other areas of developmental science a "conceptual revolution" has led to a 'development from' perspective, according to which there is no pre-specified developmental pathway. Rather, every developmental step, including even behaviors previously considered instinctual or innate (e.g. Blumberg 2005 – see references to Gottlieb's research), is constructed from the complex and dynamic interaction between environmental stimuli, genotype, and the organization of the nervous system in a particular developmental stage.

As Moore (2002: 65) notes, research strategies that observe only early hormones and behavioral outcomes leave "lots of unexplored territory and many possible pathways, perhaps convoluted ones, from the early hormones and end points of interest." Indeed, given the complexity of the role of early hormones in the developmental process that is becoming apparent even in non-primate animals, it is not clear whether it is even plausible to predict that in humans fT levels (independently of sex) will predict later neurological or behavioral outcomes. With this in mind, we turn to the empirical evidence for associations between fT, brain structure, and E/S profile.

3.2   fT and E/S profile in clinical and non-clinical populations

Baron-Cohen et al. (2005: 822) cite two types of evidence as support for the idea that fT levels correlate with E/S profile:[8]

> In humans, exposure to atypically high levels of prenatal androgens results in masculine behavior and ability patterns (Berenbaum 2001). For example, females with congenital adrenal hyperplasia (CAH), a genetic condition that elevates fetal testosterone (FT), show tomboy behavior (Hines and Kaufman 1994). Normal interindividual variation in prenatal hormone levels, measured in amniotic fluid, correlates with later sex-typed behavior (Grimshaw, Sitarenios, and Finegan 1995; Lutchmaya, Baron-Cohen, and Raggat 2002a, 2002b; Knickmeyer et al. 2005a) [Numbered citations replaced with author/ date citations for ease of reference.]

In the following two sections we examine data from females with CAH, and then studies seeking to establish correlations between indices of fT levels and later sex-typed behavior.

3.2.1   *Girls with CAH*

There are a number of important observations to make with regards to the implications of the behavior of girls with CAH for the E/S hypothesis. First, the demonstration of *any* male-typical (or 'tomboy') behavior in girls with CAH does not constitute support for the E/S hypothesis: rather, the behavior must demonstrate stronger systemizing and/or lesser empathizing tendencies. The study cited as showing tomboy behavior in girls with CAH (Hines and Kaufman 1994) observed rough-and-tumble play, and asked children to report the sex of their three preferred playmates. It is not clear that either measure relates to empathizing versus systemizing, and although Baron-Cohen (2007) has argued that rough-and-tumble play may reflect males' lower levels of empathy, it is worth noting that successful rough-and-tumble play is likely to demand quite high sensitivity to cues from one's play partner. The relevance of Hines and Kaufman's study to the E/S hypothesis is therefore unclear. Moreover, whereas CAH girls tended to report a preference for boys as playmates when compared to control girls (44.1 percent vs. 11.2 percent), there were no differences between CAH girls and control girls for rough-and-tumble play.

Second, there is a difficulty in interpreting studies showing an enhanced preference of girls with CAH for male-typical activities (for a comprehensive review of these data, see Jordan-Young 2010). This is because such research has made no attempt to investigate whether girls with CAH are drawn to some intrinsic quality in boyish toys and activities, or whether they are drawn to them simply by virtue of the fact that they are associated with males (Bleier 1986; Fine 2010a; and for general discussion of issues with measurement of sex-typed interests, and arguments regarding the potential psychological effects of the intrusive medical management and social expectations experienced by this clinical group, see Jordan-Young 2010). For example, girls with CAH score more similarly to boys than do unaffected female controls on the Pre-School Activities Inventory (PSAI, Golombok and Rust 1993) which taps interest in traditionally feminine toys and activities, including jewelry, pretty things, dressing up in girlish clothes, and pretending to be a female character (Hines et al. 2003). Likewise, women with CAH asked to recall their childhood activities responded significantly differently from controls on a questionnaire that, among other items, asks about use of cosmetics and jewelry, hating feminine clothes, the gender of admired or imitated characters on TV or in movies, and whether they dressed up more as male or female characters (Meyer-Bahlburg et al. 2006). A study of children with a condition causing either partial or complete androgen insensitivity (46,XY karyotype) found that greater prenatal androgen exposure led to less interest in activities like ballet, gymnastics, playing hairdresser, working with clay, and dressing up as a fairy, a witch, or a woman, but more interest in basketball, playing spaceman, and dressing up as an alien, a cowboy, a man, or a pirate (Jürgensen et al. 2007). It is unclear to us what form of brain masculinization could lead to a cognitive predisposition for dressing up as an alien rather than a witch, lack of interest in jewelry and cosmetics, or masculine costumes over feminine ones.

Studies of toy preferences suffer the same confound. It could be argued that male-typical toys such as vehicles and construction toys facilitate systemizing more than do female-typical toys such as dolls and tea sets, which may offer more opportunity for empathizing. However, it is not clear why differences between girls with and without CAH (or indeed sex differences) are not seen for gender-neutral toys like puzzles and sketchpads, which would also appear to facilitate systemizing more than empathizing (Fine 2010a). As Bleier (1986: 150) pointed out in her critique of early studies in this area, "authors and subsequent scientists accept at face value the idea of tomboyism [such as play preferences, clothing preferences, career interests, and so on] as an index of a characteristic called *masculinity*, presumed to be as objective and innate a human feature as height and eye color. Yet 'masculinity' is a gender characteristic and, as such, culturally, not biologically, constructed." By failing to specify *a priori* what properties of toys or activities will be differentially appealing to boys and girls, researchers interested in the hormonal origins of gendered toy preferences can simply replace toys that fail to elicit the expected sex difference in preference (Pasterski et al. 2005: see 269). So while there is evidence that girls with CAH are drawn to 'masculine' activities and toys, relative to unaffected controls, so far researchers have failed to adapt their methodologies in response to Bleier's criticism.

There has also been research interest in the question of whether girls with CAH show superior mental rotation abilities. Although a recent meta-analysis suggests that girls with CAH have enhanced mental rotation skills (Puts et al. 2008; although see Jordan-Young 2010: 304 for a criticism of this conclusion), this may be a consequence of their greater male-typical play. Videogames enhance spatial skills (Dorval and Pépin 1986; Feng, Spence, and Pratt 2007; Cherney 2008) and there is evidence suggestive that play behavior likely to be differentially experienced by the sexes may also enhance spatial skills (Sprafkin et al. 1983; Baenninger and Newcombe 1989; Levine et al. 2005). Recent studies have also investigated personality traits in girls with CAH. However, so far the findings have been somewhat inconsistent. Thus, older girls and women with CAH report less social skills, tender-mindedness, and interest in infants than unaffected relative controls (Knickmeyer et al.

2006a; Mathews et al. 2009). However, these studies found no differences in social communication ability and dominance (which includes traits such as aggression, authoritativeness, and competitiveness; for a rejection of increased aggression associated with CAH, see also Jordan-Young 2010). Moreover, self-report measures may correspond poorly to actual behavior (as noted in section 2.1), and maternal reports may be biased by knowledge of the child's clinical status.

3.2.2 *fT and E/S profile*

The second category of evidence cited by Baron-Cohen and colleagues refers to studies that try to establish a link between fT exposure and "ability patterns" (Baron-Cohen, Knickmeyer, and Belmonte 2005: 822). There are two important points worth making about this empirical approach. First, as Hines (2004) has argued, a role for prenatal testosterone can only be expected for behaviors for which there are genuine differences between the sexes. As discussed earlier (see section 2.2), in humans some purported sex differences are under dispute, or contingent on social-contextual factors. Second, while both amniotic testosterone, or aT (sampled from the amniotic fluid during amniocentesis), and maternal testosterone, or mT (sampled from the mother's blood), have been used as proxies for fT exposure, there is currently no satisfactory evidence that either is related to actual fT exposure. In their review of this issue, van de Beek et al. (2004) suggest aT as the best index of fT exposure, but they also acknowledge the lack of much understanding of the relationship between levels of T in the amniotic fluid – the main source of which is fetal urine – and in the fetal blood. Indeed, as Knickmeyer et al. (2005b: 521) acknowledge, "there is no direct evidence to either support or contradict" the assumption that aT is correlated with the levels of testosterone acting on the fetal brain. Likewise, the relationship between maternal T and fetal levels is unclear. One clinical study that measured fT directly did find that it correlated with maternal T (Gitau, Adams et al. 2005). However, maternal T levels are not higher in women carrying boys than in those carrying girls, which suggests that "maternal serum androgen levels are not a clear reflection of the actual exposure of the fetus to these hormones" (van de Beek et al. 2004: 664).

It is a cause of concern that claims may be made about the prenatal, hormonal origins of sex differences on the basis of supposed biological markers of fT exposure that, remarkably, have unknown relationships with actual fT exposure. Despite this, a growing number of studies have investigated relationships between aT or maternal T and later cognitive or social abilities. In terms of evaluating these studies, it is worth noting that four criteria should be fulfilled in order to claim support for the E/S hypothesis. First, the dependent variable(s) should be plausibly characterizable as part of an E or S skill set. Second, the dependent variable should be methodologically soundly measured. Third, the dependent variable should show a reliable sex difference in the predicted direction. Finally, correlations between the fT proxy and the dependent variable should be seen within the sexes, as well as in the group as a whole (otherwise fT may be confounded with the effects of gender socialization).

Table 4.1 summarizes the data from all such studies. We note that in not a single study are all these criteria satisfied. A detailed critique of each study can be found in the Appendix, where we briefly discuss first, in chronological order, the studies that relate aT (or mT) to purported measures of empathizing, followed by studies concerned with systemizing, then gender-typical play behavior.[9] Based on the analysis of this literature, the evidence concerning "[n]ormal interindividual variation" (Baron-Cohen, Knickmeyer, and Belmonte 2005: 822), both that provided by Baron-Cohen and colleagues as well as other relevant work, yields a scattered and inconsistent picture. (Concern has also been expressed regarding inconsistencies in the treatment of statistical outliers and statistical modeling procedures in the analysis of aT data by Baron-Cohen and colleagues (Jordan-Young 2010: see 219 and endnote).) Regularly, behaviors are tested that appear to assess something other than E or S ability, methodologies are often weak and sample sizes inadequate, behavioral differences on performance tests are not reliably and consistently observed, and functions relating fT and behavior are often different from the predicted one, present only in one sex, explained by sex, or completely absent.

3.3   Sex differences in the brain

The E/S hypothesis predicts a relationship between fT level and brain structure, and requires that these structural differences have implications for E/S function. To our knowledge, no research has investigated relationships between fT and brain structure in humans. We therefore focus here on the prediction that there are functionally significant sex differences in the brain. By way of support for this aspect of the hypothesis, Baron-Cohen et al. (2005: 820) begin by referring to sex differences in brain size (citing Giedd et al. 1996), "a difference that is driven more by white matter than by gray" (citing Allen et al. 2003, and Lüders et al. 2005), relatively larger female corpus collosum size (citing Allen et al. 2003), and larger amygdala volume in boys (citing

Caviness et al. 1996) and possibly also men (citing Goldstein et al. 2001),[10] greater numbers of neurons in the male cerebral cortex (citing Pakkenberg and Gundersen 1997), that are more densely packed (citing Rabinowicz et al. 2002) although with exceptions in certain regions (citing Witelson, Glezer, and Kigar 1995). They go on to suggest that some of these structural differences "indirectly suggest a pattern of increased local connectivity and decreased interhemispheric (or long-range) connectivity in the male brain" (2005: 820). They then argue that studies showing more bilateral activation in females during language-related tasks (Shaywitz et al. 1995; Baxter et al. 2003), and a magnetoencephalography (MEG) study of grocery choices made by eight men and eight women in a shopping simulation (Braeutigam et al. 2004) reporting "increased phase locking between frontal and parietal sites in women", also suggest a stronger skew toward local connectivity in males.

Before turning to the question of what implications, if any, such structural differences have for function, there are two important points to be made about the structural claims themselves. First, on average, males have larger brains than females, and there are currently unresolved questions regarding whether structural differences in the brain are due to size rather than sex *per se*. Thus it has been argued that brain size, not sex, is the main variable affecting ratios of gray to white matter volumes (e.g. Lüders, Steinmetz, et al. 2002; Im et al. 2008). Recently, Lüders et al. (2009) found that the ratios of gray and white matter, relative to total brain volume, did not differ between men and women matched for brain size. (They did, however, find some regional volume differences in their matched groups, with larger gray matter volumes in women than men.)

A second issue is that isolated findings of particular sex differences in the brain may be spurious. A particular problem for sex differences research arises from the practice of testing for sex differences by default. As Kaiser et al. (2009: 54) have noted, classifying by sex is a "natural default" and "seemingly effortless and obvious in brain research." The concern is that false positive results arising from sex comparisons are reported, while true negatives are not (Maccoby and Jacklin 1974; for discussion specifically in relation to neuroimaging research, see Fine 2010a, 2010b). That spurious results can lead to a misleading impression of the viability of a hypothesized sex difference has been well demonstrated by two purported sex differences cited by Baron-Cohen et al. (2005): in the corpus callosum, and in the degree of lateralization of language function. A meta-analysis of 49 post-mortem and MRI investigations of the corpus callosum concluded that, even controlling for

Table 4.1 Summary of studies investigating aT/ mT and E/S ability

Dependent variable	Purported E/S measure	Study	Behavioral sex difference	Relationship with aT[a]	Relationship with aT within sexes
Vocabulary[b]	E	Lutchmaya et al. (2002b) (volume 24: 418–424)	Yes (higher for girls)	Yes	No
Eye contact	E	Lutchamaya et al. (2002a) (volume 25: 327–335)	Yes (higher for girls)	Yes (linear and quadratic)	None for girls; linear and quadratic for boys
Social relationship skills[b]	E	Knickmeyer et al. (2005a)	A trend favoring girls	Yes (negative)	No
Mental, affective, and intentional terms in triangle movie	E	Knickmeyer et al. (2006b)	Yes for affective (higher for girls) and neutral (higher for boys) terms	No for mental or affective terms, yes for intentional (negative) and neutral (positive) terms	No for mental, affective, and neutral terms. Intentional terms: none for girls, trend for boys
EQ[b]	E	Chapman et al. (2006)	Yes (higher for girls)	Yes (negative)	Negative for boys; none for girls
Reading the Mind in the Eyes test	E	Chapman et al. (2006)	No	Yes (negative)	Negative for both boys and girls
Block building task and embedded figures[d]	S	Finnegan et al. (1992)	No	Analyzes were not carried out	Negative for block building in girls, none in boys. None for embedded figures
Mental rotation	S	Grimshaw et al. (1995)	No differences in accuracy	No	Positive for girls who used a rotating strategy; negative for boys[e]

Restricted interests[b]	S	Knickmeyer et al. (2005a)	Yes (boys had more restricted interests than girls)	Yes (positive)	None for girls, positive for boys
SQ-C[b]	S	Auyeung et al. (2006)	Yes (boys scored higher than girls)	Yes (positive)	Positive for both sexes[f]
Block design	S	Auyeung et al. (2009a)	No	No	No
Pre-school Activities Inventory (PSAI)[b] (measure of sex-typical behavior)		Hines et al. (2002)[c]	Yes (boys scored higher than girls)	Analyzes were not carried out	Positive for girls, none for boys
Gender-typical play[b]		Knickmeyer et al. (2005b)	Yes (girls scored higher on femininity scales and boys scored higher on masculinity scales)	No	No
Gender-typical play		van de Beek et al. (2009)	Yes (preference for specific toys)	No	No
Pre-school Activities Inventory (PSAI)[b]		Auyeung et al. (2009b)	Yes (boys scored higher than girls)	Yes (positive)	Yes (positive for both sexes)

Notes:

a = data from both sexes pooled together; an aT effect can be explained by sex if sex is not removed from the analyzes.

b = data were based on mothers' report.

c = maternal T.

d = the authors employed a variety of cognitive tests in their study, some of which are difficult to summarize. Here we limit our analysis to tasks that have been linked to systemizing. See the Appendix for more information.

e = the correlation became significant when two data points were removed, quite arbitrarily, from the analyzes.

f = beta values for girls have opposite signs in the text and table 3 in the original article.

overall brain size, there is no reliable sex difference in the size or shape of this structure (Bishop and Wahlsten 1997). Bishop and Wahlsten particularly note the issue of spurious results arising from small sample sizes. So while Baron-Cohen et al. acknowledge Bishop and Wahlsten's findings, it's not clear how much weight the study of 23 men and 23 women (Allen et al. 2003), cited by Baron-Cohen et al. (2005) as evidence of greater corpus callosum size in females, should be credited. Similarly, while the idea of greater male lateralization of language function has enjoyed considerable popularity (for critique of the hypothesis prior to investigation using neuroimaging technologies, see Bleier 1986), recent meta-analyzes of functional neuroimaging lateralization studies suggest that linguistic functions are not more bilateral in women compared to men (Sommer et al. 2004, 2008). Sommer and colleagues' (2008) meta-analysis of dichotic listening tasks also failed to find evidence of lateralization differences between the sexes. (If males are more lateralized for language, they should have a stronger "right ear advantage" than females for language presented to the left, language-dominant hemisphere via the right ear.) Moreover, while there have been suggestions that males are more likely to suffer aphasia following stroke damage to the left hemisphere (which would be consistent with the idea that females' greater right hemisphere language function would serve a protective effect), as Wallentin (2009) notes, the Copenhagen aphasia study of more than 1000 patients found no effect of sex or side of stroke lesion (Pedersen, Vinter, and Olsen 2004; cited in Wallentin 2009). Similarly, if linguistic functions were less lateralized in women than men, aphasic symptoms would be more frequently expected in women than men following right hemisphere lesions. This is not the case (Kimura 1983).

Beyond important questions regarding the reliability of individual reports of sex differences in the brain, another critical issue concerns the relation between structure and function. It is of course critical for Baron-Cohen's thesis that structural sex differences have functional implications for cognition and behavior relating to empathizing and systemizing.[11] However, the functional meaning of the structural differences mentioned by Baron-Cohen and colleagues (2005) remains unclear, and have not been directly associated with empathizing or systemizing skills. Baron-Cohen et al. attempt to relate structural sex differences to differences in function, but their links are hypothetical at best. For example, they tentatively suggest that a male skew toward local rather than long-range connectivity would be a disadvantage for empathizing, "because empathy activates brain regions that integrate information from multiple neural sources" (2005: 821, reference removed) and that "[t]his notion of skewed connectivity is also compatible with strong systemizing, because systemizing involves a narrow attentional focus to local information, in order to understand each part of a system."

While we would not disagree that empathizing requires integration of information from many regions of the brain, we would dispute that there is any reason why systemizing, or any other complex behavior, would require any less integration. A local focus in the mind does not imply a local focus in the brain. The complexity of the relationship between brain structure and function is immense, and as Fausto-Sterling (2000b: 118; see also Bleier 1986) has observed, "despite the many recent insights of brain research, this organ remains a vast unknown, a perfect medium on which to project, even unwittingly, assumptions about gender."

Overall then, links between purported structural differences and functional differences pertaining to E/S currently remain speculative at best. Hypothesized sex differences in lateralization, corpus callosum size, and proportions of gray and white matter are under empirical dispute, highlighting the importance of treating with skepticism isolated reports of sexual dimorphism in the brain. Moreover, the functional significance of any such differences currently remains unknown.

3.4 Summary of evidence that fT organizes functional brain 'type'

In the preceding sections we have examined three categories of evidence claimed to support the idea that (purported) behavioral sex differences in E/S profile are partially caused by the action of fT on the brain: studies of girls with CAH; studies of aT and E/S profile in the general population; and studies of brain sexual dimorphism. Our analysis shows that in no domain of research do the data provide anything like compelling support for the E/S hypothesis. Importantly, the causal links between fT, brain organization, and cognitive profile, on which the E/S hypothesis hinges, are never demonstrated. No evidence is provided to suggest how fT is responsible for structural sex differences in the brain, or how these differences are responsible for differences in E/S profile. When links are made, they are highly speculative. Moreover, the studies of both fT and E/S, and of brain sexual dimorphism, have provided patterns of results that are highly inconsistent.

4 The E/S hypothesis: summary

The E/S hypothesis attempts to explain sex differences in cognitive style and behavior in terms of fT's organizational effects on the brain. A careful analysis of the evidence provided by Baron-Cohen et al. (2005) in support of their theory, as well as additional and more recent research, reveals that such evidence is far from being convincing. Purported sex differences are irrelevant to E/S profile, under dispute, are eliminated in certain social contexts, or may be due to experiential factors. The studies of aT in humans, promising at first, have not provided reliable evidence of the role of fT on behavioral and cognitive sex differences. Furthermore, these studies are often tainted by serious methodological flaws, and the relationship between proxies for fT and actual fT exposure is unknown. Sexual dimorphism in the human brain, other than size, is not yet established, and has not been linked to sex differences in behaviors or cognitive styles, or, importantly, to fT. As previously mentioned, no clear picture emerges of what fT is purported to organize in terms of neural structures, cognitive styles, and behavior. It is of concern that Knickmeyer et al. (2008: 995) have recently claimed that "It is difficult to find any cognitive measure which we can be certain is a proxy measure of fT exposure. If we are to use a cognitive task in this way, the focus should be on tasks where multiple different methodologies implicate fT, including studies of females with CAH, males with androgen insensitivity, correlations with digit ratio, and correlations with amniotic testosterone levels (Baron-Cohen et al. 2005)." To our knowledge, no cognitive measure satisfies these constraints. Even performance on the mental rotation task, the most robust known cognitive sex difference, has not been unequivocally linked to fT or its proxies (Malouf et al. 2006; Puts et al. 2008). In this scenario, no support whatsoever seems to exist for the E/S hypothesis. The authors seem to ignore this obvious conclusion, and instead claim that no cognitive measure might be convincingly considered a behavioral proxy for fT. This approach, scientifically unacceptable, potentially sets the stage for making the E/S hypothesis impossible to test.

In addition to the empirical weakness of the support for the E/S hypothesis, we have also argued that it implicitly subscribes to a conception of development that assumes a unidirectional causal pathway from genes to structural brain changes to psychological function (see Gottlieb 1992, for a critique of this view). As a point for future consideration, developmental cognitive neuroscience is beginning to yield a picture of development characterized by a gradual increase in regional specialization and modularization of function (e.g. Johnson et al. 2005; Karmiloff-Smith 2007). In this view, brain organization emerges through development, through the complex interaction of multiple factors (including behavior itself) rather than being simply the result of maturation processes. This conception of development doesn't preclude the possibility that, during one brief period of gestation, fT can act on the developing brain in a way that has consequences for future function. However, compared with a 'development to' perspective, it is less plausible that fT levels at a single time-point might have direct and measurable effects on complex psychological function many years later. And indeed, to highlight the theme of this chapter, there is no evidence that supports the E/S hypothesis of fT-directed sexual dimorphism of brain structure and function.

Methodological rigor, measured judgment, and caution should be trademarks of scholars researching in potentially sensitive fields, such as the one of sex differences. As Baron-Cohen (2007: 160) has suggested, "the field of sex differences in mind needs to proceed in a fashion that is sensitive…by cautiously looking at the evidence and being careful not to overstate what can be concluded." In contrast with this avowed sentiment, we note a frequent lack of acknowledgment of the methodological weaknesses or inconsistency of results that limit the conclusions that can be drawn. Furthermore, the several reference errors and the frequent misrepresentation of results reveal an interpretation of the literature that not only is not cautious but often imprecise or inaccurate.

We end by noting recent evidence that accounts of gender difference that emphasize 'biological' causes are associated with increased endorsement of gender stereotypes (Brescoll and LaFrance 2004), increased self-stereotyping (Coleman and Hong 2008), stereotype threat (Dar-Nimrod and Heine 2006; Thoman et al. 2008), as well as increased confidence that society treats women fairly, reification of the gender status quo, and increased tolerance for sex discrimination in the workplace (Morton et al. 2009). Thus, the empirical and conceptual inadequacies of E/S theory, and its presentation, are of significant social, as well as scientific, concern.

Appendix

Empathizing and aT

All the studies that fall into this category were conducted by Baron-Cohen and colleagues, and they drew on a single population of children whose mothers had amniocentesis. The first study aimed to relate aT with eye contact at 12 months of age (Lutchmaya, Baron-Cohen, and Ragatt 2002a). The infant, in the company of both a parent and the experimenter, was given toys to play with, and eye contact frequency with the parent was used as the dependent variable. (While contact frequency and contact duration were correlated, the former was considered, without an explanation, a more accurate measure than the latter; see 329.) The authors considered eye contact a "marker of social development" (328), but did not explain in what sense, apart from noting that autistic individuals show fewer eye contacts than individuals without autism. However, in this particular experimental situation, in which the infants interacted with a stranger (the experimenter), eye contact with the parent could reflect shyness, fear, or concern. Indeed, given that the experimenter was a stranger, arguably a better measure of social competence would be eye contact with the experimenter. Lutchmaya and colleagues found a higher frequency of eye contact in females than males. They also found no relationship between aT and eye contact frequency in females. This result was explained by the authors in terms of small sample size (n = 30), but their data, as shown in the scatterplot, shows no relationship between the two measures. In males (n = 41), the function was quadratic, which means that a high frequency of eye contact was observed in males with low and high levels of aT. This result runs contrary to the E/S hypothesis, according to which higher levels of fT should be associated with low frequency of eye contact (as in autism). A number of methodological concerns can also be raised, especially the apparent lack of any attempt to either control or monitor the gaze behavior of either parents or the experimenter. There was also no information regarding whether the experimenter was blind to either the experimental hypothesis, or the infant's aT status. Moreover, each infant was filmed for "approximately" 20 minutes (328); as a result, the frequency of eye contact could have been overestimated in some infants or underestimated in others due to an apparently variable length of observation time.

The second study is an investigation of vocabulary size in 18- and 24-month-old infants (Lutchmaya, Baron-Cohen, and Ragatt 2002b).[12] However, as noted earlier, it is not clear that vocabulary size reflects empathizing ability. Based on mothers' report, females had a larger vocabulary size than males. An inverse relationship was found between aT and vocabulary size when boys and girls were pooled together but not within each sex. Due to small sample size, the authors did not carry out a regression analysis excluding sex.

A later study by Knickmeyer et al. (2005a) tested for relationships between aT and two subscales of the Children's Communication Checklist (CCC, Bishop 1998). The subscale most relevant to empathizing assessed 'quality of social relationships' (tapped by questions such as "is popular with other children"). There was a trend for females to score better on this subscale, as reported by mothers, but it failed to reach significance (however, the effect size was moderate). While a negative relationship was found between these scores and aT with girls and boys pooled together, no relationship was found when the analysis was run within sexes. It is noteworthy that no sex differences were found on the pragmatic subscale of the CCC (which measures how children adapt to their interlocutors during a conversation), although the authors predicted "that higher fT levels would be associated with poorer scores on the pragmatic language scale" (Knickmeyer et al. 2005a: 200).

Baron-Cohen and colleagues (Chapman et al. 2006) also explored the relationship between aT and a children's version of the Empathy Quotient (EQ-C, filled out by mothers), comprising questions such as "My child shows concern when others are upset" and "My child can easily tell when another person wants to enter into conversation with him/her." Girls were rated as higher in empathizing skills, but maternally reported EQ-C score was not validated against any social performance measure. Correlations between aT and EQ-C revealed a negative relationship between aT and EQ-C for girls and boys combined. When the two groups were examined separately, a significant negative correlation was found only in boys. Chapman et al. (2006) also made use of a performance measure, a child's version of the "Reading the Mind in the Eyes" test (Eyes-C). In this test the child is shown just the eye region of a series of faces, and is offered four multiple choice options as to what the individual is thinking or feeling. Interestingly, females did not perform better than males on the task, and the authors note that they previously failed to find female superiority on the task (Chapman et al. 2006: see 140). Analyzes revealed a significant negative correlation between aT and Eyes-C score, in both boys and girls, and in both sexes separately. However, in the absence of a sex difference in behavior, it is not clear that these findings as a whole can be taken as support for the E/S hypothesis.

Knickmeyer et al. (2006b) also used a performance measure, involving two computer-presented films in which animated shapes move in ways that convey that they have mental states (see Abell, Happé, and Frith 2000). Children were probed by an interviewer to describe the events of the animation, and prompted to do so in terms of human interactions. No information is provided as to whether or how this probing and prompting was standardized for all children (see Knickmeyer et al. 2006b: 285 for sample transcript of interview), and there is no information regarding whether the interviewer was blind either to the experimental hypothesis or aT status. The authors predicted that females would use more mental and affective state terms than boys, as well as more reference to actions between animate objects (e.g. "The big one's trying to hit the little one"), and more intentional propositions (which included mental and affective state terms referring to emotional states, beliefs, and desires). These predictions were partially supported: significantly greater affective state term use was seen in females, and there was a trend for greater female use of intentional propositions. However, females did not use mental state terms more, or make greater reference to actions between animate objects, and there was an unpredicted difference in the use of neutral propositions (which was greater in boys). The authors then went on to investigate the relationships between aT and these four dependent variables.

Analyzes revealed no association between aT and mental and affective state terms, and no correlation within either sex. For both intentional and neutral propositions, main effects of aT were seen, with higher aT being associated with less intentional proposition use, and greater neutral proposition use. For intentional propositions, a negative correlation between the two variables was seen within boys, but not girls. For neutral propositions, no correlations were seen within either sex. Summarizing their findings, Knickmeyer et al. (2006b: 288) state that they "predicted that females would use more mental and affective state terms than males" as well as more intentional propositions, and that "variation in fT levels would account for the predicted sex differences. In general, our predictions were supported." We would argue that this is an overly optimistic conclusion. Of their four predicted sex differences on the task (overlooked in their summary is their prediction that females would refer more to actions between animate objects), only one attained statistical significance (affective state term use). This variable showed no correlation with aT levels. A relationship between intentional propositions (only marginally more frequent in females) and aT was established but, within sex, a correlation was seen only in males. We would suggest that no firm conclusions can be drawn from this study.

Systemizing and aT

We turn now to the smaller number of studies that have explored relations between aT and purported measures of systemizing. The earliest is a study of four-year-old children who were assessed on a range of cognitive tasks, and scores related to aT (Finegan, Niccols, and Sitarenios 1992). In girls, where relationships with aT were observed, they were contrary to the predictions of the E/S hypothesis: relationship with classification abilities was curvilinear; higher aT was associated with lower score on counting, number facts, and block building scores. No relationships with abilities such as puzzle solving, visual-motor inte-gration, and embedded figures were found. In boys, no relationships between aT and any cognitive abilities were observed.

A later study tested seven-year-old girls and boys on a mental rota-tion task study (Grimshaw et al. 1995). As noted earlier (see section 2.1), it is unclear whether mental rotation should be understood as a measure of systemizing. The sample was small and a correlation between levels of aT and performance speed was found only in girls, and only for those girls who employed a rotation strategy (n = 12). Importantly, there were no overall sex differences in accuracy or RT (although among rotators girls were faster, whereas boys were faster among non-rotators). As noted by Hines (2007), it is performance accu-racy – that did not relate to aT – on which a sex difference is normally seen. This article therefore does not provide convincing evidence of a relationship between aT and mental rotation. More recently, Auyeung et al. (2009a) tested for a relationship between aT and block design performance (thought to assess visuospatial skill). Contrary to predic-tion, no male advantage was observed for block design performance, nor any relationship with aT.

One of the subscales from the Children's Communication Checklist (Bishop 1998) used by Knickmeyer et al. (2005a) tested restricted interests, considered associated with systemizing abilities and autism according to the E/S hypothesis. The scale inquired about the presence of specific interests (e.g. "has one or more over-riding specific interests (e.g. computers, dinosaurs) and will prefer doing activities involving this to anything else"; Bishop 1998: 891) and, once again, was filled out by mothers. The authors predicted that boys would show more restricted interests than girls and that more restricted interests would be associ-ated with higher levels of aT. A sex difference in the predicted direc-tion was found. A relationship between restricted interests scores and aT was found when the two sexes were pooled together; in within-sex analysis, a relationship was found in boys but not in girls. At page 205, the authors stated "There was a main effect of fT on this scale when the group was examined as a whole...This indicates that in both boys and girls, higher fT levels are associated with more restricted interests." This statement is inconsistent with the results; indeed, although the regression analysis for the pooled sexes indicated a positive relationship between the two variables, the correlation was not significant for girls. Moreover, Its sign was negative.

Another issue that can be raised concerns the nature of the scale items. The content of some items is clearly sex-related. For example, one item refers to large stores of factual information (e.g. names of all the capitals of the world, names of many varieties of dinosaurs), or over-riding specific interests (e.g. computer or dinosaurs). It is not clear why restricted interests for social interactions are not included, or why knowing all the names of the children in kindergarten is not an example of restricted interest. Furthermore, it is not clear why "prefers to be with adults rather than other children" is associated with restricted interests. In a nutshell, it seems that some of these items are associated with what are considered sex-typical behaviors and not restricted interests *per se*.

One final study exploring the relationship between aT and systemizing made use of a version of the Systemizing Quotient, adapted for parents to rate their children (the SQ-Child, Auyeung et al. 2006). Parents of boys gave higher ratings on the SQ-Child, on average, than parents of girls. Moreover, aT was significantly associated with SQ-Child score, and within-sex correlations were significant in both boys and girls. While this appears to provide strong support for the E/S hypothesis, inspection of the items of the SQ-Child (see Auyeung et al. 2006: S126) raises the serious question of whether it actually taps systemizing ability. In addition to the subjectivity of parental report as opposed to actual performance, very few of the items are unambiguous tests of "the drive to analyze or construct systems" (Auyeung et al. 2006: S124). At least half of the 28 items appear to tap into a drive for order, routine, or arrangement of objects. Nor is it clear in many (if not all) of the remaining items that it is a drive to systemize that is being tapped (e.g. items include knowing the difference between the latest models of game-consoles, finding using a computer difficult, enjoying working to solve a puzzle, or spending time mastering aspects of their favorite activities).

Gender-typical play

To date four articles have investigated the relationship between measures of fT and gender-typical play behavior. As with the studies with girls with CAH, discussed in section 3.2.1, no attempt has been made in this research to test a specific hypothesis regarding what it is about toys and play behavior culturally ascribed to boys versus girls that makes them differentially appealing to a more or less 'masculinized' brain. Again, too, play behaviors that fail to elicit the predicted difference between the sexes may simply be replaced (Knickmeyer et al. 2005b). The first study assessed behavior using the Pre-School Activities Inventory (PSAI, Golombok and Rust 1993), and used both maternal T and maternal sex hormone-binding globulin (SHBG) levels as potential proxies for fT exposure (Hines et al. 2002). (Since SHBG limits T's functional effectiveness by binding with it, greater levels of SHBG is used as a proxy for lower levels of unbound, functionally effective T.) Preliminary analyzes confirmed that, as noted earlier, levels of maternal T and maternal SHBG did not differ in mothers bearing male versus female fetuses, underlining its questionability as an adequate proxy for fetal exposure. Hines et al. (2002) found that, in girls only, higher levels of maternal T (but not maternal SHBG) were associated with more masculine-typical play. No other relationships were significant.

Subsequently, Knickmeyer et al. (2005b) looked for a relationship between aT and gender-typical play in four- and five-year-old children, as measured by a questionnaire about play behavior, filled out by the mothers. No relationship with aT was found in either sex, or in both sexes together. Van de Beek et al. (2009) explored relationships between both maternal and amniotic T, estradiol, and progesterone levels and actual gender-typical play in 13-month-old infants in the laboratory. They found no relationship with amniotic or maternal T or estradiol levels. Surprisingly, higher levels of amniotic progesterone were associated with a stronger preference for masculine toys. However, in contrast with the largely negative findings of these three studies Auyeung et al. (2009b), with a larger sample size, found correlations, in both sexes individually as well as pooled, between aT and PSAI score. It will be important to establish whether this result can be replicated and to investigate whether it is an intrinsic difference between 'masculine' and 'feminine' activities that is correlated with aT, or their social ascription to gender. (It is also worth noting that if aT levels are influenced by maternal T levels, then a correlation between aT and play preferences may be mediated by differential social experiences provided by mothers who are lower or higher in T.)

Notes

The authors thank Alison Nash and Rebecca Jordan-Young for their very valuable comments on an earlier draft of this chapter. The authors contributed equally to this chapter.

1. Note that this article does not refer to sex differences in mental rotation ability.
2. This citation is unclear. Baron-Cohen et al. (2005) referred to the Witkin book *Personality Through Perception* in their References list. The book was published in 1972, not 1962, and had Witkin as the only author. It is likely that the authors were referring to Witkin, Dyk, Faterson, Goodenough, and Karp (1962/1974), *Differentiation: Studies of Development* (Hoboken, NJ: John Wiley). Because of this imprecision, we have not included this citation in the References section.

3. This citation is incorrect, both here and as a reference for the claim in the same passage that girls are more likely to play with dolls. Hines et al. (1992) is a study of sexual dimorphism in the rat brain and does not discuss toy preferences in children. Although sex differences in children's toy preferences have often been observed (see Hines 2004: 17), such studies do not, in fact, isolate particular types of 'masculine' and 'feminine' toys (e.g. mechanical toys versus dolls). Thus 'masculine' toys might include vehicles, construction toys, and weapons, while 'feminine' toys might include dolls, cosmetics, and household toys. The problematic nature of the toys chosen for such studies is discussed later in the chapter.

4. It is also worth noting that Fenson et al. (1994: v) reported finding only "very small" sex differences in communicative development in 8- to 30-month-old infants, "typically accounting for 1 percent to 2 percent of the variance."

5. This article is incorrectly referenced in Baron-Cohen et al. (2005) as being published in 2001, whereas it was published in 2000.

6. The purpose of the study was to determine "if gender differences exist in response to hippocampal deafferentation" (Roof et al. 1993: 47). Rats were tested on the Morris water maze task, a measure of working spatial memory. The performance of brain-lesioned female rats was not affected by hippocampal lesions, but that of male rats was. Therefore, the study did not demonstrate sex differences in a spatial working memory test, but the differential effect of hippocampal damage in the two sexes for this type of spatial learning.

7. Note that percentages refer to presentation time, not looking time, as stated in the article.

8. Not discussed here are studies that look for correlations between the 2D:4D digit ratio and sex-typed interests, and studies looking for evidence of more masculine interests in twins with a male rather than female co-twin. These data are reviewed by Jordan-Young (2010) who concludes that they provide little evidence for a relationship between fT and sex-typed interests.

9. We note that Auyeung et al. (2009a), using two parent-report questionnaires designed to quantify autistic traits, found positive relationships between the children's scores on the scales and aT levels. However, we would argue that the items on these questionnaires are too indiscriminate to be a useful device for exploring the role of aT in E or S skills.

10. Note that, in fact, this study found no evidence for greater amygdala volume in men than women.

11. While it may be intuitive to assume that structural differences enable functional difference, it has been noted that they may also enable functional similarity, by compensating for other physiological differences (e.g. Moore 1995; De Vries 2004).

12. The reference in Baron-Cohen et al. (2005) is incorrect. It refers to a 2002 article in *Infant Behavior and Development* (vol. 25, issue 319) which describes a behavioral study of looking behavior. The correct reference is Lutchmaya, Baron-Cohen, and Raggatt (2002). Foetal Testosterone and Vocabulary Size in 18- and 24-Month-Old Infants. *Infant Behavior and Development* 24(4): 418–424.

5

Hardwired for Sexism? Approaches to Sex/Gender in Neuroscience

Rebecca M. Jordan-Young and Raffaella I. Rumiati

1 Introduction

Gender theorists and some feminist scientists approach gender as a multilevel and complex structure that shapes human relations and perceptions, cognition, and institutions, including the research questions and methods used in science (Fausto-Sterling 2000b; Risman 2004; Ridgeway 2009). Neuroscientists, on the other hand, typically approach gender as a status or a collection of characteristics that male versus female people (and sometimes other animals) have, and the goal of many neuroscience studies is to add to an ever-growing catalogue of male/female differences – both what they are, and how they arise (e.g. Hines 2004: vii). Disagreements over the nature of gender are unlikely to be resolved anytime soon, but we suggest that whether understood as a cultural frame or as an individual cognitive structure, gender is so powerful that it is difficult to get a useful purchase on how it operates. It is a bit like the sun: there is a limit to what we can learn by looking straight at it, and we might just go blind trying. Thus, we argue that a more sophisticated and ethical approach to understanding sex/gender in the brain and behavior will require the somewhat paradoxical strategy of turning away from sex/gender differences in our research.

In most of this paper, we use the composite term 'sex/gender,' which will be unfamiliar and perhaps even jarring to some readers, especially those who have worked hard to ensure that complex social phenomena related to masculinity and femininity (gender) are not simply reduced to or confused with aspects of the physical body that can be designated as 'male' or 'female' (sex). We nonetheless favor this composite term when discussing neuroscientific investigations into male/female differences or similarities in patterns of brain structure or function.

While conceptual differences between the two are important, 'sex' and 'gender' are, in practical terms, inseparable. Numerous empirical studies demonstrate the problematic task of distinguishing between sex and gender in practice (Oudshoorn 1994; Kessler 1998; Fausto-Sterling 2005; Kaiser et al. 2007). The patterning of life experiences according to social structures of gender has material effects on the body (Willis et al. 2001; Fausto-Sterling 2005, 2008). These effects show up, in turn, as biologically based 'sex differences.' Feminist epidemiologists, biologists, and other scientists increasingly replace the discrete concepts of 'sex' and 'gender' with more complex formulations, such as Nancy Krieger's notions of "biologic expressions of gender" and "gendered expressions of biology" (Krieger 2003). Thus, we adopt the term 'sex/gender' as suggested by Kaiser and colleagues, who observed that "sex is not a pure bodily and material fact, but is deeply interwoven with social and cultural constructions of gender" (Kaiser et al. 2009: 49). With this composite term, we hope to underscore the importance of problematizing bodily as well as behavioral and psychological attributions of female/feminine and male/masculine.

In the next part of the chapter, we address the dominant paradigm of sex/gender differences in contemporary neuroscience. This consists of a broad consensus that there are important 'original' sex differences in brain structure and function, organized by sex-differentiating prenatal hormone exposures (the 'hardwiring' paradigm). This paradigm shapes the work of both those who frame sex/gender differences as sweeping and largely independent of socialization, as well as those who emphasize the role of gender socialization in amplifying male/female distinctions (Baron-Cohen 2003; Eliot 2009). But we argue that this consensus is both unscientific and far from politically neutral. Evidence has long suggested that 'hardwiring' is a poor metaphor for brain development. But the metaphor may be an apt one for the dominant research paradigm, which pushes inexorably towards the 'discovery' of sex/gender differences, and makes contemporary gender structures appear to be natural and inevitable. In the last section, we begin to elaborate an alternative research program. While the question of origins can't be studied experimentally in humans, it is possible to design experiments to address questions of variability and plasticity, an approach that we argue has much greater promise from both scientific and ethical perspectives.

Before proceeding further, it is worth addressing how sexuality, the realm of erotic desires and practices, fits with sex and gender. Ideas about sexuality – including but going beyond sexual orientation – play a major role in dominant ideas about sex/gender differences. In science as in popular culture, sex, gender, and sexuality are frequently merged into the simple composite 'sex': a package deal, with both the origin and the ultimate purpose being reproduction. (Note that research has repeatedly demonstrated that heterosexuals in the contemporary U.S. context interpret 'having sex' to be synonymous with penile-vaginal intercourse (Sanders and Reinisch 1999; Bogart et al. 2000).) In this framework, if one part of the 'package' is atypical, it is frequently assumed that the other parts will also be atypical. Moreover, since sex is conceived as a binary, male/female phenomenon, being 'not typical for males' is generally read as being feminine, and being 'not typical for females' is read as masculine. Since the late nineteenth century, same-sex desires have been viewed through this lens, and homosexuals of both sexes have been understood to be intermediate sexual types, whose 'cross-sex' desires are grounded in some kind of 'cross-sex' physicality – most often the brain or the hormones (Kenen 1997; Steakley 1997; Terry 1999). Brain organization research builds upon this way of conceptualizing sex, and uses these presumed links between (bodily) sex, (behavioral and psychological) gender, and sexuality to construct research hypotheses. We do not endorse this 'package' view of sex, gender, and sexuality, but it is necessary to grasp it in order to understand the logic of brain organization research hypotheses that we describe below.

2 The 'hardwired' paradigm

2.1 Scientific shortcomings

At present, neuroscientific research on sex/gender in humans has stalled on sterile approaches encouraged by the dominant brain organization paradigm, which holds that steroid hormones at a critical period of fetal development give rise to permanent structural and functional sex/gender differences in the brain and behavior (Hines 2004; Cahill 2006; Bao and Swaab 2010). The paradigm, known colloquially as 'hardwiring,' has moved beyond the level of theory to be treated as a simple fact of human development (Jordan-Young 2010).

And yet there are many compelling reasons to reject this 'fact,' beginning with flaws in the developmental model that draw incorrect parallels between genitals and other reproductive structures, on the one hand, and the brain, on the other. According to the classic paradigm of Alfred Jost (1953), a minimum level of androgens – specifically testosterone – is necessary to direct development away from the default 'female' pathway to develop the male phenotype. In 1959, William Young and his colleagues applied Jost's model to brain development (Phoenix et al. 1959). They differentiated between the initial 'organizing' effect of hormones, which are understood to permanently determine the character of the brain and behavior as masculine or feminine, and the 'activating' effects, which essentially determine the level of later activity or expression. Multiple discontinuities suggest that this initially promising extension of Jost's paradigm to the brain is greatly limited. The brain is far less dimorphic than genitals in virtually all species studied, and behavior even less so (van den Wijngaard 1997; Bishop and Wahlsten 1997; Schum and Wynne-Edwards 2005). Moreover, behaviors that are reliably sex-differentiated in some species are not sex-differentiated in others, even in closely related species (e.g. spatial ability (Costanzo et al. 2009), tendency to monogamy vs. polygamy (Lim et al. 2005), and parenting behavior (Lonstein 2002)). Genitals – at least in most vertebrates – do have a developmental moment at which an irreversible commitment to a male or female form takes place, while data on brain development indicate far longer developmental periods and extraordinary plasticity, raising doubts about the usefulness of the organization/ activation distinction (Balaban 2006). There is also far less continuity across species in terms of the specific relationships between steroid hormones and neuro-behavioral development or function than between steroids and genital development (Resko and Roselli 1997; Tilbrook et al. 2000; Bester-Meredith and Marler 2001; Sheng, Kawano et al. 2004).

The hardwiring paradigm seems to offer an answer to the common question of how it is that widespread sex/gender differences in the brain and behavior arise. Yet that question already presupposes that sex/gender differences are in fact pronounced and wide-ranging, while the reality is quite a bit more complex. In spite of the much-trumpeted 'female brain' and 'male brain,' the brain simply cannot be 'sexed' as genitals can. Imagine that one were to take scientific photographs of the genitals of 1000 human adults, and present these photos to a team of judges without any other contextual cues as to the sex/gender of the individual to whom the genitals belong. Even if our judges were ordinary people with no special training or insights, it would be possible to sort the photographs into 'male' versus 'female' piles with almost 100 percent accuracy. This is not to suggest that there is no intra-sex variety in genital size and shape, but in a group of only 1000 people, it will be possible to clearly place almost all human genitals into one of two main types. Human brains are another matter entirely. Consider first the issue of brain structure. Some scientists claim that there are no clear-cut structural differences, others claim that there are some subtle average differences, and still others claim that sex/gender differences in the brain are dramatic (Fausto-Sterling 2000b; Nopoulos et al. 2000; Cahill 2006). When important covariates such as brain weight are controlled, and the specific meaning of 'difference' is not glossed in a way that equates aspects such as cell number and regional volume, the only structural difference that has been independently replicated is in INAH-3, a tiny cell group in the hypothalamus that is larger in men than in women (Allen et al. 1989; LeVay 1991; Byne et al. 2000, 2001). The situation is even murkier when we add the question of function. While we may speculate that INAH-3 may be related to some aspect of sexual function, no one really knows what the area does – it may be related to something as mundane and 'non-psychological' as menstruation or erectile function.

All indications are that human brains are not 'sex dimorphic' – they do not occur in two distinct forms. There may indeed be differences in the *average size* of specific regions between men's and women's brains (Goldstein et al. 2001), and many activation studies suggest that there are average differences in the way that men and women 'recruit' different regions of the brain when performing emotional and cognitive tasks (see review in Cahill 2006). In fact, with new methods for measuring small regions in living brains, and statistical approaches that allow the detection of increasingly subtle differences between groups, it seems likely that more such average differences will be reported. But these differences are unlike genital differences in two key ways: (1) they are perceptible only at the group level, rather than being distinct forms that can be identified in individuals; and (2) there is no reason to assume that these differences do not arise, at least in part, from gendered patterns of social roles and behaviors – that is, brain differences may *result* from the very characteristics that are supposedly 'hardwired' into the brain in the first place. The point is not that there are 'no sex differences' in the brain, but instead is that the analogy from genitals to brains is extremely misleading.

Another misleading aspect of the hardwiring paradigm is the way it is fueled by systematically omitting evidence that the behavioral patterns that follow early hormone exposures can and do change. As early as 1969, it was known that many of the 'organizing' effects of hormones are not actually permanent, but are easily modifiable by experience. In a little-cited study by researchers at UCLA, for example, scientists found that allowing an androgenized female rat to have just two hours to adapt to a stud male *completely eliminated* the behavioral effects of prenatal testosterone injections (Clemens, Hiroi, and Gorski 1969). Subsequent experiments have shown a great many of the sex-typed behaviors that are supposedly permanently organized by prenatal hormones can be dramatically modified or even reversed by simple and relatively short-term behavioral interventions such as neonatal handling (Wakshlak and Weinstock 1990), early exposure to pups (in rats) (Leboucher 1989), and sexual experience (Hendricks, Lehman, and Oswalt 1982), to cite just a few examples.

There are two sorts of evidence available to indicate that sexed/gendered traits presumably organized by early hormones in humans are likewise impermanent. The first sort involves group-level data indicating both variability and change in the shape of sex/gender differences in cognitive abilities, occupational interests, educational interests and attainment, and even sexual orientation (Smith 1995; Huang et al. 2000; Jorm et al. 2003; Buchmann and DiPrete 2006; Hyde et al. 2008; Hyde and Mertz 2009; National Center for Education Statistics 2009). Although indirect, such data bear on the notion of 'permanent' sex/gender differences by undermining the clarity of the classification of traits themselves as masculine or feminine. Put simply, it is difficult to see how early hormones could direct the brain toward masculine or feminine cognitive or affective phenotypes, when the masculinity or femininity of the phenotypes in question is a moving target. The second sort is recent data on individual-level capacity for change in supposedly permanent traits, even in adulthood. Particularly dramatic evidence involves the most reliably observed sex/gender difference in cognitive skill: mental rotation ability, which consistently favors males (Hyde 2005). For instance, in a study conducted among women and men college undergraduates, Feng, Spence, and Pratt (2007) found that just 10 hours of training on an action video game virtually eliminated the sex/gender difference in spatial attention and simultaneously decreased the sex/gender disparity in mental rotation ability, a higher-level process in spatial cognition, with women benefiting more than men. In contrast, control participants who played a non-action game showed no improvement.

Finally, the idea that the human brain is 'hardwired' for sex/gender can never be settled by experiments. Scientists simply cannot randomly assign human fetuses to different hormone exposures in order to determine how these affect subsequent structure and function. Instead, we must rely on various quasi-experimental designs that search for correlations between sex/gender-linked behaviors, on the one hand, and indications of early steroid hormone exposures, on the other. But evaluating quasi-experiments requires a different approach than evaluating experiments. Because we cannot control the variables, we have to do a very careful and comprehensive appraisal that places all the evidence from multiple study designs into the same picture. Different designs have different strengths and weaknesses, so it is critical to avoid piecemeal evaluation of the multiple research streams, determining whether they 'add up' to some overall positive findings, on balance (Jordan-Young 2010).

In the following paragraphs we briefly review evidence that the dominant paradigm is not well-supported empirically, which has been much more fully addressed elsewhere (Jordan-Young 2010). Here, we focus on the lack of data triangulation across study types. Brain organization studies can be broadly divided into two types. The first type is cohort studies – those that begin with some knowledge about early hormone exposures, and investigate whether categories of exposure correlate with categories of later brain function. The cohort studies comprise many studies of people with unusual hormone exposures, as from the condition congenital adrenal hyperplasia (Berenbaum 1999; Meyer-Bahlburg 2001; Hines, Brook and Conway 2004), as well as studies of offspring from hormone-treated pregnancies (e.g. Ehrhardt, Grisanti, and Meyer-Bahlburg 1977; Reinisch and Sanders 1992), and some more recent studies that track proxy measures of fetal hormones in non-clinical populations (Knickmeyer and Baron-Cohen 2006). The second type is case-control studies – those that begin with some knowledge about the behavioral or functional phenotype (the presumed outcome of the brain organization process), and work backwards to search for evidence that distinct phenotypes correlate with distinct hormones on the front end of development. The case control studies almost entirely comprise within-sex/gender comparisons of sexual minorities and cisgender (i.e. non-transgender) heterosexuals (Gladue and Bailey 1995; Lalumière, Blanchard, and Zucker 2000; Byne et al. 2001; Blanchard and Lippa 2007).

In other words, these two broad sets of studies involve studying either unusual inputs (i.e. unusual prenatal hormone exposures) or unusual 'outcomes' – that is, studies that compare people with psychosexual phenotypes that are considered distinctive, such as heterosexuals compared to homosexuals. In epidemiology, where quasi-experimental or observational studies are the norm, it is well recognized that causal associations are only established when evidence from substantially different research designs converges (Cook and Campbell 1979). Figure 5.1 shows the various associations that are examined in the cohort (solid

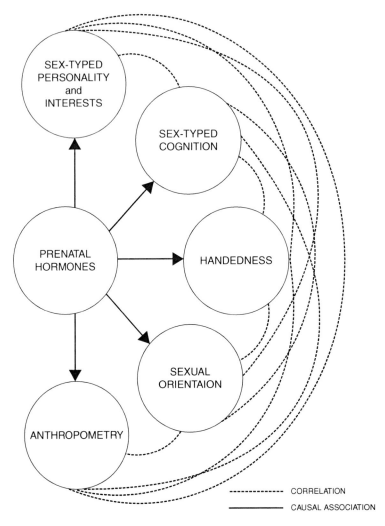

Figure 5.1   Associations predicted by brain-organization theory. Reprinted by permission of the publisher from *Brain Storm: The Flaws in the Science of Sex Differences* by Rebecca M. Jordan-Young (p. 177, Cambridge, MA: Harvard University Press), Copyright © 2010 by the President and Fellows of Harvard College.

arrows) and case-control (dashed arrows) studies bearing on the brain organization or 'hardwiring' paradigm in humans. For the paradigm to be well supported, evidence from the different designs should allow us to trace one or more complete paths from early hormone exposures, through specific psychosexual traits, and back again to early hormone exposures.

In fact, however, it is not possible to trace such complete loops, because these two types of studies give us irreconcilable data, with different designs showing associations between different specific behavioral domains, and contradicting dose-response expectations. The following figures summarize the evidence for various two-way associations between prenatal hormones and five broad domains of traits that are hypothetically sex-differentiated by hormones, as well as between these various traits.

Figure 5.2 shows the associations for genetic females. At first glance, it seems that there is one complete 'loop' of evidence supporting this paradigm, which relies especially on evidence from girls and women with congenital adrenal hyperplasia (CAH). Yet there are important problems with building the brain organization paradigm on this case. In spite of the fact that they have the highest prenatal androgen exposures of any known group of human females (and in spite of common claims that there are differences in other domains), only childhood toy preferences and adult sexual orientation are consistently different in girls and women with CAH compared to unaffected women and girls. Moreover, the much-touted increase in same-sex orientation among women with CAH is generally limited to fantasy or attraction, while rates of actual same-sex behavior are only slightly elevated, if at all, especially when women with CAH are compared to women in the general population (Sell et al. 1995; Jorm et al. 2003; Savin-Williams 2006) rather than to their own same-sex relatives (Zucker et al. 1996; Hines, Brook and Conway 2004; Gastaud et al. 2007; Meyer-Bahlburg and Dolezal 2008). The possible exception to this pattern is women with CAH who were initially assigned as male, in whom same-sex behavior and identity do seem to be elevated above population rates (Meyer-Bahlburg and Dolezal 2008).

Even these differences cannot be conclusively attributed to hormones, in part because CAH has wide-ranging effects on postnatal physiology (e.g. disrupted synthesis of mood-regulating hormones; short stature; and high rates of obesity, cystic acne, hirsutism, and male-pattern baldness) (White and Speiser 2000; Lin-Su et al. 2008; Jordan-Young in press). As a group, girls with CAH also have very unusual rearing experiences and extremely intrusive medical interventions and monitoring, due both to concerns about 'virilization' and to the difficulty of achieving hormone control in the condition (Karkazis 2008).

Notably, no behavioral differences are found in the only other group of girls and women who are known to have been exposed to high

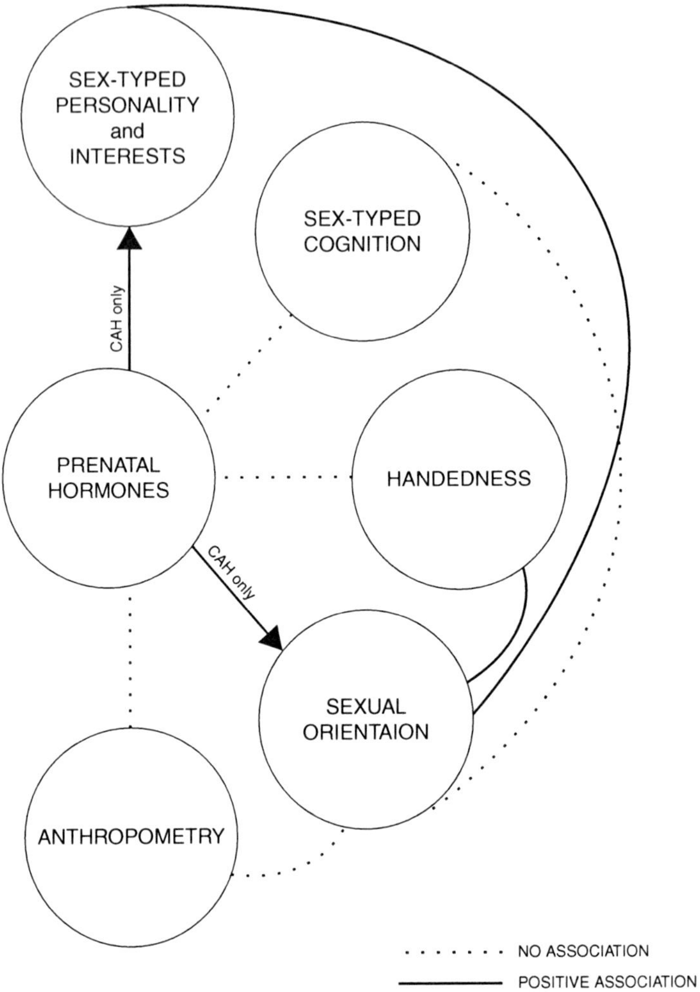

Figure 5.2 Associations observed among (genetic) females. Reprinted and adapted by permission of the publisher from *Brain Storm: The Flaws in the Science of Sex Differences* by Rebecca M. Jordan-Young (p. 190, Cambridge, MA: Harvard University Press), Copyright © 2010 by the President and Fellows of Harvard College.

levels of 'masculinizing' hormones in utero, namely those exposed to diethylstilbestrol (DES), a synthetic estrogen with androgenic properties in most species studied (Lish et al. 1992; Titus-Ernstoff et al. 2003). In particular, in spite of some early reports that DES-exposed women were more likely than unexposed comparison woman to be left-handed (Schachter 1994; Scheirs and Vingerhoets 1995; Smith and Hines 2000) or lesbian or bisexual (Ehrhardt et al. 1985; Meyer-Bahlburg et al. 1995), these associations could not be replicated when repeated with more appropriate comparison groups, including the only large, longitudinal cohort study of psychosexuality and DES exposure, which included nearly 4000 DES-exposed women (Titus-Ernstoff et al. 2003).

Figure 5.3 shows the observed associations among genetic males. Here, there is an even greater dissociation between evidence from research designs that begin by comparing people with different psychosexual profiles (case-control designs), on the one hand, and studies of hormone-exposed subjects (cohort designs), on the other. In particular, no cohort design shows a consistent correlation between prenatal androgens and *any* aspect of psychosexuality in genetic males (Jordan-Young 2010).

2.2 Ethical shortcomings

For all the reasons outlined above, the hardwiring paradigm is plainly unscientific; it is at odds with many kinds of evidence both about the nature of traits and about the actual observed associations between early hormones and sex/gender in humans. Given this, continued use of the hardwiring metaphor is also unethical.

The hardwiring paradigm locks neuroscience studies of sex/gender into a framework that implies permanence for any randomly observed correlations between sex/gender, on the one hand, and brain structure or function, on the other. It encourages ongoing material and social investment in the primacy and irreducibility of sex/gender differences. In particular, the notion of innate sex differences has led both lay observers and some scientists to suggest that social policies directed toward gender equity in education, occupation, or other aspects of social life are either useless or actually damaging (Holden 2000; Udry 2000; Hewlett 2002).

Hardwiring is an unethical metaphor because it says 'what is, must be.' That would be scientifically unsatisfying even if sex/gender were simply a domain of difference, rather than a domain of power relations and marked inequalities. But the continued existence of sex/gender inequalities adds an additional problem. The hardwiring paradigm erases the effect of the social world in producing sex/gender differences, so that sex/gender hierarchies appear natural. Neuroscientific explanations of sex/gender differences have added new allure to an old-fashioned sexism (Fine 2008b). The endorsement by neuroscientists of innate accounts of differences has inevitably reinforced the status quo

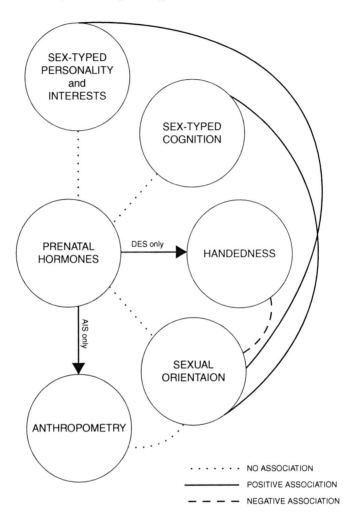

Figure 5.3 Associations observed among (genetic) males. Reprinted and adapted by permission of the publisher from *Brain Storm: The Flaws in the Science of Sex Differences* by Rebecca M. Jordan-Young (p. 191, Cambridge, MA: Harvard University Press), Copyright © 2010 by the President and Fellows of Harvard College.

and non-interventional policies. This has been amplified also by the popularization of these ideas in the press. In a study that appeared in 2004, Victoria Brescoll and Marienne LaFrance examined 290 articles taken from 29 U.S. newspapers which reflected, more or less explicitly, whether the cause of a given sex/gender difference was innate or acquired. These authors found that the ideology of the newspaper – established by taking into consideration its political view on a selection of issues (e.g. presidential endorsement and whether women should be admitted to military academies) – influenced the way in which the scientific research was addressed. More specifically, conservative newspapers were more inclined to attribute sex differences to biological cause than were liberal newspapers. Moreover, Brescoll and LaFrance further demonstrated that the type of explanation endorsed by the newspaper influenced the beliefs of the readers.

As Cordelia Fine (Fine 2010a), we (Young and Balaban 2006) and others have documented, scientists who double as popularizers of the sexed brain knit more than a few elaborations and conjectures together with neuroscientific facts to support the hardwiring paradigm (Baron-Cohen 2003; Brizendine 2006; Swaab and Garcia-Falgueras 2009). But we suggest that even careful studies of sex/gender differences, at this time, may be missing the point. Rather than continuing to build and revise the list of differences (which are inevitable so long as social life is pervasively structured by gender), the question to ask now is *why* is it that we want to know about sex/gender differences? What do we wish to do with or about them? We write this, with humility and some concern, as scientist-critics who have both written books reviewing sex/gender difference research, for audiences that we hope will be broad. So we aren't picking on others here, but raising concerns about where we hope that we might all go from here, most productively.

3 Where should we go next?

We close by considering the messages we convey by continuing to invest our scientific resources in extending, revising, or refining the catalogue of sex/gender differences. One very strong message is that sex/gender differences are crucial fundamental facts, that simply knowing about them in minute detail will guide us in important ways. Together with the pervasive belief that such differences are original, essential – that is, innate – this catalogue of differences distracts us from the extensive evidence on how the shape of sex/gender differences changes across both time and place, and can be altered by both natural experiences and deliberate interventions.

If we want to know about sex/gender differences because we are interested in empirically grounded understanding of human development and potential, we can look in two promising directions. First, we can focus directly on plasticity, instead of using it as background information against which we interpret findings of difference. We might build on Feng et al's video game intervention (described above, Feng, Spence, and Pratt 2007) by identifying some skills and traits that we can agree are desirable, and for which there seem to be reliable sex/gender differences at some point in the lifespan – mental rotation is a good example, but there are others like strong contextual verbal ability or empathy. Why not decide that we want to cultivate these skills or traits, and encourage creative research designs that would help us to establish effective strategies for doing so? Likewise, we could build upon experiments that show how invoking either positive or negative stereotypes can stimulate sex/gender differences as large as those that are usually taken to be innate (Hyde and Mertz 2009).

A second promising direction is to turn our backs on sex/gender differences. Because sex/gender differences are so mesmerizing, and because we ourselves are immersed in the "cultural frame of gender" (Ridgeway 2009), we may do much better to understand development and plasticity by looking at other kinds of variation, where our models and our interventions are less confounded by the complex and unavoidable overlay of gendered socialization and ingrained research hypotheses. Sex/gender differences exist, but so do differences between groups that we might want to define on many other dimensions – social class, occupation, development index or global region, specific training experiences, to name just a few. And each of these categories are themselves heterogeneous; more research on the ways in which sex/gender patterns in brain and behavior are specific to social class, ethnicity, and nation might provide much more illumination on the concrete mechanisms through which the social world shapes behavior, and even becomes embodied (brain) difference. Suggestive evidence in this direction is available from cross-national and ethnic comparisons of sex/gender difference in math and science tests. For example, both the size and the direction of sex/gender difference vary across ethnic groups. In the U.S., whites show the familiar pattern that boys score slightly higher ($d = 0.13$), whereas Hispanics show no discernible sex/gender difference ($d = 0.00$), and African Americans and Asian Americans show small differences favoring girls ($d = -0.02$ and $d = -0.09$, respectively) (Hyde and Linn 2006). Further, in 2008, Guiso et al. analyzed mathematical and reading test scores (from the Programme for International Student Assessment – PISA) of 276,165 male and female adolescents from 40 different countries; in particular, the mathematical gap favoring boys is attenuated, and sometimes even reversed, depending on a measure of sex equity of the country (Guiso et al. 2008). These and similar findings clearly should remind us that we are not measuring 'biological sex' when we record students' sex/gender. Instead, we are measuring a composite variable that includes sex*ism*, as well as other aspects of social structure and experiences, including regionally and ethnically specific modes of 'doing' sex/gender.

Another compelling example of dimensions of difference that might prove more tractable than sex/gender for focused study is Maguire and colleagues' fairly recent data on differences in neural structure and even function in a group defined only by occupation – namely, long-term taxicab drivers compared with those who haven't driven cabs (Maguire et al. 2000, 2003). Why not follow Maguire's lead, and think about other occupations that might involve sufficiently distinct tasks that we could trace their effects in actual structural differences or brain activation patterns?

Given pervasive gender socialization and widespread gender segregation in occupation and family responsibilities, it is utterly predictable that we would observe group-level differences between men and women in various cognitive functions. It is frankly somewhat surprising to us that we do not see greater differences and less overlap, and also would not be especially surprising to see more structural differences than there seem to be. What's the big deal? Certainly it makes a huge difference to your daily life and activities whether you are male or female, without question more difference than whether or not you are a taxicab driver. Continuing to treat findings of sex/gender difference as if they are revelations feeds the commitment to and mystification of sex/gender differences, and distracts us from serious science.

Sex/gender is, for most purposes, at best an imperfect proxy of the variables we actually need to understand. Recent analyzes by feminist epidemiologists show that studies that treat 'sex difference' as an explanation actually obscure more than they explain (Krieger 2003; Messing and Stellman 2006). Instead of treating sex/gender as the denominator of difference, it turns out to be far more informative to focus on specific mechanisms (such as hormone activity, body size differences, occupational differences, and co-morbidities) that themselves show meaningful variability within sex/gender groups that are routinely treated as homogeneous. Data on differences in neural structure and function in groups that are defined only by occupation and hobbies, including pianists and jugglers, in addition to the aforementioned taxicab drivers (Maguire et al. 2003; Driemeyer et al. 2008; Lappe et al. 2008) offer a useful start for thinking about how pervasive organization of daily tasks and social assignment of appropriate emotion, movement, and affect by gender becomes embodied as measurable 'sex difference.' Most importantly, it provides a ground for thinking about what we actually wish to do with the information we have about difference and variability. What traits do we value, and what might we wish to cultivate?

Steven Rose and colleagues (2009) wrote that "In a society in which racism and sexism were absent, the questions of whether whites or men are more or less intelligent than blacks or women would not merely be meaningless – they would not even be asked." It follows that it would be better to abstain (at least for now) from trying to deal with unanswerable questions about origins of sex/gender differences, or to continue building a catalogue of 'differences' when we know that this catalogue is neither stable nor innocent.

3.1 Acknowledgment

Chapter 5 is reprinted with permission from *Neuroethics*.

6
Re-Queering the Brain

Isabelle Dussauge and Anelis Kaiser

Are women taking contraceptive drugs brighter than women not using the birth control pill? Does testosterone make people's behavior more masculine through its effects on the brain? And can there ever be a neuro-gaydar?

Recently published neuroscientific papers use largely disparate ways to engage with no less disparate questions about sex/gender[1] and sexuality. Using fMRI, Pletzer et al. (2010) demonstrated that women taking hormonal contraceptives showed significantly larger prefrontal cortices, amongst other regions of the brain, compared to women not using contraceptives. Neuroeconomist Eisenegger and colleagues (2010) indicated that the faith in a specific effect of testosterone rather than testosterone's biological action itself made research participants believe that they were acting in a 'male way.' Neuropsychologist Ponseti et al. have proposed that although homo- and heterosexual women and men have identical brain processes of sexual arousal (2006), statistical analysis of the brain response to sexual stimuli could yield the participants' sexual orientation (2009). If we queer our gaze we begin to see that in the contemporary neurosciences there is some gender trouble going on.

1 The age of queer and brainhood

In this chapter, we dedicate our attention to the critical study of the sexed/gendered, and homosexualized brain in recent neuroscience. Starting from a feminist point of view, we aim to begin to elaborate a queer perspective for neuroscience. Our position is that a queer-neuroscientific approach has to reflexively address how neuroscience deals with the categories of sex/gender and sexuality. Current neuroimaging research on sex/gender and sexual preference seems at best limited and at worst, flawed, by the routine use of unsatisfactory notions of sex/gender and sexuality. We will see that in the sciences of the brain based on functional neuroimaging, approaching sex/gender does little else than produce differences between the sexes/genders, usually by attempting to detect and stabilize 'female' and 'male' activation patterns in the brain. We will also argue that studies of the brains of lesbians and gays are limited by their '2×2' categorization of gender and sexual orientation; not least, by their import of the dualistic framework of sex/gender research. We are going to interrogate the neuroscientific studies we review here with regard to classical issues of *innatism, determinism, reductionism,* and *essentialism,* and discuss the less classical relation between neuroimaging and causality. To conclude, we will propose to dispose of the versions of the concepts of *sex/gender* and *sexuality* currently in use in neuroscience, and build on new scientific and conceptual foundations. We will propose that theoretical insights from queer theory, especially the recognition of the performative and contextual character of sex/gender, may be used productively as a basis for a more trustworthy, and more radical, neuroscience of sex/gender and sexuality.

1.1   Queer approach

Based upon the assumption that sexual identity is not a natural given but constructed through complex heteronormative power relations and sexed/gendered norms, queer theory critically investigates the relation between sex/gender and desire (e.g. Butler 1990; Halberstam 2005). Against this deconstructive backdrop, not only queer sexualities but also any kind of sexual orientation, for instance heterosexuality, are neither innate nor stable and thus cannot be regarded as an immutable style of living.

Queer theoretical strategies highlight discourses and practices through which sex/gender and sexuality are constituted, such as speech acts, everyday social practices and the making of social norms, or the frames of production of scientific knowledge. Thus, subcultural norms and political debates, as well as medical research can be brought into focus to explore how heteronormativity makes heterosexuality – in specific forms – the dominant form of sexual desire and the determinant of sex/gender expressions, and defines sexualities other than hetero-sexualities and heterosexualized sex/gender expressions as abnormal and threatening.[2] Within this conceptual frame, one of queer theory's strategies is to explore the diversity of genders and sexualities that emerge despite and, paradoxically, as a necessary counterpart of the hegemonic heterosexual discourse. A central issue has been to theorize the processes of materialization of social norms, i.e. the processes by which individuals come to embody – and in part refashion – culturally privileged forms of sexual desire and sexed/gendered behaviors. Additionally, queer theoretical work aims to draw political implications and actively engage against practices of exclusion and oppression, starting from the point of view that there is no such thing as a natural order of gender and sexuality from which a social order should emerge. Rather, what appears as the 'nature' of gender and sexuality is the result of normative sociocultural processes of naturalization of certain forms of sexuality and gender expressions. Hence, the denaturalization of gender identity and sexual preference has been an important dimension of queer approaches toward gender and sexuality.

Biological descriptions of the human have been repeatedly used and are still often used to legitimize existing forms of oppression, which second-wave feminism confronted forcefully and queer scholarship still needs to engage with more strongly. Although the naturalization of gender identity and sexual desire is so palpably related to our material bodies and corporeal biology, attempts to introduce perspectives from queer studies into the biological, medical, and natural sciences are still few. In the field of biology, Bruce Bagemihl (1999) and Joan Roughgarden (2004) show how diverse sexuality, 'gender' roles, and procreation can be in non-human animals. Auto-critically, these authors raise the question why there is the necessity to scientifically explain and justify everything outside the (heterosexual) norm. In a similar way, Smilla Ebeling (2006) demonstrates how descriptions of queer animals can be used to legitimize queer human behavior and calls for a cautious use of primary social terms, such as 'hetero-' and 'homosexuality' and their application to biology. Evolutionary biologist Malin Ah-King (2009) reminds us that reproductive sexual practices between female and male animals are by far not the only way of sexual interaction in the non-human animal world, and that the heteronormative gaze produces a scientifically problematic bias in evolutionary-biological theories and methods. At stake are not only the political consequences of the naturalization of gender and sexuality norms, but also and centrally, the scientific character of knowledge production in biological sciences.

Beyond these undertakings of queering biology, and after the important feminist critiques of the last century's brain sciences of gender and sexuality (e.g. Fausto-Sterling 2000b, 2007; Fine 2010a; Jordan-Young 2010), to the best of our knowledge no queer research has been done in the area of neuroscience.

1.2   Braining the human

Never before in history has the brain been so present in our culture and everyday life accounts of the human (e.g. Ortega and Vidal 2007; Vidal 2009). Sociologist Nikolas Rose (2004, 2007) has emphasized that neuroscience, as a major contemporary framing of how we think of ourselves, is an instance of a power system, a biopolitical regime which regulates modern society as well as individual subjectivities (cf. Foucault 1976, 1997). Cultural historian Fernando Vidal (2009) has argued that Western societies' huge investments in neurosciences in the twentieth century has been the result of a modern ideology of 'brainhood' which equates the brain with the person and has its roots in modern Western notions of subjectivity as individual, autonomous, conscious, and detached from the world. In turn, public and private investments in neuroscience have further fueled the predominance of the 'cerebral subject' as a central cultural figure of the human (Vidal 2009). For instance, the Decade of the Brain (1990–2000) was a major event that promoted brain science both in academia and in the public (Herculano-Houzel 2002).

The intensified contemporary 'braining' of the human has been taking place not because of but in conjunction with functional neuroimaging methods. Highly elaborated technologies of brain imaging, such as fMRI, PET, SPECT, EEG, or MEG[3] have enabled neuroscientists to develop insights into the workings of the living brain. These complex and expensive evaluation tools, based on algorithmic reconstructions of brain activity, afford visualizations of the human brain and guarantee its constant, appealing, and problematic visibility in the public (Dumit 2004; Racine et al. 2005). An explosive growth of research on human neurocognitive functioning has also been concomitant to the recent diffusion and enhancement of neuroimaging techniques. The question remains whether – and how – the attempt to link cognitive and behavioral patterns with patterns of brain activation can increase our understanding of human functioning.

Living in the era of the brain means that not only people, their diseases or cognitive abilities, but also identities, religions, feelings, lived experiences, and social relations, are believed to be localizable in the brain – and potentially neuroimaged as such (e.g. Ortega and Vidal 2007). Sex, gender, and sexuality are no exception to this phenomenon. For instance, Larry Cahill (2006) has pointed out why sex difference research is mandatory to fully understand the functioning of the brain and Carina Dennis provocatively argued that the brain is "the most important sexual organ" (Dennis 2004: 390). A major concern for us is to understand what sex/gender and sexuality become when they are approached scientifically as something of the brain and studied with neuroimaging techniques – i.e. when they become 'brained.' At stake is the description of a sexed/gendered and sexualized cerebral subject.

In the following section, we will review generally accepted neurophysiological, neuroanatomical, and neuroimaging descriptions of the sexed brain. As we will argue, there are several problems with that knowledge which enjoys a status as indisputable – a main problem being that it works on the arbitrary premises of a binary system of gender.

2 Sex/gender in, not of, the brain

2.1 A canonical background: brain structures and sex/gender dimorphisms

Sex in human and non-human animals is usually described on different biological levels: genetic or chromosomal sex, hormonal sex, and morpho-structural sex in the body and brain (e.g. Fausto-Sterling 2000b). Here, we will begin by sketching neuroanatomical areas relevant to the neuroscience of sex/gender and sexuality – the latter in order to inform the review of neuroimaging studies of sexual orientation in Section 3.

It is important to bear in mind, first, that this literature is widely based on research on non-human animal models such as rats and mice and, second, that this research is oriented toward *sex differences* and not toward the investigation of what sex or gender *is* or *can be*. Hence, the notion of a binary system of sex/gender is from the very beginning interwoven with what may come later in the results and interpretation of those results.

In the brain, which 'controls' all sensory and motor bodily functions, certain regions involved in directing the activity of sexual organs are 'dimorphically different,' is what we read in the neurobiological literature canon (Kandel et al. 1996; Gazzaniga et al. 1998; Matsumoto 1999). Although biological research on the question of "How Sexually Dimorphic Are We?" (Blackless et al. 2000) as well as biology-informed literature on the biological category of sex (Fausto-Sterling 2000b; Voß 2010) strongly question this typical dualistic view (see also Kraus 2000), almost no critical literature reaches the canon of biological or medical textbooks. However, abundant research on highly complex interactions between genetic, hormonal, and cerebral processes is permanently going on, showing that what we think we know is always in a flow of corrections, differentiations, and changes. Here we summarize the main descriptions along which the brain is sexed and sexualized in neurosciences.

Central nervous system regions involved in sexual activity are the hypothalamus, the amygdala, and the sacral spinal cord, the first two being situated in *subcortical* areas of the brain and the latter at the lower end of the spinal cord. They are treated as the origin of a fundamental sexual dimorphism, which in turn is said to be developed in concordance with a genetic prenatal predisposition inscribed in the so-called sex chromosomes XX or XY. Hypothalamus, amygdala, and sacral spinal cord are instances of control and execution for sexual and reproduction enabling activities; the sacral spinal cord is in charge of triggering muscular contractions; the hypothalamus, whose nucleus preopticus is allegedly larger in men and whose nucleus infundibularis is involved in the menstrual cycle, plays a crucial role in regulating hormonal interplays; the amygdala, finally, is 'known' to be involved in the detection of sexual partners. Moreover, the amygdala, a limbic structure in the medial part of the temporal lobe, is involved in complex brain functions such as learning, memory, emotions, and anxiety.

Beside these subcortical structures of hypothalamus and amygdala involved in sexual interaction, *cortical* structures are also claimed to show distinctive sex/gender differences. In humans, the cortex is primarily active in 'mental processes' and 'higher thinking.' Higher cognitive functions, such as language, controlling, or planning are located in specialized cortical areas. Unlike subcortical sexual functioning – argued to be prenatally determined – debates on finding cortical differences between sex/gender can more easily be discussed as influenced by social learning.

Sex/gender differences are also mapped on the brain according to other systems of classification than their neuroanatomical localization and categorization. The division in brain anatomy, chemistry, and function (e.g. Cahill 2006) is common, as well as the approach of developmental genetics which, for instance, yields theories of the evolution of brain mechanisms of control of sexual behavior, or examines the effects of steroids and their receptors in brain cells.

Finally, the hormones, secretions of the gonads, stand for a large range of neuroscientific binary sexings/genderings of the brain (Fausto-Sterling 2000b), both in neuroimaging studies of sexed 'biological facts,' such as the female menstrual cycle (e.g. Gizewski et al. 2006) and of sexed mental functions such as spatial cognitive abilities (Hausmann et al. 2000; Schöning and Engelian 2007).

2.2 Current research on sex/gender in the brain

From structure to function, from single nerve cells to multimodal networks in neuroimaging studies, the brain is currently scrutinized for gender differences like never before (Kaiser et al. 2009). This is partly due to the overwhelming abundance of neuroimaging research itself, partly to the resurgent specific interest into the topic of the biology of sex/gender.

Anatomical sex/gender differences have been tested with respect to different sized brains. A great part of regional neuroanatomical female and male variations can be explained by brain size and volume differences rather than by the variable sex/gender (Jäncke et al. 1997; Leonard et al. 2008). It has also been shown that smaller brains, and not female brains *per se*, have more gray matter (Lüders et al. 2002; Leonard et al. 2008) whereas other studies demonstrated that women, but not men, with higher cerebral volume have proportionally more gray matter (Gur et al. 1999).

In *Brain Storm: The Flaws in the Science of Sex Differences*, socio-medical scientist Rebecca Jordan-Young (2010) conducts an extensive review of the published evidence for the 'brain organization theory,' the model according to which prenatal-hormonal levels categorically sex the human brain before birth as female or male, respectively. In that model, the sexed brain that people are born with subsequently directs their behavior throughout life, including sexual behavior and preference, along two main scripts – female or male. According to Jordan-Young, not only does the available evidence not support brain organization theory; as a whole, the huge range of neuroscientific results actually *disproves* the theory. As an explanation for this discrepancy between what the neuroscientific studies claim to prove and what they do actually support, Jordan-Young invokes, among other problems, methodological inconsistencies including sweeping, changing, stereotypical, and often implicit definitions of gender and sexuality.

The hormonal-structural brain studies reviewed by Jordan-Young have been conducted since the 1960s at least. In contrast, the explosive growth of the field of functional neuroimaging studies is more recent, with a steady increase of the number of publications since the 1990s with the increased availability of fMRI methods.

A high number of experiments on tasks related to defined cognitive skills as well as higher cognition have been conducted to differentiate men from women in fMRI science. Results are not unequivocal; similarities *and* differences have been shown to exist in a great number of cortical and subcortical areas. However, differences, rather than similarities, have been emphasized in experimental fMRI research. An example is the often cited (Wallentin 2009) study by Shaywitz et al. (1995) which showed in a study of human speech how men differ from women with respect to a cortical area associated with language processing known as the inferior frontal gyrus. This fMRI experiment examined three component tasks: skills in orthography, in phonology, and in semantics, respectively. In this experiment, Shaywitz and colleagues demonstrated in the inferior frontal gyrus a statistically significant sex/ gender difference, in terms of the number of activated pixels, in the phonology task. Interestingly, this one difference was foregrounded in the publication's title, where we read in a generalizing fashion: "Sex differences in the functional organization of the brain for language." Why were the other two component tasks, in which no significant difference was registered, not granted sufficient relevance as to be included in the title?

Apart from language processing, basically any mental process and its neurobiological correlate can be examined for potential sex/gender differences. For example, Jordan et al. (2002) tested women and men in their skills and brain representations in spatial orientation; Boghi et al. (2006) measured neuroscientifically the female and male ability to plan; whereas Piefke et al. (2005) recorded the performance of women's and men's memories with regard to their localization in the brain, to name only a few. Further fMRI experiments on the topic of woman/ man include, for example, examinations of olfactory processing (Royet et al. 2003), facial perception (Kranz and Ishai 2006), emotional sensation (Hofer et al. 2007) – and also, why not? – the satiety reaction to chocolate (Smeets et al. 2006). Again, significant differences as well as similarities between the sexes/genders in regional brain activation were discovered in those experiments – but mostly differences were highlighted.

2.3   Foregrounding difference

Why are differences apparently scientifically more important than similarities, and is this inevitable? Whereas exhaustive answers to these questions are beyond the scope of this chapter, we want to single out two central levels at which the foregrounding of differences takes place in neuroimaging-based knowledge production: statistical analysis and publication bias.

The production of differences in neuroimaging-based science is crucially dependent on the statistical analysis of the brain data produced in the experiments. When is a sex/gender difference a *significant* difference in neuroimaging? In fMRI research, experts from statistics, neuroinformatics, physics, neuroanatomy, or neuroradiology set the thresholds that turn a certain number of activated brain voxels into something 'different' from another number of activated voxels. The criteria and methods to set these statistical thresholds have a long history, vary across fMRI studies, and may result in the production of spurious results or in the invisibilization of differences. This issue has been the object of heated debate in the field of social neuroscience following the publication of a critical paper by Edward Vul and colleagues (Vul et al. 2009). In the field of neuroscience and gender, Kaiser and colleagues have shown that the sex/gender differences found in fMRI experiments on brain lateralization and language are highly dependent on thresholds and that, unreflexively, neuroscientists often choose a problematic statistical processing that cannot show a possible *similarity* of lateralization patterns (Kaiser et al. 2009). In other words, the choices made in statistical processing of data are a crucial site where data are transformed into similarities or differences.

Moreover, the foregrounding of sex/gender differences in fMRI research must be understood in the broader context of the problem of 'publication bias,' i.e. the fact that scientific studies that 'find' differences are far more likely to be published than those which do not (Dickersin and Min 1993; Bishop and Wahlsten 1997; Gilbody et al. 2000). In a thorough review of findings of sex/gender differences in the neuroscience of language, neuroscientist Mikkel Wallentin (2009) has recently shown that *none* of the often posited sex differences in language-related brain structures and processes has been consistently proven although the papers that claim to have detected these differences enjoy a thriving citation rate.[4] Wallentin also points to publication bias as a partial explanation for the almost compulsory orientation of neuroimaging results towards the production of sex/gender difference.

Interestingly, Wallentin proposes that putative differences may only be unveiled and understood through more detailed sociolinguistic analysis in neuroscientific experiments on language; which anticipates Deboleena Roy's general point (Roy 2011) that the problem of neurosciences of gender is not so much their backgrounding of similarities between people but rather their failure to scientifically address the concept or meaning of difference itself.

After hundreds of fMRI experiments on sex/gender in the brain, what we know is that the question of sex/gender differences in higher cognitive processes is still, at best, a matter of scholarly debate, and can certainly not be answered by saying that the male and female brain are distinctive entities. What is certain, on the other hand, is that as binary cultural *constructs*, the figures of the male and female brain enjoy a thriving social life in neuroscientific knowledge production and other cultural arenas (Fine 2010a). Among others, the neuroscientific interpretation of neural correlates of psychological processes and behavior tends to simply import such a binary framework, where patterns of brain activation often are categorized and interpreted as male or female, as we will outline in the following review of recent neuroimaging studies of sexual orientation.

3   Neuroimaging sexual orientation

The belief in a link between brain structure and sexual orientation is not new, as witnessed, for instance, in the use of lobotomy on non-heterosexuals in the 1940s and the widely publicized neuroanatomical quest for the gay brain in the 1990s. The 2000s have, in turn, brought about the more systematic mapping of possible differences in patterns of brain activation related to sexual preference. Here we review the published functional neuroimaging (PET, fMRI) studies of sexual orientation. As we shall see, all such publications use a '2×2' binary framework of sex/gender and sexuality, categorizing participants and their desire as women and men, and homo- and heterosexuals. However, not all of these studies attempt to map these neural correlates as 'male' or 'female.' Which claims are made about gender and sexual preference, and on which basis, is the object of this section.

3.1   Neurotransmitters

To our knowledge, the first published neuroimaging study of homosexuals was published in 2004 by Lean H. Kinnunen et al. (2004). With a PET experiment, Kinnunen and colleagues investigated differences in the brain metabolism of serotonin in eight homosexual and seven heterosexual men. The rationale of this study was inspired by the previous anatomical measurements of hypothalamic nuclei sizes mainly and originally in rats, as well as literature on sex differences in levels of neurotransmitters and/or metabolites, which led the authors to "hypothesize that a relationship might also exist between sexual orientation and brain neurotransmitters" (Kinnunen et al. 2004: 251). Kinnunen et al. found that the homo- and heterosexual participants' hypothalamus reacted differently to the injected substance (fluoxetine). The authors also observed differences in terms of which other brain areas "not known to play a role in sexual behavior" were activated during the experiment (Kinnunen et al. 2004: 253).

This study is interesting in the sense that it marks a shift in the privileged locus/focus of investigation of difference in brain research on the 'gay brain': from neuroanatomy (as in the 1990s) to brain function in parallel to the shift from structural MRI to fMRI. However, the authors of that 2004 investigation did not want to draw conclusions on the basis of their results: putative differences would need to be explored in more heterogeneous subject groups, confirmed, and not least important, their significance in terms of brain function would need to be assessed (Kinnunen et al. 2004: 253). The authors cautiously advanced that this study should be considered an encouragement to further exploration of differences in brain function between homo- and heterosexual men.

3.2 Putative pheromones

In two publications (Savic et al. 2005; Berglund et al. 2006), a group of researchers based at the Karolinska Institute (Stockholm, Sweden) who had previously conducted PET research on pheromone-like substances in humans, investigated the reaction of the human brain to two pheromone-like compounds in homosexual subjects as compared to heterosexual women and men. In these two PET-experiments, the subjects inhaled one compound, 4,16-androstadien-3-one (AND), extracted from some male bodily fluids (e.g. sweat and semen), and a second compound, estra-1,3,5(10),16-tetraen-3-ol (EST), extracted from some female bodily fluids (e.g. urine). The Karolinska researchers found differences between heterosexual men and women in brain response to inhalation of these two compounds; they also found differences between heterosexuals and homosexuals and claimed that homosexuals' brains showed response patterns similar to 'the opposite sex.' The anterior hypothalamus was recruited in all subjects but in different situations, upon inhalation of AND in heterosexual women and homosexual men and upon inhalation of EST in heterosexual men. Moreover, in homosexual men, additional brain regions were activated upon inhalation of EST (Savic et al. 2005). Homosexual women "did not show a differentiated pattern of activation with AND and EST" (Berglund et al. 2006: 8269). Whereas these studies confirmed that AND and EST were compounds with interesting properties to investigate, the conclusions to be drawn about sexual orientation and its relation to the brain were unclear. The authors explained that the observed differences in brain response could merely reflect an acquired sensitivity to a preferred

category of gendered bodies, or they could be the result of more fundamental biological differences.

3.3 Rest activity in the amygdala

In 2008, the same research group based at the Karolinska Institute published a PET-study (Savic and Lindström 2008) in which the research
subjects were breathing the air of the room, rather than pheromones,
while lying in the scanner. In this article it was the baseline brain activity (i.e. activity at rest) in specific brain regions that was analyzed. The
researchers interpreted their results as exhibiting the same pattern
of difference with regard to gender and sexual orientation as in their
previous studies of homosexuality reported here above: that the brain
activity patterns in heterosexual women and homosexual men showed
strong similarities, and differed from heterosexual men and homosexual women whose activity patterns showed similarities to each other.
What makes that study stand out from the others presented here is its
explicit claim to have found a structural difference between homosexuals and heterosexuals that cannot be explained by the sexual history of
the subjects, on the basis that the experimental design produced brain
data which "were not directly dependent on perception or behavior"
(Savic and Lindström 2008: 9407).[5] Instead the authors "believe that
the observed connectivity patterns reflected true biological differences"
(Savic and Lindström 2008: 9405).

3.4 Face attractiveness

Two studies by Alumit Ishai and Felicitas Kranz (Kranz and Ishai 2006;
Ishai 2007) investigated homo- and heterosexual women's and men's
brain response to human faces, and their assessment of the attractiveness of the presented faces. The authors found that the subjective rank-
ing of face attractiveness as well as the kind and intensity of response in
the distributed neural networks involved (regions in the visual cortex,
limbic system, prefrontal cortex, and reward circuitry) were as a whole
independent of the gender and sexual orientation of the participants
(Kranz and Ishai 2006: 66). They also argued that the brain response in
regions part of the reward circuitry reflected the subjects' sexual preference: "Sexually relevant faces elicit stronger neural responses in the
reward circuitry, where the value of stimuli is represented" (Kranz and
Ishai 2006: 66). Their conclusion was that attraction response to specific
faces is dependent on the sexual preference of the subjects rather than
on their gender, thus in opposition to what had been suggested by previous evolutionary-psychological studies; and that the neural networks

involved are similar in homo- and heterosexual men and women. In that sense, Kranz and Ishai's results point in the same direction as Ponseti and colleagues' study of sexual arousal in homo- and heterosexual men and women (Ponseti et al. 2006), as we shall see below.

3.5 Sexual arousal triggered by visual sexual stimuli

Four different research groups have published experimental neuroimaging work on homo- and heterosexual subjects' brain response to pictures of sexual situations, resulting in five publications as a whole. One of the studies was in women and men (Ponseti et al. 2006); and four were in men only (Safron et al. 2007; Hu et al. 2008; Paul et al. 2008; Ponseti et al. 2009).

Ponseti et al. (2006, 2009) found a general pattern of brain response to visual sexual stimuli in which subjects (homo- and heterosexual women and men) showed stronger reactions to their preferred sex. Ponseti and colleagues underscored that their neural model of sexual arousal, which involved the ventral striatum, centromedian thalamus, and the ventral premotor cortex, had what can be termed a universal character: according to their findings, the brain response to sexually preferred stimuli was similar in all groups. In other words, the brains of women, men, hetero- and homosexuals functioned similarly in terms of sexual response but were preferentially triggered by different genders.

Safron et al. (2007) found widespread and similar activation patterns in homo- and heterosexual men upon viewing of their preferred gender engaging in sexual activity (the stimuli they were presented depicted either sex between two women or sex between two men). A main conclusion was that "[i]n the whole-brain analysis, the pattern of greater evoked activity for preferred stimuli did not differ reliably across the participant groups" (Safron et al. 2007: 241). However, Safron et al. found group differences in region of interest analysis of the amygdala "with homosexual men showing category-specific activation to male sexual stimuli and heterosexual men showing tonic activation across stimulus conditions" (Safron et al. 2007: 242).

Paul et al. (2008) found that the hypothalamus was activated in both homosexual and heterosexual men when viewing their 'corresponding' sexual activity (i.e. homosexual or heterosexual sex, respectively). They also found differences between homosexual and heterosexual men in terms of which brain regions outside the hypothalamus were activated when viewing their 'corresponding' sexual activity; but they insisted on the similarity of brain response between the groups: "Taken together, our results demonstrate that brain response of heterosexual males to heterosexual stimuli is comparable to that of homosexual males to homosexual stimuli" (Paul et al. 2008: 734). However, Paul and colleagues also found a generally lower level of activation in homosexual men as compared to heterosexual men when aroused by viewing their 'corresponding' sexual activity.

One dimension that makes these three studies different from one another is the kind of pictures showed to the subjects in experiments. Ponseti et al. (2006, 2009) used visual 'sexual core stimuli,' i.e. pictures of aroused genitalia only, so as to remove interactional components from the stimuli; whereas Paul et al. (2008) used pictures of homo- and heterosexual sex respectively (which thus work as categories of preferred and non-preferred sexual activity) and Safron et al. (2007) used pictures of sexual activity between two persons involving only one gender at the time, i.e. lesbian sex and gay sex, respectively. Without going into the detailed rationale of these choices, it is important to know that the differences between Paul et al. and Safron et al. in choice of stimuli reflect an underlying difference in sexological assumptions: What turns men on? Paul et al. hypothesize that sexual arousal is triggered by viewing the kind sexual activity that the subject himself prefers to engage with, whereas Safron et al. work on the premise that men's sexual arousal is category-specific, i.e. that men get sexually triggered when viewing any sexual situation involving a person (or persons) of their sexually preferred gender.

As a whole and most strikingly, not only the methods but also the ways in which participants are aroused in the experiments (visual sexual stimulation; which films, images, and sexual practices are used), what counts as sexual or not, and the sexological theories (if any) are disparate across this body of neuroimaging studies. Implicit (and sometimes explicit) definitions of sexual desire are built into the experimental design: from the selection of participants, through the situations in which their brain activity is monitored, to the interpretation of results.

Furthermore, only a minority in the published neuroimaging research on sexual orientation (four publications out of eleven) emphasizes differences between homo- and heterosexual subjects' brain processes. A majority (six out of eleven) underscores the commonalities between the two groups; and one study does not take an explicit stance. In the next sections we will come back to whether the emphasis on sameness over difference in most of the studies is good or bad news for a queer neuroscience project.

All of the studies reviewed here function in a taken-for-granted binary framework of sex/gender. However, not all these studies interpret neural patterns of sexual arousal as either hetero-male or hetero-female; in some cases, patterns of homosexual desire are interpreted as something which does not fit in these two categories, and a few studies emphasize a 'universal' neural network of desire and attraction which would be the same for homosexual, heterosexual, female, and male desire. Whereas this partial escape from the simple sex/gender-binary framework is an improvement to a certain extent, since it acknowledges the possibility of some difference *within* gender categories, the use of sexual orientation as another categorical dimension in such studies is also problematic from a queer theoretical point of view. The binary framework used in all of the neuroscientific studies reviewed here organizes both gender and sexual orientation along a compulsory '2×2' matrix of categories of sex/gender and oriented sexual desires.

Some the studies emphasize that the neural processes of sexual arousal are common to homo- and heterosexual women and men and thereby they implicitly open up for the possibility to ask scientific questions about sexual desire other than its causes. If difference in a '2×2' framework is not relevant to the neural correlates of sexual desire, then an obvious implication is that neuroscientific knowledge about sexual preference ought to address other questions about difference and use other categorizations of desire.

Using these two short reviews of research in each area of investigation, we want to make visible now shared problems and limitations in the framing of neuroimaging investigations of sex/gender and sexual orientation.

4 Neuro-determinism and other key issues

4.1 Innatism and neuroimaging

A common (and often justified) criticism of brain research on gender or sexuality is that it attempts to find innate determinant biological causes of posited sex differences of behavior, homosexuality, or non-conforming gender identities such as transsexualism. Innatism refers, in this context, to the claim that gender and sexual orientation are inscribed in the brain in a way that people are born with; in innatist neuro-claims, the brain people are born with determines their behavior in gendered ways and also their sexual preference (see e.g. Stein 1999). Thus, innatism is a specific form of biological determinism.

For instance, Wang et al. (2007) claim that gender is an important biological determinant of vulnerability to psychosocial stress. In their study on schizophrenia, Gur and colleagues found a correlation between neuroanatomic sexual dimorphisms and behavioral differences between healthy women and men (Gur et al. 2004). They concluded that the early neurodevelopment of amygdala implied a 'feminization' of men and a 'masculinization' of women with schizophrenia. As we have seen, one neuroimaging study of sexual orientation also makes innatist claims, announcing that "[t]he results [of the experiment, structural brain differences between homo- and heterosexual] cannot be primarily ascribed to learned effects" (Savic and Lindström 2008: 9403). However, the authors of that study do not propose any clear explanation nor any concrete model for how the structural brain differences they claim to have shown could imply the posited differences in sexual behavior (sexual preference).

There are at least two central problems with innatist theories of gender and sexuality in the brain: Firstly, they do not account for the differentiation and changing character of gender and sexuality in individuals and populations (e.g. Lancaster 2006; Jordan-Young 2010); and secondly, innatist claims are weak unless an explanation is provided of the mechanisms by which a given innate structure would generate a specific sexual orientation or gendered behavior (Stein 1999).

In spite of these examples, whereas innatist claims have been strong in neuroanatomical studies of gender and sexuality (and strongly criticized as such, see e.g. Rose 1996; Stein 1999; Jordan-Young 2010), there has been a visible shift in the neuroimaging-based science of gender and sexual orientation in the last years. fMRI research, in particular, has taken the direction of a more performative understanding of what was previously regarded as immutable. This can be regarded as an opposite tendency to innatist positions. Thus, for instance, we find articles clearly saying that: "The sex differences are, in this view, not immutable and attributable to fixed differences in cerebral organization but rather may result from sex-specific preferred strategies and reactions to certain classes of cognitive problems" (Jordan et al. 2002: 2407).

Seemingly more often nowadays than before, neuroimaging articles avoid taking an explicit stance on innatism, and instead deal with the current uncertainties on the question of neurobiological sex/gender differences by focusing on methodological issues: "When holding the task constant, some methods (for example different ROIs within individual analyses) revealed sex differences while others methods did not, indicating a dependence on methodology" (Harrington and Farias 2008: 1221).

Our review of neuroimaging studies of sexual orientation reveals that almost no such studies make innatist claims, and in some cases (Ponseti et al. 2006; Safron et al. 2007) actively distance themselves from the question of causality of differences in brain processes related to sexual preference (where again, the issue of causality is cast along an additive model of biologically innate versus environmentally changing factors).

The relation between neural networks (as described by neuroimaging research) and behavior is, indeed, ambiguous. On the one hand, the rationale of neuroimaging research is crucially dependent on the assumption that brain structures have specific functions, i.e. that there is an anatomical substrate to behavioral and cognitive processes. But on the other hand, neuroimaging methods yield, at best, *correlations*, which are not relations of causality. Moreover, by studying the workings of the brain rather than the etiology of its structure, neuroimaging research keeps open the possibility of escaping innatist frames of description of brain and behavior. Not least, an underlying possibility that neuroimaging research tends to acknowledge is that the brain may be used or activated in different ways for the same behavior in different individuals;[6] or, reciprocally, the brain may be activated in similar ways associated with different behaviors, as for instance, similar networks recruited for sexual arousal in women and men, homo- and heterosexuals, upon different sexual behaviors. In other words, neuroimaging, as a frame of knowledge production, works in a tense epistemological relation with causal models of explanations of behavior.

4.2 New neuro-determinism

The epistemological question of *what* neuroimaging methods provide information about informs us about which kinds of biological determinism (innatism left aside) may be embedded in neuroimaging science of gender and sexuality. The studies reviewed here all share a trait so evident that we almost do not view it as anything special: They consider their results to give relevant information about the brain states that lead to specific behavioral outcomes. The underlying logic spells out simply: different brain states, different behaviors; which in turn implies: (different) sexed brain states, (different) gendered behaviors.

As neuroscientist and feminist scholar Sigrid Schmitz has argued, a new form of biological determinism has had a central hold in recent neurosciences. This new neuro-determinism does not concern the deep etiology (causes) of behavior, as it does not focus on the development of the individual brain due to innate or plastically shaped processes. Instead its central axiom is that the present brain constitution determines and can fully predict all actual behavioral properties. A main problem with the new neuro-determinism, Schmitz argues, is that it enables neuroimaging studies' unquestioned projection of cultural stereotypes of gender (see also Fine 2010a), such as female emotionality or male rationality, onto neuro-facts of behavior, while keeping the appearance of being liberated from the old ghosts of innatism. Furthermore, this new neuro-determinism contributes to the exaggeration of neurosciences' claims to accurately describe, explain and potentially predict human behavior and human nature (Schmitz 2010a).

4.3 Indirect biological determinism

An additional problem which deserves consideration is that of what can be termed indirect biological determinism, or biological determinism by proxy, where neuroscientific studies do not make explicit biological deterministic claims but inscribe themselves in biological-deterministic theoretical frames.

A common instance of this problem is that many studies propose interpretations of their results with reference to prenatal-hormonal theories of sex dimorphism of the brain (the 'brain organization theory' scrutinized by Jordan-Young), positing that the brain is feminized or masculinized in specific ways before birth, with a posited significant influence on behavior in the whole life of the individual. When referred to in interpretation/discussion sections of medical publications, the brain organization theory is treated as accepted knowledge – whereas it is elsewhere disputed on solid scientific grounds (Jordan-Young 2010). The common interpretations of homosexuals' brain processes as similar to those of the 'opposite sex' in neuroimaging studies, or Larry Cahill's (2006) taking innate structural sex differences in the brain for granted in his broad neurobiological review, are striking examples of how neuroimaging studies are episodically mobilized in a more general innatist argument framed by brain organization theory and vice versa.[7] Referring to brain organization theory transforms non-causal neuroimaging results into supportive elements of a determinist frame of knowledge.

Another instance of indirect biological determinism is the use in neuroimaging publications of biologically deterministic previous studies or theories as a backdrop to generate hypotheses or select and interpret regions of interest for neuroimaging investigation. Common examples are the use of teleological theories such as evolutionary psychology (also featured in Cahill 2006) or Hu et al's (2008) use of controversial or invalidated innatist studies of the neurobiology of sexual orientation.[8]

In short, from the above it seems that straightforward innatism, albeit a relevant concern, is not as problematic as could have been expected on the basis of earlier debates about, for instance, the brain organization theory or the 1990s' neuroanatomical research on the 'gay brain.' It is instead the new neuro-determinism and indirect biological determinism which haunt neuroimaging research with the specter of an almighty neurobiological description of behavior. We want to argue that in the apparent dislodging of neuro-determinism as an object of critique, other issues become apparent which are of concern for a queer feminist neuroscience. We will now turn to a few main issues in neuroimaging studies' description of gender and sexuality: reductionism, essentialism and reification. These issues are classical, in the sense that they have been raised with regards to earlier brain research; but the problems at stake in neuroimaging are specific to the configuration of brain, behavior, gender, and sexuality found in these studies.

4.4 Reductionism

All scientific research is necessarily reductionist, i.e. it works with simplifications, or 'reductions,' of the phenomena it investigates. For instance, in neuropsychological empiricism, simplifications are simply regarded as necessary steps in the process of reconstructing a manageable reality in an experimental frame. Reductionism does not negate the existence of complexities in the reality it is used to simplify, but reductions are taken either as proxies for the real or, at least, as relevant selections from the real. Therefore, whereas it is naïve to criticize scientific research simply for reducing the phenomena under study, it is relevant to ask ourselves: What specific reductions are at work in the neuroimaging science reviewed here, and what knowledge are they productive of?

The monolithic character of the sexes/genders and sexualities studied in neuroimaging-based science is a first, central reductionism. There people, behaviors, experimental tasks, and experimental outcomes are sexed/gendered and sexualized along two genders/sexes and two sexual orientations only.[9]

Moreover, the multiplicity of sexual orientations is studied only as a one-dimensional spectrum defined by the degree of attraction to the two genders. Other aspects of lived sexual attraction – *what* people are attracted to in a person, a situation, a desire, etc. – are simply ignored as irrelevant. Idealized, static, monolithic sexualities and genders are studied as if they were sufficient for a universal neuro-mapping of human sexuality.

As critical scholars have pinpointed earlier (e.g. Lancaster 2003), unfortunately, this set of '2x2' categories neither maps onto the huge variation of sexual preferences and gender behaviors that we know exist nor accounts for the multiplicity and changeability of people's preferences and behaviors.[10] Most people have many gender and sexual preferences, and change preferences along their lifetime. Reducing gender and sexuality to '2×2' categories is disrespectful and certainly not representative of human gender and sexuality.

As very few people (if any) are the bearers of idealized forms of monolithical gender and sexuality, knowledge produced on these premises is, at best, knowledge of a few people's reality. At worst, it is a knowledge that makes claims about gender and sexuality far beyond what is epistemologically honest.

4.5 Essentialism and reification

Queer theoretical studies have demonstrated and explored how gender and sexuality are performatively constructed, i.e. constituted in the repetition of gender acts and sexual acts (which, in turn, explains how the norms and social categories of gender and sexuality are maintained, among others in the social form of 'natural' categories). In contrast, the neuroimaging literature reviewed here works on the essentialist premise that gender (and sexual orientation, if addressed) exists *within* people prior to, and independently of, any action undertaken by the subjects: gender and sexual preference are treated as an ontologically permanent property of *individuals*. Epistemologically speaking, we want to argue that this is an effect of the neuroimaging studies' use of gender (female/ male) and sexual preference (homosexual/heterosexual) as fixed variables in their experimental design, including during the processing of data. The processes of gender/sex and sexual orientation – defined in queer theory as processes of the formation of the subject – are simply not *investigated* in current neuroscience, and as a result, these neuroimaging studies tell us little (if anything) about gender and sexuality; neuroimaging simply works as a means to divide people again into socially predefined black-boxes (see Roy 2011).

Moreover, in a queer theoretical framework, individual gender and sexual identities result from repeated individual gender expressions performed *in a cultural context*. Put simply, gender and sexual identity, like subjectivity, cannot exist detached from the cultural context in which we live our lives. In contrast, the essentialization and experimental design in neuroimaging studies described above implies the reification of gender and desire (i.e. their turning into things, cf. Lancaster 2003) and the disappearance of the contexts and specific objects of gender and desire (Dussauge 2010b). In the neuroscientific studies reviewed here, we witness the disappearance of everything which is not contained within the individual body: neither lived interactions with the world, cultural imaginaries, processes of meaning-making nor power relations are theoretically allowed to leave marks on the brain and/or its function; nor are they considered as relevant parts of the experimental conditions (cf. Cohn 2008).

Epistemologically speaking, we view these effects as a concrete outcome of the specific ways of framing gender and sexuality in the experimental design and apparatus (it *could* be otherwise). But gender, identities, desire, and the experience of those are lived, shared, cultural frames that are constitutive of who we are and how we live (Lancaster 2003). We do share gender identities, lives, sexual feelings, with others in complex manners; and these experiences move us, displace us and our senses of self (Ahmed 2004). Neuroimaging cannot afford to treat gender and desire as permanent, self-contained and individually enclosed things, because neurosciences cannot afford to reify gender and desire beyond recognition.

Our critical review suggests that as a whole, it is unclear how existing neuroimaging studies contribute to a better understanding of gender and sexual orientation; and as a rule, their purpose and contribution are not explicitly formulated. We can only speculate on why this is so, and observe that the current ideology of brainhood (Vidal 2009) potentially justifies the neuroscientific study of any human phenomenon. Moreover, the public fascination with neuroimaging "undoubtedly also influences the evolution of the science itself, as researchers are not isolated from wider social and cultural beliefs about the brain" (Racine et al. 2005: 160).

To coin yet another neologism, such a 'neuro-voyeurism' – our cultural desire to visualize anything in the brain – can be a destructive force, when leading to a reinforcement of representations of gender, sexuality, and narratives of gender/sexuality as less complex, fully human phenomena than they are. But we also believe that neuro-voyeurism, if taken seriously, can be pursued in more honest and constructive ways. How this could be so is the object of the final section.

5   Re-queering the brain

In the present chapter, we have pursued a critical study of the ways current neuroscience sexes, genders, and sexually orients the brain. From a feminist and queer vantage point, we have outlined problematic implications of these ways of dealing with sex/gender and sexual preference beyond the classical problem of innatism. We have especially addressed the place of neuroimaging in the production of difference. Analyzing issues of determinism, reductionism, essentialism, and reification, we have shown that studying sex/gender and sexual orientation as '2×2' stable, essential categories of the person leads to serious limitations and flaws, and directs the neuroscientific gaze away from a more enlightening understanding of the performative instantiation of sex, gender, and sexual desire.

However, as Hilary and Steven Rose once noted (Rose and Rose 2000: 9), critique is not enough and alternatives need to be put forward if the aim is a renewal of the scientific theories and methods under criticism. In this context, we do not want to leave it to the field of mainstream neuroscience, which is specialized in the brain's functioning but not in the functioning of gender, sexuality, and gender politics, to define what a female, male, lesbian, gay, transgender, intersexual, or transsexual brain 'is.' Besides, we do see a potential in neuroscientific empiricism for queer issues, which requires that we as a scientific community establish a new empirical scientific agenda based on different theoretical premises about gender and sexuality. There are many reasons to believe that neuroscience can adapt to new understandings of gender and sexuality and establish this new scientific agenda. The crucial issue is, of course, how. Here we want to conclude by presenting some strategies to attempt to re-queer the brain in the neurosciences.

First, neuroscientific research on sex/gender and sexuality needs a clearer non-deterministic approach. For this purpose, neuroscience needs not only to confront its possible determinist ghosts, for instance by using less neurocentric accounts of human behavior, but also leave behind indirect deterministic frames. Instead, as Deboleena Roy (2011) has proposed, we should attend more to how brain function influences brain structure, effectively pursuing the relation between brain structure and brain function as a two-way relation.

Second, neuroscience needs a new point of departure which de-essentializes gender and sexual preference; we propose that neuroscience should empirically work with gender and sexuality as performative processes, i.e. processes that are constituted in their repeated and contextual making. For this purpose, stable categories of gender and sexual preference have to be left behind; instead, we need to open them up and focus on diversity not only within these social categories but also within individual subjects, and we need to explore further the making of gendered and sexualized subjectivities.

Third, in neuroimaging experiments about gendered and sexually oriented behaviors, we have to re-multiply gender expressions and sexual desires and, avoiding the individualization of difference (cf. Kraus 2010a), explore what these differences are in and of themselves (Roy 2011).

Finally, an honest recentering of the level of interpretation of experimental results is necessary. Neuroscientific interpretations of experimental results need to constantly and self-reflexively ask the question of *what* the neuroimaging studies really say something about. We simply cannot afford exaggerated extrapolations – for instance on the nature or the 'effects' of gender – from fairly limited experimental results (e.g. performances on specific tasks). Or, to take another example, we may need to accept that a study of heterosexuality in very specific experimental settings is a study of a very specific instance of desire.

The argument we have tried to put forward is that people and their brains are queerer than the neuroscience of gender and sexuality; and that much of the current neuroscience of sex/gender and sexual orientation unnecessarily but effectively strips the brain from its queerness. It is by engaging critically with the rationales and methods of their gaze that the neurosciences can contribute with potentially radical new biological understandings of gender, sexuality and the brain – and this endeavor begins with re-queering the brain.

Notes

1. Gender Studies indicate that there does not exist a clear-cut distinction between *sex* and *gender* (e.g. Butler 1990). We therefore use the double-term *sex/gender* wherever applicable. In some cases though – especially in the section on sexual preference (Section 3) – we chose *gender* instead of *sex/gender* to avoid confusions with sex as in 'having sex' and thus for the sake of legibility of the text.
2. Heteronormativity refers to a system of power which declares heterosexual practices and heterosexual relations as standard and 'normal.' This normative convention implies an understanding of sex, gender identity, gender role, and sexual orientation along the lines of 'female' and 'male.'
3. fMRI: functional magnetic resonance imaging; PET: positron emission tomography; SPECT: single photon emission computed tomography; EEG: electroencephalography; MEG: magnetoencephalography.
4. Ironically, Wallentin notes that the only statistically 'significant effect' found in the meta-studies reviewed was the effect of author gender on the results of scientific studies. "This indicates that researchers bring their own preconceptions, or gender stereotypes, with them in their interpretation of data," Wallentin concludes, thereby echoing a classical point in science and technology studies (e.g. Martin 1991; Oudshoorn 1994).

5. This was also the justification of the experimental design: "Because measurements of the resting state functional connectivity are independent of user, perceptive, cognitive, or behavior related tasks, they lend themselves to studies of more crude potential neurobiological correlates to sex and sexual orientation" (Savic and Lindström 2008: 9404).
6. See Fine (2010a: 142) referring to De Vries (2004).
7. Hilary Rose formulated a similar point about 1990s' gay brain research's dependency on brain organization theory (Rose 1996).
8. About the problems of evolutionary psychology, among others its teleological character, see Rose and Rose (2000). For reviews of the criticisms of neurobiological studies of sexual orientation, see e.g. Jordan-Young (2010) and Wilson (2000).
9. Note that several neuroimaging studies of sexual orientation acknowledge the existence of more than two sexual orientations; yet their authors chose to study extreme versions of homo- and hetero-sexuality. Rebecca Jordan-Young (2010) makes a similar point and elaborates on the rationale between these choices.
10. A similar criticism of dichotomized models of gender and sexuality has been made by Elizabeth Wilson (2000) who proposes that we understand the relation between the range of sexual preferences and a gender-dichotomous society as one of *reticulation*.

7
Situated Neuroscience: Exploring Biologies of Diversity

Gillian Einstein

> I think...that we are at the stage when we can just proceed with the project, rather than having to defend it. (Longino 1992: 338)

1 Prologue

From the late 1980s to the late 1990s there was concentrated activity around feminist philosophy of science and the question: could there be a feminist science? (Richardson 2008). Early feminist approaches to science were concerned with certain assumptions within scientific methodology itself. During that period, there were exhortations for a replacement of androcentric values with feminist values (Harding 1991) and a replacing of the Kuhnian values for interpreting underdetermined knowledge with feminist 'virtues.' In contrast to Kuhn's values, the virtues as set forward by Longino were:

  (i) empirical adequacy
 (ii) novelty
(iii) ontological heterogeneity
(iv) complexity of relationship
 (v) applicability to current human needs
(vi) diffusion of power (Longino 1992: 336–337)

However, Longino, Harding, and others were concerned that if the 'scientific method' – as in setting out to falsify one's hypothesis, reducing variables, objectifying oneself and the studied, and producing generalizations that outstrip one's data based on some epistemological set of values – was not followed, then what resulted would not be science

(Harding 1987). And, what did not go forward from these reconfigurations was an empirical agenda – that is, a scientific program resulting in data of some sort.[1]

What did go forward however were trenchant analyses of masculinist science: Barad and physics (1999), Fausto-Sterling and sexual differentiation (2000b), Martin and developmental biology (1991), Haraway and immunology (1989), Weasel and immunology (2001), and Wilson and neuroscience (1998). Each has had their own approach, critique, and reinterpretation of the science using feminist approaches. Thus, without 'practicing' science, feminist philosophers created a kind of 'feminist empiricism' which takes for granted certain research practices, and demands that feminist principles prove their effective interaction with the research question at hand (Rouse 1998). I would posit that this began to change the landscape and the popular imagination, including that of philosophers of science, of what science might be; one issue with which feminist philosophers of science struggled was whether what they proposed as feminist science would be taken as science – either by scientists or perhaps even philosophers of science.

This seems as if it may no longer be at question in the philosophy of science community. Rouse in his review of developments in the history of science in the twentieth century writes that there has been within the philosophy community a contemporary widespread rejection of any pre-assumed scientific methodology "... in favor of some form of epistemological naturalism" (Rouse 1998: 85). On my reading this means that even in the history and philosophy of science, which has traditionally defined the theoretical values of the scientific endeavor, 'good' science doesn't rely on a fixed, theoretically based method and the assumption of objectivity, but rather adapts the scientific method to the natural problem at hand.

The emerging complexities as well as new epistemic developments of each science subspecialty have encouraged a once relatively unitary philosophy of science to subdivide and engage in the particularities of each field. Indeed, the history and philosophy of science has moved from judging an empirical endeavor by the classical picture of physics as science to the particularities of the underlying epistemic structures of different areas of science. Rouse remarks that the project of philosophizing about science as a whole is no longer viewed as useful to the field. In fact:

> The field has grown so rapidly since then that for many philosophers of biology in the United States today, their principal intellectual

community consists of biologists and historians, sociologists, and other philosophers of biology rather than philosophers of science in general. (Rouse 1998: 79)

Thus, a new philosophy of science might allow each field and subfield to have their say, move in their own directions and dictate their own theory. This would mean that neuroscience as biology doesn't have to be held to the accounts of physics as the ideal in science. On this view of neuroscience then there can be rejection of

> determinism, intertheoretic reductionism, and essentialism about natural kinds. The world includes multiple kinds of things, which cross-classify. The same things are subject to multiple descriptions, while the discernable regularities at "micro" levels of description are only contingently relevant to whatever regularities are manifest at more macroscopic levels. (Rouse 1998: 109)

While "quantitatively precise causal regularities" are still important, causality also encompasses a probabilistic causality and it is "... a 'promiscuous' realism of multiple and intersecting objectified divisions between natural kinds. Thus, some philosophers of biology even deny the plausibility of causal completeness as an epistemic ideal" (Rouse 1998: 109).

So on this approach, feminist approaches that demand accounts of complexity would be good science.

Another foundational concept in classic science is that hypotheses are underdetermined by evidence. That is, it is not possible to completely verify or disprove a hypothesis on the results of one or even a series of experiments. All data can do are bear on a theory relative to the society or the group within which it belongs. Thus, scientific communities make choices about what data they are going to believe or not, often unforced, although supported, by the evidence presented (Rouse 1998). It is the epistemic community that judges how good the evidence is and based on that, how good the theory about it is. This perspective becomes critically important when considering evidence gleaned by feminist approaches. Some will be acceptable to the general epistemic community; others may have to wait until there is a critical mass of scientists using these approaches, which may form its own epistemic community as well as change the playing field of other communities. Ultimately, however, their acceptance will depend on whether or not the scientific community to which it belongs accepts the evidence.

Interestingly, this has already happened in some scientific epistemic communities. Richardson chronicles how feminist ideas of gender have in fact infiltrated the epistemic community of biologists who study sex determination and how this, in turn, has modified their playing field. Geneticists studying sex determination have admitted to how wanting a reduced theory – such as one genetic switch that when 'flipped' makes you one sex and not the other with no other interposing choices in the pathway – has clouded their thinking. They are aware that sexual differentiation[2] in females might not simply be due to an *absence* of a testis determining factor located on the SRY gene of the short arm of the Y-chromosome – the 'default pathway' as it has become known. In fact, the reason we have not identified 'agency' for female sexual differentiation is because the female pathway needs further study. In other words, sex determination for XX and XY may not just be a matter of the presence or absence of a genetic switch. Richardson quotes Reed and Graves' introduction to the conference volume:

> "[W]e are gradually getting *an uneasy feeling* that [the genetic switch being on the Y-chromosome] is flawed. The history of studies of sexual differentiation exemplifies the truism to 'seek simplicity, then distrust it'...*[We] were not prepared* for the ambiguities and difficulties that would follow in trying to interpret the role of SRY in aberrant phenotypes." (Richardson 2008: 29)

As well, a number of key geneticists are beginning to acknowledge that there is no simple definition of sex – that there are diversities of human identities and sexual practices within which biological models of sex must be *contextualized*. One scientist goes so far as to say that he has realized that sex is on a spectrum. Richardson attributes this sea change in perspective to: (1) activism from outside the field; (2) the authority of a practicing geneticist who is feminist; and (3) the data, themselves (Richardson 2008).

Critically important is to have theories that match the entity under study. Rouse points out that

> Mechanics, astronomy, anatomy, and pneumostatics enjoyed unprecedented success beginning in the 17th century not because scientists finally began to do experiments, observe, and abide by the results, but because they happened upon theories to guide their research whose terms actually matched up reasonably well with the entities that were causally efficacious in the domains they studied. (Rouse 1998: 82)

This raises the important point that to study a constantly changing biology, such as women's during their reproductive lives, using static methods as has been done until the end of the twentieth century is not properly aligning the approach with the nature of the 'kind' under study. For example, consider any test of a new drug for breast cancer. The constant is the drug and the variable is the cancer. If a potential user group is women of reproductive age then 'the problem at hand' requires that the test consider at least four phases of the menstrual cycle (Becker et al. 2005). If a potential user group is pregnant women then the treatment must be tested over nine months of pregnancy. And to achieve a closer approximation one might also want to consider physiological variation in circadian rhythms. Would it, in fact, be good science to not take all this variability into account, given the population for which the drug is intended? A real understanding of this world's biological phenomena is so complex as to disallow reduction to a single variable – even when it comes to male bodies. Interestingly this approach has probably curtailed our learning about the subtleties of men's biologies as well as women's. In support of this, at the 2010 meeting of the International Congress for Gender Medicine in her keynote address, Maryann Legato referred to men as having been 'mined' for data but their biologies not really studied.

If questions must dictate methodologies then methodologies for studying women's and men's biologies must be such that they can reflect change, variation, and the particularities that a given question might encompass.

P. B. Medawar recognized this about biology, in general, as early as 1969:

> Biologists work very close to the frontier between bewilderment and understanding. Biology is complex, messy and richly various, like real life; it travels faster nowadays than physics or chemistry (which is just as well, since it has so much farther to go), and it travels nearer to the ground. It should therefore give us a specially direct and immediate insight into science in the making. (Medawar 1969: 1)

In sum, in this section, I have tried to show that while early feminist inquiry into what a feminist science would be did not result explicitly in the feminist doing of science, it did go hand-in-hand with changes in science and the epistemologies of science, which changed the playing field substantially enough that alternative approaches to science are now within the epistemic fold. This opens the gates substantially wide for feminist approaches to be brought to bear on projects taking an empirical approach. It is therefore worth exploring how an explicitly feminist science research program could now go forward and of what that might consist.

2   Introduction

2.1   Doing feminist neuroscience

This then raises the question: what it would be to *do* feminist neuroscience?

In order to tease apart the various strands of this question what follows is an account of a project to understand the neurobiological effects of female genital circumcision/mutilation/cutting (FGC), a traditional North East and West African ceremony that in its most extreme examples requires excision of the clitoris (Clitoridectomy), cutting off the labia minora (Excision), cutting the labia majora (Excision), and suturing the labia majora together to make a small hole from which urine and menstrual blood can flow (Infibulation) (WHO 1998, 2010). The project was approached from an explicitly feminist perspective asking what it would be to do neuroscientific research that would be commensurate with feminist epistemologies. To my mind this would be research into the nervous system that would give voice to areas of research previously silenced, uncover pockets of ignorance – not just 'knowledge gaps' – turn expectations about the essentialism of biology on its head, and contribute meaningfully to women's lives in all their varieties: a short agenda.

Taking to heart Sandra Harding's view:

> Thus meditation on the method question in feminism leads us to the recognition that feminism is fundamentally a moral and political movement for the emancipation of women. We can see now that this constitutes not a problem for the social science and biology that is directed by this morals and politics, but its greatest strength. (Harding 1987: 30)

And Medawar's admonition:

> If politics is the art of the possible, research is surely the art of the soluble. (1967: 97)

And, Harding's conclusion:

> The search for a distinctive feminist method of inquiry is not a fruitful one. (Harding 1987: 30)

I asked the question:

Are there neurobiological effects of the traditional practice of Female Genital Circumcision/Mutilation/Cutting (FGC)?

My hypothesis was, yes there are (Einstein 2008). Furthermore, the result of the involvement of the central nervous system (CNS) would be to embody the tradition affecting the way women with FGC walked, carried themselves, and generally, experienced the world through their bodies thus, in effect, embodying their culture. I wondered specifically if the purpose of the tradition was to instantiate a corporeal difference in the CNS between male and female that wasn't present without the procedure.[3]

The challenge was to devise an experimental paradigm that would lead me to, at least, a partial answer – or enough understanding that I could in good faith, design further experiments – or not.

2.2 The research project

FGC has been highly contested as a human rights issue and a feminist cause (Obermeyer 2005). It has been most commonly studied either from the ethnographic or the biomedical perspectives. When studied biomedically, the focus has been on reproductive health (Obermeyer 2005; WHO 2006).

Ignorance: No one had approached the repercussions from a neurobiological perspective, which is surprising because nerve and muscle are being cut – in fact, one could view it as an amputation. Using neuroscientific understandings of the plasticity of the adult primate nervous system, and the roles of experience and steroid hormones to affect that plasticity, one might expect that cutting the genitalia would have long-lasting, whole body effects via central nervous system (CNS) rewiring. From this perspective, one would expect antero- and retrograde degeneration of nerve pathways, possible nerve sprouting, and changes in somatosensory cortex which would lead to potentially chronic pain, referred sensation potentially to the leg and foot, and phantom clitoris (Einstein 2008).

Oppose the essentialist body: Such neurobiological changes of the genitals would also lead to experiential changes affecting the sensation of touch on different body regions, the sound and sense of peeing,[4] how one walks,[5] sits and carries oneself. These experiential changes would then become instantiated as the 'normal' (and perhaps, desirable) body. Changes to the central nervous system would also have the effect of making it very difficult, at least in context, of imagining any other way of being.

Contribute meaningfully to women's lives: Toronto is home to upwards to 200,000 Somali-Canadians, a demographic fact which made pursuing the neurobiological repercussions of FGC possible. Somalis still practice FGC in their natal land with upwards to 98 percent practicing excision and infibulation, which they call Pharonic circumcision. Therefore, I could assume safely at the outset that any Somali-Canadian woman who had immigrated to Canada would have Pharonic FGC.[6] These numbers made it possible for me to restrict the 'experiment' to one cultural group[7] practicing the same form of body modification for the same reasons and roughly at the same age.

Since I would be relying on the Somali community to participate, before designing or planning an experiment, I wanted to find out if members of the Somali community who had FGC thought this was a salient question. So I went to a talk by a Somali activist midwife in the Toronto community, told her my idea, and asked her what she thought of it.

Did the idea of pain and referred sensation ring true to her from both her own experience and the experience of other Somali women?

She leaned in closely while I explained what I thought might happen, listening very intently, and a look of recognition flooded her face and physical expression. Leaning toward me she said that she thought it was a very interesting idea and that she, herself, had chronic leg pain that worsened in cold weather – to me one of the possible signs of neuropathic pain as a long-term outcome of FGC.

I then talked with a colleague who does community-based research (CBR) with the Ethiopian and Tamil communities in Toronto about how to make contact with the Somali community more broadly. This led to a meeting of three Somali community health workers at a Toronto community health center. I described my ideas to them and asked their opinions. They all had the same intent expressions as the previous activist and one reported that she, too, had leg pain. As did the activist midwife they felt it was a valid question that could have important findings for their community. They especially liked the fact that it focused on their brains and not their genitalia and felt that the question of chronic pain was particularly important. They agreed to help design the study as well as to recruit participants for the study. Their response, stories, and willingness to help were validating – a far different feeling than having one's colleagues affirm that one's project is the next logical step.

These three women plus the original woman I had consulted became my community advisory board (CAG), continuing partners in the study even after giving it the intellectual 'green light.' The CAG was the critical component of the study's success because without this group I would have had a paltry understanding of the perspectives with which participants came to the study. Without the CAG as interpreters (figuratively and literally) it would have been very difficult to square my own understanding of the corporeal consequences of FGC with the important meanings that FGC held for them. For example, even in a culture that decried the tradition (Canada), many women still felt it carried social capital. As well, all felt it made them more beautiful. However, they were also curious as to what it was like for uncircumcised women. One member of the CAG in a joking moment even told me that I was not very generous and why wouldn't I lend her my clitoris for a few weeks?

Choose methods that adequately reflect the intricacies of the question: Since at the time I began there was no physiological literature indicating that the CNS of women with FGC might be affected, it seemed to me that the first step was to demonstrate that there might be changes. I set out to gain by ***external*** methods whatever evidence I could that the CNS might be affected.

But how, *from the outside*, could I determine that there might be nervous system effects *inside*? Here are some of the ways I thought about:

(1) I could ask participants directly.
(2) I could administer standardized instruments.
(3) I could carry out neurological tests of function or thresholds of sensation.

Given that I was: (1) outside the culture; (2) asking about a tradition that had been portrayed as shameful to discuss; (3) relatively certain from my reading that although there is a word for pain in Somali, it referred to sickness so great that one would be incapacitated; and given that (4) most people feel it is important to convey themselves as healthy, competent, and strong to those in power, I decided to use all three approaches.

One was qualitative from the first-person perspective and would hopefully tell me *what it is like* for them. One was a third-person perspective, quantitative and standardized to reveal a mean across a population – or, *how it appears*. The physiological measure could be either depending on whether it was averaged across a population or compared to the other two accounts of the same person. When used non-quantitatively, the physiological measure could be thought about as allowing the body to speak and as such, was also first person. I hoped that triangulating what

I learned from each approach across individual women would provide insight about the individual repercussions for each participant. This juxtaposition of methods across individuals was the paradigm for the study.[8]

Engage in reciprocity: Every aspect of the study design was reviewed by the CAG, from the issue of pain and referred sensation to all of the instruments – qualitative and quantitative. Some instruments, such as those used to assess sexual trauma, were thrown out (even though grant reviewers asked for them) because the CAG felt that since parents had sacrificed mightily to obtain circumcisions for their daughters and did it out of love, questions suggesting sexual trauma would be offensive to participants. Some instruments were modified because they were too wordy or unintelligible. We spent many sessions going over visual aids that a biomedical illustrator had made in order to have inoffensive images of the body only to throw them out because we were finally informed that, "Somalis like to talk." Others were deemed fine and we went forward. We threw out the idea of having a 'thorough' neurological work-up both because it would add too much time to the quantitative session, already two hours long.

All the chosen approaches were pre-piloted on members of the CAG and modifications made based on their relative failure and success. Through this piloting I decided to throw out the semi-structured interview and substitute a fully qualitative interview because the semi-structured version did not allow women to tell their stories in a way that did justice to the stories themselves. Through this exchange of ideas I also learned that while at the outset I hadn't wanted to pathologize FGC by making the study about pain, what was important to the CAG was for us to focus more on pain than on overall bodily sensation. Because pain is so culturally dependent, it became apparent that it was important to give the body a voice as well and to explore how different narratives about pain aligned.

2.3 The study design

After discussing, testing, and revising instruments with the CAG, I piloted the paradigm on three members of the community. After some further modification I went forward with recruitment and the two sessions, qualitative and quantitative interviews, for fourteen participants.

Each participant was invited to come to one of the GTA community health centers ordinarily providing services to Somali-Canadians. The first session consisted of a qualitative interview in which they were asked to talk about their circumcision, their current daily lives, and in what parts of their bodies they felt pain or pleasure, sensitivity or numbness. They were then invited back for a second session in which they were asked about their medical history, given some questions about pain, and participated in a physical exam for pain of the vulvar region. They could come back for the questionnaires without being physically tested and half the women did. The other half also consented to what is called 'quantitative sensory testing' (QST) of their external vulvar region. The QST made it possible to determine each individual's threshold to pain at four regions of their vulva. We learned some important, and probably generalizable, neuroscience from the study that will take us further in asking deeper questions about how the CNS is affected by other corporeal modifications and plays a role in the embodiment of culture.

Note that from a classic scientific perspective, the study design has two limitations: (1) there is a serious disconnect between the numbers usual for qualitative studies and those required for quantitative study[9] and (2) there was no control group.[10] I dealt with both of these by analyzing all the data as a within subjects design.[11]

2.4 Study findings

My study found that women who have had FGC do have experiences and test results that suggest that the practice does have effects on the nervous system and on the body as a whole. These include: (1) referred sites of pleasure with the breast and neck being the most pleasurable part of the body for many women; (2) regular times of extreme exhaustion – perhaps one might even say, pain – around their periods when they might not be able to pick up their children and/or be in bed for a week; (3) many sites of pain on their bodies – backs, abdomen, and legs – with McGill pain ratings on a scale of 0–10 of five or higher; (4) regions of their vulva with pressure-pain thresholds as low as those of women who avail themselves of vulvar pain clinics. These physiological findings were embedded in the daily lives of the study participants. For example, with these corporeal manifestations women continue to lead extremely busy lives – up at dawn and not in bed until after 11 p.m. They described taking care of their families and often working outside the home. In the face of being acutely aware of their new country's perspective on their bodies and the tradition they embodied, most participants were proud of what they had endured for their culture. Some even wished they could give it to their daughters although they had no intention of doing so. Most also said that they will never forget their circumcision and that it was the most painful experience they have ever had. Being currently citizens of a country in which the medical system was not set up to deliver babies from bodies like theirs, many had faced an ignorant and at best, insensitive, medical system during one of their most vulnerable life moments, highlighting their embodied cultural differences.

When pressed, most describe aches and pains and some, periods of weeks around menses when they were in such pain that they went to bed and it hurt to pick up their children. Like other researchers, we found that Somali women in Diaspora who have FGC have pain-filled narratives (Tiilikkainen 2001; Johansen 2002; Einstein unpublished results). For example, those immigrating to Finland characterize it as painful to wear so many clothes in the winter and to walk on ice (Tiilikainen 2001).[12] However, my study's participants regularly brushed off the importance of their pains and stated that they are in good health and feel that these aches and pains are normal. They did not have an illness identity. It would be difficult to describe any of the fourteen participants as having post-traumatic stress in the sense that while they will always remember the event of FGC, it is not an intrusive memory. Finally, while no one reported having vulvar pain, when I carried out quantitative sensory testing of the vulvar region on a subset of the women, all had regions of the vulva with extremely low pressure-pain thresholds that were commensurate with those of Canadian women who sought medical help specifically for relief of vulvar pain.

Thus, in their physiologies and their attitudes toward them, the participants of my study had embodied their culture.

3   Emergent principles

I found that unlike some studies, this study required constant, reciprocal interaction with participants as well as a constant interrogation of my methods and what I was learning in a more iterative fashion than is standard practice in a scientific experiment. Thus in addition to 'experimental' findings, there were also some research principles that emerged. I suggest that these might be helpful for further pursuit of a 'feminist' neuroscience.

3.1   New approaches can be made out of 'old' methods

I did not set out to develop new methods but because I wanted to know how women with FGC felt both socially and physiologically about their FGC, I had to develop my own approaches to studying it. Since I was triangulating between methods, I also felt strongly that each method should follow the standard in its own field as closely as possible. This required collaboration with experts in those methods from other fields as well as a constant checking of the data to ensure that they were being collected and analyzed in a way commensurate with each methodology. But it also means that one field (i.e. social science) is not subordinated or used in the service of the other (i.e. biological science) and especially, that one isn't privileged over the other. As well it means that one of my collaborators from the social sciences could look at the qualitative data and they would be rich enough for them to write a solely qualitative paper on the results.

Cobbling together methods from the social sciences and the biological sciences was disconcerting for some (i.e. grant reviewers). Because often these methods are viewed as philosophically antithetical – positivist vs. constructivist approaches – and it raised for them concerns about a potential unintelligibility of the results. However, I would argue that neuroscience, especially affective neuroscience, really must ask (however it can) the organisms being studied what it is *like* for them. After all, we are trying to learn something about the experience – which presumably doesn't only take place in the brain, and is textured by context. Even if a third person method (like *in vivo* imaging) reveals a different interpretation than what a participant says *it is like* for them, the discontinuity (or continuity) should be important to our further understanding.

Of practical concern is the question of, "When does one have enough participants?" which is answered differently for the two methodologies. In a quantitative study if the variation is high and the effect small, one would need large numbers of participants. On the other hand, traditionally, when listening closely to themes across individual stories, the numbers can be much lower. Melding these two numerical needs *is* a challenge but one that reveals a deeper understanding of the reasons for variation from a mean. This is especially important to delve into, if science is to tell us something real about biology in all its variation. What seems most revealing is to use a within subject design and compare the different measures across a single person treating each measure as a different perspective on the same question, rendering quantitative methods as qualitative.

There is also the possibility that if melding two diametrically opposed methods takes off, some interested statistician will come along and invent a statistical approach to deal with this.

3.2   The body has no independent parts

Underlying my original research question was the unstated intent to demonstrate how when one part of the body was removed, it affects the entire body via the nervous system.[13]

Since the scientific revolution we have been depending on the model of body as machine with independent parts or systems, to shape experimentation and cure. This has led to some remarkable advances in medicine: women do not have to die in childbirth anymore, if an organ is cancerous, it can be removed to life-saving effect, clogged veins can be reamed out like a sewer line to prevent the death of heart muscle, and hearts, lungs, and kidneys can be replaced to life-gifting effect. In other words, life can be wrested from death in the case of acute corporeal problems (Einstein and Shildrick 2009). But a wrench has been thrown into this 'body as machine' metaphor. After the problem is fixed, other problems pop up. Just like taking one's car into the mechanic; the gearshift is fixed but the air conditioning is damaged in the process. While the patient is saved, other parts of the body are compromised. In the best of cases such as curing a cancer, acute becomes chronic. In the worst of cases, surgery induces other problems such as neuropathic pain or phantom breast after mastectomy (Smith, Bourne, and Squair 1999; Dijkstra, Rietman, and Geertzen 2007); 'occult' incontinence after treatment for pelvic floor prolapse (Reena, Kekre, and Kekre 2007); or depression and cognitive decline after coronary artery bypass surgery, affectionately known as, 'pump head' (Newman et al. 2001).

Because the nervous system is an integrator of and integrated with the entire body and the world, as discussed previously, it is not possible to take it out of any body system's picture. But this is the case for all of what we consider 'discrete' body systems. None of them really are independent of the other; the idea that they are is a fiction that works in the worst-case scenario but it is not a truth to rely on. Freud knew this when he saw other parts of the body being recruited in the service of the emotions or, the nervous system (Taylor 2006). Thus, a practice that affects one part of the body will be owned by the entire body or, embodied through the interconnections of all body systems and the environment.

Many areas of neuroscience are already coming to this conclusion. For example, circadian biology unites nervous, cardiovascular, musculoskeletal, and reproductive systems (Moore 1997). Stress biology unites nervous, endocrine, cardiovascular, and immune systems (McEwen and Seeman 1999). Social contexts and behaviors affect sex steroid hormone expression (van Anders and Watson 2006; van Anders 2010). How can one be damaged, removed, or repaired without affecting all?

We now have corporeal phenomena that are not very well studied by Cartesian, non-contextual approaches of the classic scientific method. For example, we know that the biology of stress is not separable into cause and effect and we have developed theories that call on integrated body systems to explain a reverberating system, e.g. the hypothalamic-pituitary-adrenal (HPA) axis. We know that the mammalian body has biological rhythms and the study of circadian rhythms is an account of the cyclicity of physiological response depending on time of day, light, and dark (Moore 1997). These are only partially understood by the old 'scientific method'/biomedical model.

As well we have conditions not well understood either by the classic biomedical model, which rests on Cartesian separability of body systems. Might another view, one of the body as comprising inseparable systems *whose interactions and reciprocities need to be understood*, be a view that might help us in better treating chronic dis-orders? We need a more fluid and dynamic biomedical research paradigm to add to our research tools, providing more flexibility in gaining an understanding of the corporeal body.

> Feminists have stakes in a successor science project that offers a more adequate, richer, better account of a world, in order to live in it well and in critical, reflexive relation to our own as well as others' practices of domination and the unequal parts of privilege and oppression that make up all positions. (Haraway 1988: 579)

3.3 Corporeal hierarchies of power can be reduced

In the Cartesian model of the human body there has been a noticeable disconnect between the rest of the corporeal body and the brain. On this view, even if mind equals brain and thus, is meat, the brain still sits privileged atop our polarized body with other body systems arrayed like arms, legs, and trunk on a marionette's strings – to be pulled and moved by the brain. Information comes in. The brain processes it. An action is generated and then carried out by the peripheral nervous system. The rest of the body responds. On this view, the brain is the CEO of the body. Perhaps because of this the body itself has not been considered knowledgeable and thus, has not been thought to have its own narrative (Grosz 1994).

I proposed to look at the effect of cutting the genitals on the rest of the body via their connection with the CNS. This led to some interesting conceptual ramifications. First, it meant that *the rest of the body affects the CNS*. While it could be argued that it was in someone's brain to do the circumcision, one important outcome of the circumcision to the peripheral body affected the brain. There does exist strong evidence of this flattening of the hierarchy. For example, amputations lead to a rewiring of neural circuits and the brain's response, which leads to the phantom limb phenomena (Ramachandran and Blakeslee 1998). Further, tumors of the adrenal gland can lead to psychosis by flooding the brain with glucocorticoids (Levenson 2006). The development of the testes leads to the production of androgens and estrogens, which in turn shape the development of the brain *in utero* (Einstein 2007). Further to this point, the brain isn't the only nervous system the body has. Other nervous systems are hard at work interacting and being affected by the rest of the body. The spinal circuits and the peripheral nervous system – nerves, receptors, and far-flung neurons – as in the retina, dorsal column nuclei and enteric nervous system – all contribute to what the cerebral cortex 'knows.'

This underscores the point that body, brain, and society are in a reciprocal relationship mutually affecting each other. Activity in the world affects the body and these effects may or may not make their way to the brain but they still instantiate themselves in response, memory, language, and thought. Literally then, *the world writes on the whole body*. The Cartesian model of an unknowing and inchoate body with the brain in charge deflates.

In addition, I found that when asked, the body told us something different than the narrative produced by the brain. Women did not report genital pain but their genitals responded as if in pain. This says to me that the parts of the body other than the brain have knowledge and when given the opportunity, will speak.

3.4   Sexed bodies can be studied without essentializing reproduction

As a biologist, I believe that the body is sexed. There is a biological pathway to sexual differentiation and while it does not always produce idealized female and male bodies (Fausto-Sterling 2000b), it does play a role in establishing nervous system circuits involved (and not involved) in reproduction and shapes other tissues such as bone, heart, muscle, and immune response (Einstein 2007). Taken together these differences lead to overlapping bimodal distributions of phenotype. Societies tend to push the means of these bimodal curves as 'the normal' and disguise the variation but while the notion of sex may well be socially constructed (Fausto-Sterling 2000b; Hird 2004) it has biological manifestations that, in themselves, have wide-ranging consequences for the organism.

As a feminist, I have a strong reaction to the phenotypic differences as constituting 'essential' differences between female and male and have tried to move the idea of women's health away from these as the focus (Einstein and Shildrick 2009). However, in the project under discussion, I was asking questions about bodies that I assumed to be the bodies of women and, at first glance my question seemed placed at the essentialist core – the clitoris, ovaries, uterus, and breasts with the question redefined through the reproductive system's connections to the nervous system.[14] Via these connections the genitals are no longer the focus of the question – not essential – to the way the body ultimately feels or to the subjectivity of the person.

This actually became an advantage that was profound for the CAG and the project participants because for such a long time the gaze has been on their genitals alone – not just for women with FGC, but for women in general. The move to link the genitals with the CNS took the genital experience and moved it into the brain. In fact, I was able to start out the conversation with each woman by saying that I was not interested in her genitals; I was interested in her brain. Redirecting the questions from the genitals – a site of silence in cultures practicing FGC – to the brain – a site not previously considered, but privileged in the popular imaginary allowed participants to talk about their circumcision as well as placing the topic in what for them was a respectful space. It means that when I go back to the community to tell them about my findings, I will not be talking about 'what FGC did to their genitals and reproductive health' but about effects on the CNS, how it can change and that sometimes that change leads to pain or hypersensitivity. This is a completely different conversation than has been previously had about FGC. It encompasses the whole body and, as such, women's whole lives.

3.5 Biological diversity within categories can be revealed

Myra Hird rightly points to a disjunction between the intraspecies differences humans delight in studying in non-human animals and the tight rein kept on diversity among humans, sexual and otherwise (Hird 2004). Patricia Gowaty cites evolutionary biology as a space in which human diversity *should* be studied:

> The evolutionist in me argues with essentialist feminists and likewise with some evolutionary biologists that attention to fixed, invariant, and universal differences among women and men is likely to miss the mark most of the time... First, the diversity and variation among individuals is one of the most impressive of human 'universals,' and

anyone seeking a unified theory of human nature must account for the impressive variation among, between, and within individuals. (Gowaty 1997: 6–7)

Anne Fausto-Sterling has neatly described how variations in sunlight produce diverse musculoskeletal systems (Fausto-Sterling 2003, 2008). Donna Mergler has shown how location and diet influence cognitions (Mergler 2002).

Linda McDowell suggests that Harding's feminist standpoint theory is a place from which to start understanding difference.

> She [Harding] sets out the arguments for the construction of knowledge that recognizes differences between women – on the basis of class, age, ethnicity, sexuality and culture – in an epistemology of 'permanent partiality'. This knowledge is thus forced to grapple with questions of difference. (McDowell 1992: 412)

This is especially the case for the nervous system for which the old notion of the brain as fixed and static is no longer a tenable explanation for the observable plasticity of neural structures over a lifetime. Neural circuits change depending on our particular experience in the world. We really are all different. In fact what has served as the normative ideal is only imagined – constructed if you will. In order to fully understand human biology we will have to start from the assumption that we are all different, and then determine how much of a difference makes a difference for a given body. A biology of human diversities will underscore the full range of human kinds and how normative standards of corporeality does a disservice to all bodies.

3.6   Neuroscience can be situated

As a practicing scientist, I think of 'situatedness' much like Grosz's Moebius strip with an inside and an outside and seamless transition into the other (Grosz 1994). There is my particular place as female, Caucasian, Jew, American, professor, neuroscientist, aging, partner, daughter, mother, with all my politics, etc. There are the particularities of the population that I am studying: female, African, Muslim, Somali-Canadian, once doctors or professors or students, under 45 years, partner, sister, mother, with all their politics, etc. Harding's 'robust reflexivity' forces me to think of all these with their diversion and intersections. Reflexivity forces me to think about how all of these interact to affect the study.[15]

Situating the participants: Certainly in studying people, if one acknowledges contextual influences, the response to stimuli and measurable behaviors of experimental participants must be influenced by a participant's interaction with the investigator and her feelings about being investigated. To not acknowledge this is to turn a blind eye to the obvious and therefore to ignore an important scientific pitfall. For example, the famous memory patient, Henry M., performed much better on language tasks when studied in a nursing home – his own environment – than he did when taken out of his context and studied in a psychology lab (Skotko, Andrews, and Einstein 2005). Considering how a participant might be responding to the environment and factoring this into any interpretation of findings is a kind of second-person perspective, and keeping this in mind was important. For example, anyone interacting with participants was made aware of modesty requirements for Somali women's dress. I always wore long sleeves and a long skirt or slacks when interviewing. Individual women felt differently about having another member of the Somali community present during either of the interviews, and participants always had the option of having a Somali interpreter present or not, or, for the second interview, a Somali health care worker present or not. The qualitative interviews were carried out in an informal setting, around a small table with fruit and tea. Quantitative interviews and testing were administered in a small examination room, which was part of the same health care center. As has been thoroughly considered by the qualitative interviewing literature, I can only assume that these environments and people made a difference to comfort level and hence responses of each participant (Pini 2005; Manderson, Bennett, and Andajani-Sutjahjo 2006; Broom, Hand, and Tovey 2009).

In a study about embodiment and corporeality, there is also no doubt that the body's physiology comes to the study from a particular place which, in turn, shapes its response to the measure. Thus, historically situating participants is also important. For example, most of the participants in our study were from wealthy, educated families in Somalia. They came to Canada as part of the first immigration in the late 1980s/early 1990s. Most were abroad visiting, studying, or working when the war broke out and they simply never went home. They are healthy, engaged, energetic women with a particular sense of their place in the world. This is a very different body than those of lesser socioeconomic status, less schooling, and less privilege who had to continue to live in war-torn Somalia and who then left only to end up in refugee camps in Tanzania with eventual immigration to North America. And the meanings of their circumcision and the body on which it is played out are likely very different. We will only know this when we compare Somali women in all their differences of class, country, or city location when they had their circumcision, when and how they immigrated, whether they are being interviewed in Diaspora or their natal country.

There is also the very real question of geographic situation: how this study would go if it were carried out in Somalia with participating women being still in a country in which their FGC is validated – indeed, honored. Would they have pain? This is important to test for any further validity of the research findings. Certainly any claims will have to be located to Somali women between the ages of 18 and 45 who live in the Greater Toronto Area. Even standard neuroscientific methodologies demonstrate the necessity of restricting one's claims. Look at any paper using functional magnetic resonance imaging to explore a brain response to stimulation and if individual scans are figured one sees a plethora of data showing successful and functional brain individualities. As Michael Gazzaniga pointed out in one of his series of three distinguished lectures at Harvard University, "Feeling Free in a Mechanistic World: Where the Brain Meets the Law" (22 April 2010), no normative standard fit for legal evidence is really possible from a brain scan since there is so much variation between human brains.

Thus, in spite of the fact that we are all women immigrants to Canada and most have borne children, there was very little overlap in our situatedness. For example, the group of women I interviewed had a major change in socioeconomic and social status when they immigrated; I did not. Furthermore, when my body was encountered by the biomedical system, it was what was expected. It was very clear in our interactions that I was privileged and that whereas they had once been, they were aware that in the world's view they were not. As one of the women in my group told me, "Halima's father was the wealthiest man in Mogadishu." Or, another woman told me, "I was the first woman medical student at the University; now we are nothing." Or as another woman essentially told a Norwegian researcher, "We didn't know we were black until we came to Norway" (Johansen 2002).

With all of this in mind, I also chose to situate the participants as colleagues. I felt that they had all the knowledge about their circumcision, their histories, and their bodies and I was very grateful that they were committed to helping those without FGC to learn something generalizable from women with FGC. From my perspective, we were situated as equal partners in the study – in fact, I felt they held most of the power – and the study would have failed without this assumption. In this sense

I felt that we were all neuroscientists working on this project. We just had different knowledges about the nervous system with theirs being an invaluable first-person account.

Situating the researcher: With respect to Sandra Harding's call for a science with 'robust reflexivity,' it was important to the study that I be reflexive about the study, its effects on me, and its potential affects on the participants. To quote Elizabeth Grosz (1994):

> the conventional assumption that the researcher is a disembodied, rational, sexually indifferent subject – a mind unlocated in space, time or constitutive interrelationships with others, is a status normally attributed only to angels. (Grosz 1994: 199)

Thus, for me to walk in to the next interview without acknowledging the study's effects on me would have led to a muddying of the interactions. There were many days when I returned from the community health center and just sat in a chair and stared at the wall; I was so drained. The power of the women's stories, their pride, sorrows, and struggles made me feel so privileged and just plain lucky in my life. While I was able to overcome my initial reactions to the descriptions of the practice of FGC by coming to understand how much it meant to the women and their culture, it still left me deeply affected and was disturbing to my own sexual life.

Situating the study: I also needed to be reflexive about my expectations for the study and question many of my assumptions about what a 'scientific' study *should* be like. This led to many encounters with my expectations, my culture, and my beliefs about what is scientific. As McDowell states as she contemplates a feminist geography:

> there has been a challenge to the argument in conventional methods manuals that involvement with and participation in the lives of those who are being investigated 'biases' the results. In the collection of 'data', for example, it is not assumed that the researcher is objective or value-free, nor is she assumed to stay 'at a distance' from her subjects. As women interviewing women, commonalities of experience should be recognized and become part of a mutual exchange of views. (McDowell 1992: 405)

In order to stay 'true' to the experience of my participants, I had to question my own sense of what a 'clinical' study was about. How could I – given my strengths and weaknesses – make the study work? And I believe that with the particular participants I involved, it would have been extremely disrespectful, and downright rude, to treat them like observable objects. There could be no air of objectification about the study. For example, any belief that each participant came in as unknowledgeable as the last about the study had to be altered. In fact realizing that the participants were talking about the study amongst themselves was quite a moment (we were in a large, metropolitan center after all, not a village) – at which point I had to turn the surprise back on myself and wonder what kind of a society I lived in that I could expect to recruit participants from the public and depend on them *not* talking to each other. The study had to work with this conversation between participants.

Situating what is important to participants: Asking participants what matters to them is both a source of agency and a way of uncovering important scientific ignorance that is a result of the assumptions and prejudices of biomedicine. When carrying out a study of reproductive health in Lebanese women living in three different disadvantaged Beirut neighborhoods, the researchers asked participants to rank their health concerns. Participants ranked musculoskeletal health as their number one concern; mental health as number two; and reproductive health (the focus of the study) as number nine (Zurayk et al. 2007). I honestly do not believe I could have recruited anyone to another reproductive health study about women with FGC. It was important to the success of recruitment to study what was germane to the participants. By trying to understand something about the CNS from the outside and, therefore, pain, I learned that pain was both an unspoken problem for Somali women in Toronto and something that they wanted to understand. Therefore, they said to me that this study, unlike others in which they had participated, would 'go somewhere' because it was about *their* pain.

All of this had to be thought about, tacitly acknowledged, and negotiated in both the qualitative interview and the physical exam otherwise we would not have been able to even gather data.

4   Guideposts to feminist neuroscience practice

Based on these emergent principles, and without hardening any practices in stone, I would like to suggest some guideposts to practice that in concert might add up to a feminist neuroscience. In doing so I prefer to not refer to these guideposts collectively as a 'gender analysis' because that is large and all-encompassing as well as often used *in contrast* to biology. Instead, I choose to just lay out the details of the approach that one might or might not use for a given question. These are not hard and fast rules – neither is this a complete list. Rather what follows are things to think about as one asks questions and designs experiments. Hopefully, these guideposts can be applied to standard questions to yield new answers, as well as lead to novel questions. What is key is a spirit of commitment to the question, itself, as well as the opportunity to reveal the ignorance and presuppositions embedded in current neuroscientific practice.

- Ask a question about which you are genuinely curious about a problem to which you are genuinely committed.[16]
- Consider it in all its contexts – geography, culture, space, time, and individual biologies.
- Situate yourself and your prejudices with respect to the study.
- Clarify, as best you can, the power issues in your paradigm; try to flatten hierarchies of power.[17]
- Ask the question from multiple perspectives:
  (1) First person – find out how the participant feels about the question; what is it like for them?
  (2) Second person – how does the environment in which the question is being asked and the person asking, affect the participant's account?
  (3) Third person – how do standardized measurements and physiological responses relate to what the participant is saying – how does it appear?
- Be reflexive – how is who you are and what you are doing part of the experiment? Can you remove it or are your own particularities important to maintain? How are you projecting your own prejudices and human condition on the experimental design, environment, and interpretation?
- Consider the 'subject' of your experiment an active partner – explore their agency; marvel at their participation; ask them what they care about.
- Practice reciprocity; bear in mind that the system under study – human or non-human – will have conditions under which it will flourish and conditions under which its growth will be restricted. Giving back by ensuring that it will flourish is opening the doors to more robust response.
- Restrict claims – situated biologies are particular to their context including: culture, geography, experience, sex, gender, etc. On the other hand, don't loose sight of the possibility of learning something general from the particular.

- Display individual data points as well as statistical differences of the mean in order to do justice to individuals and their particular variations.
- Eschew the language of normativity and assume plurality.

5   Discussion

Upon reviewing earlier approaches to feminist science I believe my approach was very much in the same spirit. First, I tried to redress a wrong born of a Cartesian vision of the body comprised of separable parts. I questioned whether the Cartesian model of the separation of body and mind, which undergirds modern biomedicine, is in fact an adequate place to start in describing the biologies of women.

I selected my research project on substantive grounds with my "Personal interests and skills meld[ing], often mysteriously, with collective feminist concerns to determine a particular topic of research" (Stacey 1988: 21). This, in turn, "guided the research methods employed in its service" (Stacey 1988: 21). In doing so I used Harding's 'radical reflexivity' – at least, radical for a neuroscientist. Her admonition was, in fact, critical to the success of the study:

> A third feature contributing to the power of feminist research is the emerging practice of insisting that the researcher be placed in the same critical plane as the overt subject matter, thereby recovering for scrutiny in the results of research the entire research process. That is, the class, race, culture and gender assumptions, beliefs and behaviors of the researcher her/himself must be placed within the frame of the picture that she/he paints. (Harding 1987: 29)

In doing so I tried to reduce power structures between researcher and participant by taking simultaneously the views that: (a) we all had important knowledges for the project and (b) I was being studied as well – if not by the participants, then certainly by myself. Finally, I very much tried to apply a scientific rigor while at the same time ascertaining that the project and the methods were meaningful to those being studied. In a sense, *relational*, in the way that Evelyn Fox Keller described Barbara McClintock studying corn genetics (Keller 1983).

In fact, the principles that emerged from my study described earlier are, with the order reversed slightly, very reminiscent of Longino's feminist scientific virtues: *empirical adequacy, novelty, ontological heterogeneity, mutuality of interaction, applicability to current human needs, and diffusion of power* (Longino 1996).

As is apparent, developing feminist approaches to neuroscience must necessarily be a work in progress. Both we, as scientists, and our subject, the nervous system, are in flux within our reciprocal relationship. As we take a feminist approach to experimental design and interpretation, we change what we know. Which, in turn, changes the types of question we can ask. Some of the project might even look like 'neuroscience as usual' because there are many aspects of the nervous system and neurobiological research that are aligned with paradigms of feminist inquiry such as the importance of experience in shaping individual behavior; the situatedness of each nervous system yielding a difference that comes from each lived life.[18] The key is to explicitly carry out these principles in the (1) question; (2) design; (3) methods; and (4) interpretation of the experiment/project.

A particular place that neuroscientists using feminist approaches can make a huge contribution to neuroscience is to identify areas of ignorance. Our commitment to understanding non-normative biologies – for example, the bodies of women – is a place of novelty. As Ruth Hubbard pointed out:

> Feminists are in a good position to analyze what is wrong with science as a social institution and with the knowledge it produces. We recognize that science was begun, and has been practiced, primarily by men from the educated upper classes in Europe and the United States and that it therefore embodies their values and views about how the natural world functions and should function. (Hubbard 1992: 16)

This is actually a tremendous area of strength for neuroscience in general because instead of being the kind of critique that painstakingly reveals the next small gap in 'the literature' it takes us leapfrogging over whole topics to reveal large swaths of ignorance. It opens the doors of real discovery about that which is unknown, ignored, or silenced. As Harding points out:

> Bodies of systematic ignorance always develop alongside bodies of systematic knowledge, since asking one kind of question about natural or social relations can cognitively, technically, or simply pragmatically preclude at that time and place asking certain other kinds of questions. (Harding 2001: 516)

The politics of feminist approaches allows a questioning of *why we do not know something* (Harding 2006; Tuana 2006). This question can serve as an important source of novel questions and innovative perspectives on our results. Feminist scientists armed with the epistemics of gender theory were able to clearly see that the sex determination story made the Y-chromosome the main actor. Why was there no role for the X-chromosome? Could the SRY gene explain all variations of sexual differentiation (Richardson 2008)? Once this lacuna of ignorance was identified, studies assuming female agency in sexual differentiation revealed a number of possible genetic pathways important for XX differentiation (Hughes 2001). This, then, allows feminist scientists to adopt methods and combinations of methods that are in line with their values as feminists (McDowell 1992).

In my own study, as I was developing hypotheses for possible neurobiological outcomes of FGC, one that seemed obvious (previously discussed) was phantom clitoris. According to Ramachandran and Blakeslee (1998), the phantom would be activated with stimulation of the body region whose representation in the brain lies near the representation of the clitoris. In trying to determine which body region is represented next to the clitoris, it becomes apparent that no one has actually mapped female body regions to their representative neurons in the brain, as Wilder Penfield did for the male when he produced the 'homunculus' (Einstein 2008; DiNoto et al. 2012).[19] This is an astonishing area of ignorance to most neuroscientists when it is pointed out to them. It has repercussions for developing therapeutics for women with chronic pain after any surgery, as well as leaving empty an entire understanding of a mechanism underlying changes in the sense of one's body during menstruation, menopause, and pregnancy. Explicitly studying the plasticity of female somatosensory cortex due to steroid hormones most certainly will contribute to our understanding of plasticity of the male brain, which is also affected by hormonal changes though perhaps not as robustly, or with the same pattern (Becker et al. 2005).

Finally, by engaging in questions that interest us and by designing systematic ways of studying complex phenomena, neuroscientists taking feminist approaches may develop entirely new areas of knowledge and methods. The world requires that the particularities of the different sciences must be heeded. It does then seem that even in the philosophy of science where science *qua* science gets studied and confirmed or rejected, positivism, itself, seems no longer to be the epistemological grounding for discovery. In the words of Cordelia Fine:

> present knowledge reevaluates the whole character of past practice [and] there is no saying, in advance, how this will go. (Fine 1986: 149, in Rouse 1998: 106)

6 Conclusion

The time is ripe for renewing the project of feminist science. We have a new crop of students (male and female) who plan to become scientists and who have majored in women's and gender studies, and thus, been exposed to feminist philosophy and critiques. It would be impossible for previous work not to have left its mark on current generations (Bordo 1990). In addition, there are those in this generation who explicitly want to *do* feminist science in neuroscience, immunology, and biophysics. As well, we are currently faced with biological and, more specifically, neuroscientific problems for which the classic biomedical model and a dualist scientific method cannot provide insight: chronic conditions, disabilities, the role of the environment on biology, and the influence of biological cycles on other bodily changes (Einstein and Shildrick 2009). Classic, positivist science devoid of context will only haltingly allow us to understand the biology of the female body during the reproductive years – or any body that is subject to changes over time, place, and circumstances. From the neuroscientific perspective, much about behavior is unintelligible if context is not taken into account. The nervous system is exquisitely sensitive and malleable. For example, even songbirds know what season it is by sensitivity to light and length of day which, once encoded neurally, leads to the production of new neurons in nuclei mediating song production (Alvarez-Buylla and Nottebohm 1988). The sensation of pain is embedded in a context; furthermore, what might be painful to one person is not to another. What might be painful in one cultural milieu or geography might not be painful in another (Melzack and Wall 1996). In humans, which genes are expressed and which are unexpressed may depend on early interactions with others, which has the capacity to lead to neuropsychiatric behaviors in later life that are threatening to life itself (McGowan et al. 2009).

In these important cases, feminist theory can contribute new methods of study, as well as new interpretations. It is no longer a question of "redressing masculinist scholarship" (Stacey 1988); rather, it is a matter of finding solutions to currently insolvable problems. To assume that these feminist approaches are themselves unique to something imagined as 'women's ways of thinking' would be a grave mistake. As Longino points out:

> The problems with this approach are, first, that there's no evidence that women are inclined biologically or culturally to understand the

world in these ways; second, that even if they were, we'd still need an argument that these are traits that ought to be valued in theory construction and assessment; and third, that it creates a need to explain the endorsement of these virtues by non-feminists...if the world is such as to be more adequately understood via theories exhibiting these virtues, then they ought to be promoted as general theoretical virtues and not just as feminist. (Longino 1996: 49)

Can feminist approaches bring us to a different understanding of the natural world – a paradigm shift? I believe they can. But it will require

a doctrine of embodied objectivity that accommodates paradoxical and critical feminist science projects: feminist objectivity means quite simply situated knowledge. (Haraway 1988: 581)

Acknowledgements

Thanks to Lucy Suchman who listened carefully and supported the necessity of bringing qualitative methods into biology; Joy Johnson for pioneering conversations on methods and measures in sex/gender research; Anne Fausto-Sterling for fruitful skepticism on the idea of a feminist neuroscience forcing me to read further and question my own desires; Sari van Anders for being a scientist engaged in the project and her thought-provoking questions on the manuscript; Leeat Granek and Emily Glazer for insightful reading of early drafts; Emily Ngubia Kuria for important comments on the manuscript; and Habiba Adan, Hawa Farah, Maryan Barre, and Kowser Omer-Hashi for partnering with me in research. CIHR-IGH, HCTP grants supported the project.

Notes

1. Richardson (2008) points out that when feminist perspectives are used they have become an important epistemic resource.
2. Human sexual differentiation comprises the biological steps necessary to transform the developing embryo into a female or male phenotype, or body. This includes the formation of internal and external genitalia as well as laying the endocrinological and neurological scaffolding for reproductive behavior (Einstein 2007; Fausto-Sterling 2000b).
3. For details on the neuroscience on this see Einstein (2008). Instantiation involves affecting a change in a grouping of spinal cord neurons that innervate the muscles of the perineum that are interestingly dimorphic in rodents but not so different between female and male humans.
4. Manderson (2004) reports that de-infibulated women find the sound of their pee to be foreign and strange.

5. This has never been measured but in two personal conversations, one with Janice Boddy and another with Comfort Momoh – both well-steeped in the knowledge of women with FGC – they both report that women with FGC have a special walk.

6. However, this also made the determination of a control group impossible.

7. Of course as I encountered the stories of these Somali women I learned that cultural homogeneity is a myth.

8. There are numerous models on how to design mixed methods research (e.g. Morgan 1998; Morse and Niehaus 2007; Medlinger and Cwikel 2008; Creswell 2009). However, few if any combine physiological measures with qualitative interviewing and none are explicitly feminist with the possible exception of Medlinger and Cwikel (2008). This is discussed at greater length in a manuscript in preparation: Glazer et al.: "Women's Health and Cultural Embodiment: Intersecting Methods to Understand Pain in Somali-Canadian Women with Female Genital Circumcision/Cutting."

9. At the time of writing the qualitative results are still being analyzed and the quantitative results on pain being written up. I am not sure the quantitative study will be accepted for publication with this few participants. The quantitative data will be reported for each person and used as preliminary data for further physiological studies as well as information sessions for the community.

10. I believe this is justified because there really is no control group possible. There are scarcely any Somali women who have immigrated to Canada who do not have FGC. There are Somali women born in Canada who do not have FGC but they have been raised in a non-African culture. There are a few Somali women in Somalia without FGC but they live in a culture with very different expectations about the tradition than the countries to which their countrywomen have immigrated. I decided that the triangulation of the methods would serve as an internal control for each participant.

11. I am hoping that in the future, based on the findings gleaned from these limited numbers, I will be able to apply the QST and further neurological examination to a larger population and include uncircumcised women as well as women with FGC.

12. However, we wonder: Is walking painful in their natal countries where the climate is warm, clothes are light and loose, families are there to help with life, and having FGC is a point of pride and not shame?

13. I chose the nervous system as the unifier because I am a neuroscientist. If I were a cardiologist, I would have chosen the cardiovascular system – an immunologist, the immune system.

14. In a broad sense they are, indeed, part of the nervous system because they have transducers of external information, nerve–muscle connections, and representation in the somatosensory regions of the brain.

15. Even if one doesn't believe they are in the picture, reflexivity could be defined as simply as asking oneself what one expects from the experiment or why one is doing the experiment (both worthwhile intellectual pursuits). It could be carried further by asking even of animal models, "What human attributes am I imposing on these non-human animals?"

16. Harding underscores the importance of one's own experience in formulating and interpreting a question: "Women's [and men's] perspective on our

own experiences provide important empirical and theoretical resources for feminist research. Within various different feminist theoretical frameworks, they generate research problems and the hypotheses and concepts that guide research. They also serve as a resource for the design of research projects, the collection and interpretation of data, and the construction of evidence" (Harding 1987: 28).

17. These bullets considered together represent Haraway's "feminist versions of objectivity" (p. 190) according to McDowell (1992). They include "limited and situated knowledges, knowledges that are explicit about their positioning, sensitive to the structures of power that construct these multiple positions and committed to making visible the claims of the less powerful" (McDowell 1992: 413).

18. Consider London taxicab drivers who have larger gray matter volumes of posterior hippocampus (brain regions that play a role in spatial navigation) than bus drivers. Moreover, the cab drivers' right posterior gray matter volume increases with more navigation experience (Maguire, Woollett, and Spiers 2006).

19. While there is a growing literature on brain regions that light up with genital stimulation and orgasm (Komisaruk and Whipple 2005; Georgiadis 2006), as well as stimulation of the breast (Rothemund et al. 2005): (1) none of these have been mapped together to regions of the brain leaving the female somatosensory cortex a hodge-podge of independent sensory regions; (2) we have no idea how these regions grow or shrink with different stages of the ovarian cycle, delivery, nursing, or excision; (3) we have no idea where the internal portion of the clitoris, the ovaries, and uterus are represented (DiNoto, Newman, and Einstein 2012).

8
Cosmopolitics and the Brain: The Co-Becoming of Practices in Feminism and Neuroscience

Deboleena Roy

Thought is not arborescent, and the brain is not a rooted or ramified matter. What are wrongly called "dendrites" do not assure the connection of neurons in a continuous fabric. The discontinuity between cells, the role of the axons, the functioning the synapses, the existence of synaptic microfissures, the leap each message makes across these fissures, make the brain a multiplicity immersed in its plane of consistency or neuroglia, a whole uncertain, probabilistic system ("the uncertain nervous system"). Many people have a tree growing in their heads, but the brain itself is much more a grass than a tree. (Deleuze and Guattari 1987: 15)

1 From treachery to laughter

While teaching a class on "Sex, Gender and the Brain," or giving a presentation on feminism and neuroscience, I often begin my lectures by using a slide with which I admit to having a tenuous but productive relationship. The power point slide, which I put together in a rather obvious cut and paste aesthetic, is of an fMRI image taken from a study on gender differences in the brain. Below the fMRI image of the brain, I have inserted the words *"This is not a brain,"* in a dark brown cursive font and in clear imitation of Rene Magritte's phrase *"Ceci n'est pas une pipe"* from his painting *The Treachery of Images.*[1] When I first put the slide together a few years back, it was in the vein of providing some comic relief at the beginning of a talk, as many academics like to do, but I also intended to use the image as a launching pad for a more critical discussion at the intersection of neuroscience and feminist theory. More recently, I have turned to using the slide as an entryway into discussions around the politics of representation and questions of materiality. I continue to use the slide but I must admit, I find myself wondering what other acts of treachery this image may be evoking to unsuspecting audiences, intentionally or unintentionally on my part. I also wonder how I can move from what may begin initially as an acknowledgment of betrayals and mistrust between the humanities and sciences to a place where the irony of this slide can be shifted slightly and turned into a moment of shared laughter or humor that produces the possibility for new interdisciplinary conversations and questions regarding the matter and materiality of the brain.

As a feminist science studies scholar trained in neuroscience and molecular biology, housed primarily in Women's Studies departments, and more recently thankful for a position that was created through a joint neuroscience and humanities initiative, most of what I do on a daily basis involves the facilitation of interdisciplinary discussions. This work is undoubtedly challenging and extremely rewarding. But it would be entirely misleading on my part if I didn't reveal the fact that I frequently leave these encounters with a nagging feeling that much of what I have tried to say or do has been lost in translation. I think most scholars working at the intersection of traditionally disparate fields would say the same thing, or at least sympathize with this claim. Having done this for a few years now, however, I am more comfortable with, or perhaps have grown more accustomed to, the sum of these losses. In fact, I have come to see them as being generative in some other sense, perhaps more in line with what the philosopher of science Isabelle Stengers would refer to as a necessary consequence resulting from the attempt to create "moments of shared perplexity" (Stengers 2000a) between neuroscience and feminist scholarship. What I am less comfortable with, and what I think is partly the motivation for writing this piece, is the realization that before these generative losses ever even begin to surface, I often find myself entering into these interdisciplinary conversations between the neurosciences and feminism with a looming sense of treachery or betrayal on my part, usually played out in two distinct forms. Truth is, I know that I am up to no good, but as a career "insider-outsider" and a dedicated viral activist, my hope is that these acts of treachery will in fact infect our thinking and play a crucial role not by simply building a unified bridge between "two cultures," but rather by creating an immanent mode of engagement between the neurosciences and feminism.

To begin with, given my background and the nature of my joint appointment, I am often called on to give talks to neuroscience audiences who are interested in, or are open to, discussing current neuroscientific research findings in the context of contemporary issues of culture, society or ethics. I know now, however, in a manner that has become all too predictable, that when I enter a room full of neuroscientists or neuroscientists in training, this audience almost certainly assumes that what I am going to talk about involves some aspect of the 'female brain.' Their expectations of my expertise in this area usually range somewhere between seeing me as a proponent of the study of sex-based or gender-based differences (the distinction is often unclear) in the brain, to seeing me as perhaps somewhat of an historian of science. I am expected to recount all the challenges that women have faced in the past and continue to face as female research subjects who have been left out of neuroscience research either as clinical subjects, or as career scientists whose lives and professional accomplishments are best understood and organized through some kind of pipeline metaphor. As important as these issues are, they are not entirely aligned with the intersections of feminist theory and neuroscience that I find most useful or interesting. My representations of the intersections of these fields therefore invariably turn out not to match these audience preconceptions. I know going in that I will not properly represent the formula of [brain] + [women]. This is the first type of treachery or betrayal on my part and in these particular scenarios, I usually turn to my *"This is not a brain"* slide to draw closer attention to the politics of meaning-making. If my presentation turns to the discussion of behavioral biology or imaging technologies such as fMRIs, as it often does, I try to use this slide to draw attention to the meaning-making practices in neuroscience that move us – quite easily I might add – from depictions of structure to interpretations of function. I then suggest that we may need to consider the broader implications of these practices.

On the other hand, I am also regularly called upon by women's studies audiences to deliver an insider's report on the status of research and scientific practices in the neurosciences. On many of these occasions I find that the expectations held by these particular audiences involves showcasing the most problematic features of current developments in neuroscience research today, such as those theories of difference promulgated by the recent popularity of studies attempting to describe the 'female brain.' These audiences have come to expect a thorough discussion of the ontological, epistemological, and methodological assumptions embedded within neuroscientific research. Admittedly, my own interests at the intersections of feminist theory and neuroscience do lie more closely along these lines. However, even though there is generally a genuine interest in the direction and details of these new neurotechnologies and research developments, the questions and comments following many of these talks hover somewhere between developing more critiques of the biologically deterministic aspects of the research, to conducting even closer analyzes of the language and paradigms of neuroscience in order to expose their embedded gendered biases. With some of these audiences, I find myself wanting to steer away from those habits of repetitive and extended critique that can ultimately end up with a dismissal of the biology and all scientific evidence of biological difference. Indeed, on these occasions, I return to my *"This is not a brain"* slide and instead try to call attention to the subtleties of the scientific practices of neuroscience research. At times, I may even defend some of the scientific practices of neuroscience as valid ways of extending our reach towards biological matter that need not remain perpetually elusive. The slide then serves to highlight the idea of how in fact *"This could be a brain,"* or at least a brain that we can come to know. This approach and orientation can throw off some of my feminist audiences.[2] My voice does not properly resonate with the familiar tones of feminist critiques of biology, and therein lies the second type of treachery.

2   From two cultures to an ecology of practices

These curious acts of treachery carried out on my part are not simply due to the legacy left behind by the science wars or a result of the vast distance and lack of a common language between the humanities and the sciences. They go beyond C. P. Snow's message in *The Two Cultures* (1998) that educational systems have fallen short and have failed to train our students to become proficient in both the sciences and humanities. They represent, I think, my desire to work within an ethical field of resistance, or what the political philosopher Brian Massumi (drawing on the work of Felix Guattari), has called a "political ecology" (2002: 255). A political ecology encourages us to find ways of coming together despite our disciplinary differences. As Massumi states:

> The "object" of political ecology is the coming-together or belonging-together of processually unique and divergent forms of life. Its "object" is symbiosis, along the full length of the nature–culture continuum. (2002: 255)

My intentions are to expose the creativity of distinct practices and to produce new zones of proximity between feminism and the neurosciences through the recognition of these practices. However, these intentions also go beyond a hope of learning how to recognize and then simply tolerate the differences between these different sets of practices. In describing her approach to developing a political ecology, which she refers to as an "ecology of practices," Stengers (2000a, 2000b, 2005) describes her own efforts to reengage with physics in a way that does not simply attempt to tolerate the scientists or scientific practices of that field. In her article "Introductory Notes on an Ecology of Practices" (2005), Stengers enters into conversation with the work of Massumi. In agreement with Massumi's thoughts on developing a political ecology, Stengers argues that she is interested in developing her ecology of practices as a "social technology of belonging" that assumes "coexistence and co-becoming as the habitat of practices" (Stengers 2005: 183). While trying to reengage with physicists who during the science wars were told by the social constructivists that, "physics is a social practice like any other" (2005: 184), Stengers states

> This is how I produced what I would call my first step towards an ecology of practice, the demand that no practice be defined as 'like any other,' just as no living species is like any other. Approaching a practice then means approaching it as it diverges, that is, feeling its borders, experimenting with the questions which practitioners may accept as relevant, even if they are not their own questions, rather than posing insulting questions that would lead them to mobilize and transform the border into a defence against their outside. (2005: 184)

Stengers describes her ecology of practices as a "tool for thinking through what is happening" (2005: 185) and considering other ways of knowing without falling into the easy habit of thinking we already know what is going on and already have a clear understanding of what is wrong with a disciplinary approach that is not our own.

It is my impression that another important element of Stengers' ecology of practices involves an active monitoring of our tendency to pass judgments. If we proceed in our interdisciplinary engagements with preconceived assessments of what the practices of another discipline are, and how they are constituted, we will likely be unable to see anything differently. Stengers suggests that:

> An ecology of practices does not have any ambition to describe practices 'as they are'; it resists the master word of a progress that would justify their destruction. It aims at the construction of new 'practical identities' for practices, that is, new possibilities for them to be

present, or in other words to connect. It thus does not approach practices as they are – physics as we know it, for instance – but as they may
become ... [W]e do not know what a practice is able to become; what we
know instead is that the very way we define, or address, a practice is
part of the surroundings which produces its ethos. (2005: 186–187)

It may have to do with the fact that I have trained myself as an interdisciplinary scholar and hold a joint appointment across the 'two cultures,' but it is absolutely the case that I would not want to see either
of my scholarly interests and affiliations being dismissed as incorrect,
irrelevant or just like any other. Stengers' ecology of practices moves
my work beyond just knowing the different disciplines and tolerating
what I see as their shortcomings, to a new way of thinking about the
brain for instance, as a shared political project between neuroscience
and feminism. This approach of opening ourselves up to new possibilities of engagement, I think, also describes a characteristic gesture that
appears in Stengers' concept of cosmopolitics. In her recently translated
book *Cosmopolitics I* (2010), Stengers states:

If learning to think is learning to resist a future that presents itself
as obvious, plausible, and normal, we cannot do so either by evoking
an abstract future, from which everything subject to our disapproval
has been swept aside, or by referring to a distant cause that we could
and should imagine to be free of any compromise. (2010: 10)

In my own training to become proficient in both neuroscience and
feminist scholarship, a training which I might add is always ongoing,
the lesson of resisting a dream of a future where all that I disagree with
goes away, has been a very important one. The work of Isabelle Stengers
has influenced me a great deal in coming to this place in my thinking.
Although the feminist critiques of neuroscience will and must continue,
I now know that a practice-oriented feminist science studies approach
(e.g. Haraway 1991, 1997, 2008; Barad 2003, 2007) requires us to meet
a different kind of challenge, which is to learn to work *with* what may
have been previously dismissed.

3   Working with neuroethics

The field of neuroethics has developed over the past decade mainly in
response to the widespread use of imaging technologies such as positron emission tomography (PET) and functional magnetic resonance

imaging (fMRI) in neuroscience research. Many scholars, including myself, are interested in the development of these neurotechnologies, but are simultaneously concerned with their potential applications toward monitoring and altering brain function. Although some see the field of neuroethics as broadening our understanding of the neural bases for ethical behavior (locating which part of the brain is responsible for making us ethical) (Levy 2007), most neuroethicists are primarily concerned with the societal impacts of these new neurotechnologies. As such, they are actively trying to not only respond to the neurosciences, but to also work with neuroscientists in order to help guide the direction of this research. My own interest in neuroethics lies in including feminist and poststructuralist ethics into these discussions, particularly in those studies that examine the intersections of sex, gender and the brain.

In an article recently published in *The American Journal of Bioethics*, the authors of the brief article entitled "Women's Neuroethics? Why Sex Matters for Neuroethics," announce the need for establishing a "women's neuroethics" (Chalfin, Murphy, and Karkazis 2008). While arguing in favor of increased attention to neuroscientific work on sex differences, they also ask the following questions:

> How ought we disseminate this [neuroscientific] information into a sensitive social environment that has a history of bias and discrimination against women? What are the implications of this work for our understandings of what makes us women and men? (2008: 1)

The authors of this article are concerned about the inclusion and treatment of women as clinical subjects in recent studies using neuroimaging technologies, and rightly so. At some level, however, this concern may easily be reduced to and aligned with other 'add women and stir' projects in science, math, engineering, and technology (STEM) fields. In the case of neuroethics, for some scholars this may translate into arguments for the inclusion of women as test subjects in neuroscience experiments, such that the harm previously incurred when women were excluded from the study of certain diseases and clinical drug trials, is not repeated. This concern is of course valid. However, the authors are also responding to a recent surge in the number of scientific studies that report sex and/or gender differences in the brain compared to the number of studies that report no such differences (Kaiser et al. 2009). Unfortunately, the lack of a sex-based difference is not exciting news. Even though a similarity between male and female brain structure and physiology is in itself interesting to some researchers, for all intents and purposes this result would end up counting as a null result and likely get filed away somewhere in a lab drawer. Findings of similarities between the sexes do not exactly make the morning headlines or the front page of *Science*. So, as in the past, demonstrations of the neurological basis for sex and/or gender differences in the brain appear to have garnered a great deal of attention with the advent of new imaging technologies such as fMRI. The fMRI studies that are most popular for sex/gender differentiated analysis are those that examine for instance cognitive tasks (Bell et al. 2006; Boghi et al. 2006; Schmithorst and Holland 2007), emotional responses (Azim et al. 2005; Takahashi et al. 2006; Koch et al. 2007), and sexual behavior (Hamann et al. 2004; Gizewski et al. 2006; Goldstein et al. 2005). Several previous studies examining 'gender biology' in the brain have also used evolutionary psychology, for instance, to provide invigorated arguments in support of sociobiological theories of difference (Blum 1997; Hines 2004; Brizendine 2006). In fact, a whole field known as gender biology itself has been newly formulated in the last decade (Birmingham 2000; Zhang and Manson 2002; Giardina et al. 2006) and can be further evidenced by the 2007 launch of UCLA's Center for Gender-Based Biology (www.genetics.ucla.edu).

As I have stated before, the inclusion of women in scientific research and clinical trials is absolutely vital. However, the effort to address gender issues or gender disparities in research design has, as many feminists will point out, also unfortunately resulted in invigorated lines of deterministic biological reasoning. While I would support the idea that women should be included in the new neurosciences research, I would also suggest that making an appeal for a 'women's neuroethics' alone may not lead these authors to the answers they seek. It might also be necessary to point out that while there may be some areas of common interest, the call for a 'women's neuroethics' cannot be considered to be the same thing as a call for a *feminist neuroethics*. If the concept of 'gender difference' is to be utilized in the new neurosciences research and discussed in neuroethics circles, it would seem prudent to also include the voices and practices of those scholars who have spent a great deal of time theorizing at the intersections of ethics, gender, and difference. Without the support of decades of feminist interventions in the sciences, including a wealth of scholarship in the areas of feminist philosophy of science, feminist cultural studies of science, feminist critiques of the practices of science and feminist theorizations of gender and difference, the answers to how 'women,' or any other marginalized group for that matter, can be included as subjects in the new neurosciences research, and yet not be discriminated against, will not come easily. An important question to ask then is how did we get to this place where a call for a women's neuroethics is not in conversation with the theories and practices of current feminist scholarship? It is also interesting to note that on the website for the UCLA Center for Gender-Based Biology, not a single women's studies or gender studies scholar or department is listed as an affiliate or partner. There is most certainly something to be said about this apparent lack of practice-sharing.

I do not think that this realization of a lack of co-existence and co-becoming between the neurosciences and feminist theory comes entirely as a surprise. I also don't think that it is due to the fact that scientists are unwilling to bring their research questions into conversation with the humanities, or feminists are unwilling to step into a lab. In fact, if the direction of scholarship in neuroethics can be used as any indication, the invitation for feminists to engage with the new neurosciences research is quite obvious. While discussing the challenges of interpreting neuroimaging data for instance, Judy Illes, a leader in the field of neuroethics and former Director of the Program in Neuroethics at the Stanford Center for Biomedical Ethics, stated that the "interpretation of such findings will necessitate not only traditional bioethical input but also a wider perspective on the construction of scientific knowledge" (Illes and Racine 2005: 5). Knowingly or not, Illes appears to be sending out an open invitation to include the body of work in feminist scholarship that has already answered this call. Feminist science studies has devoted much effort to the reconfiguration of objectivity and to careful articulations of power relations in – as Illes points out – the "construction of scientific knowledge." There is an opportunity here to put feminist theory and practices into action and come into conversation with neuroscientists and neuroethicists who are obviously grappling with fundamental questions of scientific objectivity and the politics of knowledge production. The question is, how shall we proceed and how shall we present ourselves? My interest in these questions admittedly has more to do with exploring ways of bringing the fields of feminist analysis and neuroscience into closer zones of proximity rather than forming one big amalgamated interdisciplinary practice. Following the cues of Stengers' ecology of practices, I am interested in examining how feminist and neuroscientific practices may begin to impinge upon each other. As Stengers explains:

> The problem for each practice is how to foster their own force, make present what causes practitioners to think and feel and act. But it is a problem which may also produce an experimental togetherness among practices, a dynamics of pragmatic learning of what works

and how. This is the kind of active, fostering "milieu" that practices need in order to be able to answer challenges and experiment
changes, that is, to unfold their own force. This is a social technology
any diplomatic practice demands and depends upon. (2005: 195)

Our previous habits would have dictated that the immediate response
to how we can present ourselves and work with these discussions in
neuroethics would be to set forth with a series of tried and trusted feminist critiques of science. We would not necessarily pause to think about
how this practice may present itself or how it 'captures' our intended
audience. This is where I think we can enact a crucial shift in our orientation. To do this, I would suggest that Stengers' concept of cosmopolitics deserves a closer look.

4   Turning towards cosmopolitics

Several science studies scholars including Donna Haraway (2008) and
Bruno Latour (2004b) have used Stengers' concept of cosmopolitics in
order to theorize their own projects and imagine new modes of collaboration with the natural sciences. In my own crude interpretation, cosmopolitics allows us a way to keep reaching out towards the sciences,
after we have carried out our feminist critiques of science. In Deleuzian
terms, one might say that it moves us from the broken record of the
two cultures problem to working with two strata that are oriented in
such a way as to form a plane of consistency where immanent critique
becomes possible (Deleuze and Guattari 1987). In other words, we try
to create a framework for joint inquiry and learn how to ask each other
meaningful questions in a way that does not assume a transcendent
position – either to that which what we wish to know, or to other disciplinary ways of knowing. This reorientation, however, requires that we
make a motion to pause, both in the sciences and the humanities, and
carefully reflect upon our current disciplinary practices and consider
how these practices might be presenting themselves to each other.
In her recent book *When Species Meet* (2008), Haraway for instance calls
upon Stengers' cosmopolitics as a way to approach the world with a
shared appreciation of complexity. She states:

The sense of cosmopolitics I draw from is Isabelle Stengers's. She
invoked Deleuze's idiot, the one who knew how to slow things down,
to stop the rush to consensus or to a new dogmatism or to denuncia-
tion, in order to open up the chance of a common world. Stengers

insists we cannot denounce the world in the name of an ideal world. Idiots know that. For Stengers, the cosmos is the possible unknown constructed by multiple, diverse entities. Full of the promise of articulations that diverse beings might eventually make, the cosmos is the opposite of transcendent peace. (2008: 83)

I like the idea of slowing things down and taking a moment to reflect on our practices before jumping into the familiar and comfortable mode of feminist critique. I am not arguing that there is no longer a need for feminist critiques of neuroscience, but rather that as we design these critiques, we must pause and reflect carefully on the contours that will be left behind post-critique and consider whether any openings will unfold on the surface of our practices so that we may extend their reach toward the sciences. The approach of defense-causing critique has worked as a practice in many important ways, but we must begin to recognize that it has not worked or allowed further movement in others. This admission may perhaps serve to explain why, for instance, we have arrived at a place where we have a call for a women's neuroethics without even a nod to any kind of women's studies scholarship,[3] or, for that matter, a Center for Gender-Based Biology without any apparent affiliation with a gender studies program or scholar.

In her book *Cosmopolitics I* (2010), which was first published in French in 2003 and was recently translated into English, Stengers expands on her use of the term cosmopolitics. She presents it as a means to "consider" (2010: 79) that which is not in our own manner of thinking, and to come to a place where all forms of inquiry and ways of knowing are seen as having a legitimate place in the cosmos. Instead of searching for a distinction between 'truth' and 'fiction,' or science and myth, she implores us to turn towards that unknown space where we stop silencing the questions with which we are unfamiliar or uneasy. As Stengers explains:

I have named this unknown "cosmopolitics." Within the tradition of philosophy the term is Kantian in origin. The *jus cosmopoliticum* is associated by Kant with the project for "perpetual peace" corresponding to a "natural destination of mankind," in the sense of an idea that demands to be constantly pursued rather than a constitutive principle that would turn this destination in to an object of knowledge. The possible unification of all people through certain universal laws involving their possible commerce was for Kant a perspective not devoid of plausibility... Today, we have reason to complicate this point of view. Although the idea of peace among various peoples must have some significance, we need to start not like Kant from promises the West might flatter itself for propagating, but from the price others have paid for this self-definition. It is not so much peace that we have brought to other peoples and ourselves, but a new scope, new methods, and new modalities of warfare. It is, therefore, in contrast to Kant, rather than as a follower, that I borrow the term "cosmopolitics," and this contrast finds its initial expression in the constructivist approach of so-called rational practices. (Stengers 2010: 79–80)

Stengers describes the cosmopolitical space as that which permits an "ecological perspective" (2010: 35) whereby variable practices are not submitted to the pressure of forming a forced consensus but are rather able to combine in a "symbiotic agreement" (2010: 35). The arrangement of this symbiotic agreement is what Stengers refers to as "reciprocal capture" (2010) and can be thought of as the way in which two practices from disparate disciplines or modes of thought, present themselves to one another over a shared object of knowledge. Stengers states for instance:

No unifying body of knowledge will ever demonstrate that the neutrino of physics can coexist with the multiple worlds mobilized by ethnopsychiatry. Nonetheless, such coexistence has a meaning, and it has nothing to do with tolerance or disenchanted skepticism. Such beings can be collectively affirmed in a "cosmopolitical" space where the hopes and doubts and fears and dreams they engender collide and cause them to exist. That is why, through the exploration of knowledge, what I would like to convey to the reader is also a form of ethical experimentation. (2010: vii)

If as feminist scholars we are to take this idea of ethical experimentation seriously, then we must remain open to the idea that two disparate practices, such as feminism and neuroscience, can enter into an arrangement, or reciprocal capture, that in some way is beneficial to both. As Stengers notes:

[W]e can speak of reciprocal capture whenever a *dual* process of identity construction is produced: regardless of the manner, and usually in ways that are completely different, identities that coinvent one another each integrate a reference to the other for their own benefit. In the case of symbiosis, this reference is found to be positive: each of the beings coinvented by the relationship of reciprocal capture has an interest, if it is to continue its existence, in seeing the other maintain its existence. (2010: 36)

The implication of Stengers' cosmopolitics in the space where feminism and neuroscience collide is that it requires us to start thinking about coming to an understanding of the brain in new ways. It entails imagining the brain as an object of joint political value that in turn brings out the value of our own distinct practices. It is a realization that feminism itself takes shape or comes into form upon its very engagement with the brain itself. In fact, both feminism and neuroscience are co-invented by our shared relationship with the brain and with biology. What might an example of this kind of reciprocal capture between feminism and neuroscience look like? While commenting on the impact of new neuroimaging technologies used in some areas of psychology and neuroscience, science studies scholar Anne Beaulieu argues that critics should not dismiss the potential of newer brain mapping techniques so easily. Similar to Stengers in this regard, Beaulieu is interested in turning the critique around and looking for ways in which the complexities of brain mapping can be emphasized and its productive qualities brought to light. Beaulieu states:

> The past decade has seen growing interest in the use of functional brain imaging methods in research ... While these events have been critiqued as reductionist moves, I argue that they can better be characterized as productive processes. Such a characterization makes visible the expansion and reorganization of the object of study and of domains of investigation; it highlights new relations with other disciplines and institutions, and it problematizes the subsequent increased social visibility. (Beaulieu 2003: 561)

Beaulieu goes on to suggest a more reflexive approach for researchers using mapping practices, both in terms of content and context. She recommends a closer examination of what is left out of dominant paradigms of mapping experiments as well as a greater awareness on the researchers' part as to their responsibility as producers of knowledge and their social accountability. These endeavors, she argues, can "lead to a fruitful debate, beyond accusations and denials of biological reductionism" (Beaulieu 2003: 566). This, in my opinion, is a wonderful example of how a productive and "symbiotic agreement" can be imagined between feminism and the neurosciences.

5 Conclusion: capturing the female brain

In her book *The Female Brain* (2006), which was written for a popular science audience and has become a *New York Times* bestseller, Louann Brizendine states:

> Biology does represent the foundation of our personalities and behavioral tendencies. But if in the name of free will – and political correctness – we try to deny the influence of biology on the brain, we begin fighting our own nature. If we acknowledge that our biology is influenced by other factors, including our sex hormones and their flux, we can prevent it from creating a fixed reality by which we are ruled. The brain is nothing if not a talented learning machine. Nothing is fixed. Biology affects but does not lock in our reality. We can alter that reality and use our intelligence and determination both to celebrate and, when necessary, to change the effects of sex hormones on brain structure, behavior, reality, creativity – and destiny. (2006: 6)

Brizendine's book, written from the perspective of a neuropsychiatrist and founder of a Women's and Teen Girls' Mood and Hormone Clinic, promotes many theories that are based on evolutionary psychology. No one, I think, not even feminists, would deny the influence of 'biology' on the brain; however, in the argument put forward in the above quote and also ensconced in her book, Brizendine draws upon the idea of an 'innate' biology. She suggests that if only we can try to understand this biology properly, our knowledge can then be used to modify the brain (hormonally one supposes), control this biology, and then "empower us to better plan our future" (Brizendine 2006: 159). I will be the first to admit that it took a great deal of control of my own biology to sit down and get through Brizendine's book. However, my own gut reactions (irony and sarcasm included) to *The Female Brain* have become an even greater cause for discomfort for me as Stengers' ecology of practices and her concept of cosmopolitics loom large in my theorizations and in my hopes to contribute to moments of shared perplexity between feminism and neuroscience. I know that I would feel entirely at home and in good company were I to add my voice to the critical commentaries on Brizendine's work (Young and Balaban 2006; Fine 2010a), but I am also well aware that the focus of my engagement with this text must proceed in another direction. No one said that working towards "ethical experimentation" or "symbiotic agreement" was going to be easy.

One of the reasons why I think Brizendine's book is troubling for feminist audiences is that it is written in a tone as if rebuking feminism for having *caused* the general lack of understanding and biological research on hormones and their function in the brain. Brizendine traces the lack of biological information on sex differences to the desires for "free will" and "political correctness" that, according to her, mainly came out of the feminist movement in the 1970s, and that she witnessed as an undergraduate student at Berkeley. I have commented elsewhere on the relationship between feminism and biology and the role of earlier feminist critiques of science in the 1970s and 1980s, particularly those made by feminist scientists (Roy 2007), and do not wish to repeat those ideas here. I would like to pause for a moment, however, and suggest that, whether we like it or not, Brizendine is commenting here on the status of a particular moment of reciprocal capture between feminism and the neurosciences. She is giving us her take on how some of the feminist practices that came out of the women's liberation movement of the 1970s presented themselves to some of the neuroscience and endocrinology research practices that were underway at the same time. She is obviously less prepared to consider how those practices in the sciences were presenting themselves to the feminist movement, and why the critiques against biological determinism might have been initiated in the first place. It is this end of the reciprocal capture that has historically gone unexamined, or has self-proclaimed the position of not requiring a closer analysis.

While describing the power that physics has traditionally had through the establishment of "physical laws," Stengers states, "Physics, today, is haunted by laws, and as long as this is so, as long as it presents itself as the science that discovered that nature obeys laws, it will stand as an obstacle to any ecology of practices" (2010: 87). She then extends this argument to the establishment of biological laws in the neurosciences. Stengers states:

> As early as the seventeenth century, when we knew little about the brain and nothing about neurons, Leibniz stated that "mechanical reasons," based on Descartes's figures and movements, would never explain perception. This central thesis of the *Monadology* was repeated over the centuries, while figure and movement were replaced by chemical, neuronal, and synaptic interactions, introducing what was

sometimes a dry brain, a kind of electric calculator, and sometimes a wet brain, primarily hormonal and emotional. This does not mean that we have learned nothing about the biological brain but that whatever neurophysiologists and philosophers have learned, it did not modify the terms of the problem they have always confronted. (2010: 88)

The point that Stengers goes on to make here is that those who would now argue against, or criticize the mechanistic approach to knowing the brain, are up against biological "laws" that have been put in place to describe the brain as being in a "state" (2010: 90). These laws have the "power to provide a goal to scientific research, and already gives 'materialist theoreticians' the right to question the validity of statements that seem to imply a 'mind' irreducible to that state" (2010: 90). Stengers continues:

The reductionists, who, in America, are curiously referred to as "materialists," limit themselves to putting forth faulty syllogisms such as: there is nothing "in" the brain other than physical-chemical processes; physical chemistry defines states and "explains" the behavior of a system based on those states; ... The denial of "mind" by the spokespersons of the unstoppable progress of science always refers to what appears as the crowning achievement of any objective science: characterizing its object in terms of a state, which defines at each instant the interplay of everything that contributes to its behavior. Here, reciprocal capture operates as a matter of right: anyone who speaks in the name of a science, or the possibility of science, designates a reality she considers subject by right to the requirements of the approach for which she has become the spokesperson. (2010: 90–91)

As long as neuroscience presents itself as having the key to unlocking and unveiling the laws that biology and the brain obey, there will indeed be little chance for a symbiotic agreement with feminism. Not all neuroscientists, however, are busy chasing these laws. There are plenty of neuroscientists who would never approach the brain in this way and who have spent their entire careers considering the ontological status of the brain and its neurons in deep and meaningful ways. Even Brizendine in the above quote says that "[t]he brain is nothing if not a talented learning machine" and that "[n]othing is fixed" (2006: 6). I believe feminists and neuroscientists will begin to find each other again through the recognition of these "new materialist ontologies" (Coole and Frost 2010).

To conclude, what I would like to consider and suggest is that we move forward with the problem of "political correctness" raised by Brizendine. I would argue that my project, surprisingly similar to Brizendine's, has also been an attempt to move away from the perils of political correctness. But that is perhaps where the similarity ends. My goal, unlike Brizendine, is not to search for the female brain, the male brain, or the gay brain as such, but rather for what might be called a cosmopolitically correct brain. This would mean searching for those practices in neuoroscience and feminism that can come together to form a plane of consistency. My own interests in neuroplasticity and gender performativity for instance have opened up the possibility of one such shared project with a colleague in the neurosciences (Parvisi and Roy 2011). I think that feminists and neuroscientists have always had, and will continue to have, the capability of fostering a milieu of joint inquiry if they can learn to recognize and appreciate each other's efforts in coming to know the brain. As the new materialists suggest:

> For materiality is always something more than "mere" matter: [it is] an excess, force, vitality, relationality, or difference that renders matter active, self-creative, productive, unpredictable. (Coole and Frost 2010: 9)

The task at hand, then, necessary for the formulation of a cosmopolitically correct brain, is not to argue for the erasure of difference between our practices. Movement must be made from seeking to secure a position of transcending 'truth' to one of joint perplexity and 'immanent critique.' This process may involve, for all parties concerned, a reorientation to matter and to the world around us.

5.1   Acknowledgments

I would like to the thank the Clayman Institute for Gender Research at Stanford University for support during my sabbatical year during which time I conducted a portion of the research for this essay. I would also like to thank Anelis Kaiser and Isabelle Dussauge for organizing the "NeuroGenderings: Critical Studies of the Sexed Brain" conference held at Uppsala University in early 2010 and for inviting me to present portions of this chapter. Lastly, I give much thanks to Cindy Willett and the Emory students in my graduate seminar "Posthumanist Ethics and

Aesthetics" for creating many moments of shared perplexity while reading the work of Isabelle Stengers together.

Notes

1. I thank my former graduate student Monica Bradley for bringing Magritte's painting to my attention and for her own expressions of biopolitical artistry.
2. I have raised similar feminist discomforts on the question of molecular biology research. For further reading, see my article "Should Feminists Clone? And If So, How? Notes from an Implicated Modest Witness" (Roy 2008).
3. The authors of the article do, however, refer to Steven Jay Gould's *The Mismeasure of Man* (1981).

9
Linking Neuroscience, Medicine, Gender and Society through Controversy and Conflict Analysis: A "Dissensus Framework" for Feminist/Queer Brain Science Studies

Cynthia Kraus

> In order to advance towards problem resolution, what is needed is not conflict resolution, but *conflict exacerbation.* (Martinez-Allier 2002: 68, emphasis in original)

This chapter outlines a programmatic proposal linking neuroscience, medicine, gender, and society, with consequences for research, training, and action. I suggest we work with what I call a 'dissensus framework,' i.e. a critical framework centered on the study of conflicts and controversies, including their absence, unsuccessful controversies, etc. I explore how we could work with a dissensus framework, taking as an illustration the controversial question of which is the most important sex organ for gender identity formation in intersex people: their brain or their genitals? I then consider how to make a controversy and conflict-centered analysis relevant to social scientific interventions in the current debates about best practice issues in the clinical management of intersex conditions. Reflecting on the productive tensions surrounding training and multidisciplinary team-building that we have been working out since 2005 in Lausanne to improve standards of care, I end up proposing a new project that captures my overall argument: organizing the first 'Dissensus Conference' to follow up on the controversial 2005

"International Consensus Conference on Intersex," and the no less controversial "Consensus Statement on Management of Intersex Disorders" issued in 2006.

1   A dissensus framework for what?

The dissensus framework I present here is still in progress. Rather than offering a set of definite principles, my discussion seeks to invite further reflections on the critical and normative tasks of science studies scholars in relation to neuroscience and medicine. My interest in working out a theoretical and practical framework focusing on conflicts and controversies is grounded in three ongoing research projects.[1] The first one inquires into the sciences of the sexed, gendered, and sexualized brain with special interest in the ways in which the so-called organizational theory developed in the 1950s in behavioral neuroendocrinology has gained increased prominence in debates about the clinical management and definitions of intersexuality and transsexuality. The second project seeks to analyze conflicts and controversies over the prevalence of biological or psychosocial factors in gender identity formation in intersex people in order to highlight the ways in which neuro/biological knowledge claims and clinical practice are being contested or appropriated, naturalized or critically redefined in relation to activist agendas for the right of bodily integrity and self-determination. It also examines the idea that neuroscience can enlighten medical practice and make it more scientific. The third project is concerned with the question of how, and under what conditions, science and gender studies can be made relevant to clinical practice in relation to the various forms of 'lay expertise' developed by patients, relatives and activists (Epstein 1995).

The first two research projects have raised for me the question of how and why intersex and trans' activists with a feminist and queer political agenda have sought to challenge standards of care and the very definition of their 'disorders' by mobilizing plastic and idiosyncratic knowledge claims from studies of intersexed and transsexual brains. The relative silence of feminist, queer, and transgender scholars on this subject matter is neither accidental, nor incidental. Intersex and trans' activists were able to enroll the discourse of fetal brain sex in feminist-informed projects of subverting identity categories, gender and heterosexual norms, precisely *because* this appropriation is consistent with – in fact an extension of – the ways in which feminist, queer, and transgender scholars have been refuting biological determinism with plasticity arguments for "all biological levels" and not just the brain.[2] Such bio-social (nature–culture) arguments that conceive of the many intricate, productive, and feedback processes between the self, the body, and society, underscoring individual variations rather than group differences, can be considered a key idea and a long-lasting trope in the critical history of feminist science studies – though not an unproblematic one. I have discussed elsewhere the reasons why we should not simply presume that plasticity arguments innocently advance strategic/critical engagements with the biology of sex (see Kraus 2000, 2005), and that in an emerging 'plastic era,' we need more than ever to reflect critically on the undercurrents of arguments about brain plasticity, individual variations, idiosyncrasy and the like (Kraus 2010a, 2010b, 2011a). One needs in particular to consider how the apparently emancipatory discourse about one's uniqueness is no way out of 'medicalization,' and that it promotes an ambivalent politics of self-realization and a problematic theory of agency.

Some aspects of my discussion will perhaps sound polemical, but this is due to the sensitive and polemical issues touched upon. Obviously, one of them, and not the least, has to do with the most political question of what it means, and takes, to be a human subject in a society that is committed to sex/gender differences and to heterosexuality and how neuroscientific knowledge claims are an active party in this debate, reconfiguring and accrediting certain versions of the self (what I am) and forms of knowledge about who I am. One understands that the debate can be hot and the stakes high, not only because the personal is indeed political as feminists have rightly pointed out in the 1960s, but also because the political itself has become personal. This 'personal turn' is constitutive of our epistemological and political situation today, making it difficult to recast the question of the person and personal identities in non-tautological terms, i.e. from a sociological perspective, distinct from methodological individualism (Ehrenberg 2010).

The dissensus framework I argue for is a programmatic proposal that seeks to tackle this difficulty by extending the critical tradition of controversy analyzes developed in the broad field of science studies from its inception up till now.[3] Initially, controversy studies were designed to provide us with an analytical framework warranting an "axiological and political neutrality" by explaining symmetrically all protagonists' claims, agenda, and strategies regardless of which party would eventually win or lose the dispute (Pestre 2007). Such a methodological fairness has sometimes been critiqued for accrediting and supporting,

wittingly or not, the losers' side. These critiques have generated interesting questions and discussions about the kinds of politics of explanation promulgated in controversy studies, and their social uses outside
academia. For instance, authors like Sheila Jasanoff (1996) suggested
that the narrative of winners and losers was not the best explanatory
style to capture the ambivalent outcomes of scientific and technological
controversies, nor the ways in which constructionist arguments about
knowledge production were sometimes used in public and legal disputes by resourceful protagonists (e.g. tobacco companies) to make all
claims equal and reject accountability. As Jasanoff also called attention
to the fact that science studies scholars were increasingly pressured to
take sides in sociotechnical controversies, she proposed an alternative
framework centered on co-production and reflexivity:

> 'co-production' – the simultaneous production of knowledge and
> social order – provides a more satisfying conceptual framework than
> 'controversy' for understanding the relationship between science and
> society, and the scholar's role in that relationship. Political engage-
> ment is better achieved through reflexive critical scholarship than
> through identification with apparent 'winners' or 'losers' in well-
> defined but contingent controversies. (Jasanoff 1996: 393)

I agree. We certainly need to understand how knowledge production
about the brain is situated not just in time (to be studied historically)
and space (to be studied by sociology or anthropology), but also and
most importantly in relation to the production of a social order –
indeed, co-production. It also makes sense not to choose sides between
winners and losers, when identifying who is what in that process is
problematic in the first place. But Jasanoff seems to go one step further,
arguing that controversy studies have somehow become a theoretical
and practical obstacle to reflexivity and normative interventions from
a science studies perspective. Such a position may need to be updated
and reformulated in the light of today's repeated calls for (self-)critical
interdisciplinarity. Indeed, the incentive to bridge the purported gap
between the neuro- and social sciences (including the humanities) not
only illustrates the extent to which interdisciplinary has become insti-
tutionally organized, promoted and valued as a synonym of creativity and innovation, although not without ongoing controversies and
struggles for disciplinary legitimacy (see e.g. Weingart and Stehr 2000).
This particular social order of knowledge also raises challenging questions about the very object, nature, and usefulness of a social scientific

critique of neuroscience. It confronts brain science studies scholars, and not just the gender theorists in the field, with the need to clarify how we want to frame our critical practices and promote interdisciplinary dialogue and collaborations. We may ask ourselves of what and for whom is it a critique? (see also Kraus 2011a) and a "cooperation for what?" (Jasanoff 1995).

The so-called Critical Neuroscience program stands out as an interesting expression of the imperative to bridge the science gap, proposing a stimulating research program. It seeks to integrate reflexively insights from the social sciences, in particular the social studies of science, with empirical practice to improve the robustness, social relevance, and public understanding of neuroscientific research. Such (self)-critical practices are aimed at raising neuroscientists' awareness of the social dynamics and contexts in which they work and, in the long run, create a shared knowledge space between the brain and the social sciences (Choudhury et al. 2009; see also Slaby 2010). 'Socializing' neuroscience in this manner is a good idea, but steps toward a neurofeminist extension of this interdisciplinary endeavor are complicated by the problematic ways in which critical neuroscientists conceive of their critical practices. They suggest that we work and talk across the disciplines as if neuroscientists were from Mars and social scientists from Venus, while critical neuroscientists would act as "informed 'middle men' [*sic*] communicating between neuroscience and the public" (Choudhury et al. 2009: 67). They frame the question of a science gap between neuro- and social scientists, experts and the public, just as couples' guides for improving men and women's relationships conceive of the gender gap, i.e. in terms of unawareness, misunderstanding, or ignorance – all matters that can be settled through enhanced communication and better knowledge of each other's distinctive language, culture, needs, or concerns (see Gray 1992).

In the case of couples, emphasizing communication has obviously the peacekeeping function of preventing the political question of gender equality from arising. In the area of Critical Neuroscience, this suggests that the so-called science gap might involve more than misconceptions or deafness. I suggest that the Critical Neuroscience communication framework prevents politics or, rather, does preventive politics in a specific and gendered manner: by assigning social scientists to the typically feminine and highly political job of assuaging dissensus – tensions within and between disciplines, scientific controversies, political struggles, social conflicts, etc. – in the name of interdisciplinarity. The peacekeeping function of the social sciences in relation to neuroscience and the public does not just circumvent political debate. If, as argued by science studies scholars, "controversy in science and technology is not only typical and common but a normal (perhaps even desirable) product of the encounter between science and society" (Jasanoff et al. 2008: 391), and thus constitutive of good science (one can think here of the 'voodoo correlations' issue[4]), peacekeeping may as well preclude the possibility of doing better empirical research.

By contrast with a preemptive critique of neuroscience, but consistent with a feminist/queer agenda in the field of science, technology, and medicine studies, or social movement theory, or even political ecology (see introductory quote), I think that our critical and normative tasks as social scientists and scholars from the humanities are not to preempt political debate, prevent or absorb controversies and conflicts, but rather to exacerbate them through critical analysis. To this end, we need to articulate a *strong* social science perspective on neuroscience that is not domesticable for peacekeeping purposes. From such a perspective, controversies, conflicts, or any disputed issue are not epistemological obstacles to be overcome before we could have a 'proper conversation,' but the very objects of a science and gender studies analysis (nothing new or original in this regard). They are no more practical obstacles to normative interventions. Quite to the contrary, critical focus on conflicts and controversies makes it possible to reconsider whether and how we want to implement interdisciplinarity or other forms of meaningful conversations between different professional and social actors. Most importantly, from a strong social science perspective, both conflict resolution and consensus are not primary items on the critical agenda. Instead of foreclosing political debate through peacekeeping actions, it matters to keep conflicts and controversies alive, indeed to exacerbate them, in order to open up and sustain the possibility for political transformation and contestation, for objections and other forms of disagreements, productive doubts and irritating questions (see also, e.g., Pestre 2008).

To return to Jasanoff's earlier proposal, my suggestion is that we need not abandon an agonistic politics of explanation to achieve reflexivity with the aim of making science studies relevant to political matters, but quite to the contrary, we should enrich it with the study of social conflicts inherent in processes of knowledge and world making. I suggest we take the struggle for a better life as a point of entry to inquiring into the ways in which brain questions are written in a "moral grammar of social conflicts" – to borrow an expression from Axel Honneth (1996). To put it in a more sociological vein, the language of the brain has become a prominent truth-discourse about the self in contemporary

Western societies where self-realization and autonomy are valued, and concerns, complaints, claims, and struggles for recognition, are increasingly expressed in terms of mental health issues (Ehrenberg 2010). If people come to speak the language of the brain,[5] they also do it to come to terms with conflicting life situations (Ehrenberg 2004b). This is not unlike scientists from the life and social sciences, or health care professionals for that matter, who advance cerebral arguments in a confrontational context – the context of the *'subject wars'* opposing competing conceptions (rather than disciplines) of human beings, defined in primary reference either to their brain/body or their society (Ehrenberg 2004a). We can then take such struggles for recognition and/or legitimacy as interesting sites for analyzing the co-production of matters of fact and matters of concern, discursive frames and frames of action, description/perception of a situation, and prescription for transforming or coping with it through a critical framework highlighting the conflicting dimensions of social life.

2 Conflict and controversy over the most important sex organ: brain or genitals?

In January 2004, the journal *Nature* featured an article commenting on new evidence suggesting that the fetal brain is "the most important sexual organ." It is more important than sex hormones or, possibly, sex-determining genes, for understanding how one gets to know if one is male or female early in the womb. Thus, "does the fetal brain know its sex before its gonads [testis or ovary] develops?" (Dennis 2004: 391) becomes a new research question. It has the potential to explain why transsexuals feel "trapped in the wrong body" and want sex change operations. It also suggests that we can develop a biological tool to predict whether children born with 'ambiguous' genitalia will grow up "thinking, feeling, and behaving like a man or a woman," thus helping us decide which sex should be assigned at birth to prevent gender dissatisfaction at adult age (see Dennis 2004; see also Hines 2004: ix). To drive her point home, Dennis reports the case management of two genetic males with so-called ambiguous genitalia, Susan and Tony. Susan was assigned to be a girl, underwent feminizing genital surgery along with hormonal treatment, and her parents were assured she would develop normally and identify as a female. And so it happened: she is now in her twenties, married, and living happily as a woman. But things did not turn out as well for Tony who was also assigned the female sex, in keeping with the surgical and phallocentric dogma, unchallenged by the *Nature* article, that it is easier to construct a 'credible' vagina than a penis. Tony always felt unhappy as a girl, turned to testosterone treatment and switched to living as a man.

Susan's successful gender assignment is the idealized version of a theory of gender identity formation developed in the 1950s by John Money and colleagues, in particular Joan and John Hampson, from studies on 'life adjustments' by hermaphrodite infants in close collaboration with Lawson Wilkins, one of the founders of pediatric endocrinology in the 1940s, at the psycho-hormonal unit of the Johns Hopkins Hospital, Baltimore. As the theory goes, one is not born, but becomes a man or a woman early in life; one assumes a gender identity and role through social interactions, reinforcement, and learning, just like one learns how to speak one's native language. The learning process is limited in time: gender identity is established at the critical age of 18 months, and 'indelibly imprinted' (a concept borrowed from Austrian ethologist Konrad Lorenz) by the age of two to three years (Money, Hampson, and Hampson 1955a: 310, 1955b: 285). Not everyone, however, can become a man; a biological male without a 'credible' penis cannot develop into a normal man. In theory, the importance of the external genitalia was minimized, but in practice, healthy psychosexual development was said to depend primarily on the "appearance and morphology of the external genitals" (Money, Hampson, and Hampson 1955a: 308, 1955b: 288). These genital-centered recommendations have served to rationalize surgical and hormonal treatment so as to maintain and fortify the child in assigned gender (Money, Hampson, and Hampson 1955b).

Since the 1980s however, adults born with an intersex condition treated according to Money and colleagues' recommendations have been confronting health professionals with another story: bodies mutilated by unwanted genital surgery, brainwashed minds, gender-role training, medical secrecy, family secret, shame, trauma, stigma, and the desire to get their intersexed body back or to change assigned gender. Ironically, surgical and hormonal treatment to turn intersex children into heterosexual men or women just like everyone else tends to produce dissatisfaction with assigned gender – what could be called 'nosocomial transsexuality' – as an unwanted result of medical care (as in the case of Tony above). Despite ongoing debates in the medical community initiated by intersex associations, issues about optimal care for children born with an intersex condition, best criteria for gender assignment, opportunity and timing of genital surgery, informed consent, and complete disclosure have not been settled yet. Quite to the contrary, disputes over the clinical management of intersexuality have been reignited by the recent controversial "Consensus Statement" published in 2006 by the American Academy of Pediatrics that proposed renaming intersex conditions as DSD (disorders of sex development) and new guidelines for neonatal specialists (Lee et al. 2006; see also Hughes et al. 2006).

The clinical promises of fetal brain sex research make sense and are advanced in this critical context – a crisis and a critique of medicine. Such research, as the *Nature* article suggests, might help resolve the negative outcomes of gender assignments that draw the limits of medicine so far: Susan and Tony's doctors held the wrong belief that "the brain is a sexual blank slate until it comes under the influence of sex hormones" (Dennis 2004: 390). However, brain sex research is not just a new predictive tool with the aim of improving patient satisfaction; it has been a major player in redefining the clinical issues it claims to resolve as cerebral issues. In this regard, the so-called limits of medicine dramatized in the discourse of brain sex are better analyzed as a trope that serves the self-promoting rhetoric of neuroscientific progress and its claims to enlighten medical practice. In what follows, I propose to rewind part of the story[6] focusing on the mid-1960s up to the late 1990s in the United States on the controversial question of whether gender identity formation in intersex patients is more a function of their brains than of their genitals. The twists and turns of the plot can be narrated in three Acts.

2.1 Act I

The history of the intersexed brain in the so-called hermaphrodite debate is marked by a series of unsuccessful attempts at creating a scientific controversy. In 1965, Milton Diamond, a neurobiologist trained at William Young's laboratory, the founder of behavioral neuroendocrinology, proposed a 'sexuality-at-birth' theory according to which hermaphroditism (as it was called at the time) involved atypical brain development (Diamond 1965). This theory is explicitly presented as a biological refutation of the so-called 'neutrality-at-birth' theory and of the case management protocols developed in the 1950s by Money and colleagues, as mentioned above. Diamond's thesis is that *one becomes the man or woman one is born as*, and one is born with an innate sexual identity, i.e. with predispositions that are tied up to the fetal development of a brain sex. At the time, however, his 'sexuality-at-birth' was not grounded in any human evidence, but inferred from animal studies on sex development. In some classic animal experiments, the Young team has shown that prenatal hormones *organize* sexual/mating behavior (mounting as male-typical behavior, lordosis as female-typical

behavior) and somatic development (measured by a male or female morphology) in specific ways (Phoenix et al. 1959; Phoenix 1961; Young,
Goy, and Phoenix 1964). These seminal experiments established two
core principles of behavioral neuroendocrinology: first, that genes and
especially prenatal hormones organize the "neural tissues mediating
sexual behaviors" and the morphology of the whole body in a dimorphic fashion (Phoenix et al. 1959: 369); and second, that, while the two
processes occur in parallel in normal sex development, in atypical brain
and body development "the brain and the genitals can be differentiated
and develop independently" (Diamond 2002: 28–31). The developmental 'antagonism' between the brain and the genitals outlined in these
animal studies underwrites Diamond's opposition to early genital surgery in the late 1990s: *braining* intersexuality involves *degenitalizing* sex
development, sexual identity, and orientation altogether. In retrospect,
it seems obvious that Diamond would have been an ideal candidate for
an alliance with intersex activists seeking to put an end to unwanted
genital surgery. In 1965, however, it is as a biologist trained in behavioral neuroendocrinology that Diamond responds to theories that privilege family and social conditioning over our mammalian heritage. His
intervention in the hermaphrodite debate appears in this regard as a
professional statement against psychology and sexology on its way to
institutional recognition.[7] But despite Diamond's polemical tone, his
blow did not strike home, and for long time, he would be rather lonely
in the battlefield.

2.2   Act II

Fifteen years later,[8] a BBC follow-up on a patient treated by Money and
colleagues in the 1960s – the 'twin case' (now known as the John/Joan
case, see Act III) – would provide Diamond with the first opportunity
to go public and take issue with their assignment to the female gender of a boy who had accidently lost his penis before the age of two.
The BBC broadcast and a related paper in which Diamond (1982) challenged the successful outcome of this case management were produced
in the context of a potential controversy over the relative importance of
psychological and biological factors in gender identity formation. The
preeminence of prenatal sex hormones was asserted anew in studies
conducted in Santo Domingo on so-called 'penis-at-twelve' boys who
were raised as girls, but who assumed a masculine identity and role
at puberty (Imperato-McGinley et al. 1974, 1979; Imperato-McGinley
and Peterson 1976). The fact that the authors of these studies challenged the Baltimore school with contradicting hormonal evidence

fueled Diamond's cerebral arguments. A few waves indeed, but again, not enough to seriously rock the boat. From a controversy and conflict-centered perspective, it matters that we analyze why and when some controversies catch on, but also why and when others do *not*, i.e. failed controversies. I suggest that Diamond's two attempts at creating a controversy have so far been unsuccessful *in the absence* of a social conflict. Diamond remained a minor figure in the hermaphrodite debate until intersex adults got political during the decade of the brain.

2.3   Act III. Scene 1

Social conflict will arise with intersex associations emerging in the beginning of the 1980s in North America and Europe. The Intersex Society of North America (ISNA), founded by Cheryl Chase, has been the most influential in defining the intersex agenda over the last two decades, the most present in the media, the most cited in medical literature, and the first to take an overtly political stance. Indeed, intersex activists got political in explicit reference to feminism and other feminist-inspired social movements existing or emerging at the time. ISNA built up its agenda in working relationship with feminist, queer, transsexual, and transgender scholars and activists as well as more mainstream gay and lesbian organizations (see Chase 1998; Kraus et al. 2008a; Kraus 2011b).

While ISNA's initial aim was to politicize intersex issues in non-medical terms "in order to destabilize more effectively the heteronormative assumptions underlying the violence directed at our bodies" (Chase 1998: 199), the primary item on the intersex agenda is not to change society, but to put an end to unwanted genital surgery and non-consensual treatment. During the 1980s and 1990s, intersex adults and activists have been confronting professionals with patient dissatisfaction with medical care and liability for the treatment plan outlined by Money and colleagues. Early professional reactions to intersex activism were rejections. In response, ISNA's modes of action were rather confrontational, e.g. by picketing in 1996 in front of the conference building where the annual meeting of the American Academy of Pediatrics took place (see Beck 1997/1998). During the first decade of intersex activism, *there is a social conflict* between the activists and the medical community, *but still no biomedical controversy*. However, it should be noted that while ISNA was directly challenging the medical community with 'anti-medicine' arguments, it has also systematically endorsed the prevailing discourse of physical and mental health. This registers no surprise: it makes sense given the activist agenda and the target-audience (neonate specialists) in the context of a sanitary and individual-centered society. Over the years, ISNA has increasingly focused on health issues, and in particular on the many traumas resulting from clinical management. Along with the support groups asking for better medical care, such a health-oriented program will progressively trace the contours of an 'ecological niche'[9] favoring the enrollment of cerebral arguments in activist struggles for recognition of the right to their bodies, themselves.

2.4   Act III. Scene II

The point of climax takes place in the late 1990s. First, professionals began to openly express their interrogations and doubts about past practice. Second, cerebral arguments about gender identity formation in intersex people were asserted more and more in the critical context of growing acknowledgment by the medical community of intersex associations, and the need to reflect on best practice issues. And third, in the context of a now open controversy over best practice issues in the clinical management of intersex conditions, intersex activists began to use, individually and collectively, the discourse of brain sex as a political resource to confront neonatal specialists with patient dissatisfaction with standard of care and translate their interests into best practice and human rights issues.

Along with intersex activists' work of consciousness-raising, which included touring the medical establishments, two professional events are of particular significance for changing medical views. In 1997, Diamond and psychiatrist Keith Sigmundson (1997a) published an article in which they reevaluated the case management by Money and colleagues of the boy who accidently lost his penis and was surgically made into a girl (pseudonym Joan, see also Act II). Diamond and Sigmundson revealed that, against the medical expectations of the Baltimore team, Joan had switched back to living as a man since the age of 14 years after a long period of distress and was currently married to a woman with two children of her own he adopted. John (pseudonym) is described as a psychosexually healthy, socially adapted, and self-respecting man, husband and father.[10] In the John/Joan case, Diamond restates his earlier position about a fetal brain sex, but, unlike his earlier papers, it soon became a reference in professional debates about the clinical management of intersexuality. Even if John was not born with any hermaphroditic condition, but a normal boy with traumatized genitalia, the John/Joan case can be considered a 'foundational story' in neurobiological discourse about intersexuality and in the growing public awareness about this clinical issue (see in particular Colapinto 2000). The second significant event took place in 1999 in Texas. A multidisciplinary conference sponsored by the National Health Institute on "Pediatric Sex Reassignment – A Critical Appraisal" was held, bringing together "basic scientists, endocrinologists, surgeons, psychiatrists, psychologists and ethicists to discuss the management of the neonate with ambiguous genitalia" in order to reflect critically on the long-term outcomes of past practice and to allow "for better medical and emotional management of these patients in the years ahead."[11] Diamond views the Texas Conference as a historical event not just for intersex advocacy, but also for the advancement of a more scientific medicine. Finally "the brain was to be recognized as a sexual organ" (Diamond 2004: 599).

These two major events contributed to creating a biomedical controversy where there was previously an overall consensus over standards of care. In the case of both events, critiques of past practice are 'indigenous' critiques, i.e. from experts, researchers, and health care professionals, in the area of prenatal, neonatal, and postnatal sex/gender identity development. Intersex activism is not mentioned in the 1997 reevaluation of the John/Joan case; no intersex people were invited to speak at the Texas Conference. In sum, the conflict and the controversy are now coexisting, but somehow in parallel. The two will converge by presenting a common front against early genital surgery. Following on their article on John/Joan case, and on the request of some medical intersex specialists, Diamond and Sigmundson published new "Guidelines for Dealing with Individuals with Ambiguous Genitalia" (1997b). This position paper was commented on the same year in the Fall issue of ISNA's newsletter, *Hermaphrodites with Attitude*:

> The article outlines new recommendations which are very much in sympathy with ISNA's. They are expanded to include specific details for which sex to label children born with each type of condition. Diamond and Sigmundson emphasize that the child, rather than the parents, must be the patient, and stress avoidance of early surgery, respect for the child's wishes including privacy, autonomy, sexual orientation, change of sex role, and access to surgery. Most importantly, they emphasize peer support and, breaking with the tradition of the journal, include a long list of contact addresses for peer support groups. (ISNA 1997: 3)

Diamond and Sigmundson's clinical recommendations were extremely well received by all intersex associations, and the information posted on their respective websites received laudatory comments and comments expressing relief that their experiences were supported by a scientific expert. Diamond's other position papers, which call for a moratorium on genital surgery and for long-term studies assessing the outcome of past interventions to "undo the past deceptions," and which confronts the medical profession with liability and best practice issues (Kipnis and Diamond 1998; Beh and Diamond 2000), have been unanimously applauded, endorsed, and circulated by intersex associations. In this manner, Diamond is progressively singled out as one of the most prominent expert figures in the debate, the legitimate spokesperson of intersex claims to reach out the medical community, and an active ally of intersex activism against unwanted genital surgery.

Regardless of their political program and affiliation, intersex activists have, wittingly or not, contributed to promoting the discourse of brain sex, as they repeatedly invoke Diamond's expertise to voice the right to bodily integrity and self-determination. As it happens, the expert has been speaking the language of brain sex all along, *including in his commendable position papers opposing unwanted genital surgery*, where he outlines new guidelines for gender assignment, and confronts professionals with new practical, ethical and legal questions (see Diamond and Sigmundson 1997b: 2–9; Kipnis and Diamond 1998: 9/18;[12] Beh and Diamond 2000: 7/44). In return, intersex activists do not necessarily accept the prevalence of the brain over other factors in gender identity formation. Some do, but at least in their public statements, most support and advocacy groups are either agnostic (ISNA), ambivalent (Organization Intersex International – hereafter OII), or rather silent on this issue (Androgen Insensitivity Syndrome Support Group in the UK, The UK Intersex Association), although Diamond stands out for all as the intersex person's best friend.[13]

At the core of the affair is what I have elsewhere called an "anatomy of social conflict" (Kraus 2011a). This expression seeks to capture the ways in which the history of the cerebralization of intersexuality can be analyzed from a controversy and conflict-centered perspective as the history of a biological alliance bringing together neurobiology and intersex activism against the 'limits of medicine.' This alliance emerged in the contexts of a 'science war' waged by neurobiologists and other neurophiles, with Milton Diamond at the forefront, against the psychosexual theory of gender identification and role modeling, and of a 'sex war' contrasting two kinds of sex organs: the fetal brain versus the genitals. But Diamond's two first attempts to create a scientific controversy from the mid-1960s to the late 1990s were drops in a bucket. I have referred his failures to the absence of a social conflict. When the conflict arose during the decade of the brain through intersex struggles, the biomedical controversy took off in parallel. When intersex activists and neurobiologists, in particular Diamond, presented a common front against non-consensual treatments, especially genital surgery in newborns, it was not always on the same grounds. As intersex activists became more vocal about the damage of past practice on their bodies and lives, calling for the end of unwanted early genital surgery and the right of bodily integrity, neurobiology became instrumental in promoting a more compassionate and evidence-based medicine. Supporting and building on intersex activism, neurobiologists such as Diamond found an opportunity to assert, theoretically and professionally, the relevance of brain sex research for the clinical management of intersexuality (see also and again Dennis 2004). In the latest guidelines of the American Academy of Pediatrics (AAP), biological factors, and not the least the brain, are given ontogenetic precedence over psychosexual factors and socialization (see Lee et al. 2006: 489). A decade earlier, the AAP's guidelines made explicit reference to Money and colleagues' theoretical and practical framework (see AAP 1996: 590).

3 Action!

What is the usefulness of a social science critique of (neuro-)science, technology, and medicine, and in particular of gender studies? And how is this practical question related to the question of critical practices? My programmatic proposal to work with a dissensus framework seeks to address precisely these questions. I have earlier argued that the task of clarifying how we want to frame our critical practices is a prerequisite for articulating normative positions, making it possible to reconsider and redefine the conditions under which interdisciplinarity – or other interesting ways of shaping dialogue across different social worlds, of confronting perspectives, of cooperating, etc. – could be valued as a theoretical and practical solution. I have argued that it is a solution that would seek not to prevent, absorb, nor even resolve controversies and social conflicts, but rather to exacerbate them through critical analysis. If we want to make science and gender studies relevant to social science interventions, what is needed is not preemptive critiques, e.g. a peace-keeping communication framework for social scientists from Venus, but critical practices framed from a strong social science perspective centered on controversy and conflict analysis. These are, in summary, the normative – both theoretical and practical, epistemological and political – commitments involved in my dissensus framework.

Since 2005, I have initiated, and participated in, various collective projects bringing together physical and mental health profession- als concerned with the clinical management of intersex people in Lausanne and the Lake Geneva region (Switzerland), medical or social science students, parents, (ex-)patients, and intersex adults and/or activ- ists (see Kraus et al. 2008b). The projects carried out so far include: co- organizing medical, psychological and social science research seminars, conferences, and public debates; presenting ongoing research to peers, clinicians, and activists; and publishing a special journal issue with gender studies colleagues, intersex adults, and activists (Kraus et al. 2008a). More recently, I have organized an intersex class specifically designed for medical students together with a pediatric surgeon, co- teaching it with geneticists, endocrinologists, radiologists, neonatolo- gists, obstetricians, gynecologists, pedopsychiatrists, pediatric surgeons (who do not perform sex assignment surgeries on intersex newborns), ethicists, health law specialists, parents (i.e. mothers), intersex adults, and activists.

The dissensus framework I argue for can be considered a reflexive prod- uct elaborated in part through my direct participation in these projects. Of course, this does not mean that my colleagues would approve of my dissensus framework (although I can say that none of them would be surprised by the ways in which I reflect here on my actual practices), or even define our collective endeavors in these terms. However, all acknowledge, in one way or another, that the intersex question is con- troversial in many regards, that the controversy cannot be confined and contained by biomedicine only, and that we have to take into account the sometimes diverging perspectives of health professionals and the other concerned parties. Such an acknowledgment makes it possible to collaborate and discuss the most controversial issues in the clinical management of intersex conditions with the explicit aim of comple- menting/confronting our views and of building up a multidisciplinary (or call it inter-, trans-, co-disciplinary) team to improve standards of care. As I see it, here is an example of a collaboration constructed on existing and maybe irresolvable tensions between disciplinary, profes- sional, and sociopolitical conceptions of sex and gender, medicine, and society.

Teaching medical students conflicts and controversies over the clini- cal management of intersex conditions has so far not been more difficult than teaching social science students. But the later biology and medical students encounter science and gender studies in their curriculum, the more resistant they become to a critical social science perspective on their disciplines. Further, the various forms of resistance depend not only on the extent to which they have incorporated their professional norms and identity; they also vary between professional groups and areas of specialization.[14] Such resistance can sometimes complicate the teacher's task. In other instances, they can have the pedagogic virtue of making it possible to identify, express, and clarify what is the matter of disagreements in the classroom. In this manner, resistance to a strong social scientific perspective can become an opportunity to learn how to address controversial issues and consider conflicting perspectives. Students can learn to relativize[15] what they take for granted in their curriculum and future professional practice. At any case, centering one's teaching on conflict and controversies in medical training makes perfect sense in the light of the existing controversy over best practice issues within the professional community and literature. (Future) doctors cannot grasp what is at stake in the current debates if they are not aware that the best practice issues they are confronted with today are made of controversies, conflicts, and social struggles, not aware of the ways in which (ex-)patients and activists have been challenging the medical community since the 1980s and critiqued standard practice as normalizing medicine.

Interestingly, medical students in the intersex class tend to expect clinical answers and clues from (fetal) brain sex research. Most of the pediatric surgeons who are opposed to early genital surgery and who taught in this class also assume, even ground, the good clinical decision of not performing such surgeries in intersex newborns in controversial studies about a sexed and sexualized brain during embryogenesis and after birth. This should not come as a surprise. It testifies to the fact that brain sex discourse has gained increased legitimacy in the current debates about best practices issues in the clinical management of intersex newborns, They forget, however, that the discourse of brain sex can pass for a more compassionate and scientific medicine only to the extent that it has succeeded in redefining, as we have seen, the clinical issues it claims to resolve *on its own terms* (see also and again Dennis 2004). For my part, the challenge then is to try to make sure that none of them take for granted the discourse of brain sex and its promises for clinical practice, by explaining the history of the cerebralization of intersexuality, the existing but contradicting data in brain sex research, the critiques formulated by feminist neurobiologists and feminist/queer brain science studies scholars (see note 2), in order to confront them with an instructive and constructive aporia: even if we assumed that brain sex facts were robust, how good would this knowledge be for making the most difficult decision of which sex to assign to a newborn with a 'severe' intersex condition? Would brain scans be of any help to make the decision? This will have to remain a thought experiment. The reason is very simple: the machine scanner just does not work if you do not indicate the sex (either F or M) of the experimental subject.[16]

Except perhaps for teaching, the dissensus framework does not provide direct or ready-made guidelines for action. However, there are two deadly sins that social scientists and other scholars from the humanities should not commit. First of all, we are not, as critical neuroscientists would have it, "middle-men [*sic*]" (Choudhury et al. 2009: 67) communicating between laboratory researchers on sex/gender identity development, health care professionals, parents, patients, intersex adults/and activists, the so-called lay public, or even the media. We must not speak from Venus. The second sin would be to act as expert/activist spokespersons of intersex associations to reach out to clinicians. The existing gender scholarship about intersexuality tends, in political sympathy, to borrow their critical arguments from activist discourse, ISNA's in particular, and, more recently, OII's. This is no real surprise, since the reverse is just as true. Intersex activists, at least the more or less politicized ones (especially in the U.S.), make explicit references to feminist/queer/transgender scholarship and movements, and reclaim this critical/political tradition. Gender scholars who want to work with a dissensus framework, however, should dare to take issue with intersex activists, typically on the question of an 'intersexed brain.' Not taking for granted the controversial idea of a brain sex is a condition of possibility for analyzing the process of braining intersexuality, what is at stake, including the fact that feminist, intersex, and neurobiological discourses share the same problematic, but barely controversial, rhetoric of the self: idiosyncratic arguments about who we are and how each of us becomes a unique individual, that translate the 'personal turn' in politics I mentioned in the introduction. Analyzing intersex activism in this reflective manner does not disqualify its discourse or actions. Quite to the contrary, I think this critical analysis should serve to *requalify* the political work of creating controversies and conflicts, and underscore their clinical relevance. We can then bring clinicians to ask themselves: when I meet an intersex newborn or a growing child and her parents, I can ask myself, what do social scientists, parents, patients, adults, and activists have to say about this controversial and highly sensitive issue? It is a good question, because it seeks to make sense of diverging perspectives.

Even if we do not commit either of these sins, it still remains a complicated question what it means to intervene from a strong social science perspective. But practical solutions, I suggest, can emerge from this complicated situation. Complicated is not the same as confusing, because what is complicated can precisely be explicated, i.e. made explicit and be explained.[17] Making things complicated in this precise sense of the term thus defines the critical and normative agenda of a dissensus framework. Explaining and making controversies and conflicts explicit is not just an agonistic politics of explanation, it also supports a political framework. Democracy is the political regime that acknowledges the conflicting dimensions inherent to social life and provides various possibilities for expressing and making these conflicts explicit (see, e.g., Lefort 1986). Conflict exacerbation (see Martinez-Allier 2002), rather than conflict resolution or consensus, has therefore a fundamentally democratic function. If such possibilities have to be protected and kept open for all, we have a special responsibility toward those who are minoritized, marginalized, and excluded from political life and decisions (Pestre 2008).

To conclude, let me just put on the table the question of which organizational device could be imagined and operationalized through a dissensus framework. Since the 1990s, science studies scholars have been increasingly concerned with the question of science and democracy, and the active, even activist, role they could play to enhance a more direct or participative democracy (see, e.g., Latour 2004a; Pestre 2007, 2008; Hess et al. 2008). Among the various models proposed for public participation in science, technology, and medicine,[18] the consensus conferences model, developed in the mid-1970s "as a tool of medical assessment technology in the USA," and later in Europe through Danish initiatives in the 1980s (Joss and Durant 2002: 10) is of particular interest for my argument:

> A consensus conference may be described as a public enquiry at the centre of which is a group of 10–16 citizens who are charged with the assessment of a socially controversial topic of science and technology. These lay people put their questions and concerns to a panel of experts, assess the experts' answers, and then negotiate amongst themselves. The result is a consensus statement which is made public in the form of a written report at the end of the conference. (Joss and Durant 2002: 9)

Although it is a top-down process, the consensus conference model is of course not an uninteresting process. Of special interest is the fact that, in actual practice, consensus conferences and statements can produce an unsought-for, and actually inevitable, result: *dissensus* and even sometimes *more* dissensus. Such is the case of the "Consensus Statement on Management of Intersex Disorders," endorsed in 2006 by the American Academy of Pediatrics (Lee at al. 2006). The Statement was issued after the "International Consensus Conference on Intersex," held in Chicago in October 2005, which brought together basic scientists and health care professionals, but only two intersex activists. I cannot here elaborate on this latest episode, or discuss the active role of ISNA in this affair.[19] But from the activist perspective, there are two main contentious issues: the under-representation of intersex groups, and the question of whether intersexuality is a pathology. Is intersexuality a 'disorder of sex development,' as the new medical terminology has it, or is it a normal 'biological variation,' as argued by Milton Diamond (him again!) and many intersex organizations who were not invited to join the event.

Now, since both the Consensus Conference and Statement on Intersex *are* extremely controversial, and raise more problems than they solve, I suggest that we seriously consider the possibility of preparing a *dissensus* conference and statement for a change. The purpose would not be to reach a consensus, since the consensus framework presupposes that we could come to an agreement that would not be contested; that objections can be contained upstream and once for all. By contrast, the aim of a dissensus conference would be to identify and clarify what is controversial by confronting the many partial perspectives from the various actors concerned with intersexuality. The central idea behind a dissensus conference is to invite further inquiry into which kinds of concrete organizational devices could make things complicated and thus better democratic work by operationalizing the *normality*, indeed the *desirability*, of controversies and conflicts in the encounter between neuroscience, medicine, gender, and society.

3.1 Acknowledgments

I would like to thank the editors, in particular Heidi Lene Maibom and Robyn Bluhm, for their quality and much appreciated follow-up, as well as the two anonymous reviewers for helpful comments on an earlier draft. My thanks also go to Ellen Hertz for making many little differences that matter.

Notes

1. The advantages of a controversy and conflict-centered perspective in relation to these three projects have been explored elsewhere (Kraus 2011a). I submit a modified and improved version of some of these arguments here.

2. To do justice to gender scholarship, let me be precise here that the brain science question was addressed very early in the critical history of feminist science studies (e.g. Star 1979), foremost by neuroscientists or biologists (in particular Bleier 1984, 1986; Byne, Bleier, and Houston 1988; see also Fausto-Sterling 1992, 2000b; Vidal 2004). In the last three decades, most gender studies of neuroscience have tended to consider brain sex research as another example of how malestream modern science actively produces the sexed/sexualized bodies/brains it claims to discover. These studies have also tended to stress the continuity of the pervasive endeavor of sexing/ sexualizing the brain – from nineteenth-century phrenology to contemporary research. Feminist critics have not only analyzed the ways in which cerebral arguments about sex, gender, and sexuality can be mobilized to support or undermine gender equality and the rights of 'sexual minorities' (see e.g. Fausto-Sterling 1992; Stein 1993; Halley 1994; Rosario 1997), but also the very status of the alleged facts. Through a detailed analysis of the ways in which research questions were framed, materials selected, data produced, interpreted, and publicized outside the laboratory, most critics have considered the proliferating claims about a typically female, male, or gay brain as good examples of 'bad science' (Bleier 1984, 1986; Fausto-Sterling 1992, 2000b; Vidal 2004; Fine 2008a, 2010a; Jordan-Young 2010). Some have even turned the argument of brain plasticity against the very idea of a brain sex (Vidal and Benoit-Browaeys 2005; Kaiser et al. 2009), while a few and rare studies have tried to rethink feminist theorizations of the mind/body problem with neuroscientific insights, including research on the gay brain (Wilson 1998, 2000). More recently, some feminist and queer scholars, in and outside neuroscience, have also begun to inquire into the *specific* modalities in which brain researchers operationalize the identity categories of sex, gender and sexuality. These studies about 'neurosexism' (Fine 2010a) bring into critical focus *objects* and *areas* of knowledge emerging from the so-called new brain sciences and/or understudied from a gender perspective – e.g. the hype of emotional intelligence research with its empathic female brain and a systematic male brain (Karafyllis and Ulshöfer 2008), the increasing legitimacy of cerebral arguments in clinical debates about gender identity formation in intersex and transsexual people (Kraus 2011a, 2011b) or the proliferation of pop neuroscience literature (Fine 2008a, 2010a). The task of specifying the workings of neurosexism also involves analyzing new *instruments* of knowledge production, and in particular brain imaging technologies (Sommer et al. 2004, 2008; Kaiser et al. 2009; Dussauge 2010a; Schmitz 2010b). The first 2010 "Neurogenderings: Critical Studies of the Sexed Brain" conference bringing together neuroscientists, scholars from the humanities, and the field of science and technology studies stands out as an interesting and collective expression of such a renewal of gender perspectives in feminist/queer studies of neuroscience (see Dussauge and Kaiser 2009), neuroethics included (Roy 2010).

3. For a review see e.g. Pestre (2007). For a typology of disputes, see e.g. Delkin (2008). For a typology of approaches, see e.g. Martin and Richards (2008).

4. See Vul et al. (2009). This paper on the "puzzling high correlations in fMRI studies" in the expanding area of social neuroscience was formerly known as "Voodoo Correlations in Social Neuroscience" (see http://www.edvul.com/

voodoocorr.php, accessed 6 April 2011). As soon as it began circulating on the net in December 2008, this paper written by authors outside (social) neuroscience created a controversy about the (mis-/ab-)uses of statistical methods in neuroimaging, provoking many various reactions in science blogs and later in print. One critical social neuroscientist, Daniel Margulies (2010), gave a great performance talk on this issue at the 2010 Critical Neuroscience Workshop (University of Marburg, Germany, 22–24 April). According to Margulies, this kind of complex and technical discussion should not be widely publicized via the net. He contrasted the voodoo correlations controversy with an article, this time by social neuroscientists, presenting false positive fMRI results (scans indicating brain activity in a dead salmon) in order to argue for statistical corrections through multiple comparisons (Bennett et al. 2009). In the final discussion of the Critical Neuroscience Workshop, I then asked Margulies and other critical neuroscientists, whether, given the positive impact of the voodoo correlations controversy for improving statistical analysis in neuroimaging, they thought we/they should be more active in creating more controversies. Margulies thinks that the salmon study is a more elegant and effective manner than the Vul et al. article to transform research practices. Jan Slaby, a philosopher and one of the co-authors of the Critical Neuroscience manifesto, considers that we should not focus on controversies, since interdisciplinary collaboration is also very important to achieve. At any case, and even though the Critical Neuroscience project seems to have evolved in some regards since 2009 (see Choudhury et al. 2009; Slaby 2010), especially concerning the need to address political issues (personal communications with some members of the Critical Neuroscience Group at and since the 2010 workshop), controversies and conflicts remain a minor concern in the ways in which the various researchers involved in this project continue to frame their critical practices and try to address political questions.

5. In this context, it would be rather odd *not* to mobilize such a discourse. Also, let's not forget here that in people's everyday life and language, brain talk coexists with other scientific discourses about the body, the self, and society, in particular genetics and biochemistry (especially in the case of psychoactive drugs).

6. For a more detailed discussion, see Kraus (2011b)

7. Diamond's contention with Money and his colleagues should not obscure the fact that the two 'rival' theories were *not* considered mutually exclusive, but rather complementary at the time (see e.g. Phoenix et al. 1959: 370, 381). Over the years, this 'rivalry' would have to be constructed even further, because the organizational theory became an 'obligatory point of passage' for anyone, *including* Money and his colleagues (in particular Anke Ehrhardt), involved in the study of masculine and feminine behaviors in the 1970s (see van den Wijngaard 1997; see also Jordan-Young 2010).

8. For lack of space, I cannot discuss here an important controversy that took place in the 1970s between Bernard Zuger against John Money in *Psychosomatic Medicine*. For a discussion, see e.g. Fausto-Sterling (2000b: 68–69) and Castel (2003: 75–82).

9. Hacking (1998).

10. On 11 May 2004, John, real name David (formerly Bruce then Brenda) Reimer committed suicide.
11. I draw the quotes from the documents distributed to the conference attendees. I thank Dr Blaise-Julien Meyrat, pediatric surgeon at the University Hospital CHUV in Lausanne, Switzerland, for passing them to me. We have been collaborating on various projects since 2005 (see my discussion below), as he does *not* perform sex assignment surgeries on intersex newborns; neither do the other urogenital surgeons in Lausanne.
12. Diamond and Sigmundson (1997b) and Kipnis and Diamond (1998) are posted on the UK Intersex Association's website from which I indicate the page references purposefully to make my point.
13. In January 2008, the German Association of Intersexed People honored Milton Diamond for "his years of service to the intersex community and his endless commitment to their well-being and acceptance within society." Organization Intersex International also joined in, see http://www. intersexualite.org/Diamond_award.html, accessed 2 June 2009.
14. For lack of space, I cannot discuss this in more detail, but these remarks are based on a comparative observation between participants (MA and postgraduate students, interns, junior and senior MDs, etc.) from the medical, psychological, and social sciences in a research seminar on sex, gender, and intersexuality I co-organized in 2005–6 with a pediatric surgeon and a pedopsychiatrist (see Kraus et al. 2008b), and the third year medical students participating in the new intersex class (Spring 2011) I co-organized with the same pediatric surgeon. I also draw from my teaching experience from 2005–8 to first year and third year biology students (I taught an introduction to science studies with one lecture dedicated to the question of gender and science).
15. I mean 'relativize' in the strong sense of the term of making more/new sense of various situations by relating things that appear unrelated, or to unfold things that are collapsed into one another.
16. Anelis Kaiser (2010b) drew our attention to this practical requirement in her communication at the first Neurogenderings conference.
17. On the distinction between complex (primate) and complicated (human) societies, and how complicated sociotechnical assemblages can be analyzed from an actor-network theory perspective, see e.g. Latour (2005).
18. For a review and discussion of science and democracy, see e.g. Pestre (2008). For a discussion of non-institutionalized forms of participation in science and technology, in particular social movements, see e.g. Hess et al. (2008).
19. In spring 2008, ISNA dissolved and Cheryl Chase with some ex-ISNA members founded a new organization called Accord Alliance to bring professionals to put into practice the latest guidelines of the 2006 Consensus Statement.

10
Seeing as a Social Phenomenon: Feminist Theory and the Cognitive Sciences

Anne Jaap Jacobson

1 Introduction

Is seeing a social phenomenon? Are there political dimensions to the question of what can be seen? These questions are worth feminist notice, particularly since doubts about basic ways of knowing are being raised by the cognitive sciences. The problems surrounding recent doubts about human knowledge intersect with feminist concerns at many familiar points.

Recent investigations into human cognition strongly support the idea that individual human cognitive capacities are significantly less than many have been inclined to think, as we will see. The outcome is that we are not the individual knowers that we often think we are. It is then important that much in feminist thought has a context in which to place such a conclusion, since feminists are often engaged in showing how at various levels knowledge accomplishments involve the community (Longino 1990, 2002; Potter 1995; Lloyd 2000; Jaggar 2008). To put it very roughly, recent research on human cognition reveals gaps and errors, while those working on the social dimensions of knowledge are often investigating how gaps and errors get rectified in the creation of knowledge. Perhaps the most obvious of the problems are biases, such as the confirmation bias; in this case, the corresponding community role may be just to review one's work for such biases. But more generally, these two projects – the deconstruction of individual knowledge and the delineation of social knowledge – together point us toward a constructive project in understanding human cognition.

We will focus on vision. What we are learning today is that most of us are unaware of the nature of our actual visual experience and its many limitations. As (Pylyshyn 2000: 203) notes:

> less information is encoded with each glance than has been previously assumed. Research by several workers has shown that information about the properties and relative locations of small changes in a scene are rarely noticed during saccades. Nevertheless, humans have the impression of a large, panoramic scene. Such a scene does indeed exist, but it is in the real world and not in the mind.

The phenomenon Pylyshyn describes, change blindness, is further reported in Chabris and Simons (2010).

From the point of view of distinctly human interests in getting to the true facts of the case, human vision is an often faulty guide. Thus, recent research shows that our actual visual experience is very partial in comparison to the way we are inclined to think of it. Our considerably fuller perceptual reports must be drawn on resources additional to our inner experience. As such, they can be affected community contributions as much as any other statements.

2   Cognitive capacities

We can see much of Anglo-American philosophy as having inherited from the Enlightenment investigations a confidence in human cognition, where 'cognition' is understood widely to cover memory, senses, and the emotions, as well as more higher level cognitive activity such as explicit reasoning. To a considerable extent, more ordinary culture has followed with a strong faith in the senses as instruments for uncovering truths. For example, eyewitness testimony has been considered nearly incorrigible by the lay public and by judges and prosecutors. A jury may find the idea that one failed to see what was before one's eyes as simply unbelievable (Chabris and Simons 2010).

The connection between vision and the discovery of truths is reflected in many recent philosophical statements on vision. For example, the introduction to the influential collection *Perceptual Experience* (Gendler and Hawthorne 2006) takes the central problem for philosophy of perception to be reconciling the fact of perceptual errors with our view of our perceptual access to the world; here truth seems to be the aim of seeing. And in the collection Mark Johnston famously asserts that the function of sensory awareness is to disclose to our awareness the truthmakers and content providers of our sensory judgments; the senses show us what makes our judgments true (Johnston 2006). Such a claim presents as unproblematic the idea that the senses do disclose the world to us. But such views are very questionable.

> We all believe that we are capable of seeing what's in front of us, of accurately remembering important events from our past, of understanding the limits of our knowledge, of properly determining cause and effect. But these intuitive beliefs are often mistaken ones that mask critically important limitations on our cognitive abilities...As we go through life, we often act as though we know how our minds work and why we behave the way we do. It is surprising how often we really have no clue. (Chabris and Simons 2010: xii)

Sight, memory, and the grasp of causal relations are the products of evolution, which responds to such things as survival, reproduction, and, in many cases, social needs. Through much of our evolution, variations were selected on the basis of their serving the needs we share with many other species, which have little to do with human interests in the construction of factual narratives. Such constructions constitute much in our sense of ourselves, and our views on the structure and purpose of our societies, but our interest in them is an anomaly in nature. That fact shows up when we examine our cognitive capacities. For example, vision and memory give us the gist of things, but they are not well suited to the fact gathering and explaining that Western society values so highly. We may want to know just what happened, and how and where and when it happened. But, as extensive experimentation tells us, we miss out on a great deal that is right before our eyes, and what we do pick up is only partially retained by an often distorting memory.

3   Feminism and social knowledge

As we remarked above, while cognitive science has been deconstructing individual knowledge of the facts, feminist theorists have been looking at social bases for knowledge and who has it. Social factors may make us know even less, but they may also contain resources for compensating for individual deficits. Thus there are many ways in which society affects the knowledge of individuals. For example, both the means to produce knowledge and the ability to reveal the results of such production are often heavily influenced by decisions outside the control of any individual investigator. In ways discussed in many feminist-influenced works on science, even people very interested in pursuing a set of questions can find that the training needed is closed to them. In a synopsis of his forthcoming work on Victorian female scientists, Holmes (2010) notes that the female scientists were largely confined to roles that, while important, were often ancillary to the actual production of science.

And that, we may say, is just the beginning. Inquirers who resist the presence of some groups may develop theories that justify the continuation of exclusion of those groups from the community of knowers, too often with the result that knowledge about them is not developed or is distorted. Perhaps most notoriously, over the centuries many writers have claimed men are more able to do scientific research; among the most recent is Simon Baron-Cohen (Baron-Cohen 2003), whose work is discussed in a chapter in this volume.

There are, then, often communal controls on the production of and access to knowledge, which may also promote or reinforce biases in inquirers. Also important for our purposes are the positive effects the community can have. Thus a community of inquirers may correct biases in its members (Longino 1990; Potter 1995). Here we can think of a community as enhancing the members' ability to know (Lloyd 2000). Relatedly, the community may help complete projects that are too large for an individual inquirer to undertake alone, or that bring in essential pieces of expertise no one person will be able to encompass. Further, as some feminists have stressed, outsider status may confer on one situated knowledge that is not available to officially sanctioned groups of cognizers (Harding 2004). For example, those who are discriminated against may have a much clearer view of the deficits in understanding in the dominant group than that group can discern for itself.

Perhaps most philosophically challenging is the idea that the community is involved in an individual's knowledge all the way down, as it were. Could knowledge acquisition be social in the way playing chess or waltzing are? If so, then what one is doing is in part constituted by what others are doing. This view is articulated in various places by Baier (Baier 1991, 1994, 1997; Jacobson 2000) and appears to maintained by Longino in comments such as "The subject of experience, the individual, is a nexus of interpretation coming into existence at the boundary of nature and culture" (Longino 1990: 221). It is not hard to understand the thesis that knowledge of mathematics is partially constituted by the grasp of codes whose rules for use are determined by the community, and not any one individual. Seeing and remembering, we might think, are very different, since they are just a matter of the individual experiences we have. However, it can look very implausible to say that our memory reports and our perceptual reports are reports of rather full internal experiences, since it does not look as though we have such experiences. Rather, the view that we do looks like something constructed, and the construction draws on a host of factors external to us. Or so I will argue.

As we look at sensory capacities, and in particular vision, we can discern room for many roles for a community. Those good at seeing something may have needed special training, ranging from recognizing a style of painting to being able to see the affordances made possible by machinery. Seeing may deeply reflect cultural biases, since what we notice in a scene are often what stereotypical biases lead us to expect (Eberhardt et al. 2004). In addition, very importantly seeing can leave us with large gaps in our knowledge of a scene we surveyed. Bringing other witnesses together can help. Similarly, getting someone to help even in a simple search, such as finding the keys, which are in fact on one's desk, may be important to the task's success. Further, and more generally, when seeing involves recognition, that is often the result of cultural learning.

That is, I will argue, perceptual reports are not best construed as reports of internal experiences. Rather, they are contributions to shareable discourse about what is. We can consider the approach to reports of psychological states that are undertaken here to be 'analytic,' rather than 'synthetic.' A synthetic approach is based on the recognition that there is a gap between the supposed inner experience and our corresponding reports. It looks at the important ways in which community has a role in creating the material for the report. A prominent example is Sue Campbell's recent work on memory (Campbell 2003; Campbell et al. 2009) which recognizes the limited and precarious nature of the factual recording our memories do. For Campbell, an active audience can participate in the construction of a person's memory reports; memory reports can be understood as public performances shaped by interactions. Such reports also provide one a sense of one's self extended through time. We are not yet, I think, able to undertake a synthetic approach to vision; hence, I will take an analytic approach, one which examines the elements of vision to investigate how reports of visual experience contrast with the experience itself, and the ways in which the content of one's report is or can be sensitive to one's audiences, either potential or actual.

In sum, feminists have often been interested in dispatching the ideal of a solitary knower. The cognitive sciences appear happy to help. Nonetheless, the results of the wholesale questioning of a traditional conception of cognition are not always sanguine for feminists. If women are already situated as unequal in their capacity to know, their credibility may be further diminished by the new understandings. This result has actually occurred in part because the new ideas about memory have become intertwined in the public eye with the question of whether reports by women of recovered memories of sexual abuse are just the unreliable products of suggestive therapy. Sue Campbell's work in this area also highlights the extent to which women with such claims, and feminists supporting the possibility of their being true, have been dismissed as delusional or as activist zealots (Campbell 2003). Campbell concludes that the result is to deprive women of full personhood. Memories, she argues, are in part social narratives that involve the construction of selves.

Campbell's work is on a complex situation, where moral, political, and philosophical concerns intersect in creating a problem for feminists. Looking at vision gives us a chance to consider a range of issues about gaps and errors without immediately encountering political problems. As we see at the end, though, the political implications are there.

4   Vision: scope and limits

It is well to start with a number of ways vision's contribution exceeds what until recently we thought it could do. Vision has links to reactions that are important for our social behavior. The most recent research confirms the existence of 'mirror neurons' in human beings (Mukamel et al. 2010); because of them, most of us, for example, can mirror others' actions and expressed emotions, and such mirroring appears very important in numerous ways to our understanding and actions (Iacoboni 2008). Interestingly, there is very recent evidence that inhibiting our motor imitations in response to the visual uptake of facial expression degrades our ability to understand others. Thus Botox when used to suppress facial movement may do more harm socially than good (Bower 2010).

Vision is often excellent at guiding action in other ways. The magnocellular pathway in the visual system enables some highly important signals – such as ones from snakes and facial expressions – to get to the limbic system before they are recognized by any higher cognitive function (LeDoux 1996). Because of this, we can act and react very quickly. Ordinary experience reveals that vision can help us cope with complexity we would find very hard to think our way through. For example, walking along a very irregular terrain can be quite risky, but if one simply looks where one is going, the walk becomes much safer, even though it might be impossible for one to describe the variety of angles at which one places one's feet as one adjusts one's walk to the surface.

There are also many ways in which vision falls short of what we think it does. Vision does not enable us to pick up the details of our environment in the way we think it does. Thus we think we can take in a room in a glance, but in fact we pick up relatively little. In a way, this information should not be surprising. We hear stories about car accidents that occur because one driver just did not see the other car. Many of us know someone (and may be someone) who regularly fails to find keys that are in plain sight. The deliverance of unschooled common sense seems to be that one opens one's eyes and sees what is around one, but that is wrong.

It is, then, a commonplace of vision science that we get much less information at any one point in time than we tend to think we do. The visual system that produces our experience of a world of stable objects is selective in many ways. But we can understand the limitations Pylyshyn and others (see above) are interested in if we think of vision as having two great consolidation stages and two stages in which limitations are introduced by the way our attention works. In both consolidation and limitation we can encounter ways vision is restricted of which we are largely unaware.

In looking at a scene, our eyes tend to scan it by moving in saccades, which are rapid small movements punctuated by brief fixations. In such fixations, attention works to produce binding, so that qualities processed separately in very early vision are brought together in our experience. Thus, color and shape are originally processed separately, but we tend to experience colored shapes as single things. This is the first great consolidation.

We also experience a world of steady objects, but saccades give us a jerky series of very partial takes on parts of such a world. A second great consolidation is created when we transform the jerky input into an experience of objects. The second consolidation also produces partial results in comparison with the whole scene that we think we can take in. In putting the products of our short takes together it tends to be heavily selective and very object oriented. This second consolidation is sometimes said to be or to involve amodal completion.

The limits of attention add to the partiality of the results for both stages of consolidation. Thus the discontinuous nature of our saccades is compounded by our ability to bind only a limited number of elements. And a similarly restricting and interest-driven attention limits what objects we see. We are, for example, more likely to see what we expect to see, so that motorcycles and bikes are less safe to ride in areas where they are uncommon (Chabris and Simons 2010).

There has been a recent upsurge in research on the transition from saccades to objects. The 2008 *Journal of Vision*, for example, devoted an issue to new research (Martinez-Conde et al. 2008). The subsequent research that I will concentrate on (Öğmen et al. 2006; Öğmen 2007; Ayden et al. 2008), supersedes earlier distinguished research by philosophical enactivists (Noë 2004; Rowlands 2010), which stressed our intuitive grasp of the interactions among our movements and what is seen in our environment (the 'sensory-motor contingencies').

The transition from saccades to objects as it is investigated by the research we are considering is bottom-up; it is independent of any knowledge of features other than those revealed in early vision. Consequently, what we have so far gives us experiences that provide us with a world in some sense segmenting into objects. As far as what is relevant for our discussion goes, the scene is a three-dimensional partial array of colored objects and motion; we also have some changes in early visual processing that reflect our experiences of positively and negatively valenced features in the world. Action-relevant factors that might once have been matters of conscious recognition come to affect very primitive features of early sensory processing. This is particularly true of the reward signals that can show up in V1 and allow one to predict the timing of rewards (Shuler and Bear 2006; Montague 2007). We could think of such experiences as giving us a schema that is produced rapidly and that is often a very good guide to action. There is, however, a wide gap between such a schema and the contents of such perceptual reports as "I see the red light of the setting sun filtering through the black and thickly clustered branches of the elms; I see the dappled deer grazing in groups on the vivid green grass" (Noë and Thompson 2002).

Some of the added content comes in as we are able to classify objects. There is an important period in development, which is completed around 12 months, when a child moves from taking spatio-temporal continuity to be enough for the persistence of an object to taking the persistence of a kind as required (Carey and Xu 2001). Before this stage, an object that is occluded may change into any other sort of object, at least as far as the perceiver is concerned. After this stage, the perceiver grasps the predictability of kind persistence. It is here that we seem to have an individual who experiences the world as made up of stable, lasting objects.

What is also important is that the conceptual content of kind concepts, on any recent theory of concepts in psychology, is full of learned data. With classifying objects, we leave the realm of the pure sensory bottom-up processing and start to draw on the results of learning.

Amodal completion by itself gives us a kind of perceptual organization. A great deal more is provided by further conceptualization, which is learned through our social groups.

In addition to conceptualization, we have adding-in, which helps to account for the sense we have of experiencing a gap-less panorama. This last part is accomplished at least largely by experience-based adding or filling-in. Here our sense of what we see goes far beyond what we get from the consolidation of saccades and the resulting objects.

We add in descriptions of things we do see, such as "my neighbor's child," "the President of the United States," and "someone bald from chemotherapy," where what makes these descriptions true is arguably not some feature that affects our retinas. Not only may visual reports add on such descriptions, but we can also correctly put into them things we do not – in some clear sense – see at all. For example, one might say one saw someone next to the bear enclosure or over by the pond even though neither the enclosure nor the pond were visually accessible from where one stood. Though these descriptions of 'extra, unseen things' are part of descriptions of seen things, we can also add in things independently of describing other things. Thus, asked what a burgled store looked like when I entered it, I might report that the vegetables were over to the right of the door even though all I got were some unbound shapes and colors in my peripheral vision. That sort of material can be transformed into a report about things seen if we have good epistemic grounds for taking it to be that which causes in some way our experience.

The adding-in that takes us from the schema to the completed scene in fact draws on a host of factors, including surely our grasp of the relation between our environment and our movement, results from further saccading and conceptualization of its products, past experience with the location and kinds of things to be seen, cultural conventions about artifactual objects, the input of other senses, and so on and so forth. The result is that we no longer have a somewhat schematic and partial scene; rather, as our sensory reports reveal, we have a much fuller picture of the environment. We may still, however, not have the detailed grasp of the faces before us, for example. We may also completely miss out on things we do not expect, including motorcycles, or things we look for frantically, such as car keys.

5 Vision and truth

What should we say now to the idea that vision is a matter of truth-revealing inner experience? The second consolidation allows us a schematic take on the scene before us; without the inclusion of any learned material, we have some movement, some organized objects, along with some material about rewards priming us for action. There is a problem with assessing this material as correct or incorrect; the second consolidation does not cover the whole scene or provide all the details. The gaps, however, need not be in the world itself, and an accurate grasp of what is seen involves an at least implicitly employed distinction between gaps in the experience and gaps in what is experienced. The situation is quite like that of maps. Given a map with an X on it, and told that it shows where the treasure is, one does not begin to know how to look for the treasure. Even the information that the map gives of our environment is not enough. We need more of an interpretation, not just about the scale and orientation of the map, but also in many situations, we need information about, for example, how we incorporate in our plans all the things in the environment that are not on the map. Even in the wonderfully detailed survey maps of England can be seriously ambiguous. Is a broken down and decayed fence the fence on the map? Or is that a bit further on? Is this raised clump of stones the decayed burial mound or not?

We can see much of the adding-in as at least part of the interpretation of our schematic take. Such adding-in is typically automatic and very rapid. If we employ pre-verbal conceptual abilities that recent theorists drawing on sensory experience describe (Barsalou 1999; Prinz 2002), we should expect the adding on to have phenomenological import. This is because of the close connection on such accounts between sensory experience and the deployment of concepts. Consequently, as we have been stressing, what we report ourselves as seeing, and what it feels like phenomenologically to have seen these objects, are quite different from the initial schema. The initial schema is often enough for action, but it falls far short of what we ordinarily think of as what we see.

A familiar point in the philosophical literature on vision provides an important clue for how the adding or filling-in is nonetheless an appropriate thing to do. It is often said that sensory experience is transparent and that even if we try to describe its features, in fact we describe the features of objects. As Gil Harman has famously remarked:

> When you see a tree, you do not experience any features as intrinsic to your experience. Look at a tree and try to turn your attention to the intrinsic features of the visual experience. I predict that the only features you will find to turn your attention to will be features of the presented tree. (Harman 1990: 667)

What we have seen provides something of a correction on this view. Our intrinsic experience is very partial and cannot account by itself for the full description we give of our environment; rather our conceptualization and adding-in creates our understanding of the environment. To articulate our understanding is normally just to describe what is in the environment we have experienced. We learn locutions such as "I see" in the context of experiencing a world full of already named kinds. We cannot report seeing a cat unless we have mastered the reports of there being a cat. From this perspective, "I see the cat" reports an epistemic achievement, not an internal experience. We could say that the initial schema we get is more like an invitation to describe our environment than some sort of message about all that is there.

That we are as a species designed for action too rapid to require much higher level engagement (Montague and Quartz 1999; Montague 2003; Allman 2005; Montague 2007) – still less of internal debates – suggests that beliefs are a separate product caused by an action-oriented vision and a great deal of background information. To hold that in addition to the beliefs, the experience has that content appears to multiply entities without necessity.

Theorists who believe we have truth-revealing inner experience have arguments in their arsenal that I consider elsewhere (Jacobson forthcoming). Principal among these is the claim that the subjective similarities between genuine seeing, on the one hand, and illusions and hallucinations on the other, reveals an ontology needed by theories of vision. In reply I argue that the idea that subjective similarities provide an ontology for science has proved in error enough times to now be incredible.

We have seen enough to provide strong support for the idea that learned material affects our perceptual reports in a way that goes far beyond the visual data that we receive and process in early vision, the visual processing that does not draw on background knowledge and beliefs. As a consequence, much of our reporting of our visual experiences that incorporate the rich panorama are the products of a great deal of learning, including learning to employ the classifications encoded in our language. The result is the product of the physical world, our eyes and brain, and our culture. The accuracy we aim for in our reports, when that is our aim, depends on extensive practice and corrections as we learn to bring our culture and the visual input together. In the next section, we will look briefly at some of the features of vision that become highlighted when we look at it in this way.

6 The politics of seeing

Given recent research, we can see reports of our perceptual experience as close to reports of the environment. Their content draws on the resources of agreed upon classifications, themselves reflecting shared causal knowledge. The community's role in bringing out such a state of affairs is highly significant. Community reactions can also contribute to an increased accuracy in our views about what is plainly available.

Given such a role for the community, we might expect that vision is more of a site of political activity than it might have first occurred to us. And some of it is highly gendered in ways that produce different visual abilities in men and women. But other aspects react also to race, ethnicity, and class. Many of the effects we will look at are foreshadowed above.

6.1 The effects of bias

One variable in one's experience is attention, and stereotypes, conscious or not, can have a large influence on what one attends to. As a consequence, seeing may not be believing, but believing may create much of the seeing. For example, vision can reinforce stereotypes. Even implicit biases that draw on stereotypes we might not articulate can prime us for noticing items related to the stereotypes. The result is visual experiences that enact and confirm bias. For example, if we have the stereotype of black men as dangerous then we will be primed to pick out items around him that might be weapons. Perhaps worse, the more stereotypically black a man is, the more he is to be seen as dangerous (Eberhardt et al. 2004). This puts darker black men at considerable risk in the criminal justice system.

Many factors such as these reduce the evidential value of eyewitness testimony. Nonetheless, prosecutors tend to place great weight on them, and to be skeptical of any concerns that jurors may be mislead (Mukamel et al. 2010). The website of the Innocence Project tells us:

> Eyewitness misidentification is the single greatest cause of wrongful convictions nationwide, playing a role in more than 75% of convictions overturned through DNA testing. While eyewitness testimony can be persuasive evidence before a judge or jury, 30 years of strong social science research has proven that eyewitness identification is often unreliable. Research shows that the human mind is not like a tape recorder; we neither record events exactly as we see them,

nor recall them like a tape that has been rewound. Instead, witness memory is like any other evidence at a crime scene; it must be preserved carefully and retrieved methodically, or it can be contaminated. (Innocence Project)

6.2   Who sees what?

Another area of feminist concern comes into view when we realize vision is used to build potentially social narratives of what there is. This feature fits in with the fact that there can be public standards for competent seeing, and that socialization can make a large difference to a child's ability to meet them. In stereotypical situations, young men may unable to itemize the various components of diaper changing that are on a shelf, while a young woman may be lost at the sight of a car motor. It is arguable that the benefits of this arrangement are to the men. There are serious ramifications, then, for the gender-specific socialization children receive. We know, for example, that spatial imagination can be important for, among other things, doing well on various parts of the SAT exams and later pursuing careers in quantitative fields. But it looks increasingly as though spatial imagination is developed through visual interactions with the environment. Boys' games may well be more helpful here than the stereotypical girls' domestic play.

Some of the evidence that the effect is environmental is that environmental factors can correct some of the deficits. For example, women who play video games for ten hours increase their ability to rotate figures spatially so that they are close to the abilities of their male counterparts (Jing, Spence et al. 2007). IQ scores, it appears, can draw on gendered and malleable abilities.

6.3   Vision and embodiment

One final feature we can note is that the emphasis in philosophy on vision and truth-acquisition and the consequent neglect of vision's excellence in facilitating acting and social connections enacts a familiar bifurcation present in philosophy at least since Descartes. This is the divide between cognition very narrowly construed in terms of truth-seeking and bodily matters, such as actions and shared emotions. Traditionally, the body and emotions are considered outsiders in the philosophical realm, and their frequent and familiar identification with women assigns to women, on a symbolic level at least, a position on the margins of philosophy.

The appropriation of vision as a servant of those who seek truth is worth pursuing a bit. Vision's role in social connections and in action can place it on the side of the instinctive. Some more recent theorists have consigned the instinctive to the female brain, arguing that the analytical brain of men is what is needed for science and leadership, for example (Baron-Cohen 2003). We come full circle in finding that vision's excellence and women are both consigned to a 'lower order' than that needed for genuine truth-seeking.

7 In Conclusion

As Alva Noë has pointed out, it can seem natural to think of vision in terms of a photograph-like experience (Noë 2004). However, recent research makes us aware of how wrong that model is, as Noë also maintains. The product of the visual system is, in contrast to a photograph, incomplete and partial in striking ways that vary with our interests and beliefs. Vision is for meeting the organism's needs in its environment, and not for deciding complex matters of fact.

This chapter has focused to some extent on the resulting gap between perception and our ordinary view about it, much of the latter reflected in the completeness of the examples in the literature of perceptual reports. I have argued that the gap signifies the extent to which our seemingly individual views about the world are replete with influences from social contexts, particularly those in which we learn to conceptualize our environment. In acquiring terms, one also experiences agreement in judgment, a foundation for public discourse.

Arguing that we can understand perceptual reports as more like public performances than like reports on internal experiences goes on the 'analytic' side of project of providing a socially embodied theory of cognition. It is prepares us, though, for the realization that our conception of vision can disguise many ways in which vision has a political dimension. This chapter has just begun investigating that dimension.

11
Beyond Neurosexism: Is It Possible to Defend the Female Brain?

Robyn Bluhm

Over the past few years, the popular science book market has been flooded with books that purport to explain the characteristics of women and of men (as well as the way that these characteristics influence their relationships) in terms of differences in the female and male brains. This genre of pop neuroscience draws on a large body of research that looks for sex differences in neuroanatomy, endocrinology, and physiology and attempts to link these differences to psychological and behavioral differences. Cordelia Fine describes this genre as 'neurosexism'; I propose in this chapter to look more closely at whether and how such sexism occurs. I will argue that what is marketed as self-help ultimately reinforces current, gendered, social practices by reinforcing the stereotypical traits associated with women and with men.

Feminists have had good reason to be wary of the sex difference research upon which these popular books are based. A number of feminist scientists and science studies scholars have criticized the motivations, methods, and conclusions of this research, as well as the biological determinism that often underlies it. Historically, research on biological sex differences has been taken to identify 'natural' and, some conclude, immutable differences between women and men, and these differences have been used to argue for the corresponding naturalness of traditional gender roles.

Yet in contemporary society, we recognize that traditional gender roles are far from immutable, which would seem to suggest that the biological determinism and gender essentialism promoted by such sex difference research has been successfully refuted. A closer look at the pop neuroscience described above reveals that these ideas are alive and well, though the political message drawn from 'natural' sex differences has changed – at least on the surface. Although the title of one book refers to the "Fascinating and Unalterable Differences Between Men and Women" (Moir and Moir 2003), another promises to tell us not just "How We're Different" but also "What to Do About It" (Pease and Pease 2001). Sex differences, these books suggest, are real and natural, but this scientific truth is compatible with gender equality, and even, in some cases, with an empowering message. Two books in particular, Louanne Brizendine's *The Female Brain* (2006) and Mona Lisa Schulz's *The New Feminine Brain: Developing Your Intuitive Genius* (2006) argue that women's brains give them particular strengths and abilities, and that understanding how these abilities arise as a direct result of neurobiology can help women to better appreciate and draw on their natural talents.

I will argue in this chapter, however, that this supposedly liberatory message is at best equivocal, and that we still have good reason to distrust neurobiological explanations of differences between women and men, particularly when they appear in popular culture. Not only do these books present a deterministic story of development that sees sex differences as inevitable, but they also reinforce, not traditional gender roles directly, but the gender stereotypes that underlie these roles. The result is a sexism that is more insidious, but no less problematic than the overt misogyny of earlier sex difference researchers.

I will begin by briefly reviewing feminist assessments of past sex difference research and its historical relation to social movements aimed at changing traditional gender roles. This background provides a framework within which to examine the recent spate of pop neuroscience and shows why this genre should be of interest to feminists. I will then describe the way in which sex difference research is presented in these books, focusing in particular on those by Brizendine and by Schulz. Although these books purport to empower women, their defense of the 'female brain' is far from convincing.

1 Sex difference research and its social context

Biological explanations of women's inferiority are at least as old as the work of Aristotle (see Tuana 1993). At the end of the nineteenth century, however, this line of research took on a new urgency. Women in England and in the United States were beginning to demand equal access to education and the right to participate in public life. Scientists, concerned with the detrimental effects of such activities on women's health, argued that too much intellectual stimulation would divert physiological energy from women's reproductive organs to their brains, with disastrous results not only for would-be scholars, but also for the human race, as babies born to intellectual mothers would be damaged, resulting in "a puny, enfeebled race" (Maudsley 1874: 472; quoted in Sayers 1982: 18).

Not only would educating women have terrible consequences, but the effort to do so would be futile, because women were naturally intellectually inferior to men; examination of their skulls (which reflected the underlying brain) provided 'proof' of this (Fee 1979). Yet it was not entirely clear *which* characteristics of women's brains provided proof of their intellectual inferiority. Carol Tavris summarizes the difficulties experienced by scientists trying to explain the neuroanatomical basis of sex differences in intelligence:

> A century ago, scientists tried to prove that women had smaller brains than men did, which accounted for women's alleged intellectual failings and emotional weaknesses. Dozens of studies purported to show that men had larger brains, making them smarter than women. When scientists realized that men's greater height and weight offset their brain-size advantage, however, they dropped this line of research like a shot. The scientists next tried to argue that women had smaller frontal lobes and larger parietal lobes than men did, another brain pattern thought to account for women's intellectual inferiority. Then it was reported that the parietal lobes might be associated with intellect. Panic in the labs – until anatomists suddenly found that women's parietal lobes were *smaller* than they had originally believed. (Tavris 1993: 44)

The second major period of sex difference research addressed by feminist scholars began in the 1960s and continued throughout the 1970s and 1980s. At this time, the focus was on endocrinology; the idea was that exposure to different hormones during fetal development resulted in different wiring patterns for female and for male brains. According to the researchers in this field, these differences were permanent, unalterable by experience, and explained the characteristic behaviors and personality traits associated with femininity and masculinity. During this time, as well, sociobiology became popular, and was linked with research in endocrinology to show that the cause of hormonal sex differences was ultimately genetic, and thus selected for in the distant evolutionary past of the human species. Together, developmental endocrinology and sociobiology painted a linear and deterministic picture of human development and of sex differences: genes led to the production of hormones, hormones shaped the developing fetal brain prior to birth (suggesting that sex differences were 'hardwired' by the time of birth, so that 'environmental' influences on brain development were minimal), and the resulting male or female brain caused psychological and behavioral characteristics associated with being male or female.

Although the sociobiological influence during this period led to conclusions about gender roles relevant to reproduction and childrearing, the endocrinological component also influenced research on the different cognitive abilities of women and of men. After a brief period in which the 'dominance' of one brain hemisphere or the other was suggested as the root of sex differences in cognition (which foundered because the desirable characteristics associated with each hemisphere were also associated with men), it was decided that the real neuroanatomical basis for cognitive sex differences was the extent to which the two hemispheres are connected. The corpus callosum, a thick tract of fibers connecting the left and right hemispheres, was supposed to be smaller in men, with the result that their left hemisphere (responsible for logical, intellectual activity) and right hemisphere (responsible for mathematical and visuospatial abilities) worked relatively independently, allowing the special characteristics of each to develop to a high degree. Women's brain hemispheres were more tightly connected, explaining their linguistic abilities and the fact that they are more in touch with their emotions. As we shall see, this line of research is used by Schulz and by Brizendine in their defense of the female brain.

Yet, like the craniology research critiqued by Tavris and Fee, the results of investigations of sex differences in the corpus callosum have been far from unequivocal. Research has focused mainly on the splenium (the posterior fifth of the corpus callosum), with reports that both the size and the shape of this region differ between the sexes. Results between studies have not been consistent, however, and a meta-analysis published in 1997 (Bishop and Wahlsten 1997) reports that there is no difference in either the size or the shape of the splenium. Anne Fausto-Sterling (2000b) has reviewed the extensive literature on sex differences in the corpus callosum and shown that the results obtained by any given study are influenced by the methods used, which are not consistent between studies. Whether or not a sex difference was found may also depend on whether the study has used *in vivo* imaging or postmortem brains (and, in the latter case, on how the brain was preserved), on the age of the subjects, on their handedness, and, perhaps most importantly, on the way in which the corpus callosum was measured, for which there is no agreed-upon standard. Fausto-Sterling concludes that "[s]cientists have employed their immense talents to try to get rid of background noise, to see if they can more clearly tune in the [corpus callosum], but the corpus callosum is a pretty uncooperative medium for locating differences. That researchers continue to probe the corpus callosum in search of a definitive gender difference speaks to how entrenched their expectations about biological difference remain" (2000b: 145). As with the earlier research on brain size and intelligence, scientists seem to start with the unshakeable belief in cognitive gender differences and then to engage in Procrustean maneuvers in order to find the neural basis for these differences.

It is perhaps no accident that sex difference research gained a new popularity during the 1960s and 1970s. Ruth Hubbard suggests that "to be believed scientific facts must fit the world-view of the times. For this reason, since the social upheavals that started in the 1960s, some researchers have tried to 'prove' that differences in the political, social, and economic status of women and men, blacks and whites, or poor people and rich people are the inevitable outcomes of people's inborn qualities" (1992: 25). Janet Sayers and Lynda Birke both note that biological determinism was explicitly used to oppose feminist demands for equality. Birke suggests that right-wing arguments in the UK focused on the social constructionism of the 1970s Left, and proceeded to ridicule the claim that 'all' behavior was socially constructed. In this way, "the counterposed biological position acquires the status of common sense" (Birke 1986: 39). Birke also notes that sociobiology, in particular, was used by both the mainstream media and the extreme right-wing National Front to argue for the immutability of gender roles, particularly male aggression and "the 'naturalness' of women's place as wife and mother" (Birke 1986: 37).

Similarly, Sayers describes the way in which brain research on brain lateralization was used to explain women's "lack of achievement in specific professions – particularly in engineering and architecture – not in professional life in general" (Sayers 1982: 97). Although the supposed domain of women's inferiority had shrunk since the craniotomy of the nineteenth century, the remaining areas of inferiority were still held to be the result of innate, biologically determined differences in the brain. While the particular phenomena to be explained by appeal to sex differences in the brain shifted to reflect dominant gender stereotypes and expectations about appropriate gender roles, what remained constant between these two eras was the appeal to supposedly natural and therefore unchangeable differences.

The past use of research on sex differences shows that this research fits with a conservative agenda that views women's place as in the home.

Yet few people in the audiences to which current books are marketed would argue that women should not be educated, or do not belong in the workforce. The questions thus arise: why is there such an appetite now for pop neuroscience works 'explaining' sex differences? And what social and political functions do such books serve now? In the next section, I describe this genre, focusing in particular on the books by Brizendine and by Schulz, which claim to empower women by teaching them about their brains.

2   Sex difference research and pop neuroscience

In the previous section, I described the political use to which sex difference research has been put in the past and showed that the political power of this research comes from the idea that differences between women and men are biologically determined – the result of nature and not of nurture, and therefore not amenable to change by changing social practices. This deterministic framework, however, has been criticized by a number of writers, both feminist and non-feminist, who show that the linear story of genes-to-hormones-to-brain-to-behavior is insufficient to capture the complexity of neural development and that it is a mistake to view the brain as hardwired and set in its (sex-specific) ways early in life. (See, for example, Gould 1981; Sayers 1982; Bleier 1984; Lewontin, Rose, and Kamin 1985; Longino and Doell 1985; Birke 1986; Hubbard 1992; Fausto-Sterling 1992, 2000b; Rogers 2002.) Yet the linear, deterministic model of development is still commonly accepted and underlies much current research on development (see Jordan-Young 2010 for an overview and current critique of this line of research).

   In general, pop neuroscience cleaves to the story that evolution determines early development and early development in turn determines behavior. It also tends to make sweeping generalizations about the personalities and preferences of men and of women, occasionally noting parenthetically that these generalizations are averages or tendencies. Simon Baron-Cohen, for example, states early in his book that his discussion refers to "the average female, compared to the average male" (Baron-Cohen 2003: 2), though it should be noted that he still titles his book *The **Essential** Difference* (emphasis mine), suggesting that the brain differences he describes are inextricably tied to being female or male. It should also be noted that, leaving aside the problems with the deterministic framework itself, the interpretation and presentation of science conducted within the framework by pop neuroscience writers may be even more problematic. Brizendine, in particular, has come under fire for her sloppy scholarship and her tendency to use references that bear little or no relation to the claims she is making (Young and Balaban 2006; Fine 2008b, 2010a; see also several postings on the Language Log blog, listed in Liberman 2007).

Both Brizendine and Schulz are forthright in their beliefs that the female brain is fundamentally different from the male brain; that this difference is due to innate factors, with only a small contribution from cultural influences; and that because of these differences, women have special strengths, but also face special challenges. Both also see their books as providing women with information they need in order to make the most of their feminine brains. Brizendine views her book as able to help women by telling them the truth about their biological reality:

> My personal mission has been to educate interested physicians, psychologists, teachers, nurses, pharmacists and their trainees to benefit the women and teen girls they serve. I have taken every opportunity to educate women and girls directly about their unique brain-body-behavior system and help them to be their best at every age. It is my hope that this book will benefit many more women and girls than I can personally reach in the clinic. It is my hope that the female brain will be seen and understood as the finely tuned and talented instrument that it is. (Brizendine 2006: 9)

Similarly, Schulz claims that "for the last fifty years, women have had to fit their brains into a 'male' world. We have had to learn how, as the song says, 'walk like a man,' and 'talk like a man' but stay a woman inside. To accommodate those two divergent roles, our brains have had to rewire themselves" (Schulz 2006: 3).[1] She continues: "In this book, I'll tell you how, as a woman, you can keep your brain tuned in to your natural mood cycles and thought patterns, but also be able to tune in to the new challenges that you face as you go to work in the boardroom, the home, the hospital, or the office – without compromising your health" (Schulz 2006: 3–4).

What *are* the features that supposedly characterize the female brain? Perhaps not surprisingly, given both prevalent gender stereotypes and the idea that men's brains are more lateralized than women's, the female brain is supposed to be all about connection. At a social level, women are driven to connect with each other, with their mates, and with their children. At an anatomical level, this social connectedness is explained in part with reference to hormones that sculpted the brain during fetal development (emphasized by Brizendine) and the resulting physical connections between various parts of the brain (described by both authors). As noted above, both authors also view these differences as innate, shaped by our distant evolutionary heritage. In describing research that (supposedly) shows that, starting from infancy, girls are better able than boys to read faces and to hear emotional tones in voices, Brizendine says that social connection is "the main job of the girl brain, and that's what it drives a female to do from birth. This is the result of millennia of genetic and evolutionary hardwiring that once had – and probably still has – real consequences for survival" (Brizendine 2006: 21). This connectivity is also physical: "Picture, for a moment, a map showing the areas for emotion in the brains of the two sexes. In the man's brain, the connecting routes between areas would be country roads; in the woman's brain, they'd be superhighways" (Brizendine 2006: 127).

Schulz provides a breakdown of the main traits that characterize the traditional female and the traditional male brains. Women's brains have more connections between brain areas, which, according to Schulz, at least, means that men's thinking is more compartmentalized. Men are also more likely to think about only one thing at a time: "When one area of the brain is functioning, the other areas are relatively silent; you get one clear signal, while the others are relatively muted" (Schulz 2006: 21), and their brains have "less capacity for growth and change, more anatomic stability" (Schulz 2006: 19). Schulz also draws here on the research on the corpus callosum described above, which purports to show that the corpus callosum is bigger in women. According to Schulz, "[t]hese basic structural differences may explain some of the differences between men and women in how they see the world, what they pay attention to, how they remember events, and how they get in touch with their intuition" (Schulz 2006: 21). She cautions that these differences do not mean that one type of brain is superior to the other; rather they reflect different abilities acquired during our evolutionary history; men needed to adapt to perform highly focused tasks (hunting, protecting the tribe), whereas women in the Stone Age were multi-taskers, rearing children, gathering food, maintaining the cohesiveness of the family unit and connections among tribal families.

Although they both deny that they are biological determinists, Brizendine and Schulz both convey the message that women today must do battle with their Stone Age brains in order to succeed. Brizendine describes the ways in which the female brain affects women's experiences and behavior. In doing so, she consistently describes the brain – not the girl or woman inside whom the brain is located – as an agent. For example: A toddler who demands to be included in all of her parents' conversations is not spoiled: "It was just [her] brain searching for a way to validate her sense of self" (Brizendine 2006: 17). Marcie's Stone Age brain thinks that John is sexy and good-looking enough to be a good genetic bet for her offspring (Brizendine 2006: 84). The female brain has an "extreme ability to connect through reading faces, interpreting tones of voice, and registering the nuances of emotion" (Brizendine 2006: 115), though if "she's [*sic*] married or partnered with a male brain, each will inhabit two different emotional realities" (Brizendine 2006: 116). By casting the brain – with its hardwired impulses – as the agent, Brizendine seems to imply that the woman in whom the brain is located is merely a vehicle for transmitting information to and from the brain.

So far, this description of Brizendine's work seems to be perfectly congruent with the kind of deterministic thinking critiqued by feminist scholars. It seems, at many points in her book, that she believes that that we are biologically hardwired to have the desires, values, and reactions to others that characterize our sex. We are therefore all biologically determined. Yet Brizendine does not draw this conclusion from her analysis: Rather, she says, biology does not *have to* become destiny. "Biological instincts are the keys to understanding how we are wired, and they are the keys to our success today. If you're aware of the fact that a biological brain state is guiding your impulses you can choose not to act or to act differently than you might feel compelled. But first we have to learn to recognize how the female brain is genetically structured and shaped by evolution, biology and culture. Without that recognition, biology becomes destiny and we will all be helpless in the face of it" (Brizendine 2006: 6).

Despite this hopeful message, Brizendine offers no guidance for overcoming these 'compulsions.' The best that she offers is a version of the old phrase: 'forewarned is forearmed.' Now that women are delaying childbearing in order to focus on their careers, they are doomed, when they do have children, to face "an inevitable tug-of-war because of overloaded brain circuits" (Brizendine 2006: 160). Brizendine asks: "What does all of this mean in terms of a woman's innate brain biology? It doesn't mean that women should get off the path of motherhood combined with career; it just means they may benefit from getting a glimpse of all the balls they will need to juggle starting in their teen years" (Brizendine 2006: 160).

The picture painted by Schulz is even gloomier. Being a woman today, it seems, is a challenge because of the need to impose masculine styles of thought on a 'traditional' female brain, which, Schulz warns, can take a toll on a woman's mental and emotional health. "When you were born, you had a traditional female brain that combined the genetic heritage of your parents and the in utero environment in which your mother developed you until you were born. Then, as you grew up in the incubator of your childhood, that genetic heritage was molded and acculturated to life in this society" (Schulz 2006: 5). "On top of our inborn feminine wiring, we must develop or sprout new pathways in the brain – new responses, actions, and behaviors, too – to survive in jobs and careers that require a more male, compartmentalized brain style" (Schulz 2006: 16). These new pathways, though, come at a cost. The "New Feminine Brain," Schulz informs us "doesn't have all the bugs worked out of it" (Schulz 2006: 16). Like Brizendine, Schulz sees women as being largely at the mercy of their brains: "The New Feminine Brain's recently acquired brain pathways can create tension with the old brain and body, leaving a woman stuck in the middle, unable to make key decisions about her life, including vocational goals, relationships, or her place in society" (Schulz 2006: 16). The bulk of the book describes the problems that arise because of the 'bugginess' of the new feminine brain. The new neural pathways women have sprouted leave them vulnerable to depression, anxiety, obsessive compulsive disorder, and phobias, and Schulz addresses each of these in turn, with recommendations on how to treat each disorder with pharmacotherapy, psychotherapy, vitamins, meditation, etc. Behind every great New Feminine Brain, it seems, is a great therapist.

The defense of the female brain offered in these books seems to be less than inspiring. Women's brains give them unique abilities, to be sure, but these abilities mean that women must continually struggle with their natural inclinations and tendencies in order to succeed. On Brizendine's and Schulz's rendition, biology does not *prevent* women from professional accomplishment – on the contrary, women can (like the authors) achieve great success. But biology *does* mean that women's successes will be much harder achieved than men's, whether because they must adopt a masculine style of thought (as Schulz suggests) or struggle to balance their professional lives with their distinctly feminine need to focus on their relationships and to nurture their children (as Brizendine claims). In either case, the message is that women *can* do anything that they want to, but that, owing to their female brains, it will certainly be a lot of work and possibly even a hazard to their health.

One could be forgiven for wondering at this point at the popularity of these books. Why would anybody want to hear this depressing message? One reason is that it seems to resonate with readers' own experiences.

Both books are the subject of a number of glowing reviews online: "I love this book b/c it explains so much about me"[2] (on Schulz's book) or "it was...reassuring to understand my own behavior as part of being female"[3] (on Brizendine's). The reviewers also seem to slide uncritically from the accuracy of the authors' descriptions of women to the accuracy of their explanations of women's characteristics and experiences: one reader of Schulz's book says: "Women have always known that they are born multi-taskers, that they have a sixth sense and a great sensitivity. Through Schulz's findings we discover why."[4] Schulz and Brizendine are certainly saying something that their readers want to hear. But the fact that the descriptions these authors provide of women's lives and experiences ring true to the experiences of women reading the books is clearly not evidence for the truth of the 'explanations' of these experiences in terms of neurobiology. Yet these 'explanations' serve to reinforce the gender stereotypes they purport to explain; by making it seem that women's experiences are the result of their 'female' brains, these books make gender stereotypes seem natural. Women are emotional, nurturing, and concerned about relationships because of the way that their brains are wired.

Although contemporary pop neuroscience does not follow earlier discussions of sex difference research in drawing conclusions about gender *roles* on the basis of the different biologies and characteristics of women and of men, it is no less committed to the conclusion that these biologies and characteristics *are* different. As such, it does carry implications for the way that women will experience the demands of work and of family. To see how these implications are drawn out in pop neuroscience, it will be helpful to contrast the current discussion of sex differences with earlier discussions of gender and gender roles.

Popular culture has a well-recognized ability to normalize the status quo, including gender roles. In *The Feminine Mystique*, Betty Friedan (1963) expressed concerns that women's magazines keep women in the home, and as late as 1978, Gayle Tuchman argued that they portrayed the ideal woman as passive and dependent: "her fate and happiness rest with a man, not with participation in the labor force" (Tuchman 1978: 18). Like the academic and media discussions of the time, popular culture of the 1960s and 1970s served to reinforce the status quo of gender roles and relations. Recall that neuroscience was used in the late nineteenth century to argue for women's lack of intellectual ability – just as women were demanding access to education. The linear model (genes-to-hormones-to-brains-to-behavior) developed during the 1970s was used to argue for the inevitability of traditional gender roles – just as (middle-class, married) women were entering the workforce in large numbers. That is, the claims about gender difference that were supposedly supported by appeal to differences in the brain were claims that had a direct relationship to social and political issues relevant to women's equality. In both cases, women's demands for equal treatment were opposed by 'evidence' that equal treatment was not possible because of women's biologically determined characteristics and abilities, and that attempts to fulfill these demands would have detrimental effects on both society as a whole and on women who tried to go against their natures. Clearly, attempting to change gender roles would be courting disaster. Women's magazines added to this the idea that women would only be truly happy in their traditional roles.

The linear model of brain development also underlies the arguments made by Brizendine and by Schulz in support of the claim that women and men have fundamentally different natures. Both authors also say that women who have entered the traditionally masculine world by having careers are to some extent going against their instincts. Yet neither author draws the conclusion that we should maintain (or return to) traditional gender roles, nor does it seem likely that *this* claim would resonate with their readers. I suggest, though, that pop neuroscience is just as conservative as earlier discussions of the implications of (supposed) sex differences in the brain. What has changed is the social milieu that is being conserved. As Deborah Rhode notes: "Over the past several decades…women's opportunities and employment patterns have changed considerably, but traditional gender stereotypes remain much the same" (Rhode 1997: 73). By focusing on sex differences in personality and characteristics, rather than on differences in abilities, Brizendine and Schulz are able to support gender stereotypes without drawing explicit conclusions about gender roles. In other words, their focus is on women's characteristics and abilities, not (directly) on the social and vocational roles that these characteristics and abilities make suitable for women. But because these characteristics are considered to be natural and largely unchangeable, they still carry implications for social arrangements.

The question, then, is what social arrangements are being bolstered by pop neuroscience? To answer this, let us begin by looking again at the characterization of the female brain offered by Schulz and Brizendine. On their accounts, the female brain is all about connection, mainly social connection but also connections in a broader sense. Women are more in tune with their emotions and more concerned with the emotional states of others. Women are driven to have and to nurture children. And women are natural multi-taskers, able to cope with multiple demands and roles. All of this, of course, is in comparison with men, whose brains render them comparatively oblivious to their own and others' emotional needs, less focused on their children, less able to adapt to changing circumstances, and able to perform only one task at a time.

The take-home messages seem to be that (1) women are essentially nurturing, particularly when it comes to the needs of children, and (2) women are better able than men to balance conflicting or competing demands. So, how do these messages fit with the current state of gender relations and with the broader social context? Since the 1970s, women have made great progress in their work lives; it is no longer surprising that women should work (and want to work) outside the home. Yet other changes have been slower. In general, men do not seem to have been as quick to the embrace domestic and childcare responsibilities that have traditionally fallen to women as women have to enter the traditionally male public sphere. Because of this, sociologist Arlie Hochschild noted, many women work a 'second shift' upon returning home from the workplace (Hochschild and Machung 1989). Working mothers, in particular, frequently report feeling unable to balance career and home life and may drop down to part-time work or even leave the workforce. Although this phenomenon is often described in terms of women's choices (because their nurturing natures mean that they prefer to be at home?), the structure of the work world may actually force them out (Stone 2008). Even young adults, who have been raised to believe in gender equality "fear it may not be possible to forge an enduring, egalitarian relationship or integrate committed careers with devoted parenting" (Gerson 2009: 11). In short, despite the progress in gender equality made in the past few decades, we still live in what Peggy Orenstein calls a "half-changed world" (Orenstein 2001), the result of an "unfinished revolution" (Gerson 2009).

This is the status quo that Brizendine and Schulz are supporting. Again, both authors claim that they believe that women can thrive. Brizendine, for example, suggests that "Our modern challenge is to help society better support our natural female abilities and needs" (Brizendine 2006: 160). But their ultimate message is that gender equality has come just about as far as it can; remaining social problems are the result of innate differences in women's and men's natures. Brizendine even goes so far as to say that to deny these innate differences is to eschew science in favor of political correctness (Brizendine 2006: 162).

But there is another, even more problematic, aspect to this message: because women are the nurturers and the multi-taskers, it is up to them to absorb the tensions and contradictions of the half-changed world. Cordelia Fine links the appeal of pop neuroscience books with the psychological process of 'system justification,' on which "people justify and rationalize the way things are, so that existing social arrangements are perceived as fair and legitimate, perhaps even natural and inevitable" (Jost et al. 2002, quoted in Fine 2008a: 70). Fine gives the example of a woman who comforts herself with the idea that her "hardwired powers of female empathy" are the reason that she is the only one to attend to the needs of a cranky baby (Fine 2008a: 70). These examples fit with the pop neuroscience message that women are best able to nurture and to tend to the emotional needs of others.

Similarly, Amy Adele Hasinoff has examined the prevalence and function of sociobiological arguments in the popular magazine *Cosmopolitan*. She shows that, since the early 1990s, articles that use sociobiological reasoning, as well as interviews with experts in the field, have frequently appeared in the magazine. She describes the way in which men are portrayed in the magazine, as well as the way in which women are advised to respond to them. Men are "thoroughly perplexing and essentially inferior" (Hasinoff 2009: 276) to women. Moreover, "women's genetically predetermined desire to domesticate men is constantly at odds with men's supposedly primal aversion to household labor and lack of emotional intelligence" (Hasinoff 2009: 277). Since men's behavior is the result of their 'caveman biology,' and since men are the inferior sex, it is up to women to tolerate their flaws and annoying habits. Since immutable caveman biology also guarantees the failure of any efforts to effect social change, Hasinoff concludes that the message for women is that they must learn to solve their own problems, because "the social system they live in is inescapable [and] they had best make the most of it" (Hasinoff 2009: 280). Hasinoff's analysis echoes the words of Brizendine and Schulz, but she draws the seemingly inevitable conclusion that the pop neuroscientists leave implicit.

Both Fine and Hasinoff focus mainly on the implications of our 'innate biology' for interpersonal relationships. Yet appeal to this version of biology also plays a role in pop neuroscience's depiction of women's professional lives as well. As noted above, Schulz describes the necessity for women to adopt more 'masculine' strategies and behaviors in the workplace, while Brizendine warns that women (especially working mothers) will always experience a conflict between their professional and domestic lives. (This latter warning prompts Fine to worry that working mothers' brains might explode.) The impression left upon readers is that both the personal and the professional frustrations experienced by women are the result of the (innately determined) wiring of the female brain. This impression also reinforces the idea that the inescapable social system to which Hasinoff refers has shaped the professional as well as the private sphere. Rather than demand the development of family friendly policies and more flexible working conditions, individuals (particularly multi-tasking women) must learn to adjust to the demands of the traditional, masculine world of work. And what about women who do not adjust, who, in Pamela Stone's term, 'opt out' of the workplace? Or, for that matter, men who continue to put career before family? If women's and men's attitudes toward work and family are indeed hardwired, the fault is clearly not with companies and governments that fail to meet the needs of workers. As Rosaline Barnett and Caryl Rivers note, "If we believe that men and women are inevitably and innately different, we won't regard policies that limit women at work as discrimination, but rather as the logical outcome of women's 'choice' not to seek good jobs. We won't expand parental leave for fathers (as much as they might want it) because men are not 'natural' caregivers" (Barnett and Rivers 2005: 13).

Clearly, the description of women given by Schulz and by Brizendine is at the very least compatible with rationalizations of the half-changed state of society. Moreover, their insistence that women will inevitably find it difficult to cope professionally, especially when balancing their jobs with family life, because of their female brains, carries the implication that nothing is going to change. By presenting gender stereotypes as the result of innate differences between the sexes, and backing these claims with a mix of homey anecdote and scientific authority, pop neuroscience reinforces and normalizes the status quo. Although not overtly misogynistic like some earlier sex difference research (and its use in social and political debates), books like those by Brizendine and by Schulz present the most recent version of the old claim that 'biology is destiny.' Society may change, but ultimately, women, men, and the differences between them do not.

Notes

Thank you to Anne Jaap Jacobson, Heidi Lene Maibom, and Ginger Hoffman for their comments on an earlier draft of this chapter.

1. The inconsistent messages about innate ('hardwired') differences that are still somehow open to 'rewiring' is a characteristic feature both of Brizendine's and Schulz's discussions. Thanks to Ginger Hoffman for pointing this out.
2. Schulz – T. Griffin, 7 April 2008 , accessed 15 March 2011.

3. Brizendine – Aimee Fuller, 9 November 2006 (http://www.amazon.com/ Female-Brain-Louann-Brizendine/product-reviews/0767920104/ref=cm_cr_ pr_link_next_2?ie=UTF8&showViewpoints=0&filterBy=addFiveStar&pageN umber=2), accessed 15 March 2011.
4. Schulz – Jonni O'Conner, 3 September 2005 (http://www.amazon.com/New-Feminine-Brain-Developing-Intuitive/product-reviews/0743243072/ref=cm_ cr_dp_hist_5?ie=UTF8&showViewpoints=0&filterBy=addFiveStar), accessed 15 March 2011.

Bibliography

Abell, F., Happé, F. and Frith, U. (2000) Do Triangles Play Tricks? Attribution of Mental States to Animated Shapes in Normal and Abnormal Development. *Cognitive Development* 15: 1–16.

Adams, F. and Aizawa, K. (2008) *The Bounds of Cognition* (Malden, MA: Blackwell).

Ah-King, M. (2009) Queer Nature: Towards a Non-Normative Perspective on Biological Diversity. In J. Bromseth, L. Folkmarson Käll and K. Mattsson (eds), *Body Claims* (Uppsala: Centre for Gender Research, Uppsala University).

Ahmed, S. (2004) *The Cultural Politics of Emotion* (Edinburgh: Edinburgh University Press).

Alcoff, L. (1988) Cultural Feminism versus Post-Structuralism: The Identity Crisis in Feminist Theory. *Signs* 13(3): 405–436.

Alexander, G. M. and Evardone, M. (2008) Blocks and Bodies: Sex Differences in a Novel Version of the Mental Rotations Test. *Hormones and Behavior* 53: 177–184.

Alexander, G. M. and Hines, M. (2002) Sex Differences in Response to Children's Toys in Nonhuman Primates (*Cercopithecus aethiops sabaeus*). *Evolution and Human Behavior* 23: 467–479.

Allen, J., Damasio, H., Grabowski, T., Bruss, J. and Zhang, W. (2003) Sexual Dimorphism and Asymmetries in the Gray–White Composition of the Human Cerebrum. *NeuroImage* 18: 880–894.

Allen, L. S., Hines, M. et al. (1989) 2 Sexually Dimorphic Cell Groups in the Human Brain. *Journal of Neuroscience* 9(2): 497–506.

Allman, J. M., Watson, K. K., Tetreault, N. A. and Hakeem, A. Y. (2005) Intuition and Autism: A Possible Role for Von Economo Neurons. *Trends in Cognitive Sciences* 9(8): 367–373.

Alvarez-Buylla, A. and Nottebohm, F. (1988) Migration of Young Neurons in Adult Avian Brain. *Nature* 335: 353–354.

American Academy of Pediatrics (AAP) Section on Urology (1996) Timing of Elective Surgery on the Genitalia of Male Children with Particular Reference to the Risks, Benefits, and Psychological Effects of Surgery and Anesthesia. *Pediatrics* 97(4): 590–594.

Ames, D. R. and Kammrath, L. K. (2004) Mind-Reading and Metacognition: Narcissism, Not Actual Competence, Predicts Self-Estimated Ability. *Journal of Nonverbal Behavior* 28: 187–209.

Anderson, E. (2011) Feminist Epistemology and Philosophy of Science. *Stanford Encyclopedia of Philosophy* (http://plato.stanford.edu/entries/feminism-epistemology/), accessed 5 December 2011.

Auyeung, B., Baron-Cohen, S., Chapman, E., Knickmeyer, R., Taylor, K. and Hackett, G. (2006) Foetal Testosterone and the Child Systemizing Quotient. *European Journal of Endocrinology* 155: S123–S130.

Auyeung, B., Baron-Cohen, S., Ashwin, E., Knickmeyer, R., Taylor, K. and Hackett, G. (2009a) Fetal Testosterone and Autistic Traits. *British Journal of Psychology* 100: 1–22.

Auyeung, B., Baron-Cohen, S., Ashwin, E., Knickmeyer, R., Taylor, K., Hackett, G. et al. (2009b) Fetal Testosterone Predicts Sexually Differentiated Childhood Behaviour in Girls and in Boys. *Psychological Science* 20: 144–148.

Axelrod, R. (1984) *The Evolution of Cooperation* (New York: Basic Books).

Ayden, M., Herzog, M. H. et al. (2008) Perceived Speed Differences Explain Apparent Compression in Slit Viewing. *Vision Research* 48(15): 1603.

Azim, E., Mobbs, D., Jo, B., Menon, V. and Reiss, A. L. (2005) Sex Differences in Brain Activation Elicited by Humor. *Proceedings of the National Academy of Sciences USA* 102(45): 16496–16501.

Baenninger, M. and Newcombe, N. (1989) The Role of Experience in Spatial Test Performance: A Meta-Analysis. *Sex Roles* 20: 327–344.

Bagemihl, B. (1999) *Biological Exuberance: Animal Homosexuality and Natural Diversity* (New York: St. Martin's Press).

Baier, A. (1991) *A Progress of Sentiments: Reflections on Hume's 'Treatise'* (Cambridge, MA: Harvard University Press).

Baier, A. (1994) *Moral Prejudices: Essays on Ethics* (Cambridge, MA: Harvard University Press).

Baier, A. (1997) *The Commons of the Mind* (Chicago: Open Court).

Balaban, E. (2006) Cognitive Developmental Biology: History, Process and Fortune's Wheel. *Cognition* 101(2): 298–332.

Banville, J. (2006) Temple of Mysteries. *Tate Etc.* Issue 7 (http://www.tate.org.uk/tateetc/issue7/rothko.htm).

Bao, A. M. and Swaab, D. F. (2010) Sex Differences in the Brain, Behavior, and Neuropsychiatric Disorders. *Neuroscientist* 16(5): 550–565.

Barad, K. (1999) Agential Realism: Feminist Interventions in Understanding. In M. Biagioli (ed.), *The Science Studies Reader* (New York: Routledge), 1–11.

Barad, K. (2003) Posthumanist Performativity: Toward an Understanding of How Matter Comes to Matter'. *Signs: Journal of Women in Culture and Society* 28(3): 801–831.

Barad, K. (2007) *Meeting the Universe Halfway: Quantum Physics and the Entanglement of Matter and Meaning* (Durham: Duke University Press).

Barnett, R. and Rivers C. (2005) *Same Difference: How Gender Myths are Hurting Our Relationships, Our Children, and Our Jobs* (New York: Basic Books).

Baron-Cohen, S. (2002) The Extreme Male Brain Theory of Autism. *Trends in Cognitive Sciences*, 6: 248–254.

Baron-Cohen, S. (2003) *The Essential Difference: Men, Women and the Extreme Male Brain* (London: Allen Lane).

Baron-Cohen, S. (2007) Sex Differences in Mind: Keeping Science Distinct from Social Policy. In S. J. Ceci and W. M. Williams (eds), *Why Aren't More Women in Science? Top Researchers Debate the Evidence* (Washington, DC: APA), 159–172.

Baron-Cohen, S. and Wheelwright, S. (2004) The Empathy Quotient: An Investigation of Adults with Asperger Syndrome or High Functioning Autism, and Normal Sex Differences. *Journal of Autism and Developmental Disorders* 34: 163–175.

Baron-Cohen, S., Knickmeyer, R. C. and Belmonte, M. K. (2005) Sex Differences in the Brain: Implications for Explaining Autism. *Science* 310: 819–823.

Baron-Cohen, S., O'Riordan, M., Stone, V., Jones, R. and Plaisted, K. (1999) Recognition of Faux Pas by Normally Developing Children and Children with Asperger Syndrome or High Functioning Autism. *Journal of Autism and Developmental Disorders* 29: 407–418.

Baron-Cohen, S., Richler, J., Bisarya, D., Gurunathan, N. and Wheelwright, S. (2003) The Systemizing Quotient: An Investigation of Adults with Asperger Syndrome or High-Functioning Autism, and Normal Sex Differences. *Philosophical Transactions of the Royal Society of London B* 358(1430): 361–374.

Barsalou, L. W. (1999) Perceptual Symbol Systems. *Behavioral and Brain Sciences* 22(4): 577.

Batson, D. (1991) *The Altruism Question: Towards a Social-Psychological Answer* (Hillsdale, NJ: Lawrence Erlbaum Associates).

Batson, D. (2009) Empathic Concern and Altruism in Humans. The National Humanities Center's Web Project: 'On the Human' (http://onthehuman. org/2009/10/empathic-concern-and-altruism-in-humans/), accessed November 2009.

Batson, C. D. (2011) *Altruism in Humans* (New York: Oxford University Press).

Batson, D., Early, S., and Salvarini, G. (1997). Perspective Taking: Imagining How Another Feels versus Imagining How You Would Feel. *Personality and Social Psychology Bulletin* 23: 751–8.

Baxter, L. C., Saykin, A. J., Flashman, L. A., Johnson, S. C., Guerin, S. J., Babcock, D. R. et al. (2003) Sex Differences in Semantic Language Processing: A Functional MRI Study. *Brain and Language* 84: 264–272.

Beaulieu, A. (2003) Brains, Maps and the New Territory of Psychology. *Theory and Psychology* 13(4): 561–8.

Bechtel, W. and Mundale, J. (1999) Multiple Realizability Revisited: Linking Cognitive and Neural States. *Philosophy of Science* 66: 175–207.

Beck, M. (1997/1998). Hermaphrodites with Attitude Take to the Streets. *Chrysalis: Journal of Transgressive Gender Identities* 2(5): 45–50.

Becker, J. B., Arnold, A. P., Berkley, K. J., Blaustein, J. D., Eckel, L. A., Hampson, E., et al. (2005) Strategies and Methods for Research on Sex Differences in Brain and Behavior. *Endocrinology* 146: 1650–1673.

Beh, H. G. and Diamond, M. (2000) An Emerging Ethical and Medical Dilemma: Should Physicians Perform Sex Assignment Surgery on Infants with Ambiguous Genitalia? [web version]. University of Hawaii (http://www.hawaii.edu/PCSS/online_artcls/intersex/intersex00_00.html), accessed 16 January 2009.

Bell, E., Willson, M., Wilman, A., Dave, S. and Silverstone, P. (2006) Males and Females Differ in Brain Activation During Cognitive Tasks. *NeuroImage* 30: 529–538.

Bennett, C. M., Baird, A. A., Miller, M. B. and Wolford, G. L. (2009) Neural Correlates of Interspecies Perspective Taking in The Post-Mortem Atlantic Salmon: An Argument for Multiple Comparisons Correction. *Organization for Human Brain Mapping Abstracts*.

Berenbaum, S. A. (1999) Effects of Early Androgens on Sex-Typed Activities and Interests in Adolescents with Congenital Adrenal Hyperplasia. *Hormones and Behavior* 35: 102–110.

Berenbaum, S. A. (2001) Cognitive Function in Congenital Adrenal Hyperplasia. *Endocrinology Metabolism Clinics of North America* 30: 173–192.

Berglund, H., Lindström, P. et al. (2006) Brain Response to Putative Pheromones in Lesbian Women. *Proceedings of the National Academy of Sciences USA* 103: 8269–74

Bester-Meredith, J. K. and Marler, C. A. (2001) Vasopressin and Aggression in Cross-Fostered California Mice (*Peromyscus californicus*) and White-Footed Mice (*Peromyscus leucopus*). *Hormones and Behavior* 40(1): 51–64.

Biology and Gender Study Group (1988) The Importance of Feminist Critique for Contemporary Cell Biology. *Hypatia* 3(1): 61–76.

Birke, L. (1986) *Women, Feminism and Biology: The Feminist Challenge* (London: Wheatsheaf).

Birke, L. (1999) *Feminism and the Biological Body* (Edinburgh: Edinburgh University Press).

Birmingham, K. (2000) NIH Funds Gender Biology Research. *Nature America News* (http://medicine.nature.com), accessed 20 September 2007.

Bishop, D. V. M. (1998) Development of the Children's Communication Checklist (CCC): A Method for Assessing Qualitative Aspects of Communicative Impairment in Children. *Journal of Child Psychology and Psychiatry* 39: 879–891.

Bishop, K. M. and Wahlsten, D. (1997) Sex Differences in the Human Corpus Callosum: Myth or Reality? *Neuroscience and Biobehavioral Reviews* 21: 581–601.

Blackless, M., Charuvastra, A. et al. (2000) How Sexually Dimorphic Are We? Review and Synthesis. *American Journal of Human Biology* 12: 151–166.

Blanchard, R. and Lippa R. A. (2007) Birth Order, Sibling Sex Ratio, Handedness, and Sexual Orientation of Male and Female Participants in a BBC Internet Research Project. *Archives of Sexual Behavior* 36: 163–176.

Bleier, R. (1984) *Science and Gender: A Critique of Biology and Its Theories on Women* (Oxford: Pergamon Press).

Bleier, R. (1986) Sex Differences Research: Science or Belief? In R. Bleier (ed.), *Feminist Approaches to Science* (New York: Pergamon Press), 147–164.

Block, N. (2005) Action in Perception. *Journal of Philosophy* 102(5): 259–272.

Blum, D. (1997) *Sex on the Brain: The Biological Differences between Men and Women* (New York: Penguin Books).

Blum, L., Horniak, M., Housman, J. and Scheman, N. (1979) Altruism and Women's Oppression. In M. Bishop and M. Weinzweig (eds), *Philosophy and Women* (Belmont, CA: Wadsworth), 190–200.

Blumberg, M. (2005) *Basic Instinct: The Genesis of Behavior* (New York: Thunder's Mouth Press).

Boehm, C. (1993) Egalitarian Society and Reverse Dominance Hierarchy. *Current Anthropology* 37: 227–54.

Bogart, L. M., Cecil, H., Wagstaff, D. A., Pinkerton, S. D. and Abramson, P. R. (2000) Is it "Sex"? College Students' Interpretations of Sexual Behavior Terminology. *Journal of Sex Research* 37: 108–116.

Boghi, A., Rasetti R., et al. (2006) The Effect of Gender on Planning: An fMRI Study Using the Tower of London Task. *NeuroImage* 33(3): 999–1010.

Bordo, S. (1990) Feminism, Postmodernism, and Gender Skepticism. In L. Nicholson (ed.), *Feminism/Postmodernism* (London: Routledge), 133–156.

Bordo, S. (1993) *Unbearable Weight: Feminism, Western Culture, and the Body* (Berkeley: University of California Press).

Bower, B. (2010) Effects of Botox Go Beyond the Face. *Science News* 178(3): 8.

Braeutigam, S., Rose, S., Swithenby, S. and Ambler, T. (2004) The Distributed Neuronal Systems Supporting Choice-Making in Real-Life Situations:

Differences Between Men and Women When Choosing Groceries Detected Using Magnetoencephalography. *European Journal of Neuroscience* 20: 293–302.

Breedlove, S. M., Cooke, B. M. and Jordan, C. L. (1999) The Orthodox View of Brain Sexual Differentiation. *Brain, Behavior and Evolution* 54: 8–14.

Brescoll, V. and LaFrance, M. (2004) The Correlates and Consequences of Newspaper Reports of Research on Sex Differences. *Psychological Science* 15: 515–520.

Brizendine, L. (2006) *The Female Brain* (New York: Broadway).

Broom, A., Hand, K. and Tovey, P. (2009) The Role of Gender, Environment and Individual Biography in Shaping Qualitative Interview Data. *International Journal of Social Research Methodology* 12: 51–65.

Buchmann, C. and DiPrete, T. A. (2006) The Growing Female Advantage in College Completion: The Role of Family Background and Academic Achievement. *American Sociological Review* 71(4): 515–541.

Bussey, K. and Bandura, A. (1999) Social Cognitive Theory of Gender Development and Differentiation. *Psychological Review* 106: 676–713.

Butler, J. (1990) *Gender Trouble: Feminism and the Subversion of Identity* (New York: Routledge).

Butler, J. (1993) *Bodies that Matter: On the Discursive Limits of 'Sex'* (New York: Routledge).

Byne, William, Bleier, R. and Houston, L. (1988) Variations in Human Corpus callosum do not Predict Gender: A Study Using Magnetic Resonance Imaging. *Behavioral Neuroscience* 102: 222–227.

Byne, W., Lasco, M. S. et al. (2000) The Interstitial Nuclei of the Human Anterior Hypothalamus: An Investigation of Sexual Variation in Volume and Cell Size, Number and Density. *Brain Research* 856(1–2): 254–258.

Byne, W., Tobet, S. et al. (2001) The Interstitial Nuclei of the Human Anterior Hypothalamus: An Investigation of Variation with Sex, Sexual Orientation, and HIV Status. *Hormones and Behavior* 40(2): 86–92.

Cahill, L. (2006) Why Sex Matters for Neuroscience. *Nature Reviews Neuroscience* 7: 477–484.

Campbell, S. (2003) *Relational Remembering: Rethinking the Memory Wars* (Lanham, MD: Rowman and Littlefield).

Campbell, S., L. Meynell et al. (2009) *Embodiment and Agency* (University Park, PA: Pennsylvania State University Press).

Carey, S. and Xu, F. (2001) Infants' Knowledge of Objects: Beyond Object Files and Object Tracking. *Cognition* 80(1–2): 179.

Carlo, G. (2006) Care-Based and Altruistically Based Moral Reasoning. In M. Killen and J. Smetana (eds), *Handbook of Moral Development* (Mahwah, NJ: Lawrence Erlbaum Associates), 551–579.

Castel, P.-H. (2003) *La métamorphose impensable: Essai sur le transsexualisme et l'identité personnelle* (Paris: Gallimard).

Caviness, V., Kennedy, D., Richelme, C., Radenmacher, J. and Filipek, P. (1996) The Human Brain Age 7–11 Years: A Volumetric Analysis Based on Magnetic Resonance Images. *Cerebral Cortex* 6: 726–736.

Center for Gender-Based Biology (http://www.genetics.ucla.edu/gendercenter) (home page), accessed 13 March 2011.

Chabris, C. F. and Simons, D. J. (2010) *The Invisible Gorilla: Thinking Clearly in a World of Illusions* (New York: Crown Publishers).

Chafetz, J. S. (1974) *Masculine/Feminine or Human? An Overview of the Sociology of Sex Roles* (Itasca, IL: F. E. Peacock).

Chalfin, M., Murphy, E. and Karkazis K. A. (2008) Women's Neuroethics? Why Sex Matters for Neuroethics. *American Journal of Bioethics* 8(1): 1–2.

Chapman, E., Baron-Cohen, S., Auyeung, B., Knickmeyer, R., Taylor, K. and Hackett, G. (2006) Fetal Testosterone and Empathy: Evidence from the Empathy Quotient (EQ) and the 'Reading the Mind in the Eyes' Test. *Social Neuroscience* 1: 135–148.

Chase, C. (1998) Hermaphrodites with Attitudes: Mapping the Emergence of Intersex Political Activism. *GLQ: A Journal of Lesbian and Gay Studies* 4(2): 189–211.

Chatard, A., Guimond, S. and Selimbegovic, L. (2007) 'How Good are You in Math?' The Effect of Gender Stereotypes on Students' Recollection of their School Marks. *Journal of Experimental Social Psychology* 43: 1017–1024.

Cherney, I. D. (2008) Mom, Let Me Play More Computer Games: They Improve my Mental Rotation Skills. *Sex Roles* 59: 776–786.

Chi, J. G., Dooling, E. C. and Gilles, F. H. (1977) Gyral Development of the Human Brain. *Annals of Neurology* 1: 86–93.

Chodorow, N. (1974) Family Structure and Female Personality. In M. Rosaldo and L. Lamphere (eds), *Women, Culture, and Society* (Stanford, CA: Stanford University Press).

Choudhury, S., Nagel, S. K. and Slaby, J. (2009) Critical Neuroscience: Linking Neuroscience and Society through Critical Practice. *BioSocieties* 4(1): 61–77.

Clemens, L. G., Hiroi, M. and Gorski, R. (1969) Induction and Facilitation of Female Mating Behavior in Rats Treated Neonatally with Low Doses of Testosterone Propionate. *Endocrinology* 84(6): 1430–1438.

Cohen, J. and Meskin, A. (2004) On the Epistemic Value of Photographs. *Journal of Aesthetics and Art Criticism* 2(2): 197–210.

Cohn, S. (2008) Petty Cash and the Neuroscientific Mapping of Pleasure. *Biosocieties* 3: 151–163.

Colapinto, J. (2000) *As Nature Made Him. The Boy who was Raised as a Girl* (New York: HarperCollins).

Coleman, J. M. and Hong, Y. (2008) Beyond Nature and Nurture: The Influence of Lay Gender Theories on Self-Stereotyping. *Self and Identity* 7: 34–53.

Connellan, J., Baron-Cohen, S., Wheelwright, S., Batki, A. and Ahluwalia, J. (2000) Sex Differences in Human Neonatal Social Perception. *Infant Behavior and Development* 23: 113–118.

Cook, T. D. and Campbell, D. T. (1979) *Quasi-Experimentation: Design and Analysis Issues for Field Settings* (Boston: Houghton Mifflin).

Coole, D. and Frost, S. (2010) *New Materialisms: Ontology, Agency, and Politics* (Durham: Duke University Press).

Costanzo, M. S., Bennett, N. C. et al. (2009) Spatial Learning and Memory in African Mole-Rats: The Role of Sociality and Sex. *Physiology and Behavior* 96(1): 128–134.

Creswell, J. W. (2009) *Research Design: Qualitative, Quantitative, and Mixed Methods Approaches* (Thousand Oaks, CA: Sage Publications).

Dar-Nimrod, I. and Heine, S. J. (2006) Exposure to Scientific Theories Affects Women's Math Performance. *Science* 314: 435.

Darwall, S. (1998) Empathy, Sympathy, Care. *Philosophical Studies* 89: 261–282.

Darwin, C. (1871) *The Descent of Man and Selection in Relation to Sex* (New York: Appleton).

Daston, L. and Galison, P. (2007) *Objectivity* (New York: Zone Books).

Davis, M. (1983). Measuring Individual Differences in Empathy: Evidence for a Multidimensional Approach. *Journal of Personality and Social Psychology* 44: 113–126.

Davis, M. and Kraus, L. (1997) Personality and Empathic Accuracy. In W. Ickes (ed.), *Empathic Accuracy* (New York and London: Guilford Press), 144–168.

De Vries, G. J. (2004) Sex Differences in Adult and Developing Brains: Compensation, Compensation, Compensation. *Endocrinology* 145: 1063–1068.

De Vries, G. J. and Simerly, R. (2002) Anatomy, Development, and Function of Sexually Dimorphic Neural Circuits in the Mammalian Brain. In D. Pfaff, A. Arnold, A. Etgen, S. Fahrbach and R. Rubin (eds), *Hormones, Brain and Behaviour, Volume 4* (San Diego, CA: Academic Press), 137–191.

Deleuze, G. and Guattari, F. (1987) *A Thousand Plateaus: Capitalism and Schizophrenia*. Translated by Brian Massumi (Minneapolis: University of Minnesota Press).

Delkin, D. (2008) Science Controversies: The Dynamics of Public Disputes in the United States. In S. Jasanoff, G. E. Markle, J. C. Peterson and T. Pinch (eds), *Handbook of Science and Technology Studies* (revised edn., Thousands Oaks, CA: Sage Publications), 444–456.

Dennis, C. (2004) Brain Development: The Most Important Sexual Organ. *Nature* 427: 390–392.

Derntl, B., Finkelmeyer, A., Eickhof, S., Kellerman, T., Falkenberg, D., Schneider, F. and Habel, U. (2010) Multidimensional Assessment of Empathic Abilities: Neural Correlates and Gender Differences. *Psychoneuroendocrinology* 35: 67–82.

Di Noto, P., Newman, L., Wall, S. and Einstein, G. (2012) The Hermunculus: What is Known about the Representation of the Female Body in the Brain? *Cerebral Cortex* (forthcoming).

Diamond, M. (1965) A Critical Evaluation of the Ontogeny of Human Sexual Behavior. *Quarterly Review of Biology* 40(2): 147–175.

Diamond, M. (1982) Sexual Identity, Monozygotic Twins Reared in Discordant Sex Roles and a BBC Follow-Up. *Archives of Sexual Behavior* 11(2): 181–186.

Diamond, M. (2002) A Conversation with Dr Milton Diamond [web version]. For the Book: *In the Realm of the 'Phallus Palace': The Female to Male Transsexual*, ed. Dean Kotula, 35–56. Los Angeles: Alyson Books (http://www.changelingaspects.com/Technical/A%20Conversation%20with%20Dr%20Milton%20Diamond.htm), accessed 25 December 2008.

Diamond, M. (2004) Sex, Gender, Identity Over the Years: A Changing Perspective. *Child and Adolescent Psychiatric Clinics of North America* 13(3): 591–607.

Diamond, M. and Sigmundson, H. K. (1997a) Sex Reassignment at Birth: Long Term Review and Clinical Implications. *Archives of Pediatric and Adolescent Medicine* 151: 298–304.

Diamond, M. and Sigmundson, H. K. (1997b) Management of Intersexuality: Guidelines for Dealing with Persons with Ambiguous Genitalia [web version] (http://www.ukia.co.uk/diamond/diaguide.htm), accessed 25 December 2008.
Diamond, M. C. (1991) Hormonal Effects on the Development of Cerebral Lateralization. *Psychoneuroendocrinology* 16: 121–129.
Dickersin, K. and Min, Y. (1993) Publication Bias: The Problem That Won't Go Away. *Annals of the New York Academy of Sciences* 703: 135–146.
Dijkstra, P., Rietman, J. and Geertzen, J. (2007) Phantom Breast Sensations and Phantom Breast Pain: A 2-Year Prospective Study and a Methodological Analysis of Literature. *European Journal of Pain* 11: 99–108.
Dillon, S. and Rimer, S. (2005) No Break in the Storm over Harvard President's Words. *New York Times*, 19 January, Section A, Column 3, Late Edition.
Doell, R. G. and Longino, H. E. (1988) Body, Bias and Behavior: A Comparative Analysis of Reasoning in Two Areas of Biological Science. *Signs* 9(2): 206–227.
Dorval, M. and Pépin, M. (1986) Effect of Playing a Video Game on a Measure of Spatial Visualization. *Perceptual and Motor Skills* 62: 159–162.
Driemeyer, J., Boyke, J. et al. (2008) Changes in Gray Matter Induced by Learning-Revisited. *Plos One* 3(7): e2669.
Dumit, J. (2004) *Picturing Personhood: Brain Scans and Biomedical Identity* (Princeton, NJ: Princeton University Press).
Dussauge, I. (2010a) Gaying the Brain, Sex(ual)izing the Brain: Critical Approaches on Neuroimaging Studies of LG(B)(T) Desire. Paper presented at the conference on Neurogenderings: Critical Studies of the Sexed Brain. University of Uppsala, Sweden, 25–27 March.
Dussauge, I. (2010b) Sex, Cash and Neuromodels of Desire. Paper presented at the conference on Neurosociety: What Is It With the Brain These Days? Oxford, 7–8 December.
Dussauge, I. and Kaiser, A. (2009) NeuroGenderings: Critical Studies of the Sexed Brain. Call for Papers (http://www.genna.gender.uu.se/themes/bodyembodiment/news/CFP_NeuroGenderings/), accessed 14 September 2010.
Ebeling, S. (2006) Alles so schön bunt. Geschlecht, Sexualität und Reproduktion im Tierreich. In S. Ebeling and S. Schmitz (eds), *Geschlechterforschung und Naturwissenschaften. Einführung in ein komplexes Wechselspiel* (Wiesbaden: VS Verlag für Sozialwissenschaften).
Eberhardt, J. L., Goff, P. A. et al. (2004) Seeing Black: Race, Crime, and Visual Processing. *Journal of Personality and Social Psychology* 87(6): 876–893.
Ehrenberg, A. (2004a) Les guerres du sujet. Introduction. *Esprit* 11: 74–84.
Ehrenberg, A. (2004b) Le sujet cérébral. *Esprit* 11: 130–155.
Ehrenberg, A. (2010) *La société du malaise* (Paris: Odile Jacob).
Ehrhardt, A. A., Grisanti, G. C. and Meyer-Bahlburg, H. F. L. (1977) Prenatal Exposure to Medroxyprogesterone Acetate (MPA) in Girls. *Psychoneuroendocrinology* 2: 391–398.
Ehrhardt, A. A., Meyer-Bahlburg, H. F. L. et al. (1985) Sexual Orientation after Prenatal Exposure to Exogenous Estrogen. *Archives of Sexual Behavior* 14(1): 57–77.
Einstein, G. (2007) *Sex and the Brain* (Cambridge, MA: MIT Press).
Einstein, G. (2008) From Body to Brain: Considering the Neurobiological Effects of Female Genital Cutting. *Perspectives in Biology and Medicine* 51: 84–97.

Einstein, G. and Shildrick, M. (2009) The Postconventional Body: Retheorising Women's Health. *Social Science and Medicine* 69: 293–300.

Eisenberg, N. (2000) Empathy and Sympathy. In M. Lewis and J. Haviland-Jones (eds), *Handbook of Emotions* (2nd edn, New York: Guilford Press), 677–691.

Eisenberg, N. and Lennon, R. (1983) Sex Differences in Empathy and Related Capacities. *Psychological Bulletin* 94: 100–131.

Eisenberg, N., Spinrad, T. and Sadovsky, A. (2006) Empathy-Related Responding in Children. In M. Killen and J. Smetana (eds), *Handbook of Moral Development* (Mahwah, NJ: Lawrence Erlbaum Associates), 517–549.

Eisenberg, N., Shell, R., Pasternack, J., Lennon, R. et al. (1987) Prosocial Development in Middle Childhood. *Developmental Psychology* 23: 712–718.

Eisenberg, N., Schaller, M., Fabes, R. et al. (1988) Differentiation of Personal Distress and Sympathy in Children and Adults. *Developmental Psychology* 24: 766–775.

Eisenberg-Berg, N. and Lennon, R. (1980) Altruism and the Assessment of Empathy in the Preschool Years. *Child Development* 51: 552–557.

Eisenegger, C., Naef, M., Snozzi, R., Heinrichs H. and Fehr, E. (2010) Prejudice and Truth about the Effect of Testosterone on Human Bargaining Behaviour. *Nature* 463(7279): 356–359.

Eliot, L. (2009) *Pink Brain, Blue Brain: How Small Differences Grow into Troublesome Gaps – and What We Can Do About It* (New York: Houghton Mifflin Harcourt).

Epstein, S. (1995) The Construction of Lay Expertise: AIDS Activism and the Forging of Credibility in the Reform of Clinical Trials. *Science, Technology and Human Values* 20(4): 408–437.

Erwin, R., Gur, R. C., Gur, R. E., Skolnik, B., Mawhinney-Hee, M. and Smailis, J. (1992) Facial Emotion Discrimination: I. Task Construction and Behavioral Findings in Normal Subjects. *Psychiatry Research* 42: 231–240.

Fabes, R. and Eisenberg, N. (1998) Meta-Analyses of Age and Sex Differences in Children's and Adolescents' Prosocial Behavior. Manuscript partially published in N. Eisenberg and R. A. Fabes, Prosocial Development. In W. Damon (ed.), *Handbook of Child Development* (available at http://www.public.asu.edu/~rafabes/meta.pdf).

Fausto-Sterling, A. (1992) *Myths of Gender: Biological Theories about Women and Men* (revised edn., New York: Basic Books).

Fausto-Sterling, A. (2000a) The Sex/Gender Perplex. *Studies in the History and Philosophy of Biological and Biomedical Sciences* 31(4): 637–646.

Fausto-Sterling, A. (2000b) *Sexing the Body: Gender Politics and the Construction of Sexuality* (New York: Basic Books).

Fausto-Sterling, A. (2003) The Problem with Sex/Gender and Nature/Nurture. In S. Williams, L. Birke and G. Bendelow (eds), *Debating Biology* (New York: Routledge), 123–132.

Fausto-Sterling, A. (2005) The Bare Bones of Sex: Part 1 – Sex and Gender. *Signs* 30(2): 1491–1527.

Fausto-Sterling, A. (2007) Frameworks of Desire. *Dædalus* 136: 47–57

Fausto-Sterling, A. (2008) The Bare Bones of Race. *Social Studies of Science* 38: 657–694.

Fee, E. (1979) Nineteenth Century Craniology: The Study of the Female Skull. *Bulletin of the History of Medicine* 53: 415–433.

Feng, J., Spence, I. and Pratt, J. (2007) Playing an Action Video Game Reduces Gender Differences in Spatial Cognition. *Psychological Science* 18: 850–855.

Fenson, L., Dale, P. S., Reznick, J. S., Bates, E., Thal, D. J., Pethick, S. J. et al. (1994) Variability in Early Communicative Development. *Monographs of the Society for Research in Child Development* 59: 1–173.

Figdor, C. (2010) Neuroscience and the Multiple Realization of Cognitive Functions. *Philosophy of Science* 77: 419–456.

Fine, A. (1986) *The Shaky Game: Einstein, Realism and the Quantum Theory* (Chicago: University of Chicago Press).

Fine, C. (2008a [2006]) *A Mind of Its Own: How Your Brain Distorts and Deceives* (New York: W. W. Norton).

Fine, C. (2008b) Will Working Mothers' Brains Explode? The Popular New Genre of Neurosexism. *Neuroethics* 1: 79–82.

Fine, C. (2010a) *Delusions of Gender: How Our Minds, Society, and Neurosexism Create Difference* (New York: W. W. Norton).

Fine, C. (2010b) From Scanner to Sound Bite: Issues in Interpreting and Reporting Sex Differences in the Brain. *Current Directions in Psychological Science* 19: 280–283.

Finegan, J., Niccols, G. A. and Sitarenios, G. (1992) Relations between Prenatal Testosterone Levels and Cognitive Abilities at 4 Years. *Developmental Psychology* 28: 1075–1089.

Foucault, M. (1976) *Histoire de la sexualité: La volonté de savoir* (Paris: Gallimard).

Foucault, M. (1997) *Il faut défendre la société: Cours au Collège de France 1976* (Paris: Gallimard/Seuil).

Frank, R. (1988) *Passions within Reason* (New York: W. W. Norton).

Friedan, B. (1963) *The Feminine Mystique* (New York: W. W. Norton).

Gastaud, F., Bouvattier, C. et al. (2007) Impaired Sexual and Reproductive Outcomes in Women with Classical Forms of Congenital Adrenal Hyperplasia. *Journal of Clinical Endocrinology and Metabolism* 92(4): 1391–1396.

Gatens, M. (1995) *Imaginary Bodies: Ethics, Power, and Corporeality* (New York: Routledge).

Gazzaniga, M., Ivry, R. and Mangun, G. (1998) *Cognitive Neuroscience: The Biology of the Mind* (New York: W. W. Norton).

Gendler, T. S. and Hawthorne, J. (eds) (2006) *Perceptual Experience* (Oxford: Clarendon Press).

Georgiadis, J. R, Kortekaas, R., Kuipers, R., Nieuwenburg, A., Pruim. J., Reinders, A. A. and Holstege, G. (2006) Regional Cerebral Blood Flow Changes Associated with Clitorally Induced Orgasm in Healthy Women. *European Journal of Neuroscience* 24(11): 3306–3316.

Gerson, K. (2009) *The Unfinished Revolution: How a New Generation is Reshaping Family, Work, and Gender in America* (New York: Oxford University Press).

Geschwind, N. and Behan, P. (1982) Left-Handedness: Association with Immune Disease, Migraine, and Developmental Learning Disorder. *Proceedings of the National Academy of Sciences USA* 79: 5097–5100.

Geschwind, N. and Galaburda, A. M. (1987) *Cerebral Lateralization* (Cambridge, MA: MIT Press).

Giardina, Elsa-Grace V. et al. (2006) Reflections on a Decade of Experience in Implementing a Center for Women's Health at an Academic Medical Center. *Journal of Women's Health* 15(3): 319–329.

Giedd, J., Vaituzis, A. C., Hamburger, S., Lange, N., Rajapakse, J., Kaysen, D. et al. (1996) Quantitative MRI of the Temporal Lobe, Amygdala, and Hippocampus in Normal Human Development: Ages 4–18 years. *Journal of Comparative Neurology* 366: 223–230.

Gilbody, S., Song, F., et al. (2000) The Causes, Consequences and Detection of Publication Bias in Psychiatry. *Acta Psychiatrica Scandinavica* 102: 241–249.

Gilligan, C. (1982) *In a Different Voice: Psychological Theory and Women's Development* (Cambridge, MA: Harvard University Press).

Gilligan, C. and Wiggins, G. (1987) The Origins of Morality in Early Childhood Relationships. In J. Kagan and S. Lamb (eds), *The Emergence of Morality in Young Children* (Chicago: University of Chicago Press), 277–305.

Gilmore, J. H., Lin, W., Prastawa, M. W., Looney, C. B., Vetsa, Y. S. K., Knickmeyer, R. C. et al. (2007) Regional Gray Matter Growth, Sexual Dimorphism, and Cerebral Asymmetry in the Neonatal Brain. *Journal of Neuroscience* 27: 1255–1260.

Gitau, R., Adams, D., Fisk, N. M. and Glover, V. (2005) Fetal Plasma Testosterone Correlates Positively with Cortisol. *Archives of Disease in Childhood. Fetal and Neonatal Edition* 90: F166–F169.

Gizewski, E. R., Krause, E. et al. (2006) There are Differences in Cerebral Activation between Females in Distinct Menstrual Phases during Viewing of Erotic Stimuli: An fMRI Study. *Experimental Brain Research* 174: 101–108.

Gladue, B. A. and Bailey, J. M. (1995) Spatial Ability, Handedness, and Human Sexual Orientation. *Psychoneuroendocrinology* 20(5): 487–497.

Goldstein, J., Seidman, L., Horton, N., Makris, N., Kennedy, D., Caviness, V. et al. (2001) Normal Sexual Dimorphism of the Adult Human Brain Assessed by *In Vivo* Magnetic Resonance Imaging. *Cerebral Cortex* 11: 490–497.

Goldstein, J. et al. (2005) Hormonal Cycle Modulates Arousal Circuitry in Women Using Functional Magnetic Resonance Imaging. *Journal of Neuroscience* 25(40): 9309–9316.

Golombok, S. and Rust, J. (1993) The Pre-School Activities Inventory: A Standardised Assessment of Gender Role in Children. *Psychological Assessment* 5: 131–136.

Goodman, Nelson (1968) *Languages of Art: An Approach to a Theory of Symbols* (New York: Bobbs-Merrill).

Gorbet, D. and Sergio, L. (2007) Preliminary Sex Differences in Human Cortical BOLD fMRI Activity During the Preparation of Increasingly Complex Visually Guided Movements. *European Journal of Neuroscience* 25: 1228–1239.

Gottlieb, G. (1992) *Individual Development and Evolution: The Genesis of Novel Behavior* (New York: Oxford University Press).

Gould, S. J. (1981) *The Mismeasure of Man* (New York: W. W. Norton).

Gowaty, P. A. (1997) Introduction: Darwinian Feminists and Feminist Evolutionists. In P. Gowaty (ed.), *Feminism and Evolutionary Biology: Boundaries, Intersections, and Frontiers* (New York: Chapman and Hall), 1–17.

Graham, T. and Ickes, W. (1997) When Women's Intuition Isn't Greater than Men's. In W. Ickes (ed.), *Empathic Accuracy* (New York: Guilford Press), 117–43.

Gray, J. (1992) *Men Are from Mars, Women Are from Venus* (New York: HarperCollins).

Greeno, C. and Maccoby, E. (1986) How Different is the Different Voice? *Signs* 11: 310–316.

Grimshaw, G. M., Sitarenios, G. and Finegan, J. A. K. (1995) Mental Rotation at 7 Years: Relations with Prenatal Testosterone Levels and Spatial Play Experiences. *Brain and Cognition* 29: 85–100.

Grosz, E. (1994) *Volatile Bodies: Toward a Corporeal Feminism* (Bloomington, IN: Indiana University Press).

Guiso, L., Monte, F. et al. (2008) Diversity: Culture, Gender, and Math. *Science* 320(5880): 1164–1165.

Gur, R., Turetsky, B. et al. (1999) Sex Differences in Brain Gray and White Matter in Healthy Young Adults: Correlations with Cognitive Performance. *Journal of Neuroscience* 19: 4065–4072.

Gur, R., Kohler, C. et al. (2004) A Sexually Dimorphic Ratio of Orbitofrontal to Amygdala Volume is Altered in Schizophrenia. *Biological Psychiatry* 55(5): 512–517.

Hacking, I. (1998) *Mad Travelers: Reflections on the Reality of Transient Mental Illnesses* (Charlottesville: University Press of Virginia).

Haig, D. (2004) The Inexorable Rise of Gender and the Decline of Sex: Social Change in Academic Titles, 1945–2001. *Archives of Sexual Behavior* 33(2): 87–96.

Halberstam, J. (2005) *In a Queer Time and Place: Transgender Bodies, Subcultural Lives* (New York: New York University Press).

Hall, J. (1978) Gender Effects in Decoding Nonverbal Cues. *Psychological Bulletin* 85: 845–857.

Hall, J. (1984) *Nonverbal Sex Differences: Communication Accuracy and Expressive Style* (Baltimore and London: Johns Hopkins University Press).

Halley, Janet E. (1994) Sexual Orientation and the Politics of Biology: A Critique of the Argument from Immutability. *Stanford Law Review* 46: 503–568.

Hamann, S. et al. (2004) Men and Women Differ in Amygdala Responses to Visual Sexual Stimuli. *Nature Neuroscience* 7(4): 411–416.

Haraway, D. (1988) Situated Knowledges: The Science Question in Feminism and the Privilege of Partial Perspective. *Feminist Studies* 14: 575–599.

Haraway, D. (1989) The Biopolitics of Postmodern Bodies: Determination of Self in Immune System Discourse. *Differences* 1: 3–43.

Haraway, D. (1991) *Simians, Cyborgs, and Women: The Reinvention of Nature* (New York: Routledge).

Haraway, D. (1996) Modest Witness: Feminist Diffractions in Science Studies. In P. Galison and D. J. Stump (eds), *The Disunity of Science: Boundaries, Contexts, and Power* (Stanford: Stanford University Press), 428–441.

Haraway, D. (1997) *Modest_Witness@Second_Millenium.FemaleMan©_Meets_ Oncomouse™: Feminism and Technoscience* (New York: Routledge).

Haraway, D (2008) *When Species Meet* (Minneapolis: University of Minnesota Press).

Harding, S. (1986) *The Science Question in Feminism* (Ithaca, NY: Cornell University Press).

Harding, S. (1987) Is There a Feminist Method? In N. Tuana (ed.), *Feminism and Science* (Bloomington, IN: Indiana University Press), 18–32.

Harding, S. (1991) *Whose Science? Whose Knowledge?* (Ithaca: Cornell University Press).

Harding, S. G. (2004) *The Feminist Standpoint Theory Reader: Intellectual and Political Controversies* (New York: Routledge).

Harding, S. (2001) Comment on Walby's 'Against Epistemological Chasms: The Science Question in Feminism Revisited': Can Democratic Values and Interests Ever Play a Rationally Justifiable Role in the Evaluation of Scientific Work? *Signs* 26: 511–525.

Harding, S. (2006) Two Influential Theories of Ignorance and Philosophy's Interests in Ignoring Them. *Hypatia* 21: 20–35.

Harman, G. (1990) The Intrinsic Quality of Experience. *Philosophical Perspectives* 4: 31–52.

Harrington, G. and Farias, S. (2008) Sex Differences in Language Processing: Functional MRI Methodological Considerations. *Journal of Magnetic Resonance Imaging* 27: 1221–1228.

Hasinoff, A. A. (2009) It's Sociobiology, Hon! Genetic Gender Determinism in Cosmopolitan Magazine. *Feminist Media Studies* 9(3): 267–283.

Hassett, J. M., Siebert, E. R. and Wallen, K. (2008) Sex Differences in Rhesus Monkey Toy Preferences Parallel Those of Children. *Hormones and Behavior* 54: 359–364.

Hatfield, E., Cacioppo, P. and Rapson, R. (1994) *Emotional Contagion* (New York: Cambridge University Press).

Hausmann, M., Slabbekoorn, D. et al. (2000) Sex Hormones Affect Spatial Abilities during the Menstrual Cycle. *Behavioral Neuroscience* 114(6): 1245–1250.

Hausmann, M., Schoofs, D., Rosenthal, H. E. S. and Jordan, K. (2009) Interactive Effects of Sex Hormones and Gender Stereotypes on Cognitive Sex Differences – A Psychobiological Approach. *Psychoneuroendocrinology* 34: 389–401.

Hendricks, S. E., Lehman, J. R. and Oswalt G. (1982) Responses to Copulatory Stimulation in Neonatally Androgenized Female Rats. *Journal of Comparative and Physiological Psychology* 96(5): 834–845.

Herculano-Houzel, S. (2002) Do You Know Your Brain? A Survey on Public Neuroscience Literacy at the Closing of the Decade of the Brain. *Neuroscientist* 8: 98–110.

Hermans, E. J., van Wingen, G., Bos, P. A., Putman, P. and van Honk, J. (2009) Reduced Spontaneous Facial Mimicry in Women with Autistic Traits. *Biological Psychology* 80: 348–353.

Hess, D., Breyman, S., Campbell, N. and Martin, B. (2008) Science, Technology, and Social Movements. In E. J. Hackett, O. Amsterdamska, M. Lynch and J. Wajcman (eds), *The Handbook of Science and Technology Studies* (3rd edn, Cambridge, MA and London: MIT Press), 473–498.

Hewlett, S. A. (2002) *Creating a Life: Professional Women and the Quest for Children* (New York: Hyperion).

Hines, M. (2004) *Brain Gender* (Oxford: Oxford University Press).

Hines, M. (2007) Do Sex Differences in Cognition Cause the Shortage of Women in Science? In S. J. Ceci and W. M. Williams (eds), *Why Aren't More Women in Science? Top Researchers Debate the Evidence* (Washington, DC: APA), 101–112.

Hines, M. and Alexander, G. M. (2008) Monkeys, Girls, Boys and Toys: A Confirmation. *Hormones and Behavior* 54: 478–479.

Hines, M. and Kaufman, F. R. (1994) Androgen and the Development of Human Sex-Typical Behavior: Rough-and-Tumble Play and Sex of Preferred Playmates in Children with Congenital Adrenal Hyperplasia (CAH). *Child Development* 65: 1042–1053.

Hines, M., Allen, L. and Gorski, R. (1992) Sex Differences in Subregions of the Medial Nucleus of the Amygdala and the Bed Nucleus of the Stria Terminalis of the Rat. *Brain Research* 579: 321–326.

Hines, M., Golombok, S., Rust, J., Johnston, K. J., Golding, J. et al. (2002) Testosterone during Pregnancy and Gender Role Behavior of Preschool Children: A Longitudinal, Population Study. *Child Development* 73: 1678–1687.

Hines, M., Fane, B. A., Pasterski, V. L., Mathews, G. A., Conway, G. S. and Brook, C. (2003) Spatial Abilities Following Prenatal Androgen Abnormality: Targeting and Mental Rotations Performance in Individuals with Congenital Adrenal Hyperplasia. *Psychoneuroendocrinology* 28: 1010–1026.

Hines, M., Brook, C. and Conway, G. S. (2004) Androgen and Psychosexual Development: Core Gender Identity, Sexual Orientation, and Recalled Childhood Gender Role Behavior in Women and Men with Congenital Adrenal Hyperplasia (CAH). *Journal of Sex Research* 41(1): 75–81.

Hird, M. J. (2004) *Sex, Gender, and Science* (New York: Palgrave Macmillan).

Hochschild, A. and Machung, A. (1989) *The Second Shift* (New York: Viking Penguin).

Hofer, A., Siedentopf, C., Ischebeck, A., Rettenbacher, M., Verius, M., Felber, S. and Fleischhacker, W. (2007) Sex Differences in Brain Activation Patterns during Processing of Positively and Negatively Valenced Emotional Words. *Psychological Medicine* 37: 109–119.

Hoffman, M. (2000) *Empathy and Moral Development* (Cambridge: Cambridge University Press).

Hogg, M. and Turner, J. C. (1987) Intergroup Behaviour, Self-Stereotyping and the Salience of Social Categories. *British Journal of Social Psychology* 26: 325–340.

Holden, C. (2000) Parity as a Goal Sparks Bitter Battle. *Science* 289(5478): 380.

Holmes, R. (2010) *The Royal Society's Lost Women of Science* (London: The Observer).

Holter, H. (1970) *Sex Roles and Social Structure* (Oslo: Universitetsforlaget).

Honneth, Axel. (1996) *The Struggle for Recognition: The Moral Grammar of Social Conflict* (Cambridge, MA: MIT Press).

Hrdy, S. (2009) *Mothers and Others* (Cambridge, MA: Harvard University Press).

Hu, S. H., Wei, N. et al. (2008) Patterns of Brain Activation during Visually Evoked Sexual Arousal Differ between Homosexual and Heterosexual Men. *American Journal of Neuroradiology* 29: 1890–1896.

Huang, G., Taddese, N. et al. (2000) *Entry and Persistence of Women and Minorities in College Science and Engineering Education* (Washington, DC: US Department of Education, National Center for Education Statistics), NCES 2000–601.

Hubbard, R. (1992) *The Politics of Women's Biology* (New Brunswick, NJ: Rutgers University Press).

Hughes, I. A. (2001) Minireview: Sex Differentiation. *Endocrinology* 142: 3281–3287.

Hughes, I. A., Houk, C. P., Ahmed, S. F. and Lee Hughes, P. A. in collaboration with the participants in the International Consensus Conference on Intersex organized by the Lawson Wilkins Pediatric Endocrine Society and the European Society for Paediatric Endocrinology (2006) Consensus Statement on Management of Intersex Disorders. *Journal of Pediatric Urology* 2: 148–162.

Hutto, D. D. (2007) *Narrative and Understanding Persons* (Cambridge: Cambridge University Press).

Hyde, J. S. (2005) The Gender Similarities Hypothesis. *American Psychologist* 60(6): 581–592.

Hyde, J. S. and Linn, M. (1988) Gender Differences in Verbal Ability: A Meta-Analysis. *Psychological Bulletin* 104: 53–69.

Hyde, J. S. and Linn, M. C. (2006) Diversity – Gender Similarities in Mathematics and Science. *Science* 314(5799): 599–600.

Hyde, J. S. and Mertz, J. E. (2009) Gender, Culture, and Mathematics Performance. *Proceedings of the National Academy of Sciences of the United States of America* 106(22): 8801–8807.

Hyde, J. S., Geiringer, E. R. and Yen, W. M. (1975) On the Empirical Relation between Spatial Ability and Sex Differences in Other Aspects of Cognitive Performance. *Multivariate Behavioral Research* 10: 289–309.

Hyde, J. S., Lindberg, S. M. et al. (2008) Diversity – Gender Similarities Characterize Math Performance. *Science* 321(5888): 494–495.

Iacoboni, M. (2008) *Mirroring People: The New Science of How We Connect with Others* (New York: Farrar, Straus and Giroux).

Ickes, W. (2003) *Everyday Mind Reading: Understanding What Other People Think and Feel* (Amherst, NY: Prometheus Books).

Ickes, W., Gesn, P. R and Graham, T. (2000) Gender Differences in Empathic Accuracy: Differential Ability or Differential Motivation? *Personal Relationships* 7: 95–109.

Illes J. and Racine, E. (2005) Imaging or Imagining? A Neuroethics Challenge Informed by Genetics. *American Journal of Bioethics* 5(2): 5–18.

Im, K., Lee, J., Lyttelton, O., Kim, S. H., Evans, A. C. and Kim, S. J. (2008) Brain Size and Cortical Structure in the Adult Human Brain. *Cerebral Cortex* 18: 2181–2191.

Imperato-McGinley, J. and Peterson, R. E. (1976) Male Pseudohermaphroditism: The Complexities of Male Phenotypic Development. *American Journal of Medicine* 61(2): 251–272.

Imperato-McGinley, J., Geurrero, L., Gautier, T. and Peterson, R. E. (1974) Steroid 5alpha Reductase Deficiency in Man: An Inherited Form of Male Pseudohermaphroditism. *Science* 186: 1213–1215.

Imperato-McGinley, J., Peterson, R. E., Gautier, T. and Sturia, E. (1979) Androgen and Evolution of Male-Gender Identity among Male Pseudohermaphrodites with 5α-Reductase Deficiency. *New England Journal of Medicine* 300(22): 1233–1237.

Innocence Project, Eyewitness Misidentification (http://www.innocenceproject.org/understand/Eyewitness-Misidentification.php).

Intersex Society of North America (ISNA) (1997) *Hermaphrodites with Attitude. The Publication of the Intersex Society of North America* (Fall): 1–4.

Ishai, A. (2007) Sex, Beauty and the Orbitofrontal Cortex. *International Journal of Psychophysiology* 63: 181–185.

Jackson, P., Meltzoff, A. and Decety, J. (2005) How Do We Perceive the Pain of Others? A Window into the Neural Processes Involved in Empathy. *NeuroImage* 24: 771–779.

Jacobs, B., van Praag, H. and Gage, F. (2000) Adult Brain Neurogenesis and Psychiatry: A Novel Theory of Depression. *Molecular Psychiatry* 5: 262–269.

Jacobson, A. J. (2000) *Feminist Interpretations of David Hume* (University Park, PA: Pennsylvania State University Press).

Jacobson, A. J. (forthcoming) *Keeping the World in Mind* (Basingstoke: Palgrave Macmillan).

Jaggar, A. (1983) *Feminist Politics and Human Nature* (Totowa, NJ: Allenheld).

Jaggar, Alison M. (2008) *Just Methods: An Interdisciplinary Feminist Reader* (Boulder, CO: Paradigm Publishers).

Jaffee, S. and Hyde, J. S. (2000) Gender Differences in Moral Orientation: A Meta-Analysis. *Psychological Bulletin* 126: 703–726.

James, K. (1993) Conceptualizing Self with In-Group Stereotypes: Context and Esteem Precursors. *Personality and Social Psychology Bulletin* 19: 117–121.

Jäncke, L., Staiger, J. et al. (1997) The Relationship between Corpus Callosum Size and Forebrain Volume. *Cerebral Cortex* 7: 48–56.

Jansen, S. C. (1990) Review: Is Science a Man? New Feminist Epistemologies and Reconstructions of Knowledge. *Theory and Society* 19: 235–246.

Jasanoff, S. (1995) Cooperation for What? A View from the Sociological/Cultural Study of Science Policy. *Social Studies of Science* 25(2): 314–317.

Jasanoff, S. (1996) Beyond Epistemology: Relativism and Engagement in the Politics of Science. *Social Studies of Science* 26(2): 393–418.

Jasanoff, S., Markle, G. E., Peterson, J. C. and Pinch, T. (eds) (2008) *Handbook of Science and Technology Studies* (rev. edn, Thousands Oaks, CA: Sage Publications).

Jing, F., Spence, I. et al. (2007) Playing an Action Video Game Reduces Gender Differences in Spatial Cognition. *Psychological Science* 18(10): 850–855 (Wiley-Blackwell).

Johansen, R. E. B. (2002) Pain as a Counterpoint to Culture: Toward an Analysis of Pain Associated with Infibulation among Somali Immigrants in Norway. *Medical Anthropology Quarterly* 16: 312–340.

Johnson, M. H., Griffin, R., Csibra, G., Halit, H., Farroni, T., De Haan, M. et al. (2005) The Emergence of the Social Brain Network: Evidence from Typical and Atypical Development. *Development and Psychopathology* 17: 599–619.

Johnston, M. (2006) The Function of Sensory Awareness Perceptual Experience. In T. S. Gendler and J. Hawthorne (eds), *Perceptual Experience* (Oxford: Clarendon Press), 260–290.

Jonasson, Z. (2005) Meta-Analysis of Sex Differences in Rodent Models of Learning and Memory: A Review of Behavioral and Biological Data. *Neuroscience and Biobehavioral Reviews* 28: 811–825.

Jordan, K., Wüstenberg, T. et al. (2002) Women and Men Exhibit Different Cortical Activation Patterns during Mental Rotation Tasks. *Neuropsychologia* 40: 2397–2408.

Jordan-Young, R. (2010) *Brain Storm: The Flaws in the Science of Sex Differences* (Cambridge, MA: Harvard University Press).

Jordan-Young, R. M. (2011) Hormones, Context, and "Brain Gender": Evidence from Congenital Adrenal Hyperplasia. *Social Science & Medicine*. Published online ahead of print, 17 September 2011. doi:10.1016/j.socscimed.2011.08.026

Jorm, A. F., Dear, K. B. G. et al. (2003) Cohort Difference in Sexual Orientation: Results from a Large Age-Stratified Population Sample. *Gerontology* 49(6): 392–395.

Joss, S. and Durant, J. (2002 [1995]) Introduction. In S. Joss and J. Durant (eds), *Public Participation in Science: The Role of Consensus Conferences in Europe* (London: Science Museum).

Jost, A. (1953) Problems of Fetal Endocrinology: The Gonadal and Hypophyseal Hormones. *Recent Progress in Hormone Research* 8: 379–418.

Joyce, K. (2008) *Magnetic Appeal: MRI and the Myth of Transparency* (Ithaca: Cornell University Press).

Jürgensen, M., Hiort, O., Holterhus, P. and Thyen, U. (2007) Gender Role Behavior in Children with XY Karyotype and Disorders of Sex Development. *Hormones and Behavior* 51: 443–453.

Kaiser A. (2010a) Sex/Gender and Neuroscience: Focusing on Current Research. In M. Blomqvist, and E. Ehnsmyr (eds), *Never Mind the Gap! Gendering Science in Transgressive Encounters. Crossroads of Knowledge* (Uppsala: Skrifter från Centrum för genusvetenskap, University Printers), 189–210.

Kaiser, A. (2010b) The Cortical Power of Gender Differences. Paper given at the conference Neurogenderings: Critical Studies of the Sexed Brain Conference, University of Uppsala, Sweden, 25–27 March.

Kaiser, A., Keunzli, E., Zappatore, D. and Nitsch, C. (2007) On Females' Lateral and Males' Bilateral Activation During Language Production: An fMRI Study. *International Journal of Psychophysiology* 63(2): 192–198.

Kaiser, A., Haller, S., Schmitz, S. and Nitsch, C. (2009) On Sex/Gender Related Similarities and Differences in fMRI Language Research. *Brain Research Reviews* 61: 49–59.

Kandel, E., Schwartz, J. and Jessell, T. (1991) *Principles of Neural Science* (Norwalk, CT: Appleton and Lange).

Kandel, E., Schwartz, H. and Jessell, T. (eds) (1996) *Neurowissenschaften: eine Einführung* (Heidelberg: Spektrum Akademischer Verlag).

Karafyllis, N. C. and Ulshöfer, G. (eds) (2008) *Sexualized Brains: Scientific Modeling of Emotional Intelligence from a Cultural Perspective* (Cambridge, MA: MIT Press).

Karkazis, K. (2008) *Fixing Sex: Intersex, Medical Authority, and Lived Experience* (Durham, NC: Duke University Press).

Karmiloff-Smith, A. (2007) Atypical Epigenesis. *Developmental Science* 10: 84–88.

Keller, E. F. (1983) *A Feeling for the Organism: The Life and Work of Barbara McClintock* (New York: W. H. Freeman).

Keller, K. and Menon, V. (2009) Gender Differences in the Functional and Structural Neuroanatomy of Mathematical Cognition. *NeuroImage* 47: 342–352.

Kenen, S. H. (1997) Who Counts When You're Counting Homosexuals? Hormones and Homosexuality in Mid-Twentieth Century America. In V. Rosario (ed.), *Science and Homosexualities* (New York: Routledge), 197–218.

Kessler, S. J. (1998) *Lessons from the Intersexed* (New Brunswick, NJ: Rutgers University Press).

Keysers, C., Wicker, B., Gazzola, V., Anton, J.-L., Fogassi, L. and Gallese, V. (2004) A Touching Sight: SII/PV Activation during the Observation and Experience of Touch. *Neuron* 42: 335–346.

Kimura, D. (1983) Sex Differences in Cerebral Organization for Speech and Praxic Functions. *Canadian Journal of Psychology* 37: 19–35.

Kimura, D. (1999) *Sex and Cognition* (Cambridge, MA: MIT Press).

Kinnunen, L. H., Moltz, H. et al. (2004) Differential Brain Activation in Exclusively Homosexual and Heterosexual Men Produced by the Selective Serotonin Reuptake Inhibitor, Fluoxetine. *Brain Research* 1024: 251–254.

Kipnis, K. and Diamond, M. (1998) Pediatric Ethics and the Surgical Assignment of Sex [web version] (http://www.ukia.co.uk/diamond/ped_eth.htm), accessed 25 December 2008.

Klein, K. J. K. and Hodges, S. P. (2001) Gender Differences, Motivation, and Empathic Accuracy: When it Pays to Understand. *Personality and Social Psychology Bulletin* 27: 720–730.

Knickmeyer, R. C. and S. Baron-Cohen, S. (2006) Fetal Testosterone and Sex Differences in Typical Social Development and in Autism. *Journal of Child Neurology* 21: 825–845.

Knickmeyer, R., Baron-Cohen, S., Raggatt, P. and Taylor, K. (2005a) Foetal Testosterone, Social Relationships, and Restricted Interests in Children. *Journal of Child Psychology and Psychiatry* 46: 198–210.

Knickmeyer, R., Wheelwright, S., Taylor, K., Ragatt, P., Hackett, G., and Baron-Cohen, S. (2005b) Gender-Typed Play and Amniotic Testosterone. *Developmental Psychology* 41: 517–528.

Knickmeyer, R., Baron-Cohen, S., Fane, B. A., Wheelwright, S., Mathews, G. A., Conway, G. S. et al. (2006a) Androgens and Autistic Traits: A Study of Individuals with Congenital Adrenal Hyperplasia. *Hormones and Behavior* 50: 148–153.

Knickmeyer, R., Baron-Cohen, S., Raggatt, P., Taylor, K. and Hackett, G. (2006b) Fetal Testosterone and Empathy. *Hormones and Behavior* 49: 282–292.

Knickmeyer, R. C., Baron-Cohen, S., Auyeung, B. and Ashwin, E. (2008) How to Test the Extreme Male Brain Theory of Autism in Terms of Foetal Androgens? *Journal of Autism and Developmental Disorders* 38: 995–996.

Koch, K., Pauly, K., Kellermann, T., Seiferth, N., Reske, M., Backes, V., Stocker, T., Shah, N., Amunts, K., Kircher, T., Schneider, F. and Habel, U. (2007) Gender Differences in the Cognitive Control of Emotion: An fMRI Study. *Neuropsychologia* 45: 2744–2754.

Koehn, D. (1998) *Rethinking Feminist Ethics: Care, Trust, and Empathy* (London: Routledge).

Koenig, A. M. and Eagly, A. H. (2005) Stereotype Threat in Men on a Test of Social Sensitivity. *Sex Roles* 52: 489–496.

Kohlberg, L. (1976) Moral Stages and Moralization. In T. Lickona (ed.), *Moral Development and Behavior: Theory, Research, and Social Issues* (New York: Holt, Rinehart and Winston), 31–53.

Komisaruk, B. R. and Whipple, B. (2005) Functional MRI of the Brain during Orgasm in Women. *Annual Review of Sex Research* 16: 62–86.

Kranz, F. and Ishai, A. (2006) Face Perception is Modulated by Sexual Preference. *Current Biology* 16: 63–8

Kraus, C. (2000) Naked Sex in Exile: On the Paradox of the 'Sex Question' in Feminism and in Science. *The Science and Politics of the Search for Sex Differences: A Special Issue of The National Women's Studies Association Journal* 12(3): 151–177.

Kraus, C. (2005) Of 'Epistemic Covetousness' in Knowledge Economies: The Not-nothing of Social Constructionism. *Social Epistemology* 19(4): 339–355.

Kraus, C. (2010a) A Brain of One's Own: Feminism, Neurobiology and the Subversion of Identities? Paper given at the Neurogenderings: Critical Studies of the Sexed Brain Conference, University of Uppsala, Sweden, 25–27 March.

Kraus, C. (2010b) Tensions in Discourses about Nature–Culture Productions of the Self: Brain Plasticity and other Biosocial Arguments. Paper given at the 4th Christina Conference in Gender Studies – Gender, Nature and Culture, University of Helsinki, Finland, 20–22 May.

Kraus, C. (2011a) Critical Studies of the Sexed Brain: A Critique of What and for Whom? *Neuroethics*. doi: 10.1007/s12152-011-9107-7.

Kraus, C. (2011b) Am I My Brain or My Genitals? A Nature–Culture Controversy in the Hermaphrodite Debate from the mid-1960s to the Late '90s. *Gesnerus: Swiss Journal for the History of Medicine and Sciences*, 68(1).

Kraus, C., Perrin, C. and Rey, S. in collaboration with L. Gosselin, V. Guillot, A. Cocteau, C. Lamarre, E. Nagant, and Julien (2008a) A qui appartiennent nos corps? Féminisme et luttes intersexes. *Nouvelles Questions Féministes*, 27(1).

Kraus, C., Perrin, C. and Rey, S. in collaboration with L. Gosselin and V. Guillot (2008b) Edito: Démédicaliser les corps, politiser les identités. *Nouvelles Questions Féministes* 27(1): 4–15.

Krieger, N. (2003) Genders, Sexes, and Health: What Are the Connections – and Why Does It Matter?' *International Journal of Epidemiology* 32(4): 652–657.

Lalumière, M. L., Blanchard, R. and Zucker, K. J. (2000) Sexual Orientation and Handedness in Men and Women: A Meta-Analysis. *Psychological Bulletin* 126(4): 575–592.

Lancaster, R. N. (2003) *The Trouble With Nature: Sex in Popular Science and Mass Culture* (Ewing, NJ: University of California Press).

Lancaster, R. N. (2006) Sex, Science, and Pseudoscience In the Public Sphere. *Identities: Global Studies in Culture and Power* 13: 101–138.

Lappe, C., Herholz, S. C. et al. (2008) Cortical Plasticity Induced by Short-Term Unimodal and Multimodal Musical Training. *Journal of Neuroscience* 28(39): 9632–9639.

Latour, B. (2004a) *Politics of Nature: How to Bring the Sciences into Democracy* (Cambridge, MA: Harvard University Press).

Latour, B. (2004b) Whose Cosmos, Which Cosmopolitics? Comments on the Peace Terms of Ulrich Beck. *Common Knowledge* 10(3): 450–462.

Latour, B. (2005) *Reassembling the Social: An Introduction to Actor-Network-Theory* (Oxford: Oxford University Press).

Lawson, J., Baron-Cohen, S. and Wheelwright, S. (2004) Empathising and Systemising in Adults With and Without Asperger Syndrome. *Journal of Autism and Developmental Disorders* 34: 301–310.

Leaper, C. and Friedman, C. K. (2007) The Socialization of Gender. In J. E. Grusec and P. D. Hastings (eds), *Handbook of Socialization: Theory and Research* (New York: Guilford Press), 561–587.

Leboucher, G. (1989) Maternal Behavior in Normal and Androgenized Female Rats: Effect of Age and Experience. *Physiology and Behavior* 45(2): 313–319.

LeDoux, J. E. (1996) *The Emotional Brain: The Mysterious Underpinnings of Emotional Life* (New York: Simon and Schuster).

Lee, P. A., Houk, C. P., Ahmed, S. F. and Hughes, I. A. in collaboration with the participants in the International Consensus Conference on Intersex organized by the Lawson Wilkins Pediatric Endocrine Society and the European Society for Paediatric Endocrinology (2006) Consensus Statement on Management of Intersex Disorders. *Pediatrics* 118: 488–500.

Lee, S., Guajardo, N., Short, S. and King, W. (2010). Individual Differences in Ocular Level Empathetic Accuracy Ability: The Predictive Power of Fantasy Empathy. *Personality and Individual Differences* 49: 68–71.

Lefort, C. (1986) La question de la démocratie. In *Essais sur le politique, XIXe–XXe siècle*. (Paris: Seuil), 17–32.

Leonard, C. M., Towler, S. et al. (2008) Size Matters: Cerebral Volume Influences Sex Differences in Neuroanatomy. *Cerebral Cortex* 18: 2920–2931.

LeVay, S. (1991) A Difference in Hypothalamic Structure between Heterosexual and Homosexual Men. *Science* 253: 1034–1037.

Levenson, J. L. (2006) Psychiatric Issues in Endocrinology. *Primary Psychiatry* 13: 27–30.

Levine, S. C., Vasilyeva, M., Lourenco, S. F., Newcombe, N. S. and Huttenlocher, J. (2005) Socioeconomic Status Modifies the Sex Difference in Spatial Skill. *Psychological Science* 16: 841–845.

Levy, N. (2004) Understanding Blindness. *Phenomenology and the Cognitive Sciences* 3: 315–324.

Levy, N. (2007) *Neuroethics: Challenges for the 21st Century* (Cambridge: Cambridge University Press).

Lewontin, R. C, Rose, S. and Kamin, L. C. (1985) *Not in Our Genes: Biology, Ideology, and Human Nature* (London: Penguin Books).

Liberman, M. (2007) The first time? Language Log (http://itre.cis.upenn.edu/~myl/languagelog/archives/004691.html), accessed 15 March 2011.

Lickliter, R. and Honeycutt, H. (2003) Developmental Dynamics: Toward a Biologically Plausible Evolutionary Psychology. *Psychological Bulletin* 129: 819–835.

Lim, M. M., Nair, H. P. et al. (2005) Species and Sex Differences in Brain Distribution of Corticotropin-Releasing Factor Receptor Subtypes 1 and 2 in Monogamous and Promiscuous Vole Species. *Journal of Comparative Neurology* 487(1): 75–92.

Lin-Su, Y. R., Nimkarn, S. et al. (2008) Congenital Adrenal Hyperplasia in Adolescents: Diagnosis and Management. *Annals of the New York Academy of Sciences* 1135: 95–98.

Lish, J. D., Meyer-Bahlburg, H. F. L. et al. (1992) Prenatal Exposure to Diethylstilbestrol (Des): Childhood Play Behavior and Adult Gender-Role Behavior in Women. *Archives of Sexual Behavior* 21(5): 423–441.

Lloyd, G. (2000) Hume on the Passion for Truth. In A. J. Jacobson (ed.), *Feminist Interpretations of David Hume* (University Park, PA: Pennsylvania State University Press).

Longino, H. (1990) *Science as Social Knowledge: Values and Objectivity in Scientific Inquiry* (Princeton, NJ: Princeton University Press).

Longino, H. (1992) Taking Gender Seriously in Philosophy of Science. *Proceedings of the Biennial Meeting of the Philosophy of Science Association, Symposia and Invited Papers*: 333–340.

Longino, H. (1996) Cognitive and Non-Cognitive Values in Science: Rethinking the Dichotomy. In L. H. Nelson and J. Nelson (eds), *Feminism, Science, and the Philosophy of Science* (London: Kluwer).

Longino, H. (2002) *The Fate of Knowledge* (Princeton NJ: Princeton University Press).

Lonstein, J. S. (2002) Effects of Dopamine Receptor Antagonism with Haloperidol on Nurturing Behavior in the Biparental Prairie Vole. *Pharmacology Biochemistry and Behavior* 74(1): 11–19.

Lüders, E., Steinmetz, H. et al. (2002) Brain Size and Grey Matter Volume in the Healthy Human Brain. Neuroreport 13: 2371–2374.

Lüders, E., Narr, K. L., Thompson, P. M., Woods, R. P., Rex, D. E., Jancke, L. et al. (2005) Mapping Cortical Gray Matter in the Young Adult Brain: Effects of Gender. *NeuroImage* 26: 493–501.

Lüders, E., Gaser, C., Narr, K. L. and Toga, A. W. (2009) Why Sex Matters: Brain Size and Independent Differences in Gray Matter Distributions between Men and Women. *Journal of Neuroscience* 29: 14265–14270.

Lutchmaya, S. and Baron-Cohen, S. (2002) Human Sex Differences in Social and Non-Social Looking Preferences, at 12 Months of Age. *Infant Behavior and Development* 25: 319–325.

Lutchmaya, S., Baron-Cohen, S. and Ragatt, P. (2002a) Foetal Testosterone and Eye Contact in 12-Month-Old Human Infants. *Infant Behavior and Development* 25: 327–335.

Lutchmaya, S., Baron-Cohen, S. and Ragatt, P. (2002b) Foetal Testosterone and Vocabulary Size in 18- and 24-Month-Old Infants. *Infant Behavior and Development* 24: 418–424.

Maccoby, E. E. and Jacklin, C. N. (1974) *The Psychology of Sex Differences* (Stanford, CA: Stanford University Press).

Maguire, E. A., Woollett, K. and Spiers, H. (2006) London Taxi Drivers and Bus Drivers: A Structural MRI and Neuropsychological Analysis. *Hippocampus* 16: 1091–1101.

Maguire, E. A., Gadian, D. G. et al. (2000) Navigation-Related Structural Change in the Hippocampi of Taxi Drivers. *Proceedings of the National Academy of Sciences of the United States of America* 97(8): 4398–4403.

Maguire, E. A., Spiers, H. J. et al. (2003) Navigation Expertise and the Human Hippocampus: A Structural Brain Imaging Analysis. *Hippocampus* 13(2): 250–259.

Malouf, M. A., Migeon, C. J., Carson, K. A., Petrucci, L. and Wisniewski, A. B. (2006) Cognitive Outcome in Adult Women Affected by Congenital Adrenal Hyperplasia Due to 21-Hydroxylase Deficiency. *Hormone Research in Paediatrics* 65: 142–150.

Manderson, L. (2004) Local Rites and the Body Politic: Tensions between Cultural Diversity and Human Rights. *International Feminist Journal of Politics* 6: 285–307.

Manderson, L., Bennett, E. and Andajani-Sutjahjo, S. (2006) The Social Dynamics of the Interview: Age, Class, and Gender. *Qualitative Health Research* 16: 1317–1334.

Margulies, D. (2010) The Salmon of Doubt: Exploring a Recent Methodological Controversy in Social Science. Paper presented at the Critical Neuroscience Workshop: Alternatives to Neurocentrism in Philosophy and Psychiatry, Philipps-University of Marburg, Germany, 22–24 April.

Marsa, L. (2007) He Thinks, She Thinks. *Discover Magazine* (http://discovermagazine.com/2007/brain/she-thinks).

Martin, B. and Richards, E. (2008) Scientific Knowledge, Controversy and Public Decision Making. In S. Jasanoff, G. E. Markle, J. C. Peterson and T. Pinch (eds), *Handbook of Science and Technology Studies* (rev. edn., Thousands Oaks, CA: Sage Publications), 506–526.

Martin, C. and Ruble, D. (2004) Children's Search for Gender Cues: Cognitive Perspectives on Gender Development. *Current Directions in Psychological Science* 13: 67–70.

Martin, E. (1991) The Egg and the Sperm: How Science has Constructed a Romance Based on Stereotypical Male–Female Roles. *Signs* 16: 485–501.

Martinez-Alier, J. (2002) *The Environmentalism of the Poor: A Study of Ecological Conflicts and Valuation* (Cheltenham: Edward Elgar).

Martinez-Conde, S., Krauzlis, R. et al. (2008) Eye Movements and the Perception of a Clear and Stable Visual World. *Journal of Vision* 8(14): 1.

Marx, D. M. and Stapel, D. A. (2006) It Depends on Your Perspective: The Role of Self-Relevance in Stereotype-Based Underperformance. *Journal of Experimental Social Psychology* 42: 768–775.

Massumi, B. (2002) *Parables for the Virtual: Movement, Affect, Sensation* (Durham: Duke University Press).

Mathews, G. A., Fane, B. A., Conway, G. S., Brook, C. G. D. and Hines, M. (2009) Personality and Congenital Adrenal Hyperplasia: Possible Effects of Prenatal Androgen Exposure. *Hormones and Behavior* 55: 285–291.

Matsumoto, A. (1999) *Sexual Differentiation of the Brain* (Boca Raton, FL: CRC Press).

May, B., Boyle, M. and Grant, D. (1996) A Comparative Study of Sexual Experiences: Women with Diabetes and Women with Congenital Adrenal Hyperplasia. *Journal of Health Psychology* 1(4): 479–492.

McClure, E. (2000) A Meta-Analytic Review of Sex Differences in Facial Expression Processing and their Development in Infants, Children, and Adolescents. *Psychological Bulletin* 126: 424–453.

McDowell, L. (1992) Doing Gender: Feminism, Feminists and Research Methods in Human Geography. *Transactions of the Institute of British Geographers* 17: 399–416.

McEwen, B. and Seeman, T. (1999) Allostatic Load and Allostasis. In John, D. and Catherine, T. MacArthur Network on Socioeconomic Status and Health (http://www.macses.ucsf.edu/Research/Allostatic/notebook/allostatic.html), accessed 14 February 2009.

McGlone, M. and Aronson, J. (2006) Stereotype Threat, Identity Salience, and Spatial Reasoning. *Journal of Applied Developmental Psychology* 27: 486–493.

McGowan, P. O., Sasak, A., D'Alessio, A. C., Dymov, S., Labonte, B., Szyf, M. et al. (2009) Epigenetic Regulation of the Glucocorticoid Receptor in Human Brain Associates with Childhood Abuse. *Nature Neuroscience* 12: 342–348.

McIntyre, M. H. (2006) The Use of Digit Ratios as Markers for Perinatal Androgen Action. *Reproductive Biology and Endocrinology* 4: 10.

Medawar, P. B. (1967) *The Art of the Soluble* (London: Methuen).

Medawar, P. B. (1969) *Induction and Intuition in Scientific Thought* (Philadelphia, PA: American Philosophical Society).

Medlinger, S. and Cwikel, J. (2008) Spiralling between Qualitative and Quantitative Data on Women's Health Behaviors: A Double Helix Model for Mixed Methods. *Qualitative Health Research* 18: 280–293.

Mehrabian, A. (1997) Relations among Personality Scales of Aggression, Violence, and Empathy. *Aggressive Behavior* 23: 433–45.

Melzack, R., and Wall, P. D. (1996) *The Challenge of Pain* (New York: Basic Books).

Menary, R. (2010) *The Extended Mind* (Cambridge, MA: MIT Press).

Mergler, D. (2002) Review of Neurobehavioral Deficits and River Fish Consumption from the Tapajos (Brazil) and St. Lawrence (Canada). *Environmental Toxicology and Pharmacology* 12: 93–99.

Messing, K. and Stellman, J. M. (2006) Sex, Gender and Women's Occupational Health: The Importance of Considering Mechanism. *Environmental Research* 101(2): 149–162.

Mestre, M., Samper, P., Frías, M. and Tur, M. (2009) Are Women More Empathetic than Men? A Longitudinal Study in Adolescence. *Spanish Journal of Psychology* 12: 76–83.

Meyer-Bahlburg, H. F. L. (2001) Gender and Sexuality in Classic Congenital Adrenal Hyperplasia. *Endocrinology and Metabolism Clinics of North America* 30(1): 155–171.

Meyer-Bahlburg, H. F. L. and Dolezal, C. (2008) Sexual Orientation in Women with Classical or Non-Classical Adrenal Hyperplasia as a Function Degree of Prenatal Androgen Excess. *Archives of Sexual Behavior* 37(1): 85–99.

Meyer-Bahlburg, H. F. L., Ehrhardt, A. A. et al. (1995) Prenatal Estrogens and the Development of Homosexual Orientation. *Developmental Psychology* 31(1): 12–21.

Meyer-Bahlburg, H. F. L., Dolezal, C., Zucker, K. J., Kessler, S. J., Schober, J. M. and New, M. I. (2006) The Recalled Childhood Gender Questionnaire-Revised: A Psychometric Analysis in a Sample of Women with Congenital Adrenal Hyperplasia. *Journal of Sex Research* 43: 364–367.

Meyers, D. (1994) *Subjection and Subjectivity: Psychoanalytic Feminism and Moral Philosophy* (New York: Routledge).

Meynell, L. (2008a) Pictures, Pluralism and Feminist Epistemology: Lessons from 'Coming to Understand'. *Hypatia* 23(4): 1–29.

Meynell, L. (2008b) Why Feynman Diagrams Represent. *International Studies in the Philosophy of Science* 22(1): 39–59.

Meynell, L. (forthcoming) Parsing Pictures: On Analyzing the Content of Images. *Knowledge Engineering Review*.

Mikkola, M. (2008) Feminist Perspectives on Sex and Gender. *Stanford Encyclopedia of Philosophy* (http://plato.stanford.edu/entries/feminism-gender/).

Miller, C. F., Trautner, H. M. and Ruble, D. N. (2006) The Role of Gender Stereotypes in Children's Preferences and Behavior. In L. Balter and C. S. Tamis-LeMonda (eds), *Child Psychology: A Handbook of Contemporary Issues* (2nd edn., Philadelphia, PA: Psychology Press), 293–323.

Ming, G. and Song, H. (2005) Adult Neurogenesis in the Mammalian Central Nervous System. *Annual Review of Neuroscience* 28: 223–250.

Mitchell, L. and Georges, E. (1997) Cross-Cultural Cyborgs: Greek and Canadian Women's Discourses on Fetal Ultrasound. *Feminist Studies* 23(2): 373–401.

Moè, A. (2009) Are Males Always Better than Females in Mental Rotation? Exploring a Gender Belief Explanation. *Learning and Individual Differences* 19: 21–27.

Moffat, S. D., Hampson, E. and Hatzipantelis, M. (1998) Navigation in a Virtual Maze: Sex Differences and Correlation with Psychometric Measures of Spatial Ability in Humans. *Evolution and Human Behavior* 19: 73–87.

Moffat, S. D., Hampson, E. and Lee, D. (1998) Morphology of the Planum Temporale and Corpus Callosum in Left Handers with Evidence of Left and Right Hemisphere Speech Representation. *Brain* 121: 2369–2379.

Moir, A. and Moir, B. (2003) *Why Men Don't Iron: The Fascinating and Unalterable Differences Between Men and Women* (New York: Citadel Press).

Money, J. (1955) Hermaphroditism, Gender and Precocity in Hyperadrenocorticism: Psychologic findings. *Bulletin of the Johns Hopkins Hospital* 10: 66–72.

Money, J., Hampson, J. G. and Hampson, J. L. (1955a) An Examination of some Basic Sexual Concepts: The Evidence of Human Hermaphroditism. *Bulletin of the Johns Hopkins Hospital* 97: 301–319.

Money, J., Hampson, J. G. and Hampson, J. L. (1955b) Hermaphroditism: Recommendations Concerning Assignment of Sex, Change of Sex and Psychological Management. *Bulletin of the Johns Hopkins Hospital* 97: 284–300.

Montague, P. R. (2003) Uncertainty Rules. *Nature* 424(6947): 371.

Montague, P. R. and S. R. Quartz (1999) Computational Approaches to Neural Reward and Development. *Mental Retardation and Developmental Disabilities Research Reviews* 5: 86–99.

Montague, R. (2007) *Your Brain is (Almost) Perfect: How We Make Decisions* (New York: Penguin).

Moore, C. (1995) Maternal Contributions to Mammalian Reproductive Development and the Divergence of Males and Females. *Advances in the Study of Behavior* 24: 47–118.

Moore, C., Dou, H. and Juraska, J. (1992) Maternal Stimulation Affects the Number of Motor Neurons in a Sexually Dimorphic Nucleus of the Lumbar Spinal Cord. *Brain Research* 572: 52–56.

Moore, C. L. (2002) On Differences and Development. In D. J. Lewkowicz and R. Lickliter (eds), *Conceptions of Development: Lessons from the Laboratory* (New York: Psychology Press), 57–76.

Moore, R. Y. (1997) Circadian Rhythms: Basic Neurobiology and Clinical Applications. *Annual Review of Medicine* 48: 253–266.

Mora, F., Segovia, G. and del Arco, A. (2007) Aging, Plasticity and Environmental Enrichment: Structural Changes and Neurotransmitter Dynamics in Several Areas of the Brain. *Brain Research Reviews* 55: 78–88.

Morgan, D. L. (1998) Practical Strategies for Combining Qualitative and Quantitative Methods: Applications to Health Research. *Qualitative Health Research* 8: 362–376.

Morgan, M., Goddard, W. and Givens, S. (1997) Factors that Influence Willingness to Help the Homeless. *Journal of Social Distress and Homelessness* 6: 45–56.

Morse, J. and Niehaus, L. (2007) Combining Qualitative and Quantitative Methods for Mixed Method Design. In P. Munhall (ed.), *Nursing Research: A Qualitative Perspective* (Mississauga, Canada: Jones and Bartlett Publishers), 541–555.

Morton, T., Postmes, T., Haslam, S. A. and Hornsey, M. (2009) Theorizing Gender in the Face of Social Change: Is There Anything Essential About Essentialism? *Journal of Personality and Social Psychology* 96: 653–664.

Mukamel, R., Ekstrom, A. D. et al. (2010) Single-Neuron Responses in Humans during Execution and Observation of Actions. *Current Biology* 20(8): 750–756.

Nash, A. and Grossi, G. (2007) Picking Barbie's Brain: Inherent Sex Differences in Scientific Ability? *Journal of Interdisciplinary Feminist Thought* 2: Article 5.

National Center for Education Statistics (2009) Fast Facts: What is the Percentage of Degrees Conferred by Sex and Race? (http://nces.ed.gov/fastfacts/display.asp?id=72), accessed 2 March 2010.

Newcombe, N. (2010) On Tending to Our Scientific Knitting: Thinking about Gender in the Context of Evolution. In J. Chrisler and D. McCreary (eds), *Handbook of Gender Research in Psychology, Volume 1* (New York: Springer), 259–274.

Newman, M. F., Kirchner, J. L., Phillips-Bute, B., Gaver, V., Grocott, H., Jones, R. H., Mark, D. B., Reves, J. G. and Blumenthal, J. A. (2001) Longitudinal Assessment of Neurocognitive Function after Coronary-Artery Bypass Surgery. *New England Journal of Medicine* 344: 395–402.

Nguyen, H. D. and Ryan, A. M. (2008) Does Stereotype Threat Affect Test Performance of Minorities and Women? A Meta-Analysis of Experimental Evidence. *Journal of Applied Psychology* 93: 1314–1334.

Noddings, N. (1984) *Caring: A Feminist Approach to Ethics and Moral Education* (Berkeley, CA: University of California Press).

Noddings, N. (1989) Educating Moral People. In M. Brabeck (ed.), *Who Cares? Theory, Research, and Educational Implications of the Ethics of Care* (New York: Praeger), 216–232.

Noë, A. (2004) *Action in Perception* (Cambridge, MA: MIT Press).

Noë, A. (2009) *Out of Our Heads: Why You Are Not Your Brain, and Other Lessons From The Biology of Consciousness* (New York: Hill and Wang).

Noë, A. and Thompson, E. (2002) *Vision and Mind: Selected Readings in the Philosophy of Perception* (Cambridge, MA: MIT Press).

Nopoulos, P., Flaum, M. et al. (2000) Sexual Dimorphism in the Human Brain: Evaluation of Tissue Volume, Tissue Composition and Surface Anatomy Using Magnetic Resonance Imaging. *Psychiatry Research – Neuroimaging* 98(1): 1–13.

Obermeyer, C. M. (2005) The Consequences of Female Circumcision for Health and Sexuality: An Update on the Evidence. *Culture, Health & Sexuality* 7: 443–461.

Öğmen, H. (2007) A Theory of Moving Form Perception: Synergy between Masking, Perceptual Grouping, and Motion Computation in Retinotopic and Non-Retinotopic Representations. *Advances in Cognitive Psychology* 3(1–2): 67–84.

Öğmen, H., Otto, T. U., et al. (2006) Perceptual grouping Induces Non-Retinotopic Feature Attribution in Human Vision. *Vision Research* 46(19): 3234.

Orenstein, P. (2001) *Flux: Women on Sex, Work, Love, Kids, and Life in a Half-Changed World* (New York: Anchor Books).

Ortega, F. and Vidal, F. (2007) Mapping the Cerebral Subject in Contemporary Culture. *RECIIS – Electronic Journal of Communication, Information and Innovation in Health* 1: 255–259.

Ortigue, S., Bianchi-Demicheli, F., Patel, N., Frum, C. and Lewis, J. W. (2010) Neuroimaging of Love: fMRI Meta-Analysis Evidence toward New Perspectives in Sexual Medicine. *Journal of Sexual Medicine* 7: 3541–3552.

Oswald, P. (2000) Subtle Sex Bias in Empathy and Helping Behavior. *Psychological Reports* 87: 545–51.

Oudshoorn, N. (1994) *Beyond the Natural Body: An Archeology of Sex Hormones* (New York: Routledge).

Paediatric Endocrinology (2006) Consensus Statement on Management of Intersex Disorders. *Journal of Pediatric Urology* 2: 148–162.

Pakkenberg, B. and Gundersen, H. (1997) Neocortical Neuron Number in Humans: Effect of Sex and Age. *Journal of Comparative Neurology* 384: 312–320.

Parvisi, J. and Roy, D. (2011, under review) Biological Destiny? Brain Sex Differences and Neuroplasticity.

Pascual-Leone, A., Amedi, A., Fregni, F. and Merabet, L. (2005) The Plastic Human Brain Cortex. *Annual Review of Neuroscience* 28: 377–401.

Pasterski, V. L., Geffner, M. E., Brain, C., Hindmarsh, P., Brook, C. and Hines, M. (2005) Prenatal Hormones and Postnatal Socialization by Parents as Determinants of Male-Typical Toy Play in Girls with Congenital Adrenal Hyperplasia. *Child Development* 76: 264–278.

Pasterski, V. L., Hindmarsh, P., Geffner, M., Brook, C., Brain, C. and Hines, M. (2007) Increased Aggression and Activity Level in 3- to 11-Year-Old Girls with Congenital Adrenal Hyperplasia (CAH). *Hormones and Behavior* 52: 368–374.

Paul, T., Schiffer, B. et al. (2008) Brain Response to Visual Sexual Stimuli in Heterosexual and Homosexual Males. *Human Brain Mapping* 29: 726–35.

Pease, B. and Pease, A. (2001) *Why Men Don't Listen and Women Can't Read Maps: How We're Different and What to Do About It* (New York: Broadway Books).

Pedersen, P., Vinter, K., and Olsen, T. S. (2004) Aphasia after Stroke: Type, Severity and Prognosis. *Cerebrovascular Diseases* 17: 35–43.

Pestre, D. (2007) L'analyse de controverses dans l'étude des sciences depuis trente ans. Entre outil méthodologique, garantie de neutralité axiologique et politique. *Mil neuf cent. Revue d'histoire intellectuelle* 1 :29–43.

Pestre, D. (2008) Sciences et démocratie. De la participation aux choix techno-scientifiques. Paper presented at the Généalogie de la démocratie participative Conference, Ecole nationale supérieure d'architecture, Paris, 8–9 February.

Petchesky, R. (1987) Fetal Images: The Power of Visual Culture in the Politics of Reproduction. *Feminist Studies* 13(2): 263–292.

Phoenix, C. H. (1961) Hypothalamic Regulation of Sexual Behavior in Male Guinea Pigs. *Journal of Comparative Physiological Psychology* 54(1): 72–77.

Phoenix, C. H., Goy, R. W., Gerall, A. A. and Young, W. C. (1959) Organizing Action of Prenatally Administered Testosterone Propionate on the Tissues Mediating Mating Behavior in the Female Guinea Pig. *Endocrinology* 65: 369–382.

Piefke, M., Weiss, P., Markowitsch, H. and Fink, G. (2005) Gender Differences in the Functional Neuroanatomy of Emotional Episodic Autobiographical Memory. *Human Brain Mapping* 24: 313–324.

Pini, B. (2005) Interviewing Men: Gender and the Collection and Interpretation of Qualitative Data. *Journal of Sociology* 41: 201–216.

Pletzer, B., Kronbichler, M. et al. (2010) Menstrual Cycle and Hormonal Contraceptive Use Modulate Human Brain Structure. *Brain Research* 12: 55–62.

Polger, T. (2009) Evaluating the Evidence for Multiple Realization. *Synthese* 167: 457–472.

Ponseti, J., Bosinski, H. A. et al. (2006) A Functional Endophenotype for Sexual Orientation in Humans. *NeuroImage* 33: 825–833.

Ponseti, J., Granert, O. et al. (2009) Assessment of Sexual Orientation Using the Hemodynamic Brain Response to Visual Sexual Stimuli. *Journal of Sexual Medicine* 6: 1628–1634.

Potter, E. (1995) Good Science and Good Philosophy of Science. *Synthese* 104(3): 423–439.

Prager, E. and Johnson, L. (2009) Stress at the Synapse: Signal Transduction Mechanisms of Adrenal Steroids at Neuronal Membranes. *Science Signaling* 2(86): re5.

Price, C. and Friston, K. (2002) Degeneracy and Cognitive Anatomy. *Trends in Cognitive Sciences* 6(10): 416–421.

Prinz, J. J. (2002) *Furnishing the Mind: Concepts and their Perceptual Basis* (Cambridge, MA: MIT Press).

Prinz, J. J. (2006) Putting the Brakes on Enactive Perception. *Psyche* 12(1): 1–19.

Putnam, H. (1967) The Nature of Mental States. In *Mind, Language and Reality: Philosophical Papers* (Vol. 2) (New York: Cambridge University Press).

Puts, D. A., McDaniel, M. A., Jordan, C. L. and Breedlove, S. M. (2008) Spatial Ability and Prenatal Androgens: Meta-Analyses of Congenital Adrenal Hyperplasia and Digit Ratio (2D:4D) Studies. *Archives of Sexual Behavior* 37: 100–111.

Pylyshyn, Z. W. (2000) Situating Vision in the World. *Trends in Cognitive Sciences* 4(5): 197.

Rabinowicz, T., Petetot, J. M.-C., Gartside, P. S., Sheyn, D., Sheyn, T. and De Courten-Myers, G. M. (2002) Structure of the Cerebral Cortex in Men and Women. *Journal of Neuropathology and Experimental Neurology* 61: 46–57.

Racine, E., Bar-Ilan, O. et al. (2005) fMRI in the public eye. *Nature Reviews Neuroscience* 6: 159–164.

Ramachandran, V. S. and Blakeslee, S. (1998) *Phantoms in the Brain: Probing the Mysteries of the Human Mind* (New York: William Morrow).

Realo, A., Allik, J., Nõlvak, A., Valk, R., Ruus, T., Schmidt, M. et al. (2003) Mind-Reading Ability: Beliefs and Performance. *Journal of Research in Personality* 37: 420–445.

Reena, C., Kekre, A. N. and Kekre, N. (2007) Occult Stress Incontinence in Women with Pelvic Organ Prolapse. *International Journal of Gynecology and Obstetrics* 97: 31–34.

Reinisch, J. M. and Sanders, S. A. (1992) Effects of Prenatal Exposure to Diethylstilbestrol (DES) on Hemispheric Laterality and Spatial Ability in Human Males. *Hormones and Behavior* 26: 62–75.

Resko, J. A. and Roselli, C. E. (1997) Prenatal Hormones Organize Sex Differences of the Neuroendocrine Reproductive System: Observations on Guinea Pigs and Nonhuman Primates. *Cellular and Molecular Neurobiology* 17(6): 627–648.

Rhode, D. (1997) The Ideology and Biology of Gender Difference. *Southern Journal of Philosophy* 35 (Suppl.): 73–98.

Richardson, S. S. (2008) When Gender Criticism becomes Standard Scientific Practice: The Case of Sex Determination Genetics. In L. Schiebinger (ed.), *Gendered Innovations in Science and Engineering* (Palo Alto, CA: Stanford University Press), 22–42.

Richerson, P. and Boyd, R. (2005) *Not By Genes Alone: How Culture Transformed Human Evolution* (Chicago: University of Chicago Press).

Ridgeway, C. L. (2009) Framed Before we Know it: How Gender Shapes Social Relations. *Gender & Society* 23: 145–160.

Risman, B. J. (2004) Gender as a Social Structure: Theory Wrestling with Activism. *Gender & Society* 18: 429–450.

Robinson, F. (1999) *Globalizing Care: Towards a Politics of Peace* (Boston, MA: Beacon Press).

Rogers, L. (2002) *Sexing the Brain* (New York: Columbia University Press).

Roof, R. L., Zhang, Q., Glasier, M. M. and Stein, D. G. (1993) Gender-Specific Impairment on Morris Water Maze Task after Entorhinal Cortex Lesion. *Behavioural Brain Research* 57: 47–51.

Rosario, V. (1997) Homosexual Bio-histories: Genetic Nostalgias and the Quest for Paternity. In *Science and Homosexualities* (New York: Routledge), 1–25.

Rose, H. (1996) Gay Brains, Gay Genes, and Feminist Science Theory. In J. Holland and J. Weeks (eds), *Sexual Cultures: Communities, Values, and Intimacy* (Basingstoke: Macmillan).

Rose, H. and Rose, S. (2000) *Alas, Poor Darwin: Arguments against Evolutionary Psychology* (London: Jonathan Cape).

Rose, N. (2004) Becoming Neurochemical Selves. In N. Stehr (ed.), *Biotechnology, Commerce and Civil Society* (Somerset: Transaction Publishers), 89–128

Rose, N. (2007) *The Politics of Life Itself: Biomedicine, Power, and Subjectivity in the Twenty-First Century* (Princeton: Princeton University Press).

Rose, S., Ceci, S. and Williams, W. M. (2009) Should Scientists Study Race and IQ? No: Science and Society Do Not Benefit. *Nature* 457: 786–788.

Roskies, A. (2008) Neuroimaging and Inferential Distance. *Neuroethics* 1: 19–30.

Rothemund, Y., Schaefer, M., Grüsser, S. M. and Flor, H. (2005) Localization of the Human Female Breast in Primary Somatosensory Cortex. *Experimental Brain Research* 164: 357–364.

Rotter, N. and Rotter, G. (1988) Sex Differences in the Encoding and Decoding of Negative Facial Emotions. *Journal of Nonverbal Behavior* 12: 139–148.

Roughgarden, J. (2004) *Evolution's Rainbow: Diversity, Gender and Sexuality in Nature and People* (Los Angeles: University of California Press).

Rouse, J. (1998) New Philosophies of Science in North America: Twenty Years Later. *Journal for General Philosophy of Science/Zeitschrift für allgemeine Wissenschaftstheorie* 29: 71–122.

Rowlands, M. (2010) *The New Science of the Mind: From Extended Mind to Embodied Phenomenology* (Cambridge, MA: MIT Press).

Roy, D. (2007) Somatic Matters: Becoming Molecular in Molecular Biology. *Rhizomes* 14 (http://www.rhizomes.net/issue14/roy/roy.html).

Roy, D. (2008) Should Feminists Clone? And If So, How? *Australian Feminist Studies* 23(56): 225–247.

Roy, D. (2010) Brain Tease: Feminist Neuroethics and the Search for a Cosmopolitical Brain. Paper given at the NeuroGenderings: Critical Studies of the Sexed Brain conference, University of Uppsala, Sweden, 25–27 March.

Roy, D. (2011, forthcoming) Neuroethics, Gender and the Response to Difference. *Neuroethics*.

Royet, J., Plailly, J., Delon-Martin, C., Kareken, D. and Segebarth, C. (2003) fMRI of Emotional Responses to Odors: Influence of Hedonic Valence and Judgment, Handedness, and Gender. *NeuroImage* 20: 713–728.

Rupert, R. D. (2009) *Cognitive Systems and the Extended Mind* (Oxford and New York: Oxford University Press).

Ryan, M., David, B. and Reynolds, K. (2004) Who Cares? The Effect of Gender and Context on the Self and Moral Reasoning. *Psychology of Women Quarterly* 28: 246–255.

Rydell, R., McConnell, A. and Beilock, S. (2009) Multiple Social Identities and Stereotype Threat: Imbalance, Accessibility, and Working Memory. *Journal of Personality and Social Psychology* 96: 949–966.

Safron, A., Barch, B. et al. (2007) Neural Correlates of Sexual Arousal in Homosexual and Heterosexual Men. *Behavioral Neuroscience* 121: 237–248

Sanders, S. A. and Reinisch, J. M. (1999) Would You Say You "Had Sex" if...? *JAMA: Journal of the American Medical Association* 281: 275–277.

Savic, I. and Lindström, P. (2008) PET and MRI Show Differences in Cerebral Asymmetry and Functional Connectivity between Homo- and Heterosexual Subjects. *Proceedings of the National Academy of Sciences USA* 105: 9403–9408

Savic, I., Berglund, H. et al. (2005) Brain Response to Putative Pheromones in Homosexual Men. *Proceedings of the National Academy of Sciences USA* 102: 7356–7361

Savin-Williams, R. C. (2006) Who's Gay? Does It Matter? *Current Directions in Psychological Science* 15(1): 40–44.

Sayers, J. (1982) *Biological Politics: Feminist and Anti-feminist Perspectives* (New York: Tavistock Publications).

Schachter, S. C. (1994) Handedness in Women with Intrauterine Exposure to Diethylstilbestrol. *Neuropsychologia* 32(5): 619–623.

Scheirs, J. G. M. and Vingerhoets, A. (1995) Handedness and Other Laterality Indexes in Women Prenatally Exposed to DES. *Journal of Clinical and Experimental Neuropsychology* 17(5): 725–730.

Schiebinger, L. (1989) *The Mind Has No Sex? Women and the Origins of Modern Science* (Cambridge, MA: Harvard University Press).

Schinzel, B. (2006a) Gender and Ethically Relevant Issues of Visualizations in the Life Sciences. *International Review of Information Ethics* 5: 19–26.

Schinzel, B. (2006b) The Body in Medical Imaging between Reality and Construction. *Poiesis & Praxis: International Journal of Technology Assessment and Ethics of Science* 4(3): 185–198.

Schmithorst, V. J. and Holland, S. K. (2007) Sex Differences in the Development of Neuroanatomical Functional Connectivity Underlying Intelligence Found Using Bayesian Connectivity Analysis. *NeuroImage* 35(1): 406–419.

Schmitz, S. (2010a) Rationality/Emotionality in Neuroeconomics: From References to Socio-Political Implications. Paper presented at the Neurosociety: What Is It With the Brain These Days? conference, Oxford, 7–8 December.

Schmitz, S. (2010b) Sex, Gender, and the Brain: Biological Determinism Versus Socio-Cultural Constructivism. In I. Klinge, and C. Wiesmann (eds), *Sex and Gender in Biomedicine* (Göttingen: Universitätsverlag Göttingen), 57–76.

Schöning, S. and Engelien, A. (2007) Functional Anatomy of Visuo-Spatial Working Memory During Mental Rotation is Influenced by Sex, Menstrual Cycle, and Sex Steroid Hormones. *Neuropsychologia* 45(14): 3203–3214.

Schulte-Rüther, M., Markowitsch, H., Shah, N., Fink, G. and Piefke, M. (2008) Gender Differences in Brain Networks Supporting Empathy. *NeuroImage* 42: 393–403.

Schulz, M. L. (2006) *The New Feminine Brain: Developing Your Intuitive Genius* (New York: Free Press).

Schum, J. E. and Wynne-Edwards, K. E. (2005) Estradiol and Progesterone in Paternal and Non-Paternal Hamsters (Phodopus) Becoming Fathers: Conflict with Hypothesized Roles. *Hormones and Behavior* 47(4): 410–418.

Scott, J. W. (1986) Gender: A Useful Category of Historical Analysis. *American Historical Review* 91(5): 1053–1075.

Sell, R. L., Wells, J. A. et al. (1995) The Prevalence of Homosexual Behavior and Attraction in the United-States, the United-Kingdom and France: Results of National Population-Based Samples. *Archives of Sexual Behavior* 24(3): 235–248.

Shapiro, L. A. (2004) *The Mind Incarnate* (Cambridge, MA: MIT Press).

Shapiro, L. A. (2011) *Embodied Cognition* (New York: Routledge).

Sharps, M. J., Price, J. L. and Williams, J. K. (1994) Spatial Cognition and Gender: Instructional and Stimulus Influences on Mental Image Rotation. *Psychology of Women Quarterly* 18: 413–425.

Shaywitz, B. A., Shaywitz, S. E., Pugh, K. R., Constable, R. T., Skudlarski, P., Fulbright, R. K. et al. (1995) Sex Differences in the Functional Organization of the Brain for Language. *Nature* 373: 607–609.

Sheng, Z. J., Kawano, J. et al. (2004) Expression of Estrogen Receptors (Alpha, Beta) and Androgen Receptor in Serotonin Neurons of the Rat and Mouse Dorsal Raphe Nuclei: Sex and Species Differences. *Neuroscience Research* 49(2): 185–196.

Shepard, R. N. and Metzler, J. (1971) Mental Rotation of Three-Dimensional Objects. *Science* 171(3972): 701–703.

Shuler, M. G. and M. F. Bear (2006) Reward Timing in the Primary Visual Cortex. *Science* 311(5767): 1606–1609.

Silas, J., Levy, J., Nielsen, M., Slade, L. and Holmes, A. (2010) Sex and Individual Differences in Induced and Evoked EEG Measures of Action Observation. *Neuropsychologia* 48: 2417–2426.

Simerly, R. (2002) Wired for Reproduction: Organization and Development of Sexually Dimorphic Circuits in the Mammalian Forebrain. *Annual Review of Neuroscience* 25: 507–536.

Sinclair, S., Hardin, C. D. and Lowery, B. S. (2006) Self-Stereotyping in the Context of Multiple Social Identities. *Journal of Personality and Social Psychology* 90:, 529–542.

Singer, T. and Lamm, C. (2009) The Social Neuroscience of Empathy. *Annals of the New York Academy of Science* 1156: 81–96.

Singer, T., Seymour, B., O'Doherty, J., Stephan, K., Dolan, R. and Frith, C. (2004) Empathy for Pain Involves the Affective but Not the Sensory Components of Pain. *Science* 303: 1157–1161.

Singer, T., Seymour, B., O'Doherty, J., Stephan, K., Dolan, R. and Frith, C. (2006) Empathic Neural Responses are Modulated by the Perceived Fairness of Others. *Nature* 439: 466–469.

Skoe, E. (2010) The Relationship between Empathy-Related Constructs and Care-Based Moral Development in Young Adulthood. *Journal of Moral Education* 39: 191–211.

Skoe, E. and Diessner, J. (1994) Ethics of Care, Justice, Identity, and Gender: An Extension and Replication. *Merrill-Palmer Quarterly* 40: 272–289.

Skotko, B., Andrews, E. and Einstein, G. (2005) Language and the Medial Temporal Lobe: Evidence from H.M.'s Spontaneous Discourse. *Journal of Memory and Language* 53: 397–415.

Slaby, J. (2010) Steps Towards a Critical Neuroscience. *Phenomenology and the Cognitive Sciences* 9(3): 397–416.

Smeets, P., de Graaf, C. et al. (2006) Effect of Satiety on Brain Activation during Chocolate Tasting in Men and Women. *American Journal of Clinical Nutrition* 83: 1297–1305.

Smith, H. and Sowden, M. (1996) Base-Modification mRNA Editing through Deamination: The Good, the Bad and the Unregulated. *Trends in Genetics* 12(10): 418–424.

Smith, L. L. and Hines, M. (2000) Language Lateralization and Handedness in Women Prenatally Exposed to Diethylstilbestrol (DES). *Psychoneuroendocrinology* 25(5): 497–512.

Smith, T. M. (1995) *The Educational Progress of Women: Findings from 'The Condition of Education 1995'* (Washington, DC: National Center for Education Statistics, Office of Educational Research and Improvement).

Smith, W. C., Bourne, D. and Squair, J. (1999) A Retrospective Cohort Study of Post Mastectomy Pain Syndrome. *Pain* 83: 91–95.

Snow, C. P. (1998) *The Two Cultures* (Cambridge: Cambridge University Press).

Sober, E. and Wilson, D. S. (1998) *Unto Others* (Cambridge, MA: Harvard University Press).

Sommer, I. E., Aleman, A., Bouma, A. and Kahn, R. (2004) Do Women Really Have More Bilateral Language Representation than Men? A Meta-Analysis of Functional Imaging Studies. *Brain* 127: 1845–1852.

Sommer, I. E., Aleman, A., Somers, M., Boks, M. P. and Kahn, R. S. (2008) Sex Differences in Handedness, Asymmetry of the Planum Temporale and Functional Language Lateralization. *Brain Research* 1206: 76–88.

Spelman, E. (1988) *Inessential Woman: Problems of Exclusion in Feminist Thought* (Boston: Beacon Press).

Sprafkin, C., Serbin, L., Denier, C. and Connor, J. (1983) Sex-Differentiated Play: Cognitive Consequences and Early Interventions. In M. Liss (ed.), *Social and Cognitive Skills: Sex Roles and Children's Play* (New York: Academic Press), 167–192.

Spreckelmeyer, K. N., Krach, S. et al. (2009) Anticipation of Monetary and Social Reward Differently Activates Mesolimbic Brain Structures in Men and Women. *Social Cognitive and Affective Neuroscience* 4(2): 158–65.

Stacey, J. (1988) Can There be a Feminist Ethnography? *Women's Studies International Forum* 11: 21–27.

Star, S. L. (1979) Sex Differences and the Dichotomization of the Brain: Methods, Limits and Problems in Research on Consciousness. In Ruth Hubbard and Marianne Lowe (eds), *Genes and Gender: Pitfalls in Research on Sex and Gender* (New York: Gordian Press).

Steakley, J. D. (1997) Per scientiam ad justitiam: Magnus Hirschfeld and the Sexual Politics of Innate Homosexuality. In V. Rosario (ed.), *Science and Homosexualities* (New York: Routledge), 133–154.

Steele, C. M. (1997) A Threat in the Air: How Stereotypes Shape Intellectual Identity and Performance. *American Psychologist* 52: 613–629.

Steele, J. R. and Ambady, N. (2006) 'Math is Hard!' The Effect of Gender Priming on Women's Attitudes. *Journal of Experimental Social Psychology* 42: 428–436.

Stein, E. (1993) Evidence for Queer Genes: An Interview with Richard Pillard. *GLQ* 1(1): 93–110.

Stein, E. (1999) *The Mismeasure of Desire: The Science, Theory, and Ethics of Sexual Orientation* (Oxford: Oxford University Press).

Stengers, I. (2000a) Another Look: Relearning to Laugh. *Hypatia: A Journal of Feminist Philosophy* 15(4): 41–54.

Stengers, I (2000b) *The Invention of Modern Science* (Minneapolis: University of Minnesota Press).

Stengers, I. (2005) Introductory Notes on an Ecology of Practices. *Cultural Studies Review* 11(1): 183–196.

Stengers, I. (2010) *Cosmopolitics I* (Minneapolis: University of Minnesota Press).

Sterelny, K. (2003) *Thought in a Hostile World* (London: Blackwell).

Stoller, R. J. (1968) *Sex and Gender: The Development of Masculinity and Femininity* (London: Hogarth).

Stone, P. (2008) *Opting Out? Why Women Really Quit Careers and Head Home* (Berkeley: University of California Press).

Swaab, D. F. and Garcia-Falgueras, A. (2009) Sexual Differentiation of the Human Brain in Relation to Gender Identity and Sexual Orientation. *Functional Neurology* 24: 17–28.

Takahashi, H. et al. (2006) Men and Women Show Distinct Brain Activations during Imagery of Sexual and Emotional Infidelity. *NeuroImage* 32(3): 1299–1307.

Tangney, J. and Dearing, R. (2002) *Shame and Guilt* (New York: Guilford Press).

Tavris, C. (1993) *The Mismeasure of Woman* (New York: Touchstone Books).

Taylor, S. E. (2006) *Health Psychology* (New York: McGraw-Hill).

Terry, J. (1999) *An American Obsession: Science, Medicine, and Homosexuality in Modern Society* (Chicago: University of Chicago Press).

Thirion, B., Pinel, P., Mériaux, S., Roche, A., Dehaene, S., and Poline, B. (2007) Analysis of a Large fMRI Cohort: Statistical and Methodological Issues for Group Analyses. *NeuroImage* 35(1): 105–120.

Thoman, D. B., White, P. H., Yamawaki, N. and Koishi, H. (2008) Variations of Gender-Math Stereotype Content Affect Women's Vulnerability to Stereotype Threat. *Sex Roles* 58: 702–712.

Thomas, G. and Maio, G. R. (2008) Man, I Feel Like a Woman: When and How Gender-Role Motivation Helps Mind-Reading. *Journal of Personality and Social Psychology* 95:, 1165–1179.

Tiilikainen M. (2001) Suffering and Symptoms: Aspects of Everyday Life of Somali Refugee Women. In M. S. Lilius (ed.), *Variations on the Theme of Somaliness* (Turku, Finland: Centre for Continuing Education), 309–317.

Tilbrook, A. J., Turner, A. I. et al. (2000) Effects of Stress on Reproduction in Non-Rodent Mammals: The Role of Glucocorticoids and Sex Differences. *Reviews of Reproduction* 5(2): 105–113.

Titus-Ernstoff, L., Perez, K. et al. (2003) Psychosexual Characteristics of Men and Women Exposed Prenatally to Diethylstilbestrol. *Epidemiology* 14(2): 155–160.

Trivers, R. (1971) The Evolution of Reciprocal Altruism. *Quarterly Review of Biology* 46: 35–57.

Tuana, N. (1993) *The Less Noble Sex: Scientific, Religious, and Philosophical Conceptions of Woman's Nature* (Bloomington: Indiana University Press).

Tuana, N. (2006) The Speculum of Ignorance: The Women's Health Movement and Epistemologies of Ignorance. *Hypatia* 21: 1–19.

Tuchman, G. (1978) Introduction: The Symbolic Annihilation of Women. In G. Tuchman, A. K. Daniels and J. Benét (eds), *Hearth and Home: Images of Women in the Mass Media* (New York: Oxford University Press), 3–18.

Udry, R. (2000) Biological Limits of Gender Construction. *American Sociological Review* 65(3): 443–457.

van Anders, S. M. (2010) Social Modulation of Hormones. In L. F. Barrett, B. Mesquita and E. Smith (eds), *The Mind in Context* (New York: Guilford Press), 65–80.

van Anders, S. M. and Watson, N. V. (2006) Social Neuroendocrinology: Effects of social Contexts and Behaviors on Sex Steroids in Humans. *Human Nature* 17: 212–237.

van de Beek, C., Thijssen, J. H. H., Cohen-Kettenis, P. T., van Goozen, S. H. M. and Buitelaar, J. K. (2004) Relationships between Sex Hormones Assessed in Amniotic Fluid, and Maternal and Umbilical Cord Serum: What is the Best Source of Information to Investigate the Effects of Fetal Hormonal Exposure? *Hormones and Behavior* 46(5): 663–669.

van de Beek, C., Van Goozen, S. H. M., Buitelaar, J. K. and Cohen-Kettenis, P. T. (2009) Prenatal Sex Hormones (Maternal and Amniotic Fluid) and Gender-Related Play Behavior in 13-Month-Old Infants. *Archives of Sexual Behavior* 38: 6–15.

van den Wijngaard, M. (1997) *Reinventing the Sexes: The Biomedical Construction of Femininity and Masculinity* (Bloomington: Indiana University Press).

Vidal, C. (2004) Cerveau, sexe et idéologie. *Diogène* 208: 146–156.

Vidal, C. and Benoit-Browaeys, D. (2005) *Cerveau, sexe et pouvoir* (Paris: Belin).

Vidal, F. (2009) Brainhood, Anthropological Figure of Modernity. *History of the Human Sciences* 22: 5–36.

Voracek, M. and Dressler, S. G. (2006) Lack of Correlation Between Digit Ratio (2D:4D) and Baron-Cohen's 'Reading the Mind in the Eyes' Test: Empathy, Systemising, and Autism-Spectrum Quotients in a General Population Sample. *Personality and Individual Differences* 41: 1481–1491.

Voß, H.-J, (2010) *Making Sex Revisited: Dekonstruktion des Geschlechts aus biologisch-medizinischer Perspektive* (Bielefeld: Transcript-Verlag).

Voyer, D., Voyer, S. and Bryden, M. P. (1995) Magnitude of Sex Differences in Spatial Abilities: A Meta-Analysis and Consideration of Critical Variables. *Psychological Bulletin* 117: 250–270.

Vul, E., Harris, C. et al. (2009) Puzzlingly High Correlations in fMRI Studies of Emotion, Personality, and Social Cognition. *Perspectives on Psychological Science* 4(3): 274–290.

Wakshlak, A. and Weinstock, M. (1990) Neonatal Handling Reverses Behavioral Abnormalities Induced in Rats by Prenatal Stress. *Physiology and Behavior* 48(2): 289–292.

Walker, L. (2006) Gender and Morality. In M. Killen and J. Smetana (eds), *Handbook of Moral Development* (Mahwah, NJ: Lawrence Erlbaum Associates), 93–115.

Wallen, K. (2005) Hormonal Influences on Sexually Differentiated Behavior in Nonhuman Primates. *Frontiers in Neuroendocrinology* 26: 7–26.

Wallentin, M. (2009) Putative Sex Differences in Verbal Abilities and Language Cortex: A Critical Review. *Brain and Language* 108: 175–183.

Walton, G. M. and Spencer, S. J. (2009) Latent Ability: Grades and Test Scores Systematically Underestimate the Intellectual Ability of Negatively Stereotyped Students. *Psychological Science* 20: 1132–1139.

Walton, K. (1990) *Mimesis as Make-Believe: On the Foundations of the Representational Arts* (Cambridge, MA: Harvard University Press).

Walton, K. (2008) *Marvelous Images: On Values and the Arts* (Oxford: Oxford University Press).

Wang, J., Korczykowski M. et al. (2007) Gender Difference in Neural Response to Psychological Stress. *Social Cognitive and Affective Neuroscience* 2: 227–239.

Watson, N. V. and Kimura, D. (1991) Nontrivial Sex Differences in Throwing and Intercepting: Relation to Psychometrically-Defined Spatial Functions. *Personality and Individual Differences* 12: 375–385.

Weasel, L. (2001) Dismantling the Self/Other Dichotomy in Science: Towards a Feminist Model of the Immune System', *Hypatia* 16: 27–47.

Weingart, P. and Stehr, N. (2000) *Practising Interdisciplinarity* (Toronto: University of Toronto Press).

Westermann, G., Mareschal, D., Johnson, M. H., Sirois, S., Spratling, M. W. and Thomas, M. S. C. (2007) Neuroconstructivism. *Developmental Science* 10: 75–83.

White, P. C. and Speiser, P. W. (2000) Congenital Adrenal Hyperplasia Due to 21-Hydroxylase Deficiency. *Endocrine Reviews* 21(3): 245–291.

Wicker, B., Keysers, C., Plailly, J., Royet, J-P., Gallese, V. and Rizzolatti, V. (2003) Both of Us Disgusted in My Insula: The Common Neural Basis of Seeing and Feeling Disgust. *Neuron* 40: 655–64.

Willats, J. (1997) *Art and Representation: New Principles in the Analysis of Pictures* (Princeton: Princeton University Press).

Willis, E., Miller, R. et al. (2001) Gendered Embodiment and Survival for Young People with Cystic Fibrosis. *Social Science and Medicine* 53(9): 1163–1174.

Wilson, D. S. (2002) *Darwin's Cathedral* (Chicago: University of Chicago Press).

Wilson, E. A. (1998) *Neural Geographies: Feminism and the Microstructure of Cognition* (New York and London: Routledge).

Wilson, E. A. (2000) Neurological Preference: LeVay's Study of Sexual Orientation. *SubStance* 29: 23–38.

Witelson, S. F., Glezer, I. and Kigar, D. L. (1995) Women Have Greater Density of Neurons in Posterior Temporal Cortex. *Journal of Neuroscience* 15: 3418–3428.

World Health Organization (1998) *Female Genital Mutilation: An Overview* (Geneva: WHO).

World Health Organization (2010) Female Genital Mutilation. Fact sheet No. 241 (http://www.who.int/mediacentre/factsheets/fs241/en/), accessed 28 December 2010.

World Health Organization Study Group on Female Genital Mutilation and Obstetric Outcome (2006) Female Genital Mutilation and Obstetric Outcome: WHO Collaborative Prospective Study in Six African Countries. *The Lancet* 367: 1835–1841.

Yan, G. N., Gold, S. J., Iredale, P. A., Terwilliger, R. Z., Duman, R. S. and Nestler, E. J. (1999) Region-Specific Regulation of RGS4 (Regulator of G-Protein–Signaling Protein Type 4) in Brain by Stress and Glucocorticoids: *In Vivo* and *In Vitro* Studies. *Journal of Neuroscience* 19(10): 3674–3680.

Yang, C.-Y., Decety, J., Lee, S., Chen, C. and Cheng, Y. (2009) Gender Differences in the mu Rhythm during Empathy for Pain: An Electroencophalographic Study. *Brain Research* 1251: 176–184.

Young, I. M. (2005) *On Female Body Experience: "Throwing Like a Girl" and Other Essays* (New York: Oxford University Press).

Young, R. M. and Balaban, E. (2006) Psychoneuroindoctrinology. *Nature* 443: 634.

Young, W. C., Goy, R. W. and Phoenix, C. H. (1964) Hormones and Sexual Behavior. *Science* 143(3603): 212–218.

Zhang, S. and Manson, J. (2002) Women's Health and Gender Biology: The Late But Welcome Arrival of Evidence-Based Research. *Nutrition in Clinical Care* 5(6): 269–271.

Zucker, K. J., Bradley, S. J. et al. (1996) Psychosexual Development of Women with Congenital Adrenal Hyperplasia. *Hormones and Behavior* 30(4): 300–318.

Zurayk, H., Myntti, C., Salem, M. T., Kaddour, A., el-Kak, F. and Jabbour, S. (2007) Beyond Reproductive Health: Listening to Women about their Health in Disadvantaged Beirut Neighbourhoods. *Health Care for Women International* 28: 614–637.

Name Index

Baron-Cohen, Simon 9, 73–104, 106, 219, 235
Batson, Daniel C. 59, 62–64, 68, 70

Chase, Cheryl 203, 215

Deleuze, Gilles 175, 184
Diamond, Milton 84, 201–7, 212, 214, 215

Eisenberg, Nancy 66, 69, 79

Gilligan, Carol 6, 56–59

Hampson, John and Joan
  See John/Joan case
Haraway, Donna 146, 159, 172, 174, 184

ISNA/Intersex Society of North America 203–5, 212, 215

John/Joan case 200, 202, 204–5

Koehn, Daryl 58, 62

Lennon, Randy 66, 79

Money, John 1–2, 200–4, 207, 214

Noe, Alva 229

OII/Organisation International Intersex 206, 210

Reimer, David
  See John/Joan case

Stengers, Isabelle 9, 176, 179–80, 183–88, 190, 192
Summers, Larry 32

Young, William 108, 201–2

Subject Index

abstraction 11–12, 24, 27–28

blood oxygen level-dependent (BOLD) signal 22–24
bottom-up 223
brain
  activity/activation 34, 38–39, 43–44, 53, 69, 119, 124, 128, 132, 134
  development 42, 49, 73, 84, 97, 106, 108, 160, 202, 233, 235
  female 11, 26–27, 42, 73, 74, 91, 108, 109, 127, 130, 177, 213, 229, 230–42, 244
  gay/homosexual/lesbian 122, 133, 139, 142, 213
  imaging 11–12, 21–27, 40, 46, 53, 68, 124, 127–31, 175, 177, 182, 187
  intersexed/transexual 194, 201, 210
  male 11, 26–27, 42, 73, 74, 76, 79, 88, 91, 102, 108, 109, 127, 130, 170, 213, 229, 230, 232, 236–37, 242
  organization research/studies/ theory 3, 84, 96, 105–9, 111–13, 127, 138, 241
  sexual differentiation/ dimorphism 31, 33, 36, 42–53, 54, 84–85, 95, 108–9, 121, 125–27, 136, 181, 234, 241
  structure 35, 83, 90, 95, 115, 129, 137, 142

care, ethics of
  see ethics of care
co-becoming 175, 179, 183
communication
  Children's Communication Checklist 101
  Neurotransmitters 45
  Social 89, 197
conflict (social) 71, 193–215

consensus conference/statement 194, 211–12
controversy 193–215
corticosterone 36
cosmopolitics 175, 180, 184, 186–89, 191
culture 2, 3, 6, 8, 16, 79, 151, 155–56, 162, 167–68, 178, 195, 219, 238

degeneracy 40, 55 n16
democracy 211, 215 n18
depiction 11–29, 177
determinism; neuro-determinism 2, 135–39, 142, 147, 189, 194, 230, 234
difference
  see brain, sexual differentiation/ dimorphism; gender, gender differences
dissensus conference 193, 212
DSD/disorders of sex development 201
dualism 50, 54 n6,7

emotional contagion 68, 69–70
empathy 9, 59–61, 63–65, 66–70, 71–72, 77, 79, 87, 94, 243
environment; environmental enrichment; environmental stress 2, 10, 35–36, 57, 85–86, 224–26
essentialism 24, 27
ethics of Care 6, 9, 56–72, 79

female genital cutting (FGC) 150–56, 161, 164–69, 170, 173 n5,8,10,11,12
feminist science 145–46, 149–50
fetal brain 85, 89, 107, 194, 199, 204, 233
functional magnetic resonance imaging (fMRI) 124, 127–31, 136, 143n3, 164, 175, 180–82, 213n4
  see also brain, imaging

functionalism 55

gender
  gender differences 2, 9, 11, 31–37,
    67, 105, 107–110, 118, 127–29,
    181–82, 234
  gender essentialism 27, 140–41, 230
  gender identity 1, 79, 123, 193–94,
    200–06
  gender rôle 7, 123, 230–233,
    240–241
  gender stereotypes 7, 31, 97, 234,
    240
  gender theory 170
genetic determination 3, 35–36, 85,
  148, 232, 238
genitals 107–09, 159–61, 199–202

hard-wired; hard-wiring 33–34, 36,
  52, 54 n8, 73–74, 105–20, 233,
  235, 238, 243–44
heteronormative 122–23, 203
heterosexuality 123, 132
homosexuality 123, 132, 135
homunculus 170
hormones (sex) 3, 84–86, 89, 107–16,
  126, 151, 170, 188–89, 199,
  201–2, 232–33, 235–36, 240

individualism 195
inferential gap 12
innate; innatism 2–4, 35–36, 79–82,
  85–86, 115, 117, 122, 135–38,
  188, 201, 236–38, 242
interdisciplinary (research) 176, 180,
  196–98
intersex 142, 193–94, 200–10, 211

linear Model
  see brain, organization theory

machine-made images 11–12, 17–20
magnetic resonance imaging (MRI)
  see neuroimaging
materiality 176, 191
mathematics; mathematical
  cognition; mathematical
  reasoning 43–45, 78, 84, 118, 219
mechanical objectivity 11, 18, 27–28

memory 43, 50, 55 n19, 104 n6, 126,
  156, 163, 217–18, 220–21, 228
multiple realization 37–39, 52, 54

nervous system 126, 150–51,
  160–62, 171
neuroendocrinology
  (behavioral) 194, 201–2
neuroethics 180–83
neurogenesis 35, 42
neuroimaging 9, 11, 27, 121–22,
  130–37, 138–42

object from nowhere 12, 21, 24, 26

pain 38–39, 60, 68, 154–56,
  158, 166
personal distress 61, 63–65, 68–71
perspective taking 63, 66–67, 69, 72
photographs 17–19
physicalism 37, 38, 50, 54
plasticity (brain plasticity) 25, 36,
  106, 108, 118, 151, 162, 170, 191,
  194–95, 213
practices 122, 123, 197, 207
  ecology of practices 9, 178–80,
    183–84
  feminist practices 146,
    182–83, 189
principles of generation 13–14,
  19–20
psychosexual 111, 115, 200, 206
public
  participation 211
  understanding of science 23, 28,
    124, 141, 197

Queer; queer theory 121–23, 140–42,
  194, 209, 213

reductionism 8, 122, 139, 187
reification 97, 139–40
representation 12–14, 20, 24,
  170, 176

science studies/ STS 176, 180, 183,
  194 95, 209, 211, 213, 230
sexing the brain 11, 24, 27,
  126, 213

sexual orientation 9, 106, 121, 122,
    130–36, 140, 205
similarity (as opposed to difference) 9,
    14, 46, 49, 129, 133, 181
    see also brain differentiation;
    gender, gender différences
surgery 158, 170, 199, 200, 202–7, 298
sympathy 9, 58–65, 66, 68, 70

testosterone 42, 73, 76, 83–86, 96,
    107, 110, 121, 200

trained judgment 16, 18–21
transgender (studies) 111, 142,
    194, 210
transparency 12, 17, 19–22, 28
transsexualism 135, 194,
    199–203

ultrasound 12–17, 20–24

visual cortex 132
voodoo correlations 198, 214

CPSIA information can be obtained at www.ICGtesting.com
Printed in the USA
LVOW10*1225261013

358738LV00008B/297/P